The Darker Side of the Renaissance

The Darker Side
of the Renaissance

Literacy, Territoriality,
and Colonization

WALTER D. MIGNOLO

Ann Arbor
THE UNIVERSITY OF MICHIGAN PRESS

Copyright © by the University of Michigan 1995
All rights reserved
Published in the United States of America by
The University of Michigan Press
Manufactured in the United States of America
♾ Printed on acid-free paper

1998   1997   1996   1995   4   3   2   1

A CIP catalogue record for this book is available from the British Library.

Library of Congress Cataloging-in-Publication Data

Mignolo, Walter.
    The darker side of the Renaissance : literacy, territoriality, and
colonization / Walter D. Mignolo.
        p.   cm.
    Includes bibliographical references (p.   ) and index.
    ISBN 0-472-10327-X (alk. paper)
    1. Latin America—Historiography. 2. Indians—Historiography.
3. Renaissance—Spain. 4. Latin America—History—To 1600.
5. Language and history—Latin America. 6. Indians—Writing.
7. Writing—History. 8. Cartography—Spain—History. 9. Latin
America—Maps—History.   I. Title.
F1409.7.M56   1995
980'.013—dc20
                                                              94-36501
                                                              CIP

Contents

Preface

I

The argument that follows cuts across the current distinction between the Renaissance and the early modern period. While the concept of *Renaissance* refers to a rebirth of classical legacies and the constitution of humanistic scholarship for human emancipation and *early modern period* emphasizes the emergence of a genealogy that announces the modern and the postmodern, the darker side of the Renaissance underlines, instead, the rebirth of the classical tradition as a justification of colonial expansion and the emergence of a genealogy (the early colonial period) that announces the colonial and the postcolonial. Thus, rather than a lineal succession of periods I conceive the coexistence of clusters (Renaissance/darker side of the Renaissance; early modern/colonial period; enlightenment/darker side of the Enlightenment; modern/colonial period). In other words, the Renaissance is conceived in this book together with its darker side and the early modern together with the early colonial period.

Why the "Darker side of the Renaissance" and the sixteenth and seventeenth centuries and not, for instance, the late eighteenth or late nineteenth centuries when the largest portion of the world was under colonial rules? One of the reasons is that my field of expertise is not English but Spanish/Latin American/Amerindian cultural histories. But more important are the facts that the legacies of British imperialism and French and German colonial expansion are not only indirectly related to my professional training but to my personal experiences as well. And we all know how important personal experiences are in postcolonial theorizing. For instance, what I conceive in this book as the modern/colonial period (according to the previous genealogies) is a moment in which English, French, and German constitute themselves as the languages of modernity and of the "heart of Europe" (according to Hegel), relegating Castilian and Portuguese as languages not well suited for scientific and philosophical discourses. When Réné Descartes in Amsterdam, toward 1630, merged literacy with numeracy and redirected the notion of scientific rigor and philosophical reasoning in French, the Castilian and Portuguese languages remained attached to the heavy literate and humanistic legacies of the European Renaissance. If we could detect a reorientation of philosophical and scientific discourses toward the beginning of the seventeenth century, it would be worthwhile to note that such reorientation was attached to specific languages (the languages of the modern period: English, German, French) and coincided with the moment in which Amsterdam began to replace Seville as the Western center of economic transactions at the closure of the Renaissance/early modern/colonial period and the opening up of the Enlightenment/ modern/colonial period.

Why then did I write this book in English and not in Spanish? Writing in Spanish means, at this time, to remain at the margin of contemporary theoretical discussions. In the world in which scholarly publications are meaningful, there are more readers in English and French than in Spanish. Like students writing a dissertation in a "minor literature," it requires a double effort: to know the canon and the corpus. To write in Spanish a book that attempts to inscribe Spanish/Latin American and Amerindian legacies into current debates on the Renaissance/early modern period and into colonial legacies and postcolonial theories means marginalizing the book before giving it the possibility of participating in an intellectual conversation, which, since the eighteenth century, has been dominated by German, French, and—more recently—by English. I will have more to say about the issue a couple of paragraphs below when I introduce Gloria Anzaldúa's contribution to theorizing colonial legacies.

The legacies of the Spanish Empire in the Americas are what connect the fifteenth and sixteenth centuries with the present, be that present the plurilingual and multicultural Andean or Mesoamerican societies in Latin America or the emerging Latino cultures in the United States. Thus, my justification for focusing on the early colonial period and the darker side of the Renaissance (instead of on the British Empire) is that my own situation—contrary to thinking from and about colonial Australia, New Zealand, or India—at present is connected with the legacies of the Spanish Empire, with the more recent U.S. imperial expansion to Latin America and Latin American migrations toward the United States. Finally, the need to re-inscribe the legacies of the "darker side of the Renaissance" and the "early colonial period" into current discussions on colonial legacies and postcolonial theories emerges from the need to decolonize scholarship and to de-center epistemological loci of enunciation. I agree with all of those insisting that colonialism is not homogeneous, that we should pay more attention to the diversity of colonial discourses, that postcoloniality cannot be generalized, and so forth. It is precisely because I agree with the need to diversify colonial experiences that I am interested in diversifying loci of enunciations from where colonial legacies are studied and re-inscribed in the present. It would be misleading to assume, in other words, that postcolonial theories could only emerge from the legacies of the British Empire or be postulated as monological and theoretical models to describe the particularities and diversity of colonial experiences; it would be misleading to assume, also, that only the theoretical legacies of the languages of modernity (French, German, English) are the ones with scientific legitimacy. Inscribing the languages of the Early colonial period (Spanish, Portuguese, Quechua, Aymara, Nahuatl) into the theoretical languages of modernity is a first step toward intellectual decolonization and *the denial of the denial of coevalness* (see infra).

My position on this issue is neither that of personal interest nor bending toward the defense of national languages, cultures, and traditions. On the contrary, it is founded in my strong conviction that one of the rich avenues of postcolonial theorizing is, precisely, to open up the possibilities of diverse and legitimate theoretical loci of enunciation and, by so doing, to relocate the monologic and universal subject of knowledge inscribed in the modern/colonial period (i.e., Amsterdam as the new economic center and Descartes as the paradigmatic example of the modern mind). If the Spanish Empire declined in the modern/colonial period and Castilian became a second-class language in relation to languages of European modernity (French, English, and German), it was, mainly, because Castilian had lost its power as a knowledge-generating language. It became a language more suited for literary and cultural expressions at the moment that knowledge was articulated by stressing the primary qualities of reason in philosophical ideas and scientific arguments and by suppressing the secondary qualities conveyed in feelings and emotions. A fracture within the Romance languages took place in the modern period: while French maintained the expressive flair attributed to the Romance languages, it was also the language of philosophical rigor and of one of the colonial powers of modernity. This fracture was emphasized after World War II, when the planet was divided into three ranked areas and Castilian (and Portuguese) became a (two of the) third world language(s). The situation was maintained and reinforced by the coincidence of the division of the planet in three ranked economic and linguistic areas and the massive migration of the Spanish-speaking population from Latin America and the Spanish Caribbean toward the United States. Part of the Francophone world (with the exception of Canada) began to share with Spanish its belonging to the Third World (see, e.g., Fanon's Black Skin/White Masks), while maintaining at the same time the status of French as a first world language.

The rationale just outlined is strictly relevant to the location of the emergence of "comparative ethnology," the "ethnographic reason," the constitution of the "myth of modernity," and the configuration of the "postcolonial reason"—in other words, for the articulation of understanding the past and speaking the present. Anthony Pagden (a British historian whose field of expertise is the Spanish empire) located the emergence of comparative ethnology in the Renaissance/early modern/colonial period, while Jean-Loup Amselle (a French anthropologist whose field of expertise is French colonial expansion in Africa) located the emergence of ethnographic reason in the Enlightenment/modern/colonial period (Pagden 1982). Pagden's "comparative ethnology" and Amselle's "ethnographic reason" are two sides of the same coin: they are the rational articulation of cultural differences by a European observer (or, if you wish, by different kinds of European observers), since in neither case the discursive rationalization of a non-European observer (or, if you wish, of different kinds of non-European observers) is taken into account. While two sides of the same coin, "comparative ethnology" and "ethnographic reason" are significantly different (Amselle 1990). Beyond the difference in period in which the two are located, the first is forged by a British historian having the Spanish Empire as his field of expertise, while the second was forged by a French anthropologist having French colonial expansion as his field of expertise. In the first case, the scholarly identification is with Europe, and Pagden made his position publicly explicit in later publications. It is clear, on the other hand, that Amselle's identification is primarily with a discipline (anthropology) and implicitly with France as a country rather than with Europe as a transnational entity. While I find Pagden's and Amselle's contributions interesting and helpful, I cannot inscribe myself in their programs. I find, instead, a more compatible grounding in Enrique Dussel's (a philosopher from Argentina) articulation of countering modernity from a colonial perspective. Dussel's equivalent of Pagden's "comparative ethnology" and Amselle's "ethnographic reason" is the "myth of modernity," which is articulated as follows:

Modernity includes a rational "concept" of emancipation that we affirm and subsume. But, at the same time, it develops an irrational myth, a justification for genocidal violence. The postmodernists criticize modern reason as a reason of terror; we criticize modern reason because of the irrational myth that it conceals. (Dussel 1993: 66)

By locating the emergence of modernity toward the end of the fifteenth century and with the European "discovery" of a "New World," Dussel places the accent on the early modern/colonial period when Europe moves from a peripheral situation in relation to Islam, to a central position in relation to the constitution of the Spanish Empire, the expulsion of the Moors, and the success of trans-Atlantic expansion. In that configuration, the Americas become the first periphery of the modern world and part and parcel of the myth of modernity. By lining myself up with Dussel instead of with Pagden or Amselle, I attempt to emphasize the need to make a cultural and political intervention by inscribing postcolonial theorizing into particular colonial legacies: the need, in other words, to inscribe the "darker side of the Renaissance" into the silenced space of Spanish/Latin America and Amerindian contributions to universal history and to postcolonial theorizing.

The scenario I just described could be recast in terms of two stages (early modern/colonial and modern/colonial periods) of Western expansion and globalization. These two stages have something in common: an increasing tendency toward organizing hierarchies in a time frame. Although this tendency was at its inception at the end of the sixteenth century when José de Acosta ranked writing systems according to their proximity to the alphabet as point of arrival, Amselle placed the emergence of this powerful and transformative idea in Lafitau's *Moeurs des sauvages americains comparées aux moeurs des premièrs temps* (1724): the complicities between the replacement of the "other" in space by the "other" in time and, by the same token, the articulation of cultural differences in chronological hierarchies. Fabian christened this transformation *the denial of coevalness*. What shall retain our attention here is that the replacement of the other in space by the other in time was partially framed in terms of boundaries and frontiers. At the end of the fifteenth century frontiers were constructed not only in geographical terms and related to the extensions and the limits of the Atlantic Ocean but also in terms of the boundaries of humanity. The ordering was not yet openly chronological, but it became clearly so in the eighteenth century. The first thrust of this book is, then, the articulation of differences both in space and time, as well as the uses of space and time as the means by which cultural differences are articulated. Thus, while the *denial of coevalness* emerged as one of the main conceptual consequences of the growing privilege of time over space in the organization and ranking of cultures and societies in the early modern/colonial period, *the denial of the denial of coevalness* is one of the major tasks of postcolonial theorizing.

The third stage of Western expansion and globalization, of which we are part and parcel, is currently located after World War II. Some of the landmarks of this third stage are the movements of decolonization in British, French, and German colonies; the growing expansion of the United States, and the substitution of all forms of territorial colonialism by global marketing and finances. While the subject I am writing about is located in the first stage of globalization, the writing subject is located in the third. Thus, a second thrust of the book is (I have already argued) understanding the past and speaking the present. In the present being spoken (which also speaks of us), theories articulating the global are theories speaking the present in a postmodern and postcolonial world. If postmodern and postcolonial are suspicious expressions either because we are not out of modernity or colonialism or because by using them the preference that modernity attributes to time over space is reinforced, I would like to emphasize that, in spite of all the ambiguities, postmodernity and postcoloniality designate (in my argument) the locations of two different modes of countering modernity. If "deconstruction" is a mode or operation associated with the former, "decolonization" is the corresponding one associated with the latter.

Gloria Anzaldúa (1987), theorizing on borders, boundaries, and places of cultural contact, provides more theoretical insights that I can develop here. I will just mention a few of them. First, there is the double re-inscription of Spanish. On the one hand, Anzaldúa re-inscribes Spanish (a third world language) into English (a first world language) by stressing the difficulties of taming a wild tongue. Curiously enough, the concept of "taming a language" (akin to Nebrija's philosophy of language, which I analyze in the first chapter) is recast by Anzaldúa as a strategy of resistance, while in Nebrija "taming a language" is a strategy of control, government, and colonization. On the other hand, Anzaldúa re-inscribes the Aztecs' concept of painting and writing (*Tlilli, In Tlapalli* [The red ink, the black ink]) and, by so doing, she contests Nebrija and Aldrete (who I also analyze in the first chapter) by denying that writing is representation of sound (Nebrija), and that languages are bound to one territory (Aldrete). In the second place, by linking language and gender Anzaldúa allows for geocultural and chronological reconfigurations—geoculturally because Hispanic

America is (in Anzaldúa's work) extended to and inscribed within the United States and chronologically because the notion of Hispanic America blurs the boundaries between the colonial and the neo- or postcolonial, since Spanish was the official language of both the colonial empire as well as of the neo- or postcolonial nations on the one hand, and it is spoken in Latino communities in United States on the other. Furthermore, the links Anzaldúa established between gender and language allows for the displacements of geocultural concepts such as America, Our America, Hispanic America, Latin America, etc., as far as all these concepts are founded in and by discursive formations presupposing masculinity as the constitutional subject of geocultural categories. Instead, Anzaldúa displaces the accent from the delimitation of geographical spaces to their borders, locations in which languages (Spanish, English, Nahuatl) and gender (male, female, homosexual, heterosexual) are the conditions of possibility for the creation of spaces-in-between as a different way of thinking. Anzaldúa's great theoretical contribution is to create a space-in-between *from where* to think rather than a hybrid space *to talk about,* a hybrid thinking-space of Spanish/Latin American and Amerindian legacies as the condition of possibility for Spanish/Latin American and Amerindian postcolonial theories. In this regard, Anzaldúa's "borderlands" join forces with Rodolfo Kusch's concept of "phagocytosis" (upon which I elaborate in the introduction), with Dussel's "myth of modernity," and with Abdelkebbir Khatibi's "une pensée autre." Khatibi, like Anzaldúa, constructs a transdisciplinarity space for thinking about colonization *from* the personal inscription (linguistic and personal) in colonial legacies rather than writing *about* colonization from the rules of a disciplinary game. Such are the places from where I intend, in writing this book, to speak the present by theorizing the past.

II

During the time that this book has been in production, a number of significant articles and books have been published. I would like to mention only a handful directly impinging on the general line of my argument. Enrique Dussel (to whom I referred above) published "Eurocentrism and Modernity," the first of his Frankfurt Lectures (Dussel 1993a), and an entire book about the myth of modernity (Dussel 1993b). Dussel's arguments in both publications are an extension of his early work on the philosophy of liberation on which I comment in the introduction. Edward Said's *Imperialism and Culture* appeared (or at least it got into my hands) in the fall of 1993. The book is extensive and controversial, and I cannot do justice here to it nor to the polemic surrounding it. I will limit myself to two aspects related to my own argument.

The reader of Said's book will find that the emphasis I placed on comparative strategy reverberates on Said's contrapuntal analytic strategy. The same reader may not immediately think of Fernando Ortiz's "contrapunteo" of sugar and tobacco. When I read Said's *Imperialism and Culture* I assumed, indeed, that his contrapuntal analysis was borrowed from Ortiz. Fernando Coronil proved me wrong (Coronil in press). By so doing, he was also able to bring to the foreground the fact that two critics of the complicities between anthropology and imperialism, fifty years apart from each other, were both thinking contrapuntally, and their models were both derived from music: classical music in Said; Cuban and liturgical popular musical tradition in Ortiz. My own restitution of comparative strategy comes also from another "third world" intellectual, R. Pannikar (1988), a historian of religions who looks at the modern (classical) comparative methodological tradition implementing a modern (colonial) emerging methodological and epistemological comparative strategy by asking who is comparing what, why, and how. By reframing comparative strategy in colonial legacies and by introducing the comparing subject into the act of comparing, he disrupted the idea that cultures are monologic entities that a scientific mind observes, dissects and compares. Comparative strategy thus reframed becomes the analysis of processes of transculturation (another concept introduced by Ortiz) of which the comparing subject is part and parcel: Ortiz as well as Said (Coronil and myself, too, for that matter) have different intensities and forms of investments with colonial legacies that prompt their (our) analysis and critique of colonialism: for instance, while Ortiz does not have to deal with the question of exile, Said cannot avoid it (Mudimbe 1994). Hence the need to look at the interactions between people, institutions, and cultural production aligned by relations of power and domination, and the need to look at postcolonial theories in their connection with colonial legacies.

Consequently, this book was conceived and constructed at the intersecting legacies of both the Renaissance/early modern period, on the one hand, and the early colonial/Amerindian, on the other. At first glance (e.g., the table of contents), its organization benefits from the order and symmetries established during the Renaissance. However, I have avoided a chronological narrative moving from the beginning to the end of the story. I benefited from reading ancient Mesoamerican codices and attempted to present the narrative and the arguments in a layered form. First, the core period explored runs from 1570 to 1630, with a flashback to the beginning of the sixteenth century when truly mixed cultures began to emerge, and then toward the eighteenth century when the Spanish empire began to crumble, a Creole intelligentsia to flourish, and the influence of Amerindian population to diminish. Questions of language, memory, and space are presented in successive discursive organization, although in a coexisting chronological and conceptual order. The lineup of the book also follows the double logic. At first glance, again, the privilege is given to language and time over space. Such a modern and Western hierarchy could be interpreted otherwise if space, instead of being looked at only in the final part of the book, is read instead as an overarching concept in which language and time are included. In this respect, the relevance of space in Amerindian cultures and legacies is highlighted and modern Western obsession with time neutralized. In connection with the locus of enunciation, what I attempt to do is less to describe and narrate how colonization of languages, memories, and space took place and were implemented than to *identify the spaces in between produced by colonization as location and energy of new modes of thinking whose strength lies in the transformation and critique of the "authenticities" of both Western and Amerindian legacies.* This is the reason why in writing this book I was more interested in exploring new ways of thinking about what we know than to accumulate new knowledge under old ways of thinking. Thus, the reader can find here the reason for the lengthy introduction and afterword framing the six chapters and emerging from the debris and the silences in each of them.

In reading the final proofs of the book I realized that I frequently used the word "tradition." What I said in the previous paragraph and my insistence in understanding the past and speaking the present invites an understanding of "traditions" not as *something* that is there to be remembered, but the *process of remembering and forgetting* itself. That is why this book is part and parcel of the process of the reconfiguration of traditions. "Traditions" would be, in this sense, a multiplexed and filtered ensemble of acts of saying, remembering, and forgetting. In such enactments, "traditions" are the loci were people are bonded in communities by languages, eating habits, emotions, ways of dressing, and organizing and conceiving themselves in a given space (country or border) by constructing an image of both the self and the other. This is why, I would like to insist, I am more attentive to the emergence of new identities than to the preservation of old ones, and territoriality is conceived as the site of interaction of languages and memories in constructing places and defining identities. "Colonial semiosis" is the expression I use to suggest processes instead of places in which people intereact. A performative concept of semiotic interactions allows me to conceive colonial encounters as a process of manipulation and control rather than of transmission of meaning or representation. I am not looking for representations but, rather, for processes and semiotic interactions.

In the spring of 1994 Homi Bhabha's much awaited book, _The Locations of Culture,_ was released. At that time, I had read almost all the articles that became chapters of the book, with the exception of the introduction and the conclusion. I have already devoted elsewhere (Mignolo, "The Postcolonial Reason," forthcoming) several pages comparing Dussel's and Bhabha's contribution to the criticism of modernity from a colonial and postcolonial perspective. Here I would like to underline just two aspects strictly relevant to my project and the line of reasoning I am trying to articulate in this preface. In the first place, Homi Bhabha's countering modernity stems from the experiences and legacies of the British Empire in India and—in consequence— from the endowment of the second stage or globalization from the Enlightenment to World War II. As such, his theorizing is deeply entrenched in the linguistic history of modernity and the predominance of English and French. I found "natural," for instance, the intellectual and emotional enthusiasm that Terry Eagleton expressed for the book (_The Guardian,_ February 1994), an enthusiasm that I myself tend to place in Kusch's criticism of occidentalism, in Dussel's criticism of modernity, and in Anzaldúa's critical location between Aztec speech and writing legacies, between Castilian as a colonial language vis-à-vis Nahuatl and English; as a new colonial language replacing and displacing the role of Castilian in the complex histories and contemporary genealogies of the early modern and the early colonial periods. Their arguments spring from the legacies of the Spanish empire, and, consequently, their theorizing is deeply rooted in the language and history of modernity and the displacement of Castilian as a language proper to knowledge and philosophical reasoning.

Secondly, I share with Homi Bhabha his emphasis on the "spaces in between," a concept that I learned from Ortíz's notion of "transculturation"; from Kusch's notion of "cultural phagocytosis"; from the Brazilian novelist and cultural critic Silviano Santiago's notion of "the inter-space" (_entre-lugar_) of Latin American literature elaborated in the early seventies; from Anzaldúa's notion of "borderland"; from the word _nepantla,_ coined by Nahuatl speakers in New Spain during the sixteenth century to designate the inter-space between cultures; from Khatibbi's notion of "une pensée autre" and the transformation of "bi-lingual" into "bi-language," which places the accent

in the spaces in between rather than in the two poles implicit in the
notion of bilingualism. What all these examples have in common is
their inscription in the early colonial period and the fact that they are
rooted in the displacement of Castilian and Portuguese languages in
the history of modernity. Khatibbi may look like an exception. However, the fact that French colonial language is, in Khatibbi, transcultu-
rated with Arabic, and that Arabic is the language upon which
Castilian built its triumphal moment in the early modern period,
makes me feel Khatibbi to be a thinker closer to the one I just quoted
than to Amselle, for example, whose conceptualizations are invested
in the history of French languages and cultures and its colonial expansion. What all of this amounts to, in other words, is the foregrounding
of history of language in the modern period and the linguistic inscriptions of theorizing in the realm of a variegated spectrum of colonial
legacies.

III

As many other people doing research and writing books, I have a long
list of debts. Several times I attempted to reconstruct the moments, in
chronological order, that brought me to this point. Perhaps the departure was when I listened to Alton Becker's interpretation of the Javanese shadow theater and read one of his articles (Becker 1980).
Becker showed me that it was impossible to understand Javanese
shadow theater from the categories traced by Aristotle to describe and
prescribe Greek tragedy. The need to compare and at the same time
undo the premises upon which comparative strategy was founded
became clear to me at the blink of an eye. It was also Becker with
whom, toward 1974–75, I was able to talk about the works of Umberto Maturana and Francisco Varela and about the contemporary
relevance of Ortega y Gasset's conceptualization of a "new philology." Next I met Lemuel Johnson, when we both were members of
the College Curriculum Committee at the University of Michigan.
Johnson helped me, without him knowing it, to put what I learned
from Becker into the context of colonization. Bringing the European
Renaissance into the scenario of comparing Javanese shadow theater
and Greek tragedy and that of colonization was indeed an easy task
since, at that time, I was doing research on Renaissance historiography
and the histories of the Indies. This, in retrospect, was the triad that
put this book in motion.

The first time I tried to put the teaching of Becker and Johnson to
good use was while I was doing research at the John Carter Brown

Library. Norman Fiering, its director, was organizing an interdisciplinary conference on "The Book in the Americas." It was June,
1986 and the conference was being planned for June, 1987. I presented my ideas to Fiering in rough form and defined my contribution
to the conference as a comparative analysis of the "book" in European
and Amerindian societies at the time of the encounter. He encouraged
me to submit a written version of my ideas; the paper was accepted,
celebrated by some, and looked at with suspicions by others. It went
through several revisions before becoming chapter 2 of this book under the new title "The Materiality of Reading and Writing Cultures." I
am in debt to Paul Gehl and Michael Palencia Roth for the time they
took to read the piece and make valuable critical comments. I am also
thankful to Elizabeth Hill Boone for making me believe that my approach to writing and the book was interesting and original.

In writing chapter 2 I became aware of the complicities between
the history of the book and the history of writing during the European
Renaissance. I was fortunate to have met Ignacio Osorio Romero in
Mexico in 1981. His knowledge of the classical tradition in Mexico, his
insights in reading the complex process of education during the colonial period against the grain, from schooling to the university, from
the Franciscans to the Jesuits, were very much responsible for the
shape and content of chapter 1. I was able to bring into a different
context what, previously, I had learned from other experts in the Spanish and European Renaissance: Luisa López Grigera, Francisco Rico,
Juan Bautista Avalle Arce, and Eugenio Ascencio (see Boone and Mignolo 1994).

After writing chapters 1 and 2, I returned to my previous research
and publications on Renaissance historiography and the histories of
the Indies. I immediately realized that I had to reframe the issue in
comparative terms and in colonial situations. Chapters 3 and 4 are the
outcome of rewriting what I had already published on the topic (Mignolo 1981, 1982, 1985, 1987) as well as of reframing what I had already
published on the relationships among history, literature, and fiction
(Mignolo 1981, 1985, 1993). The first departure from what I had already written up to that point came with my increasing interest in
literacy. I was fortunate enough to work for about four years, first in a
reading group, and then as co-teacher of two graduate seminars on
literacy, with Deborah Keller-Cohen, Anne Ruggles Gere, and Bruce
Mannheim at the University of Michigan. The dialogue with col-
leagues in linguistics, psychology, English, education, and anthropology enormously widened my literary perspectives on literacy. An interdisciplinary and international conference took place at the University
of Michigan ("Literacy: Interdisciplinary Conversations," Fall 1991),

in which I was able to verbalize the connections between literacy and historiography. My contribution to the conference proceedings ("Literacy and Colonization: Writing Histories of People without History") allowed me to articulate literacy and historiography and to move from the brighter to the darker side of the Renaissance. A previous attempt was made in 1989 when I was invited by Nancy Farriss to participate in a workshop on "The Colonization of Languages: Verbal and Non-Verbal," organized by the Latin American Center and the University of Pennsylvania. There I met Serge Gruzinski, whose *La colonizasion de l'imaginaire. Sociétés indigènes et occidentalisation dans le Méxique espagnole, xvème–xviiième siècles* (1988) greatly changed my view on the historiography of the Indies. Gruzinski's book and the exchange of information and ideas entertained thereafter, together with my reading (during the same years) of the concept of literature and history in Edouard Glissant's *Caribbean Discourse* (1981) and Ranajit Guha's piece on Indian historiography and subaltern studies (Guha 1988), contributed to my rewriting of the piece I presented at the workshop organized by Nancy Farriss. A year later I sent the paper to Raymond Grew, who encouraged me to submit a revised version to *Comparative Studies in Society and History*. The article was published under the title "On the Colonization of Amerindian Languages and Memories." Neither of the two articles I just mentioned are published as such in the book. They are dispersed, so to speak, all over chapters 2, 3, and 4.

My interest in maps goes back to 1981 when I met René Acuña in Mexico. He was editing the ten volumes of the *Relaciones Geográficas de México*, published by the Universidad Autónoma de México between 1982 and 1989. My interests and curiosity were expanded in 1986, at the John Carter Brown Library, when I was studying European cartography of the sixteenth century and discovered the world map that the Italian Jesuit Mateo Ricci made in China toward the end of the sixteenth century. The entire chapter 5 has been organized around this map and the maps of the *Relaciones Geográficas*. I am indebted to Susan Danforth for her endless patience in trying to understand my project and in finding the material I needed.

In June, 1987, during the conference "The Books in the Americas" (also at the John Carter Brown Library), I met Bryan Harley, with whom I remained in touch until his death in December, 1991. Bryan's strange combination of cartographic erudition and theoretical sophistication shaped my perception of maps more than I can do justice to in this preface. It was natural that being interested in maps I decided to spend some time at the Newberry Library and take advantage of their wonderful Renaissance and Ayer collections as well as their Hermon

Dunlap Center of the History of Cartography. There I met David
Bouisseret, director of the center, Jerry Danzer, and David Woodward. Their generosity and wisdom largely contributed to what the
reader will find in chapters 5 and 6. Finally, I am indebted to the
confidence and enthusiasm of Doris Sommer and Benitez Rojo for
inviting me to present my preliminary ideas on the issues, in the fall of
1989, at Amherst College. Nina Scott, who attended the talk and
listened to the first version of what is now chapter 5, encouraged me to
present it again the following year at the University of Massachusetts.
I did. A preliminary version of chapter 5, under the same title, was
published in the conference proceedings (Cevallos-Candau et al.
1994).

Chapter 6 has a different though related history, and again the John
Carter Brown Library is in the picture. Julio Ortega invited me to
participate in an NEH seminar in June, 1991. I presented there a rough
version of what is now chapter 6. A first version was printed by Ran-
dolph Macon Woman's College in their series of Philip Thayer Memorial Lectures. A second version was published in the first issue of
Latin American Colonial Review (1992) and, corrected and enlarged,
became what is now chapter 6. Although much of what went in this
chapter was a product of my previous research at the John Carter
Brown and the Newberry Libraries, I also benefited from the help and
generosity of David Bosse at the Clements Library (University of
Michigan), who always found the missing pieces and hidden information.

I have outlined some of my many debts articulated around significant moments in the process of doing research and writing the book. I
have many other no less significant debts, both to institutions and
persons. In the first place I shall mention the year I spent at the Institute for the Humanities at the University of Michigan as A. Bartlett
Giamatti Faculty Fellow (July 1991–June 1992), where I was able to
write and rewrite parts and wholes of the book. The leadership of its
director, James Winn, and the wisdom of the Fellows, both faculty and
graduate students, greatly enhanced the general perspective in which I
framed the main thesis of the book.

In the fall of 1992 I co-taught a graduate interdisciplinary seminar
with Fernando Coronil ("Beyond Occidentalism: Rethinking How
the West Was Born"), which greatly influenced what I wrote in the
afterword. I owe thanks to Anton Shammas for sharing with me his
ideas about writing and the book in Arabic history and about the space
in between the Islamic and European worlds. I am indebted to Fatma
Müge Goçeck for sharing with me her knowledge and ideas about

literacy in the Ottoman empire and its relations to Europe. Piotr Michalowsky was always a source of information about the history of writing in ancient Mesopotamia and a bundle of energy when it came to discussing theories of writing and representations.

Last but not least, there are a series of debts owed to those who helped not in the ideas discussed or information introduced in the book but in its very production, in the "materiality of reading and writing cultures." George Baudot introduced me—in the early 1970s and in Toulouse—to the beauty of the Nahuatl language and the stories told by the mendicant friars in early colonial Mexico. I owe more than I can express to the enthusiasm of LeAnn Fields, Executive Editor at the University of Michigan Press. When I had just a general idea of the book and perhaps a draft version of two chapters, some time in the fall of 1988, LeAnn made me believe in the relevance of the project. I am not exaggerating in saying that perhaps without that initial enthusiasm this may not have been a book but a series of articles published in different journals. I am enormously indebted to Marianne Grashoff, who, with patience and savoir faire, read and reread draft after draft of the entire book, making valuable editorial recommendations at the level of the sentence and paragraph, identifying repetition or ideas not clearly expressed, as well as underlining what she found interesting and appealing. When I began writing the book I worked closely with Noel Fallows, then a graduate student at the University of Michigan, now an assistant professor at Tulane University. Fallows's mastery of English and his experience in editing his own father's articles made my life much, much easier. He also translated from Spanish into English several quotations from sixteenth- and seventeenth-century authors. When Fallows was out of reach, Maureen Dyokas (also a graduate student at the University of Michigan) took his place in translating from Spanish into English. I shall add that both Fallows and Dyokas were very seriously interested in translation and already had experience of their own in that field. When I came to Duke University in January, 1993, I had to deal with the difficult task of obtaining reproduction permissions for all of the ninety-four illustrations. It was a task in itself, probably very much like gathering information and writing an extra chapter. I am indebted to Kristin Pesola, Lisa O'Neil, and Debbera Carson for their superb job. I wish to thank the anonymous employees at the University of Michigan Library who so diligently processed my constant requests for information, articles, and books and sent them to me via e-mail or through campus mail. Ellen McCarthy and the editorial team at the University of Michigan Press were a model of efficiency, care, and patience in the last stage of the book. Finally, Anne Wylie, Andrea Wylie Mignolo, and Alexander Wylie Mignolo, the people with whom I live, were kind in excess over the years, understanding that "Oh, he is still writing the book" when I had to leave home to do research or stay away to write.

On Describing Ourselves Describing Ourselves: Comparatism, Differences, and Pluritopic Hermeneutics

This book is about the colonization of languages, of memories, and of space that took place when the "fourth part" of the world, the New World, began to emerge in the European consciousness. The book focuses mainly on central Mexico, or Anáhuac, although examples are also drawn from colonial Yucatán and colonial Peru. Chronologically, the accent is placed on the sixteenth century, although examples from Amerindian cultures of today are invoked to show that colonization is not behind us but has acquired a new form in a transnational world. Linguistically, the focus is on Castilian and Amerindian languages (mostly Nahuatl), although some of the conclusions will illuminate the diversity of colonial experiences in the Americas. Overall, the study offers a view of the Spanish (as well as the European) Renaissance from the perspective of its colonies and, by doing so, joins other efforts to rethink the boundaries of the Renaissance by charting early modern studies. While Renaissance studies are oriented toward the Mediterranean and often assume the continuity of the classical tradition, studies of the early modern period turn toward the Atlantic and the Pacific and advocate the perspective of the colonies.[1]

The book is divided into three parts, each comprising two chapters. The first part explores the philosophy of writing in the European Renaissance as a decisive factor in the politics of language implemented by the Crown and the religious orders in the New World. It also brings to light some of the difficulties Europeans had in understanding writing systems alien to their own practices. Chapter 1 focuses on Elio Antonio de Nebrija's philosophy of writing, developed during the late fifteenth and early sixteenth centuries, and his influence on the writing of grammars of Amerindian languages; and on José de Aldrete's essays on the origin of the Castilian language, from the early seventeenth century. Nebrija, a pioneer man of letters credited with introducing the Italian Renaissance into Spain, articulated a philosophy of writing based on the celebration of the letter and the interrelations between alphabetic writing and the writing of history. He is less commonly known for the ideological program attached to his two grammatical treatises, a Latin grammar (1481) and a Castilian grammar (1492). From Nebrija's political philosophy of language follow, on the one hand, the necessity to trace the origins and the frontiers of the Spanish languages (an effort entertained by Aldrete) and, on the other, the necessity, first, to teach Castilian language and customs to Amerindians and, second, to convert them to Christianity. The first task was in the hands of the Crown, the second in the hands of friars and missionaries.

Chapter 2 revolves around concepts of writing and the book and examines the *Coloquios y doctrina christiana* (a dialogue among twelve Franciscan friars and a handful of Mexican wise men that took place in 1524, was written down, and was transcribed by Bernardino de Sahagún around 1565). The *Coloquios* is a paradigmatic example with which to analyze the connections among the Renaissance philosophy of language, the idea of the book, and the warranty of truth grounded in writing. The argument moves from the question of the letter to the question of the book in colonial situations and explores cultural assumptions behind the frustrations, misunderstandings, and power relations established between persons with different writing systems, different sign carriers (i.e., vehicles of inscriptions—books, Peruvian quipus, papyri), and, above all, different *descriptions* of writing and sign carriers. I accent how people (Castilians as well as Amerindians) described their own social interactions and cultural production. I emphasize that Castilian descriptions of Amerindian interactions either suppressed Amerindians' own self-descriptions or, when the Castilians did listen to the Amerindians, incorporated Amerindians' self-descriptions into their own (I will return to the topics of self-description and representation in this introduction, as well as in the conclusion). The materiality of writing, together with its conceptualization across cultures, is brought into focus to spotlight its underpinning of the colonization of Amerindian languages. In this second chapter philological and comparative analysis is first tested. The materiality of the sign carriers (such as textiles on the Peruvian quipus) are analyzed, together with the descriptions the Amerindians and Castilians built around their own writing systems and sign carriers.

The second part is devoted to the colonization of memory and begins where the first part left off. The celebration of the letter and its complicity with the book were not only a warranty of truth but also offered the foundations for Western assumptions about the necessary relations between alphabetic writing and history. People without letters were thought of as people without history, and oral narratives were looked at as incoherent and inconsistent. Chapter 3 focuses on history as one of the main discursive practices in the European Renaissance and as a Western regional construct with pretensions to universality. The chapter moves from the Western conceptualization of history to the reevaluation of Amerindians' means of recording the past, then into a detailed analysis of the contribution made by an Italian knight, Bernardo Boturini Benaducci, who arrived in Mexico during the first half of the eighteenth century, and to Francesco Patrizi. Patrizi, a little-remembered Italian rhetorician of the second half of the sixteenth century, is brought into the picture because of the similarities between his and Giambattista Vico's conception of recording memories by using visual means. Vico was also Boturini's inspiration. Boturini's main work, *Idea de una nueva historia general de la America Septentrional* (1746), completed a process by which alphabetic writing was elevated as the most desirable system but led to a debate on writing systems during the eighteenth century and opened the doors for a reconsideration of the different writing systems of the world. The writing of history, and the very concept of historiography, however, was not challenged by such changes in the Western conception of writing and its history.

Chapter 4 is concerned with genre and the organization of knowledge. The idea of history and of recording the past is compared with letter writing (*epistola*), another crucial discursive genre in the European Renaissance, and with encyclopedic organization of knowledge. Then, both are compared with Amerindians' ways of organizing knowledge. The chapter opens with Peter Martyr's *Epistolary* and *De orbe novo decades* as early examples of the connivance between letter writing and history and follows with Bernardino de Sahagún's monumental work, the *Florentine Codex* (a three-volume manuscript finished toward 1578, in Nahuatl and Spanish), and the *Historia de la Nueva España,* a work containing the text of the *Florentine Codex* in Castilian. Printed in the nineteenth century, it provides the main example by which to explore the complicitus among writing, discursive genres, and the organization of knowledge. The encyclopedia as a Western genre with similar examples in Chinese and Arab cultural history,[2] whose influence on Sahagún's work has been well documented, is explored to understand the colonization of memory accomplished by rendering in alphabetic writing and in Renaissance discursive genres the information Amerindians passed on to Sahagún but had already organized in their own system of genres. Sahagún captured the content of information, but not its organization. To underline both the mobility of the center and the histories of the peripheries, an Amerindian "encyclopedia" written during the sixteenth century is examined. The *Books of Chilam Balam* (from the Yucatán peninsula) is taken as the main example to reflect on alternative views of organizing knowledge and on the transformation of Amerindian traditions during the colonial period.

Thus, while chapter 3 discusses one case of colonization of memory, highlighting the Spanish deed over Amerindian customs, chapter 4 explores another, the suppression of the Amerindians' own categories for organizing knowledge. The politicization of hermeneutics proves to be necessary to account for the colonization of one system by another. Colonization does not imply a devouring march, by which everything in Amerindian cultures was suppressed by Spanish pedagogical, religious, and administrative institutions. I insist, first, on the coexistence of languages, literacies, memories, and spaces; second, on the dominance that makes it possible for one of the coexisting elements to occupy a position of power over the others as if it were the only truth; and third, on the need of the politicization of hermeneutics to deal with these questions. Finally, the case of Sahagún also illustrates the relevance of the locus of enunciation, a category that brings to awareness the act of understanding I am performing and the act of understanding performed in the past, which becomes the object to be understood in the present. Thus, understanding the past and speaking the present take a new twist with this example.

The third part of the book examines the colonization of space. Chapter 5 takes as its main example Mateo Ricci's *mappamundi* (ca. 1584) and looks into the coexistence of differing geographical framings during the sixteenth and early seventeenth centuries. Here issues are again raised of the power relations between the organization and colonization of space. Chapter 6 focuses on López de Velasco's maps of the West Indies (1574), which at the time included the Spanish colonies and extended from Florida to the Philippines. Also examined is the intellectual context of the emergence of a fourth part of the world in both the European consciousness as a whole, and in the Council of the Indies in particular, with its need to administer the newly "discovered" and colonized lands and people. Once again, I bring into focus the issue of coexistence and power relations in con-

trolling and implementing a given conceptualization of space. Once
again, my analysis does not imply that the colonization of space
devours non-Western conceptualizations, but that it banishes them
from the view of those who belong to the same culture as the mapmaker. The idea that what is different is wrong or less is perpetuated.
The colonization of space and the colonization of languages mean
that dominant views of languages, of recording the past, and of charting territories become synonymous with the real by obstructing possible alternatives.

Thus, if scholarship cannot represent the colonized faithfully or
allow the subaltern to speak, it can at least break up a monolithic
notion of the subaltern and maintain an alternative discursive practice, parallel to both the official discourse of the state, for which maps
represent territories and histories account for the truth of events,
and the established discourse of official scholarship, in which the
rules of the academic game are the sound warranty for the value
of knowledge independent of any political agenda or personal interest.[3]

The book is as much about understanding the past as it is about
speaking the present. I am trying to understand the past, although this
is not a historiographical study proper. This understanding is a communal and dialogic enterprise, not solitary and monologic; the drive
toward understanding arises not only from disciplinary and rational,
but also from social and emotional, imperatives. The past cannot be
rendered in a neutral discourse. Bound to a given discipline, any conception of it will be laid out according to rules for scholarly or scientific
reports within the discipline. Scholarly discourses (as well as other
types of discourse) acquire their meaning on the grounds of their
relation to the subject matter as well as their relation to an audience, a
context of description (the context chosen to make the past event or
object meaningful), and the *locus* of enunciation from which one
"speaks" and, by speaking, contributes to changing or maintaining
systems of values and beliefs. For Foucault, the *locus enuntiationis*
(*mode d'enonciation* in his terminology) was one of the four components of the discursive formations he conceived in terms of social roles
and institutional functions.[4] Foucault was mainly concerned with the
disciplinary and institutional grounding of discursive formations and
gave less attention to the personal history of the understanding subject
(Is it male or female? With which ethnic group does she or he identify?
To what social class does he or she belong? In which particular political
configuration is she or he speaking or writing?). It was not in his
horizon to raise questions about the locus of enunciation in colonial
situations. Thus, from the perspective of the locus of enunciation,

understanding the past cannot be detached from speaking the present, just as the disciplinary (or epistemological) subject cannot be detached from the nondisciplinary (or hermeneutical) one. It follows, then, that the need to speak the present originates at the same time from a research program that needs to debunk, refurbish, or celebrate previous disciplinary findings, and from the subject's nondisciplinary (gender, class, race, nation) confrontation with social urgencies. I certainly do not advocate the replacement of disciplinary with political underpinnings, but I attempt to underline the unavoidable ideological dimensions of any disciplinary discourse, particularly in the realm of the human sciences.

Following these considerations, the book has been written from the perspective of a literary scholar born and raised in Argentina, a country steeped more in a postcolonial history with a large component of European immigration, than in any colonial experiences or Amerindian traditions. As a literary scholar, I became interested in rereading the texts and events of the conquest and colonization of the New World from the perspective of the spread of Western literacy rather than from the formulas provided for literary interpretation. As a Latin American and an Argentinian, I became interested in the fusion of horizons between the present as it was spoken by the canonized ancestors of the Spanish culture in Latin America and the present we (Latin Americans and scholars of today) elect to speak. This fusion of horizons should not necessarily be friendly but could be critical (for instance, tracing back a genealogy that puts me, as a son of Italian immigrants, at odds with the Spanish tradition in Latin America). By bringing this piece of autobiography into the foreground, I have no intention of promoting a deterministic relationship between place of birth and personal destiny. I do not believe that someone born in New York will be a broker, anymore than someone born in San Luis Potosí will be a miner or someone born in Holland a miller. But I bring to the work those parts of my background that make me particularly sensitive to issues of bilingualism and of cross-cultural understanding: my living first in a predominantly Spanish nation, Argentina, that did not coincide with my own status as the son of Italian immigrants and second in another, the United States, where becoming a citizen solves a great many practical matters but does not erase one's memories. Consequently, the effort to critically examine oneself is imperative because literary scholarship remains intermingled with national and linguistic identities. The links between the past, which I strive to understand, and the present, which motivates me to speak and write, are not always obvious. Thus the constant need for new interpretations (understanding the past and speaking the present), be they of texts, events, actions, or ideas.

What I have referred to in the title of this book as the darker side of the Renaissance could be framed in terms of an emerging field of study whose proper name oscillates between *colonial discourse* and *colonial semiosis*.[5] Both expressions are employed by those whose main interest is the understanding of the relationship between discourse and power during colonial expansion. The expression colonial discourse has been defined by Peter Hulme as all kinds of discursive production related to and produced in colonial situations, from—to use his own examples—the Capitulations of 1492 to *The Tempest*, from royal orders and edicts to the most carefully written prose.[6] *Discourse* used in this sense has an enormous advantage over the notion of literature when the corpus at stake is colonial. While *colonial literature* has been construed as an aesthetic system dependent on the Renaissance concepts of poetry, *colonial discourse* places colonial discursive production in a context of conflictive interactions, of appropriations and resistances, of power and domination. Significant texts such as the *Popol Vuh* (Book of council, a Maya-Quiche narrative of origins)[7] as well as many others of the same kind now acquire a new meaning: instead of being considered pre-Columbian texts admired for their otherness, they now become part and parcel of colonial discursive production. It could not be otherwise, since the *Popol Vuh* as we have it was written alphabetically around 1550. How could a text alphabetically written be pre-Columbian if Amerindians did not have letters, as all missionaries and men of letters constantly remind us? How then could such a text not be related to the European Renaissance when the celebration of the letter became one of its foundations? The original *Popol Vuh*, destroyed during the conquest, was written in Quiche, certainly a language not very popular in the European Renaissance, but quite common in the colonies where major Amerindian languages (such as Nahuatl, Zapotec, and Quechua) competed with Latin and Spanish and challenged the continuity of the classical tradition and the spread of Western literacy.

However, when pushed to the limit, the notion of colonial discourse,[8] desirable and welcome as it is, is not the most comprehensive one we can concoct to apprehend the diversity of semiotic interactions in colonial situations and, thus, to shed more light on the darker side of the Renaissance. The notion of discourse, although it embodies both oral and written interactions, may not account for semiotic interactions between different writing systems, such as the Latin alphabet introduced by the Spaniards, the picto-ideographic writing system of Mesoamerican cultures, and the quipus in colonial Peru.[9] If we were to use the term *discourse* to refer to oral interactions and reserve *text* for written ones, we would need to expand the latter term beyond alphabetic written documents to include all material sign inscriptions.[10] By doing so we would honor the etymological meaning of *text* (weaving, textile),[11] which began to lose its original meaning when alphabetic writing and the Renaissance celebration of the letter obscured the more generous medieval meaning.[12] The expression *colonial semiosis* indicates, on the one hand, a field of study parallel to other well-established ones such as colonial history or colonial art. But, on the other hand, it intends also to indicate a change in our understanding of the construction of a New World during the sixteenth century, a perspective in which the darker side of the Renaissance is brought into light and a change of voice in which the European Renaissance is looked at from the colonial periphery.[13] Among other things, this book is an essay on colonial semiosis as a field of study.

The introduction of colonial semiosis as a field of study goes together with the need for a philological and comparative approach to its understanding. Introducing philological procedures at this point might not generate much enthusiasm among readers interested in cultural and subaltern studies or in rethinking popular cultures, who would expect a more ideological grounding. I believe, however, that a "new philology" is of the essence to contextualize cultural objects and power relations alien to the everyday life of the scholar and, mainly, to (re)construct the knowledge and beliefs that Spaniards and Mexicas had about their own semiotic interactions and perceived the practices and beliefs of the other. The new philology to which I subscribe revolves around two axioms: (1) every word is exuberant, because it says more than intended; (2) every word is deficient, because it says less than expected. The two axioms were proposed by Ortega y Gasset, who (like Bakhtin during the same years) was reacting against Saussurean linguistics and moving toward a more pragmatic understanding of language.[14] Instead of looking into the logic of Saussure's "language system," Ortega y Gasset turned his attention to "the saying of the people" [el decir de la gente]. However, neither Ortega y Gasset nor Bakhtin faced the problem of a new philology or a dialogical imagination that would satisfactorily deal with the comparison between events and artifacts from radically different cultures,[15] much less with colonial situations in which comparative studies implied bringing to the foreground cultural domination, resistance, adaptation, and hybridization. My emphasis is on events and cultural artifacts in themselves as well as on the discourses by which events and artifacts

are conceptualized from within and outside a given community.
Descriptions, in this study, are as crucial as the objects or events
described. The question of who describes what, when, and for whom
guides my reflections throughout this book, both when I describe
Mexica or Spanish self-descriptions, or Spanish descriptions of the
Mexica, as well as when I describe *myself* describing Mexica or Spanish
descriptions of themselves or of each other. I take philology to be an
analytical tool for describing descriptions, either foreign to or far removed in time from the point of view of the understanding subject.

It is not necessary for an analytical procedure to be affiliated with
philosophical and ideological positions. The fact that philology during the eighteenth and the nineteenth centuries was increasingly associated with hermeneutics should be looked at in its historical con-
tingencies rather than its ontological or logical necessities. *Scientia*,
before the emergence of the human sciences,[16] was understood in the
context of discursive practices related to logic (or dialectics) and rhetoric. Thus, if hermeneutics in the twentieth century detached itself
from the interpretation of discourse and text to embrace the larger
spectrum of the human sciences,[17] it is possible to rethink the traditional ties between hermeneutics and philology in understanding
cross-cultural semiotic practices.

Two main reasons support a comparative approach to colonial situations from the perspective of the human sciences:[18] first, because
the very definition of colonial semiosis implies the coexistence of interactions among and cultural production by members of radically different cultural traditions; second, because the very act of understanding traditions that are not ours (i.e., are not the one to which the
understanding subject belongs) implies a comparative perspective between what is understood and the act of understanding itself. Thus, I
do not perceive contradictions in using philological procedures and
comparisons to deal critically with colonial situations when, in fact,
the methods I am proposing as a decolonizing venture have been
forged by members of the same cultures that produced the colonial
expansion. Neither do I assume that philology will be a more suitable
approach to the study of the European Renaissance than the study of
European colonial expansion and the encounter with persons from
non-Western cultural traditions. Since I am dealing with signs, I need
philological procedures. Since I am dealing with colonial situations,
however, I am not necessarily forced to carry on the ideological background attached to the methodological procedure itself. In fact, philology and comparatism should allow us to look at the European
Renaissance by locating the understanding subject in the colonial peripheries. This is all that can be said at this point. The remainder of the

book will either convince or disappoint you with regard to these claims.

Let me expand, however, on the advantages of philological and comparative approaches and justify my belief that such a method can also prove beneficial in the domain of colonial cultural studies, rethinking popular cultures, and building postcolonial theories. In the first place, colonial semiosis implies the coexistence of "high" and "low" cultures. It also implies power relations between, on one hand, the group of people controlling the politics and the economy and, on the other, the subaltern communities. In the second place, a philological approach is necessary for understanding colonial semiosis on two levels: first, for critically distancing the understanding subject from his/her own upbringing, memories, and sensibility; and second, for critically approaching the conceptualization of semiotic practices alien to the culture in which he or she places him- or herself. This methodological problem, common to anthropologists, is also relevant to those who work with signs or traces of the past rather than with people in the present. *Map* and *geographer* are, for instance, common names to an educated Western citizen. But *amoxtli* and *tlacuilo* are not usually so (see chaps. 5 and 6). Although map and geographer are also notions common to scholarly discourse there is a temptation to talk about "Amerindian maps."[19] It is necessary to understand how Amerindians understood a "map," and at this point, philology needs to be complemented with a comparative approach. Since *map* and *amoxtli* were names by which different cultures and communities designated the graphic and material objects in which territory was described, a comparison between their form and uses in their respective cultural context is of the essence. The situation becomes even more complex when we realize that *amoxtli* could also be translated as "book" and *tlacuilo* as "scribe" (see chap. 2). Map in the Middle Ages meant "napkin, signal cloth" and, by extension, the material on which graphic signs are inscribed. *Amoxtli* referred both to the tree from which the solid surface to write on was made ("paper") and to the entity in which the written material was kept together ("book"). *Amoxtli* and "signal cloth" were, then, solid surfaces upon which signs of territoriality were inscribed. Thus, while territoriality was common to both Spanish and Amerindian ethnic groups, maps and *amoxtli* were culture-relative names for graphic objects in which territoriality was represented. A geographer was distinguished from a historian in a culture in which writing and mapping became clearly different activities. This was not necessarily so, however, in a culture in which the *tlacuilo* painted both the pictographic signs in which past memories were preserved and those in which spatial boundaries were traced. That is why a Nahuatl noun that could be translated as the Spanish *pintura* was applied to

both writing and mapping. A possible solution is to introduce a theoretical concept, such as "territorial organization, or territorial conceptualization" authorizing a comparative analysis of Spanish maps and Amerindian *amoxtli.*

If philological and comparative analysis is the necessary approach to understanding colonial semiosis because of coexisting systems of descriptions and coevolutionary processes, with differing degrees and levels of interference and hybridization, it cannot be justified from the perspective of a philosophical hermeneutic,[20] which implicitly or explicitly grounded both philology and comparatism in the modern era.[21] The understanding of "our" tradition, in which the foundation of philosophical discursive hermeneutics rests, implies that the tradition to be understood and the understanding subject are one and the same; a universal tradition is understood by a universal subject who, at the same time, speaks for the rest of humanity. Contrary to the monotopic understanding of philosophical hermeneutics, colonial semiosis presupposes more than one tradition and, therefore, demands a diatopic or pluritopic hermeneutic, a concept I borrow from Raimundo Panikkar.[22] This book is also a venture in pluritopic hermeneutics as a mode of understanding.

What I am proposing is certainly not new. Enrique Dussel has developed a similar perspective in order to deal with a similar problem: the tensions between the Western philosophical tradition as practiced in the European centers of education and in third world universities.[23] Dussel proposes an "analectic," as an alternative to a "dialectic," method. Modifying Levinas's position according to his own experience in and of Latin American history, Dussel moves toward a politicization of phenomenology by introducing the notion of *people* as an alternative to *Dassein* in phenomenological reflection. Criticized harshly by Marxist thinkers who at first embraced his "philosophy of liberation," he has also been blamed for his metaphysical concept of *people* (even if grounded in the Argentinian experiences of the 1970s and in Latin American history)[24] and for his own totalizing conception of analectic.[25] Yet he has been recognized for politicizing phenomenology as an oppositional way of thinking rooted in the perspective of the historical, marginalized, and oppressed Other (Indians, proletarians, women). Although I agree with those who have disapproved of Dussel for proposing a methodological alternative that remains within the monotopic perspective he attempted to debunk, I would like to capitalize on his move toward a decolonization, or liberation (in his own words) of thoughts.[26] Consequently, there is an important distinction to be made between Dussel's analectic and the concept of a pluritopic hermeneutic I am developing here. While Dussel's analectic allows for a radical rethinking of the object to be understood, described, or interpreted, pluritopic hermeneutics also calls into question the positionality and the homogeneity of the understanding subject. One has the impression that Dussel remains within a representational concept of knowledge that questions the conceptualization of the Other as a subject to be understood, without questioning the understanding subject itself. However, his contribution to the construction of disciplinary postcolonial loci of enunciation should not be dismissed.[27]

It is not the whole picture of philosophy of liberation as practiced by Dussel that I am interested in, but in his politicization of phenomenology and the introduction of analectic as an alternative locus of enunciation. Such a move has put Dussel at odds with Marxist thinkers, since he sees analectic as a better alternative to dialectic and a philosophy of liberation as an alternative to Marxism.[28] My particular problem with Dussel is that the introduction of analectic results in conceiving the margins as fixed and ontological rather than as a movable and relational concept. Dussel, however, is not a solitary voice claiming the right of the margin to speak, produce, and transmit knowledge. The African writer and literary critic Ngugi Wa Thiong'O has articulated a similar idea in a different manner. Thiong'O speaks of alternative centers, instead of centers and periphery. By analyzing Conrad's *Heart of Darkness* and Lamming's *In the Castle of My Skin*, Thiong'O concludes that Conrad is criticizing the empire from the very center of its expansion, while Lamming is criticizing it from the center of resistance. Edward Kamau Brathwaite supported this idea by talking about and reading his poetry. A crucial moment of his search for a rhythm and a voice, which corresponds with his living experience in the Caribbean, came when the skidding of a pebble on the ocean gave him a sound and a rhythm he could find by reading Milton or Shakespeare. A second crucial moment came when he perceived the parallels between the skidding of the pebble on the ocean and the calypso, a rhythm he could find by listening to Beethoven.[29]

Michelle Cliff, on her part, indirectly joins these claims when she states that one of the effects of assimilation in the Anglocentrism of British West Indian culture "is that you believe absolutely in the hegemony of the King's English and in the form in which it is meant to be expressed. Or else your writing is not literature; it is folklore and can never be art. . . . The anglican ideal—Milton, Wordsworth, Keats—was held before us with an assurance that we were unable, and would never be enabled, to compose a work of similar correctness. . . . No reggae spoken here."[30] While Thiong'O, Lamming, and Brathwaite simultaneously construct and theorize alternative centers in what have been considered the margins of colonial empires, Latinos in the United States and Black Americans are demonstrating that either the margins are also in the center or, as Thiong'O puts it, that knowledge and aesthetic norms are not universally established by a transcendent subject but are universally established by historical subjects in diverse cultural centers. Gloria Anzaldúa, for instance, has articulated a powerful alternative aesthetic and political hermeneutic by placing herself at the crossroads of three traditions (Spanish-American, Nahuatl, and Anglo-American) and carving a locus of enunciation where different ways of knowing and of individual and collective expressions meet.[31]

But perhaps the best example of a pioneering effort to understand colonization in the New World, and particularly in the Andes, by practicing a pluritopic hermeneutics—without giving it a name—was provided by the Argentinian philosopher Rodolfo Kusch.[32] For political reasons, Kusch was teaching at a northern Argentinian university, Salta, during the 1960s. Northern Argentina had in the past been part of the Inca empire, and Kusch realized how much of the Inca legacy remained in twentieth-century Peru, Bolivia, and northern Argentina. He began to practice a comparative ethnophilosophy, moving from the system of thoughts practiced by the Inca elite in the sixteenth century (under Spanish rule) and by peasants of Amerindian descent to the Western philosophical tradition practiced in Europe and rehearsed in the colonial periphery. Kusch's analysis, moving from one tradition of thought to the other, was not just an exercise in pluritopic hermeneutics but, I will venture to say, the minimal step to be taken for the constitution of differential loci of enunciation and the establishment of a politic of intellectual inquiry that will go beyond cultural relativism.

Kusch's philosophical inquiry was motivated by a need felt by Latin American intellectuals since the second half of the nineteenth century, the need to discover or to invent the cultural identity of America, an ambiguous noun that sometimes implies South or Latin America and sometimes the entire American continent, including the Caribbean. Kusch uses it in both senses, indicating the differences between Amerindian and European legacies in South, Central, and North America. His main argument revolves around the distinction between causal and seminal (from "semen, seed, origin, source") ways of thinking as they refer to two generic conceptual frameworks (and their aftermath), enacted and illustrated in the West. The first is a rational thinking in the Enlightenment tradition in a capitalistic economy. The other, enacted by the Amerindians of colonial times and peasants of

Amerindian descent today, is a rational thinking in the tributary economic systems in Mesoamerica, a variety of ways of living under Western economy since the sixteenth and seventeenth centuries. If there is a dichotomous laying out of Kusch's investigation, the dichotomy ends once he compares Amerindians of yesterday with peasants of today, European thinking of yesterday and today, people in the city and in the country, the middle class in the urban centers both north and south of the Atlantic and the Pacific. Kusch's analysis goes back to the ways of thinking before the early modern period when the seminal, in the upcoming West, was anchored in religion. He begins by locating, in the West, two modes of thought at the same time that he underlines the liberation from religious thinking proclaimed by the ideologues of modernity, from the Renaissance to the Enlightenment. How these two modes of thinking interact in the history of America (his paradigmatic examples are Bolivia, Peru, Argentina, and Chile and, more specifically, the high plateau of the limits between Bolivia and Peru, on the one hand, and Buenos Aires, on the other) is what Kusch attempts to disentangle by means of conceptual analysis intermingled with personal experiences in northern Argentina and southern Bolivia as well as analysis of the middle class on the outskirts of the city of Buenos Aires. In the dialectic between causal and seminal ways of thinking, Kusch finds, as well as founds (without naming it), "a third space" in which a pluritopic hermeneutics could be practiced. Kusch uses the "us" as a member and participant in the society driven by causal ways of thinking. As an Argentinian philosopher, he is able to go beyond a surface of dichotomous oppositions and find the seminal pattern that connects the hidden underground of Western thought with explicit Amerindian attitudes, which have resisted the assimilation to causal thinking, even though peasants of Amerindian descent live within a hybrid context in which the commodification of "art crafts" in Sunday farmers' markets does not erase seminal attitudes maintained among the members of their own communities. By comparing alternative philosophies in his own and neighboring countries with the same official language (Spanish) and similar linguistic Amerindian configurations, Kusch is no longer the outsider trying to understand the Other from far away. The Other for Kusch is part of his own country, part of his own everyday life and community. "Us" and "they" are subsumed in a third space in which both become "we," the members of this country, the inheritors of a colonial legacy.

In a larger context, Kusch is—like the Amerindians with whom he converses and upon whom he reflects—a member and participant of the Americas. He is not an anthropologist who, after finishing his two or three years of fieldwork, will expend the rest of his life in a first-world environment writing about his or her distant friends, making a career out of his or her extended fieldwork. Therefore, the exercise of a pluritopic hermeneutics is more than an academic exercise. To Kusch it is a reflection on the politics of intellectual inquiry and a strategy of cultural intervention. "Writing cultures" acquires a whole new meaning when intellectual inquiry is part of the culture shared by the self-same and the other, by the subject of study and the understanding subject.

Thus, the pluritopic hermeneutic I am trying to articulate moves toward an interactive concept of knowledge and understanding that reflects on the very process of constructing (e.g., putting in order) that portion of the world to be known.[33] It is fashionable nowadays to tell a story from different points of view to show how relative the invention of reality is. What a pluritopic approach emphasizes is not cultural relativity or multiculturalism, but the social and human interests in the act of telling a story as political intervention. The politics of enacting and of constructing loci of enunciation are at stake, rather than the diversity of representations resulting from differential locations in telling stories or building theories. At this point the ethical dimension of knowledge and understanding should be introduced. For pluritopic understanding implies that while the understanding subject has to assume the truth of what is known and understood, he or she also has to assume the existence of alternative politics of location with equal rights to claim the truth. The ethical problem arises when the ideal relativism in which examples like this one have been cast overlook the fact that coexistence of perspective does not always take place without a display of power relations and sometimes violence. Thus, if the epistemological and ontological aspects of a pluritopic understanding could be dealt with in terms of relativism, its ethical dimension invites one to look at the configuration of power. Cultural relativism may be an important step in understanding cultural differences, but Kusch's practice suggests that it falls short if it is not analyzed in the context of power and domination. From this point of view, the colonization of languages, of memory, and of space to be analyzed in the following chapters sheds light on the very process of understanding.

Colonial situations invite one to rethink the hermeneutical legacy. If hermeneutics is defined not only as a reflection on human understanding, but also as human understanding itself,[34] then the tradition in which hermeneutics has been founded and developed has to be recast in terms of the plurality of cultural traditions and across cultural boundaries. Panikkar casts his concept of diatopical hermeneutics, from which I depart, as follows:

Diatopical hermeneutics is the required method of interpretation when the distance to overcome, needed for any understanding, is not just a distance within one single culture . . . , or a temporal one . . . , but rather the distance between two (or more) cultures, which have independently developed in different spaces (topoi) their own methods of philosophizing and ways of reaching intelligibility along with their proper categories.[35]

One aspect distinguishes Panikkar's concept from my own: the kind of "different spaces" implied in colonial situations. Thus, colonial situations and colonial semiosis present a hermeneutical dilemma for the understanding subject interested in the hierarchy established by the domination of one culture (its history, institutions, and individuals) over another. Historically, the analysis of colonial situations has been studied and narrated from points of view prevalent in different domains of the colonizing cultures, even when the interpreter advocates the rights and goods of colonized cultures. Colonial semiosis brings the following dilemma to the fore: what is the locus of enunciation from which the understanding subject comprehends colonial situations? In other words, in which of the cultural traditions to be understood does the understanding subject place him- or herself by constructing his or her locus of enunciation? How can the act of reading and the concept of interpretation be rethought within a pluritopically oriented hermeneutics and the sphere of colonial semiosis? These questions are not only relevant when broad cultural issues such as colonial situations and colonial semiosis are being considered, but also when more specific issues such as race, gender, and class are taken into account. It is in this sense that Dussel's analectic is a necessary complement to a pluritopic hermeneutic emphasizing the locus of enunciation and challenging the universality of the understanding subject.

Gadamer clearly states the goals and justifications of philosophical hermeneutics:

My thesis is—and I think it is a necessary consequence of recognizing the operativeness of history in *our* conditionedness and finitude—that the thing which hermeneutics teaches us is to see through the dogmatism of asserting an opposition and separation between the *ongoing, natural tradition* and the reflective appropriation of it. For behind this assertion stands a dogmatic objectivism that distorts the very concept of hermeneutical reflection itself. In this objectivism the understander is seen—even in the so-called sciences of understanding like history—not in relationship to the

hermeneutic situation and the constant operativeness of history in   17
his own consciousness, but in such a way as to imply that his own
understanding does not enter into the event.[36]

The Mexican historian and philosopher Edmundo O'Gorman
deserves reconsideration at this point for his contribution to the de-
centering of the knowing and understanding subject and contributing
to the construction of a postcolonial locus of enunciation.[37] I have no
quarrel with and, indeed, enthusiastically endorse Gadamer's criticism
of a positivistic conception of knowledge and understanding on the
same grounds that I accept O'Gorman's criticism of positivistic historiography (both come from the same source: Heidegger's critique of
historiographical understanding).[38] The position I take in this book
distances itself, however, from Gadamer at the same time that it approaches that of O'Gorman and assumes the paradox that a model of
thought so much centered in the Western philosophical practices
(such as philosophical hermeneutics) engendered a counterdiscourse
and a critic of Western historiography from the colonial centers (to
follow Thiong'O's approach). Thus, Dussel's analectics and O'Gorman's invention depart from the philosophical tradition engendering
them to become alternative methodologies for understanding social
processes and cultural artifacts outside the scope of a philosophical
hermeneutics or a universal pragmatics. It is on Dussel's and O'Gorman's philosophical moves, rather than on their entire philosophical
positions, that I would like to capitalize. Let's take another step in this
direction.

Gadamer's notion of an "ongoing, natural tradition" presupposes a
monotopic hermeneutic in which the locus of enunciation of she or he
who understands belongs to the same tradition invented by the very
act of understanding. On the contrary, colonial situations depart from
the unified and hegemonic arrangements of an evolutionary (civilizing) process that began in Greece and reached those countries that
accepted it as their own origin. From the perspective of colonial situations, it is helpful to remember that, toward the eleventh century,
Latin Christendom and Muslim Arabia were both coinheritors of the
Greek; and that Latin and Arabic were the languages of secular and
sacred wisdom. Thus, if hermeneutic is restricted to "our ongoing
natural tradition" and that tradition is the Greco-Latin one, then hermeneutic is regional and restricted to one specific kind of tradition.
On the other hand, if hermeneutic could be extended beyond the
Greco-Roman legacy to understand non-Western traditions, then it
could not be monotopic but pluritopic. That is to say, the idea that an
understanding subject located in the "natural, ongoing tradition" of

the West is in a position to understand non-Western legacies must be rejected if the understanding subject does not call into question the very act of understanding and, instead, projects a monotopic understanding over multilingual and pluricultural worlds. When Gadamer reads in the Romantics the desire to overcome the classics and discover the charms of the past, the far, the alien (the Middle Ages, India, China, and so on),[39] he redefines hermeneutics in the context of intercultural understanding, although the understanding subject remains located in one specific culture, one that claims the right to intercultural hermeneutic understanding:

> Hermeneutics may be defined as the attempt to overcome this distance in areas where empathy was hard and agreement not easily reached. There is always a gap that must be bridged. Thus, hermeneutics acquires a central place in viewing human experience. That was indeed Schleiermacher's intuition; he and his associates became the first to develop hermeneutics as a foundation, as the primary aspect of social experience, not only for the scholarly interpretation of texts as documents of the past, but also for understanding the mystery of the inwardness of the other person. This feeling for the individuality of persons, the realization that they cannot be classified and deduced according to general rules or laws, was a significant new approach to the concreteness of the other.[40]

Overcoming the classical tradition and encountering the far and the alien did not change the monotopically conceived hermeneutic, for the understanding subject and his or her locus of enunciation maintained a European position. The question of how an Indian or a Chinese could understand the far and the alien was never asked, much less how encounters between Europeans and Chinese (see chap. 5) or between Europeans and Amerindians in the sixteenth century could be understood today, and by whom and from where such an understanding was achieved. For understanding sixteenth-century encounters during the expansion of Christianity and European political and economic power would be a different enterprise if undertaken from the perspective of members of conflicting groups in power (who had the ability to speak and be heard) in Europe, China, or (Latin) America. Monotopic hermeneutics served to maintain the universality of European culture at the same time that it justified the tendency of its members to perceive themselves as the reference point to evaluate all other cultures. What European countries such as Spain and Portugal attained during the sixteenth and seventeenth centuries (and what was carried on by England, France, Germany, and Holland during the eighteenth and nineteenth centuries) was the economic and political power that made possible the universalization of regional values.

Colonial situations imply a plurality of traditions (instead of an "ongoing natural one"), call for a redefinition of Gadamer's philosophical hermeneutics, and invite a pluritopic, instead of a monotopic, hermeneutics. While in Dussel's hermeneutics the philosopher remains the voice of Knowledge and Wisdom, and in his case, the Knowledge and Wisdom of the People, in a dialogic understanding the role of the philosopher or scholar is as much to talk as it is to listen to other voices talking about experiences alien to him or her. If "natural" traditions are questioned and regionalized (i.e., there are as many natural traditions as there are communities inventing them), then the universal position of the understanding subject can no longer be maintained. Race, gender, class, and nationality are all important dimensions in the process of understanding oneself as well as in the disciplinary process in which the question, What is to be understood? is answered.

However, if a pluritopic understanding of colonial semiosis requires a comparative methodology, we might, then, easily fall into the trap that comparative understanding is in itself a product of colonial expansions,[41] or that it began with Herodotus; or perhaps even before, with Homer or the Ionian writers.[42] I prefer to think that if comparative processes need an origin, it—like many others—should not be looked for among the Greeks but among some of the features common to living organisms. Discerning differences by identities, and vice versa, also seems to be a feature of human intelligence,[43] and, consequently, so are comparative attitudes.[44] Why should comparatism be interpreted as a Greek invention instead of as a human need for (better) adaptation and survival? Comparative categories formulated in disciplinary terms are what we might attribute to the colonial expansion of the fifteenth through seventeenth centuries, which implies that only the Western foundation of knowledge was an authorized way of knowing, comparing, and formulating comparative categories. Furthermore, it would be possible to argue that most comparative studies (of literatures, religions, languages, histories, cartographies, etc.) are founded on a monotopic hermeneutics. Consequently, an alternative comparatism grounded on a pluritopic hermeneutics is at the same time a need and a challenge: a need, because colonial situations are defined by the asymmetry of power relations between the two (or more) poles to be compared; and a challenge, because an alternative methodology must deal with and detach itself from the presuppositions of the established methodological and philosophical foundations from which it departs: in this case, comparatism and monotopic hermeneutics.

David Wallace has observed that one of the chief historical markers of the Renaissance is the "discovery" and colonization of the fourth and final continent, the New World; and the most powerful redefinition of the Renaissance paradigm took place in nineteenth-century Europe, amid (and as part of) the carving up of African, Asian, and Australian territories between European powers,[45] that is to say, during the last stage of imperial expansion. But the fourth part of the world was known as such only from the perspective of European cosmography. Muslim and Chinese conceptions of the earth, as we will see in chapter 5, did not divide the known world in the same way. Nothing in nature itself divided the world in four parts; rather it was a human invention within a particular cultural tradition. Since scholars in the growing field of colonial discourse have to account for a complex system of semiotic interactions embodied in the spread of Western literacy, a concept such as colonial semiosis has the advantage of removing one from the tyranny of the alphabet-oriented notions of text and discourse, and the disadvantage of adding to an already vast and sometimes confusing vocabulary. On the positive side, it defines a field of study in a parallel and complementary fashion to such preexisting terms as colonial history, colonial art, colonial economy, and so on. However, the notion of colonial semiosis reveals at the same time that language-centered colonial studies are moving beyond the realm of the written word to incorporate oral and nonalphabetic writing systems as well as nonverbal graphic systems and that parallel notions such as colonial art or colonial history should be rethought from the perspectives opened up by a pluritopic hermeneutic.

If signs have neither defined properties nor teleologically divine or intentionally human orientations but acquire such qualities when they enter into a network of descriptions by those who, in one way or another, use them, then what are the criteria for validating one description over another? The question is neither new nor insignificant. The simple answer I would like to risk here is: performance, not correspondence. It is the function of the description rather than the accuracy of the representation. Enacting is performing, not looking for correspondences with the world or for the true meaning of a sentence, a text, an object, an event. Performing means both having the skill and knowing how to use it, for skill alone is not enough to make a person a good player, a superstar, or the leader of the community. The point I am trying to make is that scholars studying the culture (whether national, ethnic, or gender) to which they belong are not necessarily subjective, just as scholars studying cultures to which they do not belong are not necessarily objective. Since I believe that theories are

not necessarily the instruments required to understand something
that lies outside the theory, but, on the contrary, that theories are the
instruments required to construct knowledge and understanding (in
academia they would be called "scholarly or scientific descriptions"),
my use of "subjective" and "objective" constitutes examples, not epistemological statements.

From the point of view of either a constructivist epistemology, in
which the world (or the text) is constructed by the subject as "representation,"[46] or a performative (enactive) one, in which the nervous
system constitutes itself as a subject of knowledge and understanding
in a constant process of self-definition and self-adaptation,[47] it will be
true that the personal (individual) and social situation of the knowing
subject will be played within the rules and procedures of a discipline
(even in the case in which they will be contested) as well as within the
community of which the scholar is a member. Constructing or performing knowledge and understanding implies, in the final analysis,
that the living organism in any of its possible descriptions (nervous
system, person, self, scholar, scientist, etc.) prevails in its interactions
with the world at the same time that it competes with and cares for
other living organisms of the same species in its dialogue and relations.

The opposite would be true for an "objective" notion of knowledge: the order of the world and disciplinary rules will prevail over the
organism's needs, personal obsessions, and human interests. Accordingly, in neither case could we say that a better (deeper, more accurate,
more trustworthy, more informed, etc.) knowledge or understanding
is attained. For if we approach knowledge and understanding from a
constructivist or a performative point of view (even taking account of
the differences between them, and limiting it to the actual configuration of disciplinary enterprises), the audience addressed and the re-
searcher's agenda are equally relevant to the construction of the object
or subject, as are the information and models available to the understanding subject. Thus, the locus of enunciation is as much a part of
the knowing and understanding processes as are the data for the
disciplinary (e.g., sociological, anthropological, historical, semiological, etc.) construction of the "real." Consequently, the "true" account
of a subject matter, in the form of knowledge or understanding will be
transacted in the respective communities of interpretation as much for
its correspondence to what is taken to be real as for the authorizing
locus of enunciation constructed in the very act of describing an object
or a subject. Furthermore, the locus of enunciation of the discourse
being read would not be understood in itself but in the context of
previous loci of enunciation that the current discourse contests, cor-

rects, or expands. It is as much the *saying* (and the audience involved) as it is what is *said* (and the world referred to) that preserves or transforms the image of the real constructed by previous acts of saying.

This book is interdisciplinary (or multidisciplinary, as some would prefer) in content and method. By interdisciplinary I mean that practitioners of several disciplines converge in studying a situation or in solving a problem; or a practitioner of a discipline borrows from and relates his or her findings to other disciplines. In both cases, a rethinking of problems, questions, and methods that had been asked by previous scholars in their own disciplines takes place. Expanding disciplinary boundaries is a tendency of our time, clearly described by Clifford Geertz, that postmodern thinkers constantly dwell upon.[48] The force behind this tendency is an issue in which I will not get involved at this point. However, I would like to state, succinctly, how this situation impinges on the position I am taking in this book.

My disciplinary training combined the history of literature, discourse analysis, and semiotics under the label "theory of literature." Semiotics (or semiology, which I prefer, for its ties with philology) and discourse analysis have lost the glamor they enjoyed twenty years ago. They have, however, set an agenda of questions to be asked and problems to be solved. The semiological perspective introduced into the agenda of the social sciences and the humanities raises questions related to meanings and interpretations, focusing on the production, transmission, reception, and postprocessing of signs. Certainly, Peirce's semiotics was to logic what Saussure's semiotics was to linguistics. Lotman's approach to the semiological perspective introduced, instead, a context labeled "the semiotic of culture," which I perceive as compatible with cultural studies.[49] Bakhtin's contributions in this respect were by no means negligible: ideological questions were introduced, genres were approached from a semiological perspective, and the old debate between hermeneutic and epistemological, between natural and human, sciences, introduced by Dilthey, was recast.[50] Derrida's own work, in the late 1960s and early 1970s, owes a great deal to the semiological approach, even if he placed himself in opposition. *De la grammatologie* could not have been conceived without the widespread diffusion of Saussurean semiological linguistics and its adaptation by Lévi-Strauss in theoretical anthropology.[51] Finally, in this genealogy of debts, Foucault's concept of discursive formation emerged from the need to go beyond the abstract signifier/signified approach to language and the need to look not at abstract linguistic codes regulating speech, but at the functioning of discourse in history and society.[52] This approach is not unlike that of Bakhtin. These are some of the references I have in mind when I talk about semiotics. However, none of the above formulations contemplated colonial situations in their discussions of either the abstract or the historical aspects of signs and discourses. Thus, the need to introduce the notion of colonial semiosis.

Sign production and transmission across cultural boundaries and negotiations between oral discourses and different kinds of writing systems open up new horizons for which the scholar can hardly find a tradition in literary studies. Descriptions and explanations of human communication across cultural boundaries confront the scholar with the limits of a linear notion of history and invite him or her to replace it with a nonlinear history; to replace causal relations with a network of connections; to accept that the "same" object or event is conceived quite differently in different cultures and that it is not enough to say that any abstract thought or knowledge-driven activity in non-Western cultures is like science or philosophy and, furthermore, that there are narratives and songs that are like oral literature. The crux of the matter is that when cultural differences go beyond common memories expressed in different languages, we have no alternative but to understand the differences in relation to our own identity and to look at ourselves as others. While this is, indeed, a very difficult thing to do, it is precisely what the human sciences (social sciences and the humanities) attempted: to invent a (meta)language by means of which we could become observers of our own interactions. The problem is that the traditional epistemological distinction between participant and observer is not sufficient, since, as participants, we are already observers. We are, so to speak, observers twice over. Let me elaborate on this distinction.

I have tried to cast it in terms of participant/observer and scholar (scientist)/observer with the help of Maturana's distinction between descriptions and explanations, and the role played by the observer in each of them.[53] There is an important difference, clearly visible although not explicit, in Maturana's notion of observer. Simplifying a rather complex argument, I would venture to say that, according to Maturana, we who conceive ourselves as human beings become observers of our interactions, and, in the process of becoming conscious observers, we generate descriptions and representations of that which we have observed. Speech is, perhaps, one of the most powerful semiotic means to increase the domain of communicative interaction, but it also allows the participants in the speech to reflect upon speech itself and about speaking interactions. Briefly, to be human (following this logic) is not only to interact semiotically but to use language to generate descriptions of the domain of interactions in which we are participants. On the other hand, if speech is a means to describe our semiotic interactions, it is not the only one. We also have writing and other ways of using sounds and signs to interact as well as to describe our own interactions. Whether speech (and alphabetic writing) are the most powerful sign systems for communicating and describing our communications is not a problem I will pursue here. Language (in whatever manifestation, not only speech and alphabetic writing) allows for a domain of interactions at the same time that it allows the observer to describe his or her own interactions as participant, either in semiotic-communicative or any other kind of social interactions. The fact that I am interested in the former should not allow us to forget that we, as rational animals, not only interact but have invented sign systems to describe our interactions. Thus, a performative concept of cognition not only impinges on our description of the world, but also on the descriptions of our (human) descriptions of the world. We not only use a tool; we also justify its uses as selected from among many possibilities. The use of the tool is as ideological as the descriptions invented to justify its use.

But at still another level, Maturana's observer is no longer the person who describes but she or he who explains. This second observer is the scientist: "As scientists, we want to provide explanations for the phenomena we observe. That is, we want to propose conceptual or concrete systems deemed to be intentionally isomorphic to (models of) the systems that generate the observed phenomena."[54] Thus, the first interesting aspect emerges when comparing the goals of the scholar (scientist)-observer and the functions of models and explanations in scientific practices with the goals of the participant-observer and the function of definitions and descriptions in the practices of everyday life. The challenge of the human sciences is not only what has always been pointed out, the coalescence of the object of study with the subject studying it, but the positionality and politicization of the understanding subject and his or her drive to know or understand. A more complex set of problems has to be resolved when the scholar or social scientist has to negotiate his or her own cultural world as conceived in everyday practice; the conceptual scheme of the disciplinary (meta)language with the cultural world and the conceptual scheme of the disciplinary (meta)language of other social worlds. In our century, anthropologists began to realize that the Azande may not have disciplinary practices called anthropology. However, if the Western anthropologist can "observe" the Azande and describe their customs both as a participant-observer and a member of a different culture, and as scientist-observer of a disciplinary world called anthropology, the possibilities of "being observed," at various levels, are certainly open to consideration,[55] as is the question of replacing the Azande's own self-description with the more authoritative and scientific one provided by anthropological training. This point takes us back to our previous consideration of the mobility of the center, the power to speak or write, and the construction of loci of enunciation. What follows is an effort to understand otherwise, to shake up the patterns of understanding inherited from the European Renaissance and the French Enlightenment, by playing them against the disarticulation and rearticulation of knowledge inherited from colonial and neo-colonial legacies.

Part I

The Colonization of Languages

Chapter 1

Nebrija in the New World: Renaissance Philosophy of Language and the Spread of Western Literacy

Looking Back from Bernardo José de Aldrete: The Linguistic Unification of Spain and the Linguistic Diversity of the Indies

Toward the end of the fifteenth century, a philosophy of language based on the celebration of the letter and of vernacular languages began to emerge in Europe. Elio Antonio de Nebrija played an important role in this development by writing one of the first grammars of a vernacular language, Castilian, and the rules of its orthography. Both treatises, the grammar of Castilian (1492) and the rules for orthography (1517), included substantial prefaces in which Nebrija laid out the historical significance of the invention of the alphabet and the import of language in the consolidation of the Spanish empire. When Nebrija was writing his grammar of Castilian, the kingdom of Castile, under the authority of Isabella and Ferdinand, was becoming the strongest in the Iberian Peninsula, though the Moors still had control of Granada and Columbus had yet to submit his project to an increasingly powerful and busy queen.

One hundred years after Nebrija's contribution to anchoring Castilian language by writing grammars, vocabularies, and orthographic rules, Bernardo de Aldrete, like Nebrija from Andalusia, published his *Origenes de la lengua castellana* (1606).[1] Although several essays and treatises celebrating the virtues of Castilian had already been published during the sixteenth century, Aldrete's contribution was a narrative of its origins.[2] Nebrija's grammar had been published in Salamanca, one of the most important centers of learning in the kingdom of Castile during the time of Ferdinand and Isabella. Aldrete's work appeared in Rome, and he underlined the fact that the first treatise on the origin of Castilian language was published in the place where the language itself originated. He did not miss an Æopportunity to defend his main thesis, that Castilian derived from Latin and was corrupted by the Visigoths during their conquest of the Iberian Peninsula from the end of the fifth century to the end of the seventh.[3]

Recognition that the Visigoths were vanquishers and yet adopted the language and culture of the vanquished did not prevent Aldrete from defending a second thesis: throughout the history of humankind, conquerors have inflicted their language on the conquered. One of Aldrete's chapters expresses the thesis in its title, "The Vanquished Receive the Language of the Vanquishers, Surrendering Their Own with Their Land and People." In this chapter, Aldrete deals with the examples of the Iberian Peninsula and the (West) Indies.[4] In the Iberian Peninsula the nucleus of his argument was provided by the differences between the Romans and the Arabs (or the Moors). Arabic was obviously the language used in all those territories the Moors had under their control: Castilians under the Moors lost not only their language, but sometimes their religion, and often their lives (*La lengua castellana,* book 1, chap. 22, p. 139). But the Arabs left significant portions of the peninsula in which people were able to preserve their sense of territoriality by preserving their religion, Christianity, and their language, Castilian. Aldrete differentiates the invasion of the Moors from that of the Romans. The Romans invaded the *entire* territory and of course imposed their language. Aldrete had two important reasons to distinguish between the two invasions. One of Aldrete's points was historical: because the Romans invaded the entire peninsula, Romans and Castilians became one and the same people ("con los romanos con los cuales se hizieron unos los Españoles"), a legacy so strong that even the Visigoths could not alter it. A second point was religious: the origin of the Castilian language in the Iberian Peninsula went together with the expansion of Christianity. Aldrete recognized religion as the most important ally for maintaining or changing a language.[5] Consequently, since Latin was the language linked to Christianity, Aldrete perceived that the corruption of Latin by the Visigoths did not alter the more profound connection between Latin and Christianity, which was transferred to modern vernacular languages and resulted in a clear distinction from Hebrew, which was linked to Latin through the Bible, and Arabic, the language

of the Moors, the Koran, and the "other." Although the Moors occupied the Iberian Peninsula for almost eight centuries (from the
eighth to the fifteenth) and, like the Romans, had alphabetic writing
and a religion of the Book, Castilian language derived from Latin
while the Arabic influence was only registered at the lexical level (*La
lengua castellana*, 167). Two religions, related to two different languages, coexisted in the Iberian Peninsula for almost eight centuries
(*La lengua castellana*, 175) and, most importantly, the Arabic language and the Islamic religion never succeeded in replacing Castilian
and Christianity (*La lengua castellana*, 164–75). The argument allowed Aldrete to explain the expansion of Castilian language beyond
the boundaries of the Castilian kingdom to reach Navarra, Es-
tremadura, and Andalucía and to justify its connivance with Christianity by stressing the fight against the Moors.

The complicity between language and religion had not been
stressed by Nebrija at the beginning of Castile's role as an imperial
power. Queen Isabella's perception of Castile united under Christianity, however, was a legacy transferred by Aldrete's time a century
later from the philosophy of the state to the philosophy of language.
Aldrete was responding to this double endowment when he stressed
that the Arabs—contrary to the Romans—not only had a different
language but also a different religion. Expanding the language and
reconquering territories were part and parcel of a double legacy that
had its roots in the early months of 1492, when the ejection of the
Moors combined with the publication of Nebrija's grammar.

What Aldrete has to say about the West Indies is mainly derived
from the Jesuit father José de Acosta, who spent a long part of his life
in Peru. Acosta received fresh information from the Jesuits in Mexico
about the Mexica culture and history and published his *Historia natural y moral de las Indias* in 1590. Acosta's book and Francisco López
de Gómara's *Hispania vitrix*, published in 1555, were two of the most
widely read and translated books during the sixteenth century. The
Jesuit Acosta had a different agenda than Gómara, Hernán Cortés's
private chaplain. The first had a strong interest in understanding matters natural and human in the Indies. The latter chose to celebrate the
victory by describing the lands, the people, and, mainly, the Spaniards'
deeds. Following Acosta's *Historia*, Aldrete realized that there were
two "monarchies" in the Indies, one of the "Ingas, o Incas del Pirú,"
and the other in New Spain, belonging to the kings of Mexico.

Aldrete was particularly interested in learning from Acosta's report
that Quechua was the official language (*runasimi*, "the general language")[6] of the Inca empire and that Nahuatl in Mexico had a similar
function for the Aztec (or Mexica, as they prefer to call themselves)
empire. Both were languages that the conquerors imposed upon the

conquered. Aldrete found these examples extremely useful. The expansion and colonization of language by the Incas and Mexicas supported his thesis that the vanquisher always inflicted its language upon the vanquished, as did the expansion and colonization of language by the Spaniards. Since Aldrete was interested in supporting his thesis and indirectly justifying colonial expansion, he did not point out this time the differences between the colonization of language by ancient Mexicas and Incas and the colonization of language by Spaniards, as he did when distinguishing the Roman from the Arabic invasions of the Iberian Peninsula. The blind spots of his argument show that Aldrete was interested in establishing the Greco-Roman tradition in language and the Holy Roman legacy in religion. Aldrete did not doubt that there was a particular distinction and rightness in such legacies, and he never doubted that such a distinguished linguistic and religious tradition should be expanded to the Spanish dominions in the Indies. His contribution to the emerging and expansive idea of Western civilization merits an examination that it has not yet received.

Unlike those who in the first years of the colonization observed and described linguistic habits and performances, Aldrete was less concerned with the Amerindian lack of letters than with the fact that the Castilian tongue was not spreading as fast as he would have liked.[7] Relying on Acosta, he emphasizes that the Incas were able to force their language on their conquered territories and that "Guainacapa" (Huayna Capac), the Inca king under whose governance Quechua had expanded,[8] is to be credited for the successful linguistic expansion (*La lengua castellana*, book 1, chap. 22). His main interest in this example, however, is not with a linguistic ethnography of Amerindian languages but rather with the poor achievements to date in spreading the Castilian tongue. He moves, then, from the celebration of Huayna Capac's success to a description of the territorial reorganization carried out by the Spaniards. In one dense paragraph he provides a summary of the ten audiencias (geographic and administrative units) in which the Indies had been divided under the Spanish rule, from Mexico and La Florida, in the northeast of the Spanish dominions, to the Antarctic and the Philippines, the southwestern extreme. By the time Aldrete was writing, the Council of the Indies (the central institution for Spanish administration of the New World), founded in 1524, had gone a long way in the administration of the Indies. In 1571, under Philip II, López de Velasco was appointed official cosmographer, and by 1574 he had finished his *Descripción y demarcación de las Indias Occidentales*,[9] a manuscript of about one hundred and fifty folios with fourteen maps, which was reproduced in different forms until the first half of the eighteenth century (see chap. 6). Aldrete's summary of the

Spanish domains closely follows López de Velasco's description and mapping of the Indies, which was published in an expanded version by Herrera y Tordesillas, who replaced López de Velasco and became the official chronist of Philip II.[10]

Aldrete, however, was neither a historian nor a geographer. He was interested in the spread of Castilian over the new organized territories. And territorial organization was—in Aldrete's scheme of things—intimately tied up with language. If he mentions with pride the Spaniards' achievements in the administration and remapping of the territory, he is less enthusiastic about Spanish accomplishments in the teaching of Castilian to the Amerindian population, which would give territoriality a new dimension: not just the drawing of geographic boundaries and the implantation of administrative offices and administrators, but that which comes with memories shared and stored in a common language. Aldrete reported that, according to the information he gathered from the Indies, some *Indios principales* (noble persons) had as good a pronunciation as the native Spanish. However, he observed, Amerindians in general ("los Indios") did not speak very much Spanish because they preferred their own language, and because no one was seriously pushing them to do so ("Los Indios, aunque como e dicho, comunmente lo saben, i entienden, pero vsan lo poco por la aficion que tienen a su lengua, no auiendo quien los obligue a vsar la agena" (*La lengua castellana,* book I, chap. 22). In criticizing his own peers for not being prompt and active enough in teaching Castilian, he reclaims the example of linguistic policies implemented by Huayna Capac in Peru and the Romans in the Iberian Peninsula, who were able and willing to spread their language effectively in all their conquered territories ("De parte de los nuestros no a auido diligencia para la introducción de la lengua, por que si la vuiera auido, como la pusieron los Romanos, o "Guainacapa," sin duda en todas ellas se hablara, como dice el Padre Acosta"). Aldrete is confident, nevertheless, that God and the Spanish Crown would succeed in spreading the Castilian tongue in the Indies, despite the lack of interest shown so far by the Spaniards ("Pero no dudo, que continuandose, con el favor de nuestro señor, el govierno de España, que en mui breue tiempo an de hablar la Castellana todos, sin que de parte de los nuestros aia diligencia" [book I, chap. 22]).

There was another difference between the Roman colonization of Spain and the Spanish colonization of the Indies that interested Aldrete. With a calm and ghastly conviction, Aldrete states two main, interconnected differences: first, that the Iberian Peninsula was invaded by several communities before the arrival of the Romans, while no foreign nation had invaded the Indies before the Spaniards; second, that the Amerindians, "those people" ("aquella gente"), not only lacked any kind of letters, and consequently science and literature as well, but also the civility ("policía") that in Aldrete's mind went together with letters. Without interruption, Aldrete concludes by adding that they live like beasts, naked.[11] There is a complex connection, taken for granted in Aldrete's associations, between the fact that the Indies had not been invaded before the Spaniards, their lack of letters and civility, and their nakedness, that allows him to correlate the Amerindians with the beasts. It was already difficult—if not impossible—for Aldrete to understand that the materiality of alphabetic writing and the ideology built around the concept of the letter were not the only warranty of science and civility, and that if a community had not been invaded by a nation coming from east of the Mediterranean, where the origins of alphabetic writing were located, they did not have a chance to enjoy the "benefits" of the letter.

It is striking for a twentieth-century reader of Aldrete that the sentence following the argument just described begins by introducing a causal link ("because") that connects language with clothing: Aldrete states blatantly that because they lacked letters, most Amerindians were naked or seminaked. He adds that with the exception of the Amerindian nobility ("indios principales") who dressed like Spaniards ("Los principales andan totalmente vestido a la Española, i traen sombreros, que antes no vsauan, i tambien çapatos" [book 1, chap. 12]) and spoke good Castilian, those who lived in isolated towns ("los Indios") still went naked. One can surmise the following logic: that if they were naked they did not speak Castilian or did not speak it very well. There is an implicit connection perhaps taken for granted: linguistic behavior and good manners are signs of the civilizing process. If speech was used to distinguish the self-same from the other (or "barbarians" from those who do not speak "our" language), it acquired a new dimension in the cluster of principles to regulate social behavior that can be dated to the end of the fifteenth century and the first decades of the sixteenth century, and that Erasmus and Vives were major contributors to during the kingdom of Charles I of Spain.[12] Not civilization but *civility* (*civilitas*) was the word coined to justify a new code of social behavior and, at the same time, to distinguish between those who used or were aware of it from those who were out of the game.[13] Norbert Elías interprets Erasmus implying that the connections between language and clothing were related with reading and writing: "reading has sharpened seeing, and seeing has enriched reading and writing."[14] This enigmatic formula could be understood by elaborating on the increasing tendency of people to observe themselves, enhanced by the encounter with and the

dissemination of icons and descriptions of people unknown until recent times. Such tendency was sharpened by reading and writing,
which expanded the domains of description of oneself and the other.
It is in this precise sense that reading and writing sharpened seeing,
and that seeing has enriched reading and writing. In this sense also the
connection between language and clothing in Aldrete can be explained. Clothing and speaking were at the same time signs in which
good "policía" (civility), or the lack of it, could be identified, and they
were signs whose reading allowed the construction of social identities
by the perception of social differences. Aldrete could not avoid a perspective that was imbedded in the culture of the time: a feeling of
civilitas, the way people look, the way people speak, the way human
beings should behave.[15] Descriptions of Amerindian social life and
personal conduct were influenced by the code of social and bodily
behaviors that had been building up since the end of fifteenth-century
Europe (fig. 1.1).

Aldrete also takes for granted the connection between alphabetic
writing and civility. In the same way that he perceives an association
between speech and dressing, he assumes a stronger link between
speech and writing. It is difficult to decide whether the assumption
that there was a necessary connection between speech and writing
allowed him to debunk the idea that Castilian language preceded the
Roman invasion; or whether he had to come up with such a hypothesis
in order to defend his theory that Castilian language was born from
the debris of a Latin corrupted by northern invaders (the Visigoths).
Whatever his reasons, he argues that

> When a nation receives another *language,* it also jointly admits the
> *letter* with which the language is written, and if it loses its spoken
> *language,* it also loses the form of the *letter* with which it is writ-
> ten. . . . The point is that nobody who writes Latin, as he should,
> writes in Greek letters, nor vice versa: and the same is true of all
> languages that have a particular form of letter. Thus *whoever receives
> a new language also receives the letter with which it is written, and if
> they lose the language, they also lose the characters of that language.*
> And that is how the letter was lost in Spain, as well as the books. (*La
> lengua castellana,* book 3, chap. 18; italics mine)

> [Recibiendo una nacion otra lengua, con ella viene, que admita
> juntamente la letra con que se escriue, i si pierde el lenguage, pierde
> tambien la forma de la letra, con que lo escriuia. . . . El punto esta
> en que nadie, que escriua, como deue, el Latin lo escriue con letras
> Griegas, ni por el contrario: i lo mismo en todas las lenguas que

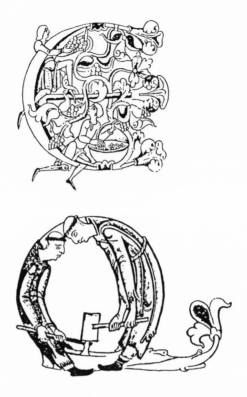

Fig. 1.1.   The alphabet and manual labor in the Middle Ages. Courtesy of
Bibliothèque Municipale de Dijon.

tienen particular forma de letra. Con lo qual los que reciben nueua
lengua, tambien la letra, con que se escriue, i si la pierden, tambien
los caracteres propios della. I assi se perdio la letra de España con la
lengua, i libros.]

In Aldrete's paragraph I perceive two main theses: the first asserts that
every spoken language presupposes the letter as its written counterpart. The second, inferred from the first, is that any particular language
(like Greek or Latin or Castilian) is so strongly tied to the letter that it
would be impossible to write in one language with the letters belonging to the other, because no one who writes Latin would write it in
Greek letters. Aldrete does not mention the writing of grammars of
Amerindian languages, a practice by that time already very well
known; by means of these grammars, languages alien to alphabetic
writing were written in the Latin alphabet.[16] Such practices offered
obvious counterexamples to Aldrete's hypothesis (although he could
have defended his thesis by saying that Amerindian languages were
not written at all and therefore not linked to any kind of letters). Even

if his thesis could be defended in those cases in which a given language derived from Latin, it would be more difficult to justify the translation of Amerindian speech to Latin letters.

But it is not necessary to prove Aldrete right or wrong, since understanding the game he was playing, the social forces nourishing it, and the complicity between knowledge, human interests, and locus of enunciation is more relevant to my goals. His defense of the continuity of the classical tradition is perfectly articulated in the double genealogy he traces: not only spoken Latin but Latin letters derived from Greek (*La lengua castellana,* book 3, chap. 28).[17] The thesis holds its force as long as the colonization of Amerindian languages, by modeling them according to the Latin grammar, is ignored. Aldrete constructs his model within a larger framework articulated by Nebrija a century earlier. The framework was bounded, at one end of the spectrum, by Latin as the language of learning and civility, and by Castilian as the language of the nation. At the other end is the belief in the power of the letter to tame the voice, to preserve the glory of the prince and the memories of a nation, and to upgrade the social and cultural processes of the Amerindians, who, even though they were not barbarians, had not yet been blessed with the most marvelous human invention, which, as Nebrija had argued, was the letter.[18]

Looking Forward from Elio Antonio de Nebrija: The Invention of Letters and the Need to Tame the Voice

A few years after the marriage of Queen Isabella of Castile and King Ferdinand of Aragon and Sicily in 1469, a landmark in the story of one of the most powerful empires in human history, Nebrija was back in Spain after his ten-year residence in Italy, where he absorbed the ideas of the time, including the ideals of the *studia humanitatis.* More than twenty years would elapse between the marriage and the glorious day in which Granada would be reconquered and a colonial empire in a still unknown land would begin to grow. The year 1479 was, however, a turning point in the rapid changes Isabella and Ferdinand were imposing on a chaotic kingdom controlled by powerful noblemen. Economic control over the nobles and compilation of the Royal Ordinances gave to the future Catholic kings a solid foundation to move from reorganization to the building of the Castilian kingdom. During the following years the court of Ferdinand and Isabella began to distinguish itself from earlier Spanish courts. One difference lay in the influence of humanistic education. Isabella had not been exposed to humanistic studies as a child. As an adolescent in the isolated castle of

Arévalo, she learned sewing, embroidering, and horseback riding, and the rudiments of a general education were provided by a local priest. Isabella had ambitions of something different for her children, and she surrounded herself with a full hand of intellectuals who would become well known in the history of Spanish letters. The Italians Pietro Martire d'Anghiera (Peter Martyr) and Marineo Siculo tutored her children in philosophy and theology. Several years later, these men would be at the prestigious University of Salamanca teaching Latin, rhetoric, and grammar next to Nebrija. During the early 1480s, when Peter Martyr was in the court of the crown of Castile, Nebrija published his influential *Introductiones latinae,* which helped introduce the *studia humanitatis* in Spain and began what Francisco Rico has termed Nebrija's fight against the "barbarians."[19]

During the early months of 1492, Queen Isabella and Nebrija were the protagonists of a well-known anecdote in the history of Spanish culture: the moment in which Nebrija offered to Queen Isabella the grammar of Castilian, whose advantages he carefully described in the prologue:

> Now, Your Majesty, let me come to the last advantage that you shall gain from my grammar. For the purpose, recall the time when I presented you with a draft of this book earlier this year in Salamanca. At this time, you asked me what end such a grammar could possibly serve. Upon this, the Bishop of Avila interrupted to answer in my stead. What he said was this: "Soon Your Majesty will have placed her yoke upon many barbarians who speak outlandish tongues. By this, your victory, these people shall stand in a new need; the need for the laws the victor owes to the vanquished, and the need for the language we shall bring with us." My grammar shall serve to impart them the Castilian tongue, as we have used grammar to teach Latin to our young.[20]

It comes as no surprise that Queen Isabella did not immediately understand what use a grammar of a vernacular language could possibly have. Although she was aware of the prestige that would be brought to the tongue by a grammar, which until then had been restricted to the languages of the Scriptures (Hebrew, Greek, and Latin), she had not yet made the connection between language and power via colonization. It was Ferdinand, after all, who had his eyes on Aragon and Castile's expansion over Europe, not Isabella, who was mainly interested in the unification of Castile. The possibility of thinking about outlandish tongues across the Atlantic was not even a utopian dream. Such issues were the task of the humanist (*litteratus*) and

man of letters (*jurisperitus*) rather than a mother and a woman of
arms. Nebrija, indeed, had his plans very well charted.

The concise and powerful argument advanced in the introductory
notes to his *Gramática castellana* are well known, and it is not necessary to go into detail here.[21] It is worthwhile to remember, however,
that one of the remarkable features of Nebrija's work was his claim for
a pact between "armas y letras" at the precise moment the kingdom of
Castile was becoming a modern state ruled by men of letters. The
flourishing of the arts, especially the art of languages, or *grammatica,*
is rhetorically emphasized by Nebrija, who contrasts the image of a
new beginning with the ruins left by the enemies of the Christian faith:

> Now that the Church has been purified, and we are thus reconciled
> to God, now that the enemies of the Faith have been subdued by
> our arms, now that just laws are being enforced, enabling us all to
> live as equals, what else remains but the flowering of the peaceful
> arts. And among the arts, foremost are those of language, *which sets*
> *us apart from the wild animals: language, which is the unique dis-*
> *tinction of man, the means for the kind of understanding which can*
> *be surpassed only by contemplation.*[22]

It is to speech that Nebrija primarily refers. That language, and
language alone, distinguishes human beings from other living systems
is a belief upon which an ideological network was built. The elevation
of language authorized the efforts by philosophers and men of letters
to expand upon a linguistic foundation; in the early modern period,
this implied a complex network in which the medieval trivium (grammar, rhetoric, and logic) and the modern *studia humanitates* complemented the spread of Western literacy in an array of forms: from teaching reading and writing in Latin and vernacular tongues to writing
grammars of tongues alien to the Greco-Latin tradition.

Nebrija introduced humanist ideas in Spain, and, as a humanist, he
knew that the power of a unified language, via its grammar, lay in
teaching it to barbarians, as well as controlling barbarian languages by
writing their grammars. Erasmus had not yet reinterpreted the meaning of *civilitas,* but it is easy to imagine that the idea was already in the
air. Bringing civilization to the barbarians meant different things from
different loci of enunciation, of course. One suspects that the Visigoths, seen as barbarians by the Romans, had an image of themselves
as the civilizers, even if they admired and adopted Roman laws, languages, and customs. But these were the terms in which Nebrija spoke
of his present to Isabella. In our own time, we understand Nebrija's

effort to civilize as the ideological seed of what would become a gigantic campaign to colonize Amerindian languages by either writing their grammars or by teaching Castilian to the native speakers.[23]

To understand Nebrija's strategy requires understanding that his argument rested both on a philosophy of language, whose roots could be traced back to Saint Augustine and the merging of Platonic and Christian traditions (applied to justify the need for a unified language to counteract the plurality of tongues after Babel), and on Lorenzo Valla's *De elegantia latinae linguae* (1435–44), written to save Christian Rome from linguistic and cultural illiteracy. Saint Augustine's strong belief in one original language came from the evidence provided by the Scriptures and from his Platonic theoretical framework. As a neoplatonist and a Christian, Saint Augustine's reading of the Holy Book assumed an original unity from which the multiplicity of things came. The original and unified language, according to Saint Augustine, was not named because it was not necessary to distinguish it from other human languages. It could simply be called human language or human locution.[24] However, human language was not enough to keep human beings happy and free from transgressing the law, as expressed in the project of building a tower to reach heaven. The multiplication of languages that caused the division of people and communities attained the number seventy-two, and each of them had a name. At this point it became necessary to find a name for the primordial language to distinguish it from the rest. Saint Augustine had good reasons to believe that the original language was Hebrew. Even forty years after Nebrija composed his Latin grammar, Vives (familiar with Saint Augustine's work and responsible for the critical edition orchestrated by Erasmus) was delineating *la questione de la lingua* in terms of the contrast between the primordial language spoken by Adam and the Tower of Babel as the event that initiated linguistic diversity.[25]

While Vives was acquainted with Saint Augustine and was developing a philosophy of language that would be implemented, directly or indirectly, by the missionaries colonizing Amerindian languages or by historians looking for some connection between Amerindian and sacred and classical tongues,[26] Nebrija was rewriting Valla's program, outlined in the preface to his *De elegantia latinae linguae.* We owe to Ascencio the report on the relationships between Valla's program to save Rome and Nebrija's program to expand the Spanish empire.[27] When he was in Italy, Nebrija became acquainted with Valla's reevaluation of letters as a means to save the Holy Roman Empire from total ruin.[28] Valla realized that rebuilding an empire could not be accomplished solely by means of arms. He intended, instead, to achieve his goals by the expedient of letters. By contrasting the Latin of his ancestors with the expansion of the Roman Empire, and by underlining the strength of the language as a unifying force over geographical and political conquests, Valla foresaw the Roman recovery of its lost power and, as a consequence, predicted a unified Italy playing a central role in the future of the new emerging nations.

Certainly it was difficult for Nebrija before and during 1492, when he wrote his preface to the Castilian grammar, to anticipate much about the colonization of the New World and the Philippines. Like Queen Isabella, he was probably thinking about a unified Castile after the reconquest of Granada. And perhaps like Ferdinand, he was anticipating that Aragon and Castile would increase the control and colonization of the Mediterranean and northern Europe. The intriguing royal marriages that Ferdinand and Isabella planned for their children make clear that even at the turn of the century, the royal eyes were looking north rather than west.[29] Still, Nebrija was not alone. Nebrija was able to persuade Queen Isabella that her destiny was not only to conquer but also to civilize. He had in Isabella a decisive and determined companion who was not happy just to chase the Moors out of the peninsula and to request the Jews' conversion to Christianity. She originated the Spanish Inquisition, paradoxical instrument to achieve a Christian and linguistic unification.

One can surmise that Nebrija's earlier Latin grammar, written with the intention of civilizing Castile, was the foundation, grammatically as well as ideologically, for his Castilian grammar. Ideologically, Nebrija was concerned with the unification of Castile and the expansion of the Spanish empire. Linguistically and philosophically, he was obsessed with the control of the voice by mediation of the letter. The liaison between the voice and the letter, which we will see expanded in Aldrete, was already an idea fermenting in Nebrija. His famous axiom: to write as we pronounce and to pronounce as we write.[30] In the description of the parts into which Latin and Castilian grammars are divided, Nebrija presented a theory of the letter that was at the same time a theory of writing. Nebrija began his grammars and later on his rules for Castilian orthography by devoting several paragraphs to the concept of the letter. He assumed that the alphabet was one of the greatest achievements of humankind, and he was constantly looking into the history of writing and the invention of letters to support his belief. An example from the *Gramática castellana* in which he merges the invention of letters with the origin of history shows that Nebrija had more than a linguistic agenda in his speculations on alphabetic writing:

Among all the things that human beings discovered through experience, or that were shown to us by divine revelation in order to polish and embellish human life, nothing was more necessary, nor benefited us more, than the invention of letters. Such letters, which by a common consent and the silent conspiracy of all nations have been accepted, have been invented—according to those who wrote about antiquity—by the Assyrians; with the exception of Gelio, who attributed the invention of letters to Mercury in Egypt.[31]

In his *Reglas de ortografía en la lengua castellana*, "compuestas por el maestro Antonio de Lebrixa," he insists:

Among all the things that human beings discovered through experience, or that were shown to us by divine revelation in order to polish and embellish human life, nothing was more necessary, nor benefited us more, than the invention of letters. It seems that this invention originated from the fact that before letters were discovered, images were used to represent the things which people wanted to record, such as the figure of the right hand stretched out which meant generosity, and the closed fist which meant avarice, and the ear denoted memory; knees meant mercy; a coiled snake indicated the year, and so on. But since this business was endless and very confusing, the first inventor of letters—whoever that was—looked at the amount of different voices in his language, and made as many figures or letters; by means of these figures, when placed in a certain order, he represented all the words he wished, as much for his memory as for speaking with those who were not present and those who were about to come. *Thus the letter is nothing more than a trace or figure by means of which the voice is represented.*[32]

The passage shows Nebrija's perseverance in his theory of the letter for more than twenty-five years, as well as the semiotic context in which the letter was conceptualized. Its superiority over other writing systems was measured by the distance between the graphic sign and the voice. If the ear signified memory, the figure of the right hand stretched out meant generosity, and the closed fist meant avarice, it was not possible to use such signs to control the voice. They were either fixed categories of meaning or signs open to various interpretations. A language whose destiny is to unify a native territory and to subjugate a conquered people could not, in Nebrija's perception, be left open to the variations of speech.

The celebration and history of the letter were followed by Nebrija's
pharmakon or remedy: once the letter was defined as the instrument
to tame the voice, he became concerned with correcting and maintaining their complicity. A successful cure for the inconsistencies between sound and letter depended on the grammarian's success in
taming the voice. Otherwise, speakers would pronounce in one way
and write in another, just the opposite result from that for which the
letters were invented. Nebrija's reasoning stated an a priori need (i.e.,
the letters were needed to tame the voice) to explain a long and complex historical development (i.e., the invention of graphic signs to
fulfill different communicative, cultural, and social needs); and then
he forced himself to find a remedy for a situation whose ideology he
contributed to framing.

Nebrija thought that without letters language deteriorated. Aldrete, we have seen, was less convinced than Nebrija that the letter was
a preventive cure. Languages die, states Aldrete, and with the death
the letter disappears. Aldrete seems to lean toward the priority of
speech over writing, Nebrija the reverse. Since Aldrete had the opportunity to read and listen to missionaries and men of letters who reported about Amerindian cultures and societies, he retains their impression that lack of letters is equated with a lack of civilization. And
since he is interested in defending his thesis that the vanquisher imposes its language on the vanquished, Aldrete pays more attention to
Mexica and Inca linguistic expansion prior to the Spanish colonization of Mexican and Incan population.

Looking West: Spreading Literacy by Writing
Grammars, Laws, and Edicts and Teaching How
to Be a Good Christian

Nebrija and Aldrete established a solid foundation for the spread of
Western literacy in the colonial world by combining grammar,
orthography, and the origin of Castilian in an ideological complex.
Origin, for Aldrete, did not yet have the evolutionary and progressive
connotations that it would acquire more than a century later with
Condillac and Rousseau.[33] During the eighteenth century the question of origin expanded from the national tongue to human language,
and the barbarian languages became primitive ones by which to measure the evolution from the simple to the complex. The question of
the original language was for Saint Augustine an issue of hierarchy,
decided by its place in theological discourse and the organization of
human knowledge. The original language was simply the best. For

Nebrija and Aldrete the same pattern was still at work, and the grammar and genealogy of a language were framed not in evolutionary
terms but as prestigious legacies. That is, a linguistic and synchronic
hierarchy was at work during the sixteenth and early seventeenth centuries. Konrad von Gesner's definition of barbarian languages offers a
paradigmatic example of a frame of mind familiar to Nebrija and Aldrete. Gesner considered every language barbarian except Greek,
Latin, and Hebrew, the oldest of them all and the language implanted
by God.[34]

Writing, however, was conceived according to an evolutionary
model. When Nebrija celebrated the invention of alphabetical writing, he described the period before the invention of the letter: "before
letters were discovered, images were used to represent the things
which people wanted to record, such as the figure of the right hand
stretched out, which meant generosity, and the closed fist which
meant avarice, and the ear denoted memory."[35] Another example is
given in Juan Bautista Pomar, a descendant on the maternal side from
the Texcocan nobility and son of a Spaniard, who was born in 1535 in
New Spain. In *Relación de Texcoco* (1582) the philosophy of language
that celebrates the letter and treats it as an evolutionary stage beyond a
previous sign system is so entrenched that Pomar applies it to measure
the Amerindian level of cultural achievements. In his report on the
education of the Amerindian nobility, he writes,

> Procuraban los nobles para su ejercicio y recreación deprender al-
> gunas artes y oficios, como era pintar, entallar en madera, piedra u
> oro, y labrar piedras ricas y darles las formas y talles que querían, a
> semejanza de animales, pájaros y sabandijas. Aunque estas piedras
> estimaban, no era porque entendieran de ellas alguna virtud o pro-
> piedad natural, sino por la fineza de su color y por haber pocas de
> ellas. Otros a ser canteros o carpinteros, y otros al conocimiento de
> las estrellas y movimientos de los cielos, por los cuales adivinaban
> algunos sucesos futuros. *Υ se entiende que si tuvieran letras,*
> *llegaran a alcanzar muchos secretos naturales; pero como las pinturas*
> *no son muy capaces para retener en ellas la memoria de las cosas que se*
> *pintan, no pasaron adelante, porque casi en muriendo el que más al*
> *cabo llegaba, moría con él su ciencia.*[36]

> [The nobles would, for their exercise and recreation, attempt to
> learn some arts and trades, such as painting, sculpting in wood,
> stone, or gold, and working precious stones and giving them the
> forms and sizes they wanted, in the likeness of animals, birds, and
> vermin. Although they valued these stones, it was not because they

understood them to have some natural virtue or property, but
rather for the fineness of their color or because they were scarce.
Others were stonemasons or carpenters, and others had knowledge
of the stars and movements of the heavens, by which they divined
future events. *And it is clear that if they had possessed letters, they
would have come to grasp many natural secrets; but as paintings are
little capable of retaining in them the memory of the things painted,
they did not advance, because almost as soon as the one who had made
the most progress died, his knowledge died with him.*][37]

The spread of Western literacy, of which Pomar is an example as
well as a convinced agent, thus took conflicting directions as it was
supported by different and sometimes conflicting ideas about languages, writing, and cultural ideologies. Spoken languages were
somewhat detached from writing when the question of origin was
discussed. But writing came into the picture when the consolidation
of vernacular languages, whose classical legacies placed them next to
nonbarbarian languages, needed the letter to tame the voice and
grammar to control the mobility of the flow of speech. Writing was
then the end result of an evolutionary process, one of the highest
achievements of human intelligence. Pedro de Gante, a relative of
Charles I and the first Franciscan to arrive in Mexico after the fall of
Tenochtitlán, expressed his reactions to the Mexicas in a famous letter
addressed to Philip II reporting on the difficulties that the missionaries
had in learning Amerindian languages because they were "people
without writing, without letters, without written characters, and
without any kind of enlightenment" ("era gente sin escriptura, sin
letras, sin caracteres y sin lumbre de cosa alguna").[38]

The philosophy of language shared by these men provided a model
for the interpretation of Amerindian writing systems at the same time
that it justified writing the grammars of Amerindian languages as a
means to teaching reading and writing. Spreading literacy meant
teaching Amerindians what the Western man of letters understood by
reading and writing. Reading and writing, of course, are not necessarily what the missionaries understood as such: They understood a
kind of negotiation with signs that the Mexicas conceived in terms of
painting and telling oral stories by looking at the painting.[39] Thus the
Amerindian relations with written signs had to be changed.

Writing grammars of Amerindian languages was a complex process
with more at stake than just the cognitive issue suggested in the previous paragraph. There were, first, the technical implications of using
the Latin alphabet to transcribe sounds of languages alien to the
Greco-Latin tradition. And there were also ideological aspects of uni-

fication, which Nebrija clearly stated as a goal in his grammars—neither of which was free, however, of conflict with the missionaries' goals in writing grammars of Amerindian languages, as we shall see.

Franciscan missionaries, de Gante among them, arrived in New Spain in 1524, two years after Nebrija's death, and seven years after the publication of his *Reglas* under the governance of Charles V; the Jesuits followed in 1572, under Philip II. The Franciscans set foot in Mexico a few months after the fall of Tenochtitlán to Cortés's army. It was Cortés, in fact, who requested from Charles V spiritual assistance to Christianize the indigenous people, not necessarily to Hispanize them. A Castile unified under one religion and one language was the ideal of Isabella and Nebrija, but not necessarily of Charles V, who lived in Flanders until he was seventeen years old and was far removed from his grandparents, particularly his grandmother's, ideal. As Holy Roman Emperor his energies were invested in Europe rather than in the linguistic and religious unification of Castile. This shift in attention is evident, for example, in Charles's treatment of Cardinal Jiménez de Cisneros, confessor of Queen Isabella since 1492 and the most powerful figure in the religious configuration of Spain, who was dismissed as regent when Charles V took possession of the Crown of Castile and Aragon.

The Franciscans not only learned indigenous languages, they also wrote their grammar. A glance at Amerindian language grammars written by Castilian friars in Mexico during the sixteenth and seventeenth centuries shows that the majority of them began with a discussion of the letters of the alphabet and by identifying those letters Amerindian languages did not have. None of them showed any concern with the script of the classic civilizations in the central plateau. Their common interest in identifying the missing letters indicates that celebrating the invention of writing and finding its origin were no longer issues and that writing systems that did not call immediate attention to the representation of sounds were of no interest. The new preoccupations expressed by the grammarians suggest that the letter had been promoted to an ontological dimension with a clear priority over the voice as well as any other writing systems (fig 1.2). The classical tradition was inverted, and the letter no longer had the ancillary dimension attributed to it by Aristotle (*De interpretatione*) but had become the voice in itself, while nonalphabetic writing systems were suppressed. The discontinuity of the classical tradition during the encounter with Amerindian languages emerged in the common and repeated expression "esta lengua carece de tales letras" (this language lacks such and such letters). If, indeed, the person who made such an assertion was not presupposing that the letter was not located in the

voice but "outside" of it, missionaries and men of letters would have
pointed out what class of sounds a particular Amerindian language
had instead of noticing what it lacked.

The Jesuit Horacio Carochi, in his well-known *Arte de la lengua
mexicana* (1645), begins his work by noting that the Mexican language lacks seven letters and, in the next section, urges those learning
the language to pronounce it correctly.[40] There is an understandable
paradox, but a paradox nonetheless, between the assertion that a language lacks a given number of letters in relation to an alphabet created
for a nonrelated language and the urge to pronounce it correctly. Of
course Amerindian languages did not lack letters but implied different
ones, namely those that were not within the sound system of the
Romance languages. But the friars' program consisted of taming
(Nebrija and Carochi use the word *reducir*) the Amerindian lan-

a

b

Fig. 1.2.   *a*, The alphabet in geometric projection during the Renaissance;
b, the alphabet and book illumination during the Renaissance

guages, not analyzing the connection between picto-ideographic writing and speech, which was of a different kind than that between speech and alphabetic writing. The conviction that Latin was a universal linguistic system and that the Latin alphabet was an appropriate tool to represent sounds of languages not related to it was expressed by the Dominican Domingo de Santo Tomás (1499–1570), in the prologue to his grammar of Quechua: "This language is so in agreement with Latin and Castilian in its structure that it looks almost like a premonition (prediction) that the Spaniards will possess it."⁴¹ And naturally he follows by linking language and territory. Not only is Quechua a sophisticated language, observes Domingo de Santo Tomás, but it is also the language through which the rulers as well as the people communicate in the entire Inca territory, which he estimated to be more than one thousand miles long and several hundred wide (11).

There is a revealing ambiguity in the history of the spreading of Western literacy by, among other means, writing grammars of Amerindian languages that I would like to explore in the remainder of this chapter. The ambiguity is related to whether it was Nebrija's Latin or Castilian grammar that provided the model to write grammars of Amerindian languages. And it is revealing because of Nebrija's ideology, underlying each grammar. Both the friars, who undertook the task of composing grammars of native languages, and contemporary scholars who have studied the history, politics, and ideology of alphabetization and conversion during the colonial period recognize Nebrija's influence. But it is not clear to what extent and in what capacity his presence in the New World left its mark. I should indicate why I think we are faced with an important issue here, how an ideology of language changed, even came into conflict with its own effects, as it was carried out by different agents in the New World. We should distinguish between two levels of Nebrija's influence. One is technical and relates to the model offered by his Latin and Castilian grammars to those who were interested in writing grammars of the native languages. The second is political and ideological and relates to the programs Nebrija attached to his grammar of Latin, on the one hand, and to his grammar and orthography of Castilian, on the other. Let's take these issues one at a time, first the relative influence of the Latin or the Castilian grammar on the technical level.

It is common to find among Nahuatl specialists assertions such as the following:

In one sense it is important to stress that Antonio de Nebrija's linguistic model, as much in his *Arte* as in his *Diccionario,* both

published in the final decade of the fifteenth century, was the fore-   49
most contribution in contemporary Europe and an inspiration for
other works of a similar nature in the Old World, and not long after   *Nebrija in the*
in the American continent as well.[42]   *New World*

The date mentioned ("the final decade of the fifteenth century")
indicates that the *Gramática castellana* is referred to. The views of this
Nahuatl specialist contrast, however, with observations made by specialists in neo-Latin in New Spain. According to their findings, the
expression "el arte de Antonio" referred, during the colonial period,
to Nebrija's Latin grammar.[43] The study of Mexican libraries during
the sixteenth century has shown that the phrase refers to the Latin but
not to the Castilian grammar, and that it is the Latin and not the
Castilian grammar that had been found in monastic libraries.[44]
Scholars who have studied the impact of Nebrija in Europe have underlined the extraordinary success of the Latin grammar (*Introductiones latinae*, 1481) and the curious neglect of the Castilian grammar.
The *Introductiones* went through no less than fifty editions during the
author's lifetime, while the *Gramática castellana* fell into almost complete oblivion and was never reprinted until the second half of the
eighteenth century, already an important indication that Castilian was
the language of communication but not of learning. The disparity
between the initial lack of interest in the Castilian grammar during
Nebrija's time and the increasing attention it received after the nineteenth century is due, according to Francisco Rico, to the growing
impact of the classical formula "language is the companion of the
empire," revamped in the Italian and Spanish Renaissance.[45]

Let's also remember the *Arte de la lengua castellana y mexicana*,
published in 1571 by Alonso de Molina. In his prologue, the author
reports that the first part of his grammar is devoted to a morphology of
the Mexican language and that he follows the model of the Latin and
Castilian grammars. Therefore, he divides the sentence of the Mexican language into eight parts. This indication is most valuable since we
know that Nebrija was clear in saying that the Latin sentence is divided
into eight parts, the Castilian into ten. So we can conclude that Molina
followed the Latin grammar, although, to complicate the mystery
further, he does not seem very concerned about making the distinction between the two grammars. This is probably because, at the technical level, when there are grammatical models of two languages that
are closely connected, it does not make much difference which one is
used to write the grammar of a language totally unrelated.

I am more interested in exploring the ideological implications of a

politics of language implemented by the Crown that had its grounding in Nebrija's prologue to his grammar of Castilian than in an empirical description of hundreds of grammars of native languages in
search of the traces of Nebrija's impact. In any event, we have enough
information to assert that, on the technical level, the Latin grammar
was the one really used in the New World colonies. If, however, the
technical differences between the two possible models were negligible
when it came to writing grammars of the native language, we cannot
ignore their ideological differences if we aim to understand the complex politics of language in colonial times. Each grammar represented
an ideological program that impinged on the justification and implementation of spreading Western literacy in the New World. Let's first
quickly review Nebrija's two programs, one associated with the Latin
grammar, one with the Castilian, in order to turn, then, to the teaching of literacy in New Spain.

Let's go back briefly to Nebrija's return from Italy in the early years
of an increasingly powerful Castilian kingdom, and to the impact that
Valla might have had in his thinking about the transformation of
Castile. It has been pointed out repeatedly that in the Iberian Peninsula Nebrija was one of the pillars of the continuity of the classical
tradition. In the prologue of the 1481 edition, Nebrija justifies the
need for a Latin grammar in Castile as a foundation of the *studia
humanitatis*.[46] The program is not original, certainly. It comes from
Italian humanism and, particularly, from the influence of Valla's *De
elegantia latinae linguae*.[47] In 1481, Nebrija emphasized the need to
know Latin, "the foundation of our religion and Christian Republic."
Beyond being the language of religion and the Christian republic,
Latin was also the language of knowledge and *scientia*.[48] Furthermore, according to Nebrija, Latin was necessary because the law was
formulated in that language, and he was persuaded that it is in and by
the law that human beings can live together in a society and build a
civilization. There is no indication that Nebrija believed the law could
have been formulated in a language that was not Latin or in a writing
system that was not alphabetic. Nebrija also considered Latin the necessary foundation of medicine, on which our health depends (fig. 1.3).
Once again, it might not have occurred to him that Incas and Mexicas
had their own medicine, and he could not anticipate that two Amerindians, from the Colegio Santa Cruz de Tlatelolco in Mexico, would
write in Nahuatl a medical treatise based on Amerindian wisdom,
translate it into Latin, and send it to Charles I of Spain (fig. 1.4).[49]
Nebrija's program and examples clearly show two sides of his philosophy of language: his belief, first, that to have law, medicine, religion,
and civilization, human beings need Latin; and, second, his goal of

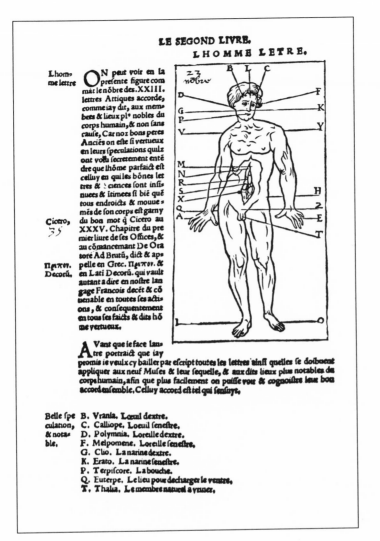

LE SEGOND LIVRE.
LHOMME LETRE.

Lhom-
me lettre

ON peut voir en la
prefente figure com
mæt le nôbre des.XXIII.
lettres Attiques accorde,
comme iay dit, aux mem-
bres & lieux pl° nobles du
corps humain,& non fans
caufe, Car noz bons peres
Anciês on efte fi vertueux
en leurs fpeculations quilz
ont vofu fecretement enté
dre que lhôme parfaict eft
celluy en qui les bônes let
tres & fciences font infi-
nuees & itimees fi bié que
tous endroicts & mouue-
mês de fon corps eft garny
du bon mot q Cicero au

Cicero,
35

XXXV. Chapitre du pre
mier liure de fes Offices,&
au cômancemant De Ora
toté Ad Brutû, dict & ap-
pelle en Grec. Πρπον. &

Πρπον.
Decorû,

en Latí Decorû. qui vault
autant a dire en noftre lan
gage Francois decét & cô
uenable en toutes fes actions , & confequentement
en tous fes faicts & dits hô
me vertueux.

AVant que ie face lau-
tre portraict que iay
promis ie veulx cy bailler par efcript toutes les lettres ainfi quelles fe doibuent
appliquer aux neuf Mufes & leur fequelle, & aux dits lieux plus notables du
corps humain,afin que plus facilement on puiffe voir & cognoiftre leur bon
accord enfemble, Celluy accord eft tel qui fenfuyt.

Belle fpe
culation,
& nota-
ble.

B. Vrania. Loeuil dextre.
C. Calliope. Loeuil feneftre.
D. Polymnia. Loreille dextre.
F. Melpomene. Loreille feneftre.
G. Clio. La narine dextre.
K. Erato. La narine feneftre.
P. Terpifcore. La bouche.
Q. Euterpe. Le lieu pour decharger le ventre,
T. Thalia. Le membre naturel a vriner,

Fig. 1.3.   The alphabet and the human body during the Renaissance

constructing a Castilian territory grounded on the idea of civility (in
terms of religion and *studia humanitatis*). Thus a new culture, from
the perspective of Italian and Castilian humanism, should be housed
in the Crown of Castile and based on the knowledge of Latin and the
classical tradition. This program grew, year after year, from 1481 to
1522, when Nebrija died. The fight against the barbarian implied, in
this context, the fight against the scholastic mentality and ignorance
of Latin. It is in the second program, represented by the Castilian
grammar and orthography, that we perceive the merging of two of the
principles already analyzed: "to speak as we write and to write as we

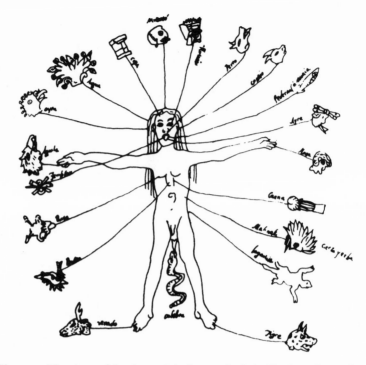

Fig. 1.4.   The signs of the day and the human body in Mexica culture after the conquest. Foto Biblioteca Vaticana.

speak" and "language as companion of the empire." How much of this was relevant in the colonization of the New World? What are the signs of the discontinuity of the classical tradition in the process of the expansion of the Spanish colonial empire? Let's take a closer look at both programs in New Spain (from approximately 1520 to 1650), beginning with the Hispanicizing of the natives.[50]

Looking Forward from Nebrija's Linguistic Programs and Backward from Aldrete's Concerns: The Difficulties of Teaching Castilian

From the sixteenth to the eighteenth century the kings of Castile proclaimed and disseminated all over the New World hundreds of laws promoting the "Castilianization" of the Amerindian population. Teaching a language that has both spoken and written versions implies not only teaching to speak, but teaching to read and write. Consequently, the dissemination of Western literacy took, among others, the form of laws and edicts that were circulated among administrative and religious institutions, as well as the practice of teaching reading and writing skills.[51] Furthermore, the missionaries contributed to the spread of Western literacy by writing hundreds of grammars of Amerindian languages and adapting hundreds of doctrines from the Christian tradition.[52] The first program, the Latinization of Castile as a model, found in the New World (more specifically, in New Spain) three different houses. The first, and most transitory, was the College of Santa Cruz de Tlatelolco, where Castilian was used, although Nahuatl and Latin were taught.[53] The second was the University of Mexico, founded circa 1550, where Cervantes de Salazar occupied the first chair of Latinity (grammar and rhetoric).[54] Finally, the College of San Pedro and San Pablo was founded a few years after the arrival of the Jesuits in Mexico (1572).[55]

Since the promulgation of the Laws of Burgos (1512–13), the *encomenderos* (concession holders) were asked to teach the Indians how to read and write Castilian. In 1526 Charles V also ordered that the natives be instructed about the purposes and programs that the Crown of Castile was in the process of implementing for New Spain. In 1535 a fundamental law was proclaimed by which school education for the sons of Mexica chiefs and principal lords was mandatory.[56] The schooling was to be supervised by the friars instead of the *encomenderos,* and the Amerindians selected for schooling were supposed to learn "Christianity, decent morals, good government, and the Castilian language." Charles V proclaimed the same law a second time in 1540; Philip II followed suit in 1579. In 1619 and 1620 the law was yet again circulated.[57] A cursory glance at the Leyes de Indias since the promulgation of the Laws of Burgos and the creation of the Council of the Indies (1524) shows that throughout the colonial period, until the eighteenth century, the aphorism *la lengua compañera del imperio* was a concern of the Crown and a reality at the level of the norms.

On the other hand, the first program, as applied in the New World, included teaching Castilian to the Amerindians, and in practice it offered more difficulties than Nebrija's triumphant account suggested. Because it was contrary to the teaching goals implemented by the Mendicant friars and the Jesuit orders during the colonial period, the Hispanicizing of the Amerindians remained at the level of edicts, royal orders, and laws. The two enemies of the implementation of Nebrija's program in New Spain were the friars, who were convinced that their goals would be better achieved if they learned and wrote grammars of Amerindian languages instead of teaching Castilian to the natives and, second, the conviction at the university and the Jesuit colleges that the *studia humanitatis* was the best model of education to civilize the New World colonies.[58] And though in the well-known Concilio III

Provincial Mexicano (1585) and III Concilio Provincial de Lima (1583) an agreement to teach Castilian to the Amerindians was reached, it is not altogether clear that a decisive turn in the politics of language took place. In the *concilio* it was recommended that, following the authority of the Tridentine Ruling, Christian doctrine would be taught in Castilian to the children of Spaniards, to Black slaves, and to the Chichimec; but to the Quechua- and Nahuatl-speaking peoples Christian doctrine should be taught in their own languages.[59]

The Mendicant friars were less interested in teaching Castilian to the Amerindians than in converting them to Christianity. Castilian was the language of everyday transactions but not necessarily of formal schooling.[60] The Jesuits taught Castilian in their missions, where they were teaching good customs as well as Western crafts. Higher education was generally reserved ethnically, to the children of Spaniards, and socially, to those born in the higher niches of society. During the second half of the sixteenth century, concern for educating the Amerindians was replaced by concern for the Creole population; the aim was to avoid sending Creole children to study in the nearest metropolis.[61] The incongruous goals of the Crown and the friars as well as the social transformations taking place in centers such as Mexico or Lima revealed that a curious inversion of Nebrija's programs was taking place: while Nebrija proposed learning Latin as means of unification and consolidation of the Christian republic, the friars in the New World had the option of Amerindian languages as a means to fulfill the same goals. The model of the Renaissance philosophy of language placed Amerindian languages in the category of "adventitious," below the range of the paradigm offered by Greek, Latin, and Hebrew and, of course, of those vernacular languages born from such prestigious ancestors, as Aldrete emphatically argued. However, Amerindian languages (especially in Nahuatl and Quechua, as lingua francas of a large number of Amerindian communities) became instruments of Christianization and acquired, in some sectors of the colonial society, a currency comparable to Castilian and Latin. The Colegio Santa Cruz de Tlatelolco remains as a paradigmatic example of the linguistic trilogy (Nahuatl, Latin, Castilian) of colonial Mexico that challenged the linguistic trilogy of the Old World (Greek, Latin, Hebrew) and suggested a new break with the continuity of the classical tradition. In this case, the influence of the first Nebrija, the Nebrija concerned with the Christian republic, seems quite obvious, although it was no longer Latin, as the language of knowledge and wisdom, but Nahuatl that served the purposes at hand (fig. 1.5). The will to insert Amerindian languages in the curriculum, next to the classical ones and to organize

at the same time literacy campaigns to integrate the already marginal
Amerindian population in a liberal society, shows the double bind of
the Creole mentality in societies deeply steeped in Amerindian traditions. Thus, the appropriation of Castilian as the language of the nation went together with the discontinuity of the Greco-Roman tradition by the incorporation of the history and languages of ancient
Mexico. After Mexican independence, in 1821, the legacy was such
that a handful of liberal thinkers defended the idea that Nahuatl, Ta-
rascan, and Otomi should be learned together with Latin.

Thus, writing grammars as well as preaching and writing sermons
and vocabularies of Amerindian languages had priority over teaching
Castilian for the Mendicant friars and, later on, for the Jesuits. And
when Castilian was taught, it was not in the context of higher education, where Latin was the paradigm. While de Gante's curriculum
in the Franciscan hands at the beginning of Western education in
Mexico consisted of reading and writing, singing, arithmetic, and
Christian doctrine, in the Jesuit missions reading and writing complemented the teaching of Western manual labors. Literacy became, in
the second part of the sixteenth century, just one more component in
the total process of Westernizing the Amerindians in the Jesuit missions. From the point of view of the early Franciscan friars in Mexico,
the fight against the devil was more important than the socialization of

Fig. 1.5.   Writing without letters: Mayan
glyph

colonized communities and their consolidation in the Spanish empire. In 1570 the Franciscans had already convinced Philip II that in New Spain Nahuatl was indeed the companion language of the empire. In the same year Philip II announced in a royal order (Cedulas Reales, 47. Archivo General de la Nación, Mexico) that Nahuatl would be the official language of the Amerindians. What is remarkable in this case is not the implicit assumption that language and human territoriality could be settled by royal decrees rather than by human nature and human memories, but the fact that Philip II modified a previous decree, published by Charles V in 1550, as well as his own edict of 1565, which established that Castilian would be taught to the Amerindians.[62] When the III Council determined to integrate Castilian into the curriculum (in 1583 in Lima and 1585 in Mexico) and to teach the language to Amerindians, social conditions had already dramatically changed. New pedagogical institutions oriented toward the education of an increasing Creole population had overpowered the pedagogical institutions oriented toward the education of an increasingly marginal Amerindian population.

It was in the context of the education of an expanding Creole population that Nebrija's program, stated in the introduction to his Latin grammar, was revamped almost a century later. The traces of the first Nebrija (i.e., the program justifying his *Introductiones latinae*) are obvious in the library of the College of Santa Cruz de Tlatelolco. Mathes, who made a library inventory, found that between 1535 and 1600 approximately a dozen of the three hundred books in the library were written in Castilian and the rest in Latin.[63] Three books written by Nebrija were part of the collection. One of them was an edition of his Latin grammar printed in Granada in 1540. It comes as no surprise, then, that *Indios latinistas* graduated from the College of Santa Cruz de Tlatelolco. We know that being taught Latin did not require just learning a foreign language, but learning a whole body of knowledge and system of thought. The well-known *Badianus Codex* (1552) remains as a paradigm of the *studia humanitatis* to the Amerindians. The true title of the *Badianus Codex* is *Libellus de medicinalibus indorum herbis* (fig. 1.6). It was written by an Indian, Martín de la Cruz, a doctor, not so much by training as by experience, and the text was translated into Latin by Juan Badiano, also a student at Santa Cruz de Tlatelolco. The existence and influence of the *colegio* were—as I have already pointed out—transitory, although extremely relevant from 1536 to the last years of the sixteenth century, when teaching Latin and *studia humanitates* to the Amerindians was perceived as a dangerous enterprise. When the Jesuits arrived in Mexico, in 1572, the teaching of Latin and the humanities changed direction and was targeted toward the Spanish and Spanish-descendant population, rather than to the children of the Amerindian nobility.[64]

Thus, the actuality of Nebrija was more discernible during the seventeenth century among the Jesuits, and, once again, not because of his Castilian but because of his Latin grammar. We should bear in mind that while, on the one hand, grammars, vocabularies, sermons, and Christian doctrines were written in Latin and the humanities were taught to the children of the Amerindian nobility, Castilian was mainly an instrument of communication, not of scholarly learning. There was no exception to this reality among the Jesuits. Osorio Romero has collected an impressive amount of information about the libraries and curricula of the Jesuit colleges, and I would like to stress two of his findings.

First, Vicencio Lanuchi, well known for his knowledge of Latin, Greek, and Hebrew, was one of the most important figures in the foundation of Jesuit studies in New Spain. Grammar was, of course, the core of a curriculum in which Latinity was the main concern. Osorio Romero quotes from a letter addressed to Pedro Sanchez

Fig. 1.6. The spread of Western literacy in central Mexico: a treatise of Amerindian medicine written in Nahuatl, in alphabetic writing, and translated into Latin (Martín de la Cruz, *Libellus de medicinalibus indorum herbis*)

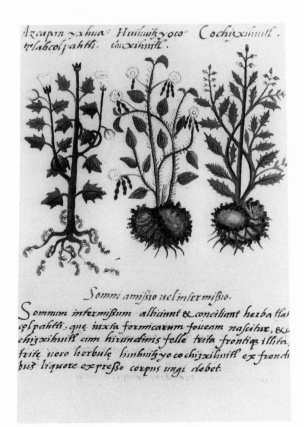

("provincial de la compañía" in Mexico) and signed by Mercuriano ("General de la Compañía de Jesus" in Rome):

En los estudios de letras humanas deseo mucho se guarde el orden, cuanto se pudiere, que aquí en Roma se tiene, que es el más útil y más compendioso de todos. El padre Vicencio Lanoche tiene pratica desto, y podrá ayudar a que así se efectúe; porque destos principios de latinidad, importa mucho el excercicio y el buen orden que acá (en Roma) se tiene.[65]

[In the study of the humanities I would like, as far as possible, to follow the same order that we follow here in Rome, which is the most useful and succinct of all. Father Vicencio Lanoche is practiced at this, and he will be able to help its being carried out; because of these principles of Latinity, the practice and good order that we follow here in Rome are of great import.]

Nebrija's program for the Latinization of Castile was not antagonistic to that of the Jesuits.[66] It comes as no surprise, then, that the Jesuits would take Nebrija's Latin grammar as one of their basic textbooks.

Second, a report written in 1586 about New Spain included a section about the Jesuit education in the city in which it was pointed out that grammar was studied in four classes: rhetoric, philosophy, two lessons on theory and one on case of conscience ("leense en este colegio gramática, en cuatro clases: retórica, filosofía, dos lecciones de teoría y una de casos de conciencia"). It was in this context that Mateo Galindo, in 1636, published the first edition of his *Explicación del libro cuarto de Antonio de Nebrija,* which was reprinted during the seventeenth and eighteenth centuries. In 1640 Tomás González published his *Explicación de las silabas sobre el libro V de Nebrija* and, in 1642, the *Explicación de la cuantidad de las sílabas sobre el libro quinto del Arte de Antonio de Nebrija.* Toward 1650, Diego de López published *Breve explicación del libro cuarto de Antonio Nebrisense;* Tomás González published *De arte rhetorica libri tres* and *Arte de Antonio,* in 1652 and 1657 respectively. It should be remembered that the "arte de Antonio" refers to the Latin and not to the Castilian grammar.[67]

We have arrived at 1657 and the publication of grammar books in Mexico, having begun in 1481 with the question of the letter. The dream of Isabella and Ferdinand was changing slowly into a concern that Spain was losing its European and Atlantic hegemony. Nebrija introduced, in his *Reglas de la ortografía en la lengua castellana,* a theory of writing in which the domain of the letter took over the domain of the voice, reversing the ancillary role of the letter with respect to the voice in the Greek philosophical tradition. This inversion was, indeed, the first manifestation of the discontinuity of the classical tradition in the modern world. The second manifestation took place the moment the modern world encountered the "other," and alphabetic writing met oral traditions and picto-ideographic writing systems (figs. 1.7, 1.8). In Castile the theory of the letter led to a theory of writing that transcended the regionality of spoken languages and colonized the voice,[68] but application of the theory in the New World led to the colonization of Amerindian languages (by writing their grammars) and the colonization of the Amerindian memories (by writing their histories, as chap. 3 will show). In the eighteenth century we still hear the echoes of the early colonization of language both in the sphere of speaking and that of writing.

More than a century after Aldrete's *La lengua,* the archbishop of Mexico, Francisco Antonio Lorenzana y Buitrón, published his classic *Cartas pastorales y edictos.*[69] In his "Pastoral V" we still hear Aldrete's complaint of the Spanish failure to teach Castilian to the Amerindians. The title of the "Pastoral V" is, appropriately, "Para que los Indios aprendan el Castellano," and in the first sentence Lorenzana claims that after more than two centuries the situation in this respect is pretty much the same as it was for Cortés, in need of "interpreters of the languages." He points out the difficulties presented by what he perceived as the multiplication of Amerindian languages in the area of Mexico, Puebla, and Oaxaca. All of this is happening, observes Lorenzana with dismay, despite the numerous laws and decrees formulated by the Crown mandating that the Castilian language be taught to the Amerindian. His dismay is complemented by a historical reasoning very similar to that expressed by Aldrete 150 years before in Seville:

No ha habido Nación Culta en el Mundo, que cuando extendía sus Conquistas, no procurase hacer lo mismo con su Lengua: Los Griegos tuvieron por bárbaras las demás Naciones, que ignoraban la suya: Los Romanos, despues que vencieron a los Griegos, precisaron á estos á que admitiesen su Lengua Latina, ó de Lacio, Campaña de Roma, con tanto rigor, que no permitían entrar para negocio alguno en el Senado, á el que hablase otra Lengua estraña.

[There has never been a Cultured Nation in the World, that when it extended its Conquests, did not attempt the same with its Language: the Greeks took for barbarians those other Nations that remained ignorant of its speech; the Romans, after conquering the Greeks, required them to accept their Latin Language—that of

a

b

Fig. 1.7.   Writing without letters. Graphic signs in central Mexico and the Valley of Oaxaca: *a*, a sign for the year; *b*, historical personages; *c*, a marriage scene. From *Picture Writing from Ancient Southern Mexico: Mixtec Place Signs and Maps*, by Mary Elizabeth Smith. Copyright © 1973 by the University of Oklahoma Press.

Latium, the Roman countryside—with such rigor that they did not allow anyone who spoke another, foreign language to conduct business in the Senate.]

While one of his reasons to teach Castilian was because the vanquisher always imposes its language on the vanquished, as Aldrete proudly insisted, the other takes a surprising turn in linguistic hierarchy. Contrary to the high esteem in which the early Mendicant friars and Jesuits held Amerindian languages, Lorenzana returns to an early sixteenth-century European linguistic philosophy in which Latin, Greek, and Hebrew are the three superior languages, to which Nahuatl could not really be compared. Lorenzana is convinced that when only one language is spoken in a nation and that language is the language of the sovereign, an expanding love and familiarity between persons are engendered, in a way that will be impossible without such a common language. While it could be accepted that sharing the same language engenders love among those persons speaking it (albeit love in two languages is also possible), it is more difficult to

accept that in Mexico that language should be the language of the sovereign living in Spain. But for Lorenzana there is no alternative, not only because of political realities but also because of the linguistic hierarchy:

Baxando ya con la consideración a los Idiomas tan varios de los Indios, ¿Quién sin capricho dexará de conocer, que así como su Nación fue bárbara, lo fue, y es su Idioma? ¿Quién podrá comparar el Mexicano con el Hebreo, y con todo ya es Lengua muerta, no obstante, que algunos dicen, que es la que habló nuestro primer Padre Adan, enseñado por Dios? ¿Quién le igualará con el Griego, que fue Lengua tan elegante y fecunda, y con todo ya es muerta, o a lo menos casi muerta? ¿Quién antepondrá el Mexicano a el Latin, en cuyo Idioma tenemos traducido todos los Libros Sagrados, de

Fig. 1.8. Translating Maya glyphs into the letters of the Roman alphabet: Diego de Landa's *Relación de las cosas de Yucatán*

Santos Padres Griegos, y quando exquisito se ha escrito en el
Mundo, y con todo ya no hay Nacion, que hable comunmente el
puro Latin?

[And now, reducing our consideration to the sundry languages of
the Indians: who could seriously fail to acknowledge that, just as
their Nation was barbarous, so was and is their Language? Who
could compare Mexican with Hebrew, in spite of the fact it is a dead
Language, even though, as some say, it is that spoken by our first
Father Adam, instructed by God? Who could equate it to Greek,
which was such an elegant and fecund Language, even though it is
now dead, or at least almost dead? Who could put Mexican before
Latin, into which language we have translated all the Holy Books of
the Holy Greek Fathers, and which is as exquisite [a language] as
has ever been written in the World, even though there is no longer
any Nation that uses pure Latin in everyday speech?]

Lorenzana introduces Castilian in this series of comparison to
lower even further the consideration of Nahuatl and, by extension, all
Amerindian languages:

A el Mexicano por sí escaso, y bárbaro, le hicieron más abundante
los Castellanos, que le aprendieron, inventando varias composi-
ciones de vocablos para adornarle: Los Indios en su Lengua no
tenían términos para los Santos Sacramentos de la Iglesia, ni para
los Misterios de nuestra Santa Fé, y aun hoy no se hallan para su
explicación los propios, y que den cabal idea.

[The Mexican (language), in itself meager and barbarous, was
made more abundant by the Castilians who learned it and invented
various compositions of words so to adorn it: in their Language, the
Indians had no terms for the Holy Sacraments of the Church, nor
for the Mysteries of our Holy Faith, and even today they cannot
find their own (words) to explain them, such as would give an exact
idea.]

Opinions such as these sound outrageous to a sensitive reader—
although they belong to the past—or to a reader suspicious of the
ways the Spaniards conducted their business in the Indies. But
Lorenzana's statements are not buried in the past, nor are they a
unique feature of Spanish colonization. The situation repeated itself
under the English, French, and German expansions during the late
eighteenth and nineteenth centuries,[70] and it is still alive today among

certain sectors of the population, who consider Amerindian languages inferior to Castilian, French, or English and cannot understand why Amerindians resist the benefits of culture and civilization. Lorenzana was writing, however, in the hub of a heated situation in which the Creole appropriation and evaluation of Mexican antiquities went together with their strong reactions against the Spaniards.

Juan José de Eguiara y Eguren (born in Mexico City in 1696), former professor of theology (1738) and dean of the University of Mexico (1749) (among the many public offices he held during his lifetime), turned down an appointment to become bishop of Yucatán in 1751 because of his age, he said, and because he was in the process of writing his *Bibliotheca mexicana,* which was published in 1755.[71] The *Bibliotheca* was, among other things, a catalog and a defense of the extraordinary cultural achievements of the ancient Mexicans as well as the Creole of New Spain. It was also a reaction against recent opinions expressed by Manuel Martí, dean of the city of Alicante, Spain. In an epistle sent to one of his young disciples who was tempted to pursue his studies in Mexico, Martí advised him to go instead to Rome, a highly civilized place, not to be compared with a barbaric Mexico. Eguiara y Eguren compiled the *Bibliotheca mexicana* to prove Martí wrong. In the preface he discusses in detail Martí's opinion and celebrates the high achievements of Mexican civilization, from the ancient Mexican to his own days. Relevant to the current discussion is his celebration of Nahuatl, with its sophisticated discourses and graphic record keeping by means of visible signs. Although Eguiara y Eguren wrote in Latin within a neoclassical mentality, both the significance of his act and the meaning of his statements could be interpreted in the context of the long history of colonization of Amerindian languages. Writing in Latin shows that the barbarians in Mexico could express themselves in Latin as well as the civilized in Spain and Rome. It also helps to authorize his words about ancient speech and record keeping. Eguiara y Eguren exemplified and described the ancient Mexican "adornment of speech" [ornato dicendi genere], praised its use of rhetorical precepts to train new orators ("rhetoricis efformaban praeceptis oratoresque olim initiandos"), and admired the eloquence favored by the abundance and tastefulness of the Nahuatl language ("divite supellectile loquendi copiosissimo et elegantissimo idiomate accurate instituebant"). Eguiara y Eguren moves from discussing speech and oral discourse to speculating about writing and graphic signs. Why, he asks, are the Mexicans not entitled to be included on the list of educated men? Why are they accused of living in the most dreadful isolation and ignorance of letters? Why are they presented as savage barbarians who abominate culture, making them not only incapable of teaching but also incapable of acquiring knowledge? (prologue, viii).

At this point, the early conflict between the Crown and the Franciscan friars becomes more complex, entrenched within the debates between Creole and peninsular linguistic and cultural ideologies.[72] While the first conflict arose from implementation of different goals (Christianization and Hispanization) by the same means (spreading Western literacy by teaching how to read and write) as contained in the two different programs expressed by Nebrija, the second led toward a radical transformation in the uses of literacy. Lorenzana and Eguiara y Eguren wrote, instead, toward the end of the Spanish domination of the Indies and approaching the independence period (fig. 1.9). After independence, the main use of literacy would be to become a good Mexican citizen instead of a good Hispanic Christian.

The early conflict between the Crown and the friars presupposed a theory of the letter and a value-laden educational philosophy claiming the superiority of alphabetic writing and of Western books as a measurement of civilization. The underlying philosophy of writing, the book, and knowledge that we saw in the educational programs of both the Franciscans and the Jesuits was not divorced from the numerous edicts and mandates published by the Crown with the intention of making Castilian available to the Amerindian and, together with teaching how to read and write in Castilian, transmitting Castilian values and manners. It is in this context that, beyond the colonization of native languages or the implementation of a linguistic politics for the expansion of the language of the empire, the theory of the letter also gave rise to a program for the interpretation of culture. The questions that Acosta directed to Tovar (to which we will return in chap. 3) could be traced back to Ramón Pané (1493) and forward to Torquemada in order to read in them all a method for the interpretation of cultures based on the lack or possession of writing and on the lack or possession of alphabetic writing.[73] The work of Eguiara y Eguren, during the first half of the eighteenth century, was part of larger changes that impinged not only on the philosophy of language but also on the philosophy of history, which will be explored in chapter 3.

Looking Back on the Previous Narrative

The New World colonies, as the case of Mexico suggests, were a linguistic and cultural mosaic. Their appearance in the eyes of Castilian interpreters was molded by the Renaissance philosophy of writing and theory of the letter.[74] The contribution of both to the discontinuity of the classical tradition took the form, first, of the colonization of the voice and, second, of the appropriation of languages and cultures outside the realm of the Greco-Roman tradition. One of the consequences was the fading out of every writing system except the alphabetic. However, contrary to Aldrete's beliefs, the death of a writing system does not imply the disappearance of a culture and its cultural construction of territoriality. Economic possession and legal control cannot be equated with cognitive mapping. Amerindian cultures continued and continue to live, nowadays, in their oral traditions, as witnessed by the hundreds of Amerindian communities in the Yucatán peninsula, Mexico, Paraguay, or in Andean Peru.[75] Amerindian languages, in other words, are also tied up with territoriality, if by territoriality we understand a sense of being and belonging beyond the administrative and legal apparatus by which the land is owned by a handful of people and the nation symbolically construed by its intellectuals. The survival, in fact, of native languages from the Rio Grande to Tierra del Fuego, as well as the cultural patterns and traditions associated with those languages, shows once more that it is in and by

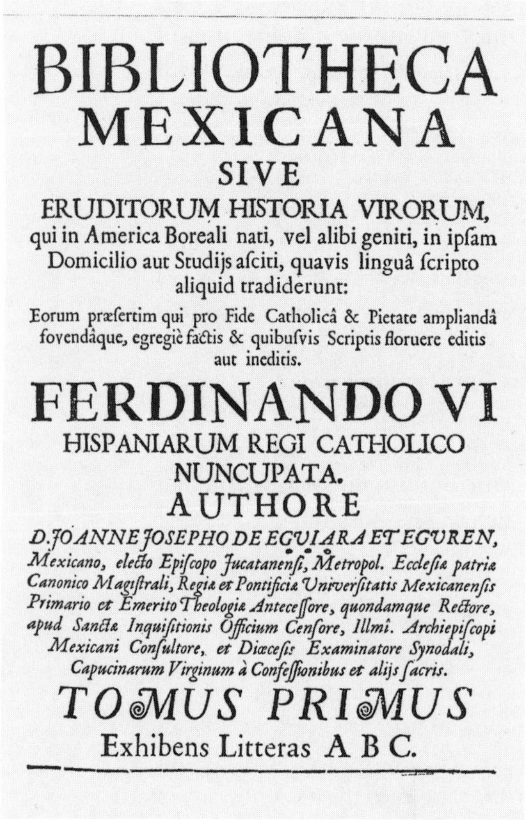

BIBLIOTHECA
MEXICANA
SIVE
ERUDITORUM HISTORIA VIRORUM,
qui in America Boreali nati, vel alibi geniti, in ipſam
Domicilio aut Studijs aſciti, quavis linguâ ſcripto
aliquid tradiderunt:

Eorum præſertim qui pro Fide Catholicâ & Pietate ampliandâ
fovendàque, egregiè faﬅis & quibuſvis Scriptis ﬂoruere editis
aut ineditis.

FERDINANDO VI
HISPANIARUM REGI CATHOLICO
NUNCUPATA.
AUTHORE
D. JOANNE JOSEPHO DE EGUIARA ET EGUREN,
Mexicano, eleﬅo Epiſcopo Jucatanenſi, Metropol. Eccleſiæ patriæ
Canonico Magiﬅrali, Regiæ et Pontificiæ Univerſitatis Mexicanenſis
Primario et Emerito Theologiæ Anteceﬀore, quondamque Reﬅore,
apud Sanﬅæ Inquiſitionis Officium Cenſore, Illmi. Archiepiſcopi
Mexicani Conſultore, et Diœceſis Examinatore Synodali,
Capucinarum Virginum à Confeﬀionibus et alijs ſacris.

TOMUS PRIMUS
Exhibens Litteras A B C.

Fig. 1.9.   Reorganizing the library: the place of ancient writing and books in the Creole cultural history of Mexico, toward the second half of the eighteenth century

language that territories are created (or invented) and not necessarily in and by the letter. Recent investigation on the ethnography of speaking has shown that the customs and traditions of communities are imbedded in their own linguistic tradition[76]. But Renaissance men of letters (*letrados*) involved in the justification of the European expansion could not have had the perspective one has today on colonized peripheries. Such men were not in a position to understand the interconnections between the letter, language, and territory. What Aldrete was clearly articulating at the height of the Spanish colonial expansion was foreseen by Nebrija when Castile had not yet ventured forth in the colonization of the New World.

Certainly, Nebrija's Castilian grammar found its home during the second half of the eighteenth century and, mainly, during the neo-colonial period. Nation building went hand in hand with the final victory of the Castilian language. Although Latin was still taught, it lost the charm and appeal it had during the colonial period. Finally, Castilian was a language to be taught and used in writing the memories of the new (national) territories. Another historical paradox: the grammar that Nebrija had intended to serve the expansion of the Spanish empire in fact served as a tool to help build the nations that arose from the liberation of the Spanish colonization.[77] A new historiography and territorial construction emerged from the ruins of the Spanish empire. In countries like Mexico, the origin of Castilian, which worried Aldrete two centuries before, was no longer an issue. Castilian also emerged from the ruins of the Spanish empire, as the language of a new historiography and territorial construction.

Chapter 2

The Materiality of Reading and Writing Cultures: The Chain of Sounds, Graphic Signs, and Sign Carriers

Who Is Naming That Object a Book?

Alejo Venegas was a well-known humanist and man of letters in the Spain of Charles I. He was the teacher of Cervantes de Salazar, who went to Mexico around 1550 and became the first professor of rhetoric at the Real Universidad de Mexico. In 1540 in Toledo Venegas published the first part of an ambitious project entitled *Primera parte de las diferencias de libros que hay en el universo*. He provided the following definition of the book:

> [A] book is an ark of deposit in which, by means of essential information or things or figures, those things that belong to the information and clarity of understanding [*entendimiento*] are deposited.[1]

Following the rules of logical discourse at the time, Venegas proceeds to analyze each component of the definition. The book is an ark, he says, because the noun is derived from the verb *arredrar* (to frighten), and the book frightens ignorance. The book is a depository because, in the same way the ark contained things, books keep the treasures of knowledge. Furthermore, things are deposited "by means of essential information" because the Divine Book contains the information and knowledge that God has of himself and through which he knows everything past, present, future, and possible. Because of his

69

divine essence, God produces and engenders the eternal Verb by means of which he creates everything. The definition also includes "things" because things are signs that bring information about something else. Finally, figures are included because of the diversity of written letters. Thus, figures basically means "written letters."

After defining the book, Venegas introduces the distinction between the "archetype book" and the "metagraph book."[2] He calls the first *exemplar* or *dechado* (rule or pattern) and the second, *trasunto* (likeness) or *traslado* (trans-lation, moving something from one place to another). The first is the uncreated book read only by the angels; the second the book read by human beings. The archetype book is the expression of the Divine Word and the container of all knowledge. God, as the supreme writer, has expressed the truth in the Book of Nature and in the Holy Book (archetype), which has been inscribed in alphabetic characters. The human book has two functions: to allow human agents to know the creator of the universe by reading his book and, at the same time, to censure every human expression in which the devil manifests himself by dictating false books.

Fig. 2.1. Writing and the materiality of sign carriers: A medieval codex

That the Holy Book was the expression of the Divine Word and the human book a container of knowledge and the inscription of the human voice in alphabetic writing was taken for granted during the sixteenth century, and the idea still has validity in communities of believers. In the sixteenth century, what missionaries and men of letters perceived in Amerindian sign carriers was molded by an image of the book to which Venegas's definition contributed. One can also surmise that the concrete examples Venegas, or any educated person in sixteenth-century Castile, had in mind were the medieval codices and the recently printed books (fig. 2.1).[3] That hypothetical person had probably forgotten what a book might have been before papyrus was replaced by vellum and the roll by the codex,[4] and perhaps forgotten also that writing did not require a book (fig. 2.2). Such a person might not have been aware that in the transformation and subsequent use of the codex form, Christianity and the reproduction of the Bible played a crucial role.[5] Thus, when a missionary, an educated soldier, or a man of letters was exposed to the artifacts the Mexicas named *amoxtli* and the Maya named *vuh*, he described them as objects folded like an accordion and translated these terms as "book" (fig. 2.3). In China and Japan, during the fifteenth century, narratives painted on folded screen and hanging scroll were very common, and the bound book familiar to European men of letters, like Venegas, was probably unknown.[6] But since Spaniards were not sure what *kind* of books the Amerindians "books" were, they feared that the words of the devil were registered in them, without suspecting that the notion of the written word might have been alien to the Amerindians[7] and the very idea of the devil questionable. The Spaniards took action consistent with what they believed a book to be and what they perceived Amerindians to have. One reaction was to burn them, perhaps with the calm and secure spirit that characterizes Diego de Landa's description:

> These people used certain characters or letters, with which they wrote in their books about their antiquities and their sciences; with these, and with figures, and certain signs in the figures, they understood their matters, made them known, and taught them. We found a great number of books in these letters, and since they contained nothing but superstitions and falsehoods of the devil we burned them all, which they took most grievously, and which gave them great pain.[8]

Misunderstanding was entrenched in the colonization of language. Landa presupposed equal means of communication and social practices in such a way that reading and writing were the same both for

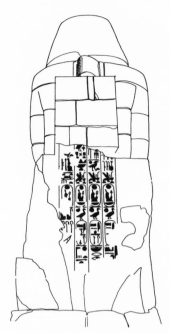

Fig. 2.2. Writing without books: *a*, graphic inscriptions on stone in ancient Egypt; *b*, inscription of a battle scene on a polychrome vase among the ancient Maya; *c*, the same scenes "unfolded"

a

b

Spaniards and the inhabitants of the Yucatán peninsula; he also pre-supposed the concept of letters among the Maya, which he distinguished from characters. Finally, because he was accustomed to seeing medieval illuminated books, he assumed that the Maya *vuh* were also written and illustrated with pictures. It did not occur to him that such a distinction might not be relevant to the Mayas. Landa around 1566 gave a description (instead of a definition) of the materiality of Maya "books." It is worthwhile when reading it to keep in mind Venegas's definition:

> They wrote their books on a long sheet doubled in folds, which was then enclosed between two boards finely ornamented; the writing was on one side and the other according to the folds. *The paper they made from the roots of a tree, and gave it a white finish excellent for writing upon.* Some of the principal lords were learned in these sciences, from interests, and for the greater esteem they enjoyed thereby; yet, they did not make use of them in public. (Italics mine)[9]

Landa might have had no choice but to talk about "their letters" and "their books," rather than think in terms of "our *vuh*" and ask what concepts the Maya used to designate the basic units of their writing; or to ask whether the distinction between painting and writing made sense for them and, consequently, what was the purpose of describing "their" books as having pictures illustrating their writing. Landa could have asked also whether the Maya distinguished "book" from "paper," since *vuh* seems to refer to the surface in which signs are inscribed and to the object created by written signs in a solid surface made out of tree bark (*vuh*). But there is still more: why did Landa believe that the materiality of Maya writing was to be understood in terms of books, and why did he not think that they could have had

c

other surfaces in which signs were inscribed and writing practiced?[10] For Landa writing was naturally conceived in terms of papers and books; and books in terms of the medieval manuscript and the printing press, which were also the examples Venegas might have had in mind some twenty-five years before Landa's report.

In Anáhuac, among the Nahuatl-speaking people, the term regularly employed to refer to the material surface on which painted narratives were inscribed was *amoxtli*. Brother Toribio de Benavente (Motolinía), who arrived in Mexico in 1524, reported on such Mexica "books." Contrary to Landa, Motolinía's description oscillates between the materiality of inscriptions and the conceptual genres he perceived in Mexicas' books. In a letter, Motolinía reported to Lord Antonio Pimentel,

> I shall treat of this land of Anáhuac or New Spain . . . according to the ancient books which the natives had or possessed. These books were written in symbols and pictures. This was their way of writing, supplying their lack of an alphabet by the use of symbols. . . . These natives had five books, which, as I said, were written in pictures and symbols. The first book deals with years and calculations of time; the second, with the days and with the feasts which the Indians

Fig. 2.3. Writing and the materiality of the sign carriers: a Mexica *amoxtli*

observed during the year; the third, with dreams, illusions, superstitions and omens in which the Indians believed; the fourth, with baptisms and with names that were bestowed upon children; the fifth, with the rites, ceremonies and omens of the Indians relative to marriage. Only one of all these books, namely the first, can be trusted because it recounts the truth.[11]

Borgia Steck's translation leaves out important wording from the original, namely, Motolinía's statement that only the first book can be trusted *because* the other four were invented by the devils. It is curious to note that a similar observation was made by Landa in connection with the Maya concept of time. This section translated Maya glyphs into alphabetic writing and reported that

The sciences which they taught were the reckoning of the years, months and days, the festivals and ceremonies, the administration of their sacraments, the omens of the days, their methods of divination and prophecies, events, remedies for sickness, antiquities, *and the art of reading and writing by their letters and the characters wherewith they wrote, and by pictures that illustrated the writings.*[12]

Venegas's dual typology, distinguishing between the archetype and the metagraph book, allowed an interpretation of the latter that emerged in almost every report about writing and books in the New World: it might be the book of the devil, which contained not science but superstition, not truth but falsehood. Material differences across cultures in writing practices, the storage and transmission of information, and the construction of knowledge were erased—in a process of analogy, a fight in the name of God against the devil.

The game of the word became, thus, a conceptual game that impinged on understanding across cultures (what is "behind" words such as *amoxtli, vuh,* and *book?*), on the exercise of power (who is in a position to decide whose knowledge is truth, what container and sign carrier is preferred and should be trusted?), and the colonization of language. The only artifacts that Motolinía trusted he named *xihutonal amatl* (book counting the years). *Amatl* is derived from *amoxtli,* a plant that grew in the lakes in the Valley of Mexico and from whose bark sign carriers were prepared. *Amatlacuilo* was a name for the individual whose social role was to paint on the *amatl;* it was translated as "scribe." Other expressions related to social roles in writing activities have been derived, such as *uei amatlacuilo,* which Simeon translated as "secretary or principal writer"; and also *amoxtlacuilo,* which he translated as "scribe, author." Simeon's translations of the first as "secretary" and the second as "author" suggests that *amoxtli* might have referred to "books" and *amatl* to "paper." In any case, not only was the materiality of the artifact different, but also the social role and the conceptualization each culture associated to the signs (letters or painting), the sign carrier (*amoxtli* or book), and to the social roles (*tlacuilo* or scribe), as well as the activities (writing/reading and looking at/telling a story). These conceptualizations varied according to respective traditions, cultural and social uses, and the materiality of reading and writing interactions. Spaniards, however, had the last word and took for granted that their reading and writing habits, their human and divine books, and their ways of organizing and transmitting knowledge were better and exempt from devilish design. The spread of Western literacy, then, did not only take the form of reading and writing. It was also a massive operation in which the materiality and the ideology of Amerindian semiotic interactions were intermingled with or replaced by the materiality and ideology of Western reading and writing cultures.

Writing without Words, without Paper, without Pen

Writing does not presuppose the book, although during the sixteenth-century celebration of the letter, it was narrowed down to mean just that almost exclusively. Its image is so strong in cultures of the book that those who do not belong to them, as we no longer do, are not always aware of what a book means.[13] Alternative sign carriers (like newspapers) were not yet available, and the complicity between writing and the book was such that the possibility of writing on clay, animal skin, tree bark, and the like was beyond the cultural horizon of the time. Venegas's definition of the book, very much like Nebrija's celebration of the letter, erased previous material means of writing practices or denied coeval ones that were not alphabetically based.

Keeping with examples from the Yucatán peninsula, we observe that the many Spanish descriptions and reactions to Maya writing practices were presented as if Western books and the equivalent of Western paper were the only sign carriers. The colonizers paid less attention to writing carved in stone and in pottery, which had very wide use and significant social functions.[14] The reader of such descriptions as Landa's and Motolinía's was invited to conceive Maya literacy in European terms and never the inverse, imagining what Europeans might lack if the point of reference were Maya script and sign carriers.

A few years after Landa wrote his *relación,* another Franciscan,

Antonio de Ciudad Real, observed in his report on the life of Brother
Alonso Ponce that the Maya should be praised above all other people
of New Spain for three things. He was impressed, first, by the characters and figures (he called them *letras*) with which the Maya wrote
their narratives and recorded their past (which he called *historia*). The
second noteworthy aspect was their religion and sacrificial rites
devoted to their gods (which he called *idols*). And third were the Maya
calendars, inscribed in artifacts made of tree bark. He described them
as consisting of very long strips almost a third of a *vara* (thirty-three
inches) wide, which were folded "and came to be more or less like a
quarto-bound book." He also observed the spread of Maya literacy.
Only the "priests of the idols" (*ah kins*) and every so often a noble
person understood such "figures and letters." After the conquest,
however, "our friars understood them, knew how to read them, and
even wrote them."[15]

The analogy with a quarto-bound book is indeed quite revealing.
The medieval bound manuscript was basically similar in format to the
printed book during the Renaissance. When paper was introduced in
Europe toward the end of the thirteenth century, replacing previous
sign carriers (such as parchment), it was folded in two or four (in folio
or in quarto) and then assembled in segments (fasciculus) of four to six
sheets. Medieval and Renaissance printed books acquired a very distinctive format in relation to previous rolls or scrolls. Yet one can find
in standard histories of the book the notion that the first books were
scrolls. Such expressions presuppose that a given material format (the
medieval and Renaissance book) was imperfect when invented and
finally achieved an essence that was *in potentia* since its inception. This
evolutionary model of writing and the book was to a great extent an
invention of the European Renaissance, and it was precisely the model
enacted by missionaries and men of letters when they described Amerindian writing practices and sign carriers. It is somewhat curious that
the analogy was made between Amerindian *amoxtli* or *vuh* and
quarto-bound book instead of the scroll, to which new pieces could be
added, and which could be rolled and unrolled. In his famous description, Bernal Díaz del Castillo chose instead to say that Mexican books
were folded like Castilian fabric.

I would like to elaborate on this point, taking an example from
current ways of talking about writing. An evolutionary model still
seems to prevail, according to which true writing is alphabetic writing
and is indistinguishable from the book, which, in its turn, is indistinguishable from the material form of the European medieval and
Renaissance examples.

Following David Diringer, for example, three kinds of writing can be visualized: embryo, nonalphabetic, and alphabetic. He calls the last two "pure" writing. It is possible, he says, "to count as 'writing' any semiotic mark . . . an individual makes and assigns a meaning to," and the antiquity of writing is perhaps comparable to the antiquity of speech. But a "critical and unique breakthrough into new worlds of knowledge was achieved within human consciousness not when simple semiotic marking was devised but when a coded system of visible marks was invented whereby a writer could determine the exact words that the reader would generate from the text."[16] Writing thus conceived is restricted to syllabic and alphabetic writing. If this distinction is valid from the standpoint of the history of writing, ethnography, or paleography, it is not as satisfactory from the semiotic point of view. I am less concerned with the change of *name,* whether we call an action "writing," than with a change of level directing us away from the particular lexicon and expressions of a culture linked with the representation of a particular mode of interaction and toward a disciplinary understanding, in which a *concept* is bonded to its theoretical definition. One needs, first, a theoretical definition of graphic signs and of graphic semiotic interactions before moving into a historical classification of different stages in the development of writing. Semiotically, a graphic sign is, then, a physical sign made with the purpose of establishing a semiotic interaction. Consequently, a human interaction is a semiotic one if there is a community and a body of common knowledge according to which (*a*) a person can produce a graphic sign with the purpose of conveying a message (to somebody else or to him- or herself); (*b*) a person perceives the graphic sign and interprets it as a sign produced with the purpose of conveying a message; and (*c*) that person attributes a given meaning to the graphic sign. Notice that in this theoretical definition of writing the links between speech and writing are not necessary because writing is not conceived of as the representation of speech.

In this sense writing is a communicative device common to all cultures, although its conceptualizations and uses diverge and not every member of a community has access to writing, whereas in Walter Ong's conception, writing is limited to alphabetic or syllabic systems. For its part, book is a concept united with writing only in the conceptualization of a culture in which writing is understood in the restricted sense defined by Diringer and Ong. To avoid the ambiguities caused by the use of concepts that preserve, in a disciplinary context, the same meaning they hold in cultural (nondisciplinary) expressions, a theoretical definition is needed. Before giving a definition of book, I will first attempt a description. In what follows I rely on Diringer's classic study devoted to the book before printing.[17] My own recognition of his important contribution will not prevent me from challenging some of his basic presuppositions. The most relevant of his presuppositions for the issues explored in this chapter is revealed by his consistency in using the term *book* in the restricted sense furnished by his own Western and contemporary culture and projecting it toward different times and places. Let me illustrate this statement. Diringer writes:

> *Libri Lintei* ("linen books") are mentioned by Livy not as existing in his own time, but as recorded by Licinius Macer . . . who stated that linen "books" were kept in the temple of Juno Moneta. They were not "books" in the modern sense, but simply very ancient annals and libri magistratum ("books of magistrates").[18]

Despite the caution ("they were not books in the modern sense"), Diringer translates "libri" as "books." Diringer certainly knows that *libri lintei* designates ancient chronicles of the Romans that were written on linen and preserved in the Temple of Juno Moneta. But it is not known for sure that they were books, since *libri* may have been used to designate the solid surface on which writing was performed (a possible extension from the original meaning: the inner bark of a tree). Thus, *libri lintei* could be just "writing on linen"; *libri magistratum* could be translated as "writings of the magistrates."

A second example comes from the idea that papyrus was the main writing material for books in the Greco-Roman world. Although papyrus was indeed the primary writing material, it does not follow that it was for writing books, but rather just for a multitude of writing purposes (e.g., recording data for future use, everyday human interactions, communication with gods).[19] To be inscribed and transmitted, a graphic sign certainly needs a medium. But from this point to the book is a long road. Diringer states that the Greek word *biblos* means the "pith of the papyrus stalk"; it gave origin to *biblion*, the common word for "papyrus scroll" or "papyrus roll" whose plural was *biblia*, "papyrus rolls," *tá biblía*, "the scrolls." In this case, Diringer translates "the scrolls" as the equivalent of "book."[20] With regard to the Roman lexicon, Diringer relates that the modern word "volume" derives from the Latin *volumen* (a thing rolled up); it is formed from the verb *volvere* (to roll) and renders the Greek *kylindros* (cylinder). In this context *evolvere, folia volvere* (to unroll) was often used in the sense of "to read" (*folia conjicere*). When, after all this information, Diringer relates that the term *volumen*, like *liber* (to peel the inner bark of a tree), was in common use for "book," the quotation marks do not solve the problem of the manner in which a community represents its own objects and social interactions. For an educated member of Western culture, the word *book* is associated with a body of knowledge (and representations) far from the meaning of a roll (*volumen*) of inner bark of a tree (*liber*) or the frame in which a roll was cut (*tómos*), which in all probability were among the meanings associated with these words in the Roman community.

Certainly the entire problem of the book cannot be reduced to the meaning of the words coined to designate the material aspects of writing ("roll," "cut," "unfold," "bark of a tree," etc.), and we cannot view the book only as an object (or a class of objects). With the increasing complexity of literacy, the practice of writing on *liber, boc, papyrus, biblios* changed. A change in a given practice and in the object affected by that practice was accompanied, sooner or later, with a change in the conceptualization of the practice and of the object. The meaning of the original words related to the practice of writing and the graphic sign carrier entered a process of transformation. I am mainly interested in two aspects of this transformation: (*a*) the plural of *biblion, biblia*, came to indicate sacred Scriptures and the Book par excellence;[21] (*b*) from *biblos* (the inner bark of papyrus) was formed the Greek *bibliothéke* (house of papyrus); it came to mean wisdom or knowledge.[22] In other words, the representation of the semiotic system of interaction achieved by inscribing and transmitting graphic signs on solid surfaces began to change with the increasing complexity of literacy and became strongly associated with religion and knowledge.

This long detour through the house of words leads me to believe that a more accurate translation of *amoxtli* would be *biblos, papyrus, liber*, or *boc* rather than "book" or "libro," as shown through a closer look at some of the Aztec words related to *amoxtli*.[23]

Amoxcuiloa, whose roots are *amoxtli* and *icuiloa*, to paint, to inscribe something;

Amoxcalli, whose roots are *amoxtli* and *calli*, house, room;

Amoxitoa/amoxpoa, whose roots are *amoxtli; itoa* means to say or to narrate something by heart; and *poa* means to tell, to summarize a process, to count.

The translation of *amoxitoa/amoxpoa* offered by Simeon, "lire un livre" (to read a book), is quite misleading if it is understood either in the sense of "to go over a written page with the eyes" or "to pronounce out loud what is written," for the Romance words *lire* or *leer* (to read) come from the Latin *legere*, meaning "to collect" (*lectio*, a gathering, collecting). The sense of "collecting" is absent from the Nahuatl word, and the emphasis is on "telling or narrating what has been inscribed or painted on a solid surface made out of *amoxtli*." The difference is not trivial. It gives us a better understanding of the idea of the book in nonliterate and literate societies.[24]

Now it is possible to attempt a definition of *book* that, contrary to that of the sign, will be culture specific:

a) A solid surface is a book as an object to the degree to which it is the sign carrier for some kind of graphic semiotic interaction;

b) A book as an object is also a book as a text to the degree to which it belongs to a specific stage in the development of writing ("pure writing," according to Diringer's classification) and the members of a given culture represent the system of graphic semiotic interaction in such a way that it attributes to the sign carrier (books as object) high and decisive functions (theological and epistemological) for their own organization.

According to this definition, the book as text implies "pure" writing, although "pure writing" does not necessarily imply the idea of the book. The necessary connections are founded in the presuppositions underlying cultural expressions. A rereading of the seminal chapter by Curtius, "The Book as Symbol," will show that he devotes a great deal of time to metaphors about writing and that he seems to assume that they are plain and simple synonyms of metaphors for the book.

Be that as it may, some example needs to be drawn from Curtius in order to back up our definition of the book as text. In 1948 Curtius called attention to the amount and the significance of the images that different cultures had constructed to represent their ideas about writing and the book. He begins his survey with the Greeks, noting that they did not have any "idea of the sacredness of the book, as there is no privileged priestly caste of scribes."[25] What is more, one can even find disparagement of writing in Plato. There is the familiar last part of Plato's *Phaedrus,* in which Socrates attempts to convince Phaedrus that writing is not an aid to memory and learning but, to the contrary, can only "awaken reminiscences" without replacing the true discourse lying in the psyche of the wise man, which must be transmitted through oral interactions. It should be underlined that Socrates is mainly concerned with writing in its relationship to knowledge and its transmission, but not with the "book." If one thinks of the rich vocabulary associated with graphic semiotic interactions inherited from the Greeks and also remembers that the idea of the sacred book was alien to them—for they were more concerned with "writing" than with "book"—one again concludes that to translate *biblos* as "book" implies *imposing* our meaning of book upon theirs rather than fully *understanding* their meaning of *biblos*. This observation, amounting to

[The Indians of Peru, before the Spaniards came, had no sort of writing, not letters nor characters nor ciphers nor figures, like those of China or Mexico; but in spite of this they conserved no less the memory of ancient lore, nor did they have any less account of all their affairs of peace, war, and government.]30

The quipu was considered by Acosta a valid sign for record keeping but not equivalent to writing since it could not be considered letters, characters, or figures (fig. 2.4). Acosta's definition of writing, then, presupposed that a graphic sign (letter, character, images) inscribed on a solid surface (paper, parchment, skin, bark of a tree) was needed to have writing. A bunch of knotted strings of different colors would not qualify for an insightful observer as analytically minded as Acosta. However, when Acosta has to describe what a quipu is and how it is used, he cannot avoid using the notion of writing, and, what is more, he makes a perfect analogy between writing with letters and writing with strings, colors, and knots. In Acosta's definition, "Son quipos, unos memoriales o registros hechos de ramales, en que diversos ñudos y diversas [*sic*] colores, significan diversas cosas" [Quipus are a kind of record keeping or register made out of sets of branches in which a diversity of knots and a diversity of colors mean different things]. What attracted Acosta's attention, however, was not the material appearance of the quipu, but what the Inca did with it. Acosta thought that whatever could be done with books in matters of recording the past, keeping track of the law, ritual, and business matters could be also done with the quipus ("los libros pueden decir de historias, y leyes y ceremonias, y cuentas de negocios, todo eso suplen los quipos tan puntualmente, que admira"). Thus, Acosta's hesitation between the fact that quipus were *not* writing or books, although they performed like writing and books. More striking in this respect is the analogy Acosta established with alphabetic writing:

> Y en cada manojo de éstos, tantos ñudos y ñudicos, y hilillos atados; unos colorados, otros verdes, otros azules, otros blancos, *finalmente tantas diferencias que así como nosotros* de veinte y cuatro letras guisándolas en diferentes maneras sacamos tantas infinidad de vocablos, así estos de sus ñudos y colores, sacaban innumerables significaciones de cosas.31

[And in every bundle of these, so many greater and lesser knots, and tied strings; some red, others green, others blue, others white, *in short, as many differences as we have* with our twenty-four letters, arranging them in different ways to draw forth an infinity of words:

Fig 2.4. Writing and materiality of sign carriers: *a*, an Andean quipu, *b*, a textile with an unidentified coat of arms, probably from colonial Peruvian families (sixteenth/seventeenth century?). Charles Potter Kling Fund. Courtesy, Museum of Fine Arts, Boston.

a

b

so did they, with their knots and colors, draw forth innumerable meanings of things.][32]

It seems evident after reading Acosta as well as other writers who described the quipu that not only was the material image of a roll or scroll forgotten and replaced by the quarto-bound book, but the meaning of *textum* had also faded out of the vocabulary of the time. *Texo* in Latin meant "to make" and more specifically "to weave." By transference, it was also used in the sense of "join or fit together," to interlace or to intertwine. Hence, textum invoked the idea of something woven or made into a web. It was also transferred by Roman rhetoricians to alphabetic written compositions to denote the texture of a composition (*dicendi textum tenue*). What Acosta missed, because he assumed that writing presupposed graphic signs inscribed on flat surfaces, was the tactile aspect of the quipu. Modern scholars who have recently studied them in detail observe that the quipu maker produced meaning, recorded memory, and worked with numbers by tracing figures in space. In the process of organizing or weaving strings and colors, and of knotting them, the *quipucamayoc* had to change the direction of the strings and the position of the colors relative to each other. This process, the authors observe, was not simply preparatory to the real making a record. It was an integral part of quipu making or writing. The materiality of quipu making invites interesting comparison with the brush and the stylus, the instruments of Mexica and European writing practices:

> The quipumaker's way of recording—direct construction—required tactile sensitivity to a much greater degree. In fact, the overall aesthetic of the quipu is related to the tactile: the manner of recording and the recording itself are decidedly rhythmic; the first in the activity, the second in the effect. We seldom realize the potential of our sense of touch, and we are usually unaware of its association with rhythm. . . . In fact, tactile sensitivity begins in the rhythmic pulsating environment of the unborn child far in advance of the development of other senses.[33]

The tactile sensitivity perceived today in the quipu maker would have been obscure to Renaissance men of letters who were thinking in terms of letter writing and books as the paradigmatic model of producing meaning and keeping records. Acosta, as we have seen, certainly did not miss the similarities between *guisar* (to organize or weave letters, strings, little stones, or beans) in order to produce meaning and keeping records. But he failed to see the tactile dimension in quipu making.

Quipu making was, then, an important activity in Inca society, important enough to have a social role assigned to it, that of the quipu maker. Guaman Poma de Ayala, in his *Nueva coronica y buen gobierno*, left a few drawings that illustrate what a quipu and a *quipucamayoc* look like (fig. 2.5). For Acosta to consider the *quipucamayoc* as a social role equivalent to a medieval scribe (fig. 2.6), a Renaissance secretary, or a man of letters (fig. 2.7) would perhaps have been beyond his horizons. Or perhaps he was also seeing, from a different perspective, the transformation that Guaman Poma de Ayala saw when he depicted an Inca colonial secretary (fig. 2.8); this, we can imagine, resulted from the social transformation of the ancient quipu maker in the colonial society.

In medieval Europe (as well as in the Islamic world), the practice and conceptualization of writing were closer to physical labor than an intellectual pursuit (see fig. 1.1). *Dictare* was the verb that described the activity that today one would describe as *writing* and composition. The generation of a text began with the dictation that the *scribe* inscribed in wax tablet; after corrections introduced by the *dictator*, it was transcribed in parchments. Writing, then, required not only a skill in which all parts of the body were engaged, but also the skill to prepare the instruments (stylus, feather, ink, parchments, etc.). The transformation from the *dictator* and the *scribe* to the consolidation of both activities in one person began to take place perhaps toward the sixteenth century.[34] However, the idea that writing implied the voice did not vanish as quickly as one might suppose after the transformation of reading brought about by the multiplication of manuscripts, during the early fourteenth century, and the invention of the printing press, in the second half of the fourteenth century. Titu Cusi Yupanki reported in 1570 how people from northern Peru witnessed the arrival of the first Spaniards and described them as bearded men who talked to themselves looking at pieces of white fabric.[35]

In Anáhuac, the *tlacuilo* was the social role equivalent to the Peruvian quipu maker, the medieval scribe, or the Renaissance secretary (see fig. 6.19). He did not deserve as much attention from the Spanish writers, however, as those who had the wisdom of the word (*tlamatinime*, in Nahuatl; *amauta*,[36] in Aymara and Quechua; *qo ru naoh*, in Maya-Cachiquel), translated as "orators" or "philosophers" by Spanish chronists. Sahagún, for instance, who did such a thorough job in researching and describing Mexica culture, devoted an entire book, out of the twelve in his *Florentine Codex* (1578),[37] to rhetoric and moral philosophy. The *tlacuilo* was practically hidden in a chapter he devoted to the craftsmen and disguised under the name of the "oficiales de la pluma" [feather craftsman] (fig. 2.9). The *Mendoza Codex*, gathered by mandate of Viceroy Mendoza toward 1550, has the *tlacuilo* and his son in the context of artisans in Mexica society (fig. 2.10).[38]

Fig. 2.5. Writing and social roles: Andean *quipucamayocs* and the administration of the Inca empire

Francisco de San Antón Muñón Chimalpaín, born around 1579 in Chalco-Amaquemecan,[39] left several *relaciones,* written in Nahuatl and in Latin script, about the origin, peregrination, and memories of people of his area. In his "Octava Relación" (Eighth relation), Chimalpaín described in detail his sources as well as the process of writing about them. He specified that the information came from "five parts or books, from ancient painted papers, very old and painted by elder and dear nobles from the towns of Tzacualtitlan Tenanco Chiconcóhuac, they wrote them before I arranged them, and wrote this story" [De cinco partes o libros, de antiguos papeles pintados muy viejos hechos por los antiguos queridos nobles que fueron de Tzacualtitlan Tenanco Chiconcóhuac, antes que yo los arreglara, fue compuesta esta historia]. The reference to five units or parts (also called "libros" by Chimalpaín) reminds us of Motolinía's classification of Aztecan "books" or *partes* (pieces). What those pieces might have been can be surmised by what Chimalpaín refers to as five units of painted *amoxtli*. He describes, furthermore, where the information comes from:

Estos viejos relatos fueron hechos durante el tiempo de los señores nuestros padres, nuestros antepasados. *Y estas pinturas del pueblo y*

Fig. 2.6. Writing and social roles: a scribe in medieval Europe. Courtesy of Bibliothèque Municipale de Dijon.

la historia de los linajes antiguos fueron guardados mientras a Dios plugo darle vida, por Don Diego Hernández Mochintzetzalohuat-zin, Príncipe reinante quien se hizo español y murió en Ce-Calli, 1545.

Entonces, el papel pintado y la historia de los linajes antiguos fueron dejados a su querido hijo el señor don Domingo Hernández Ayopochtzin, quien se *instruyó en la cuenta de los libros y pintó un libro escribiéndolo con letras,* sin añadirle nada, sino como un fiel espejo de las cosas que de allí se trasladó.[40]

[These old stories were made during the time of the lords our fathers, our ancestors. And these paintings of the people and the history of the ancient nobility were kept, as long as it pleased God to grant him life, by Don Diego Hernández Mochintzetzalohuat-zin, reigning Prince who became a Spaniard and died in Ce-Callí, 1545.]

Fig. 2.7. Writing and social roles: a Renaissance man of letters

Then, the painted paper and the history of the ancient nobility were left to his beloved son, the esteemed Don Domingo Hernández Ayopochtzin, who instructed himself in the telling of the books and then painted a book, writing it in letters, adding nothing, but rather as a faithful mirror of the things translated from there.]⁴¹

In the same way that the proper names are already a clear manifestation of colonial semiosis, so are the vocabulary and the cognitive structures of those who lived, thought, and narrated between the world of the painted *amoxtli* and the alphabetic written books. The learning process alluded to by Chimalpaín ("se instruyó en la cuenta de los libros," [learned to interpret the books]) also indicates the superposition of two kinds of schooling: the old one, in which a part of learning was to look at and to interpret the books; and the new one, in which Chimalpaín himself was educated and learned to replace the *pinturas*

Fig. 2.8. Writing and social roles: a colonial secretary, a possible transformation of a *quipucamayoc*

by alphabetic writing, and to move speech toward written prose. The fact that Chimalpaín still maintained in his writing the repetitive structure of the oral is indicative of the fractures of colonial semiosis in the transition from oral narratives, in which repetition is a part of everyday speech, to an alphabetic written prose (in both the Latin and Spanish, from which Chimalpaín learned to write in Nahuatl). By the sixteenth century, this repetition had already clearly established its distinction with versification. Even in modern Spanish translation the echoes of a rhythmic speech could be heard: "el papel pintado y la historia de los linajes antiguos" [the painted paper and the lineage history], "ahora yo he pintado, he escrito con letras un libro" [to paint a book, writing it with letters]; "el me lo prestó, el libro de sus antepasados, me lo proporcionó" [he loaned it to me, the book of his ancestors, he made it available to me].[42]

If there were at least five ancient books, as Motolinía and Chimalpaín mentioned, perhaps the *tlacuilo* was not just one single person, generally trained to paint any of them, and perhaps there was a division of labor and a division of training also. Don Fernando de Alva Ixtlilxochitl was a descendant of the same Texcocan family who hosted Pedro de Gante around 1523. What emerges from the words of

Fig. 2.9.   Writing and social roles: a *tlacuilo* among the feather artisans

Mexican chronists such as Chimalpaín and Ixtlilxochitl is what the
Spanish chronists had some difficulties in understanding (or at least in
sorting out in a way that would still be satisfactory for today's reader):
that both Spanish and Amerindians recorded their past as well as their
wisdom in graphic and oral forms; that both equally treasured those
records, even if they had different perspectives on the values that
should be attributed to the oral and the written; and that the quipus in
the Andes and the painted signs in Mesoamerica were the equivalent
of letters. The Spanish never understood that, if the Amerindians
lacked letters, they themselves by the same token lacked quipus and
amoxtli. And while the Spanish had men of letters, the Incas had
quipucamayoc and Mexicas *tlacuilo*.

Ixtlilxochitl and Chimalpaín left an extensive description of their
working methods. Ixtlilxochitl's written Spanish was quite impressive,
even though he always criticized the Spanish interpretation of Mexican history. As a historian writing in agreement with the conventions
of Western historiography and alphabetic writing, he found his source
of information in ancient painted *amoxtli* as well as in oral reports and
the memories of the elders (*huehue*). In order to find out the truth
about the past of New Spain, Ixtlilxochitl could not trust the contradictory opinions of various authors (most, if not all, Spaniards) who
wrote its history. He decided to look into the painted records of the
Mexicans themselves, as well as to the songs they used to register their
memories ("y de los cantos con que las observaban, autores muy
graves en su modo de ciencia y facultad"). The authority, according to
Ixtlilxochitl, was in the hands of the "most distinguished and wise
people" [gente muy ilustre y entendida], who looked at the events as
carefully and intelligently as "the most serious and trustworthy authors and historians of the world" [los más graves y fidedignos autores
y históricos del mundo]. Ixtlilxochitl backed up his assertion by saying
that the distinguished and wise people he trusted as the ultimate authority had for each genre of record keeping their scribes (*escritores,
tlacuilo*):

unos que trataban de los anales poniendo por su orden las cosas que
acaecían en cada año, con día, mes y hora. Otros tenían a su cargo
las genealogías y descendencias de los reyes y señores y personas de
linaje, asentando por cuenta y razón los que nacían y borraban los
que morían, con la misma cuenta. Unos tenían cuidado de las pinturas de los términos, límites y mojoneras de las ciudades, provincias, pueblos y lugares, y de las suertes y repartimientos de las
tierras, cuyas eran y a quién pertenecían. Otros, de los libros de las
leyes, ritos y ceremonias que usaban en su infidelidad; y los sacer-

dotes, de los tiempos, de sus idolatrías y modo de su doctrina idol-
átrica y de las fiestas de sus falsos dioses y calendarios. *Y finalmente,
los filósofos y sabios que tenían entre ellos, etaba a su cargo el pintar
todas las ciencias que sabían y alcanzaban, y enseñar de memoria
todos los cantos que observaban en sus ciencias e historias; todo lo cual
mudó el tiempo con la caída de los reyes y señores,* y los trabajos y
persecuciones de sus descendientes y la calamidad de sus súbditos y
vasallos.[43]

a

b

[some dealt with the annals, placing in order the things that had occurred in each year, [recording the] day, month and hour. Others, were in charge of the genealogies and descent of the kings and lords and persons of noble birth, noting faithfully, those who were born and erasing those who died, in the same manner. Some took care of painting the limits, boundaries and borders of the cities, provinces, towns and villages; and the parceling and distribution of lands: whose they were and to whom they belonged. Others [looked after] the books of laws, rituals and ceremonies that they practiced in their unbelief; and the priests [recorded] the times of their idolatries and the manner of their idolatrous doctrine, and the feasts of their false gods and calendars. *And finally, the philosophers and wise men among them were entrusted with painting all the knowledge they possessed and had attained, and with teaching from memory all the chants they observed in their histories and lore; all of which time altered with the fall of the kings and lords,* and the labors

The Materiality of Reading and Writing Cultures

Fig. 2.10. Writing and social roles: *a*, a *tlacuilo* and his son, among other artisans; *b*, weaving in Anáhuac; *c*, and in the Andes

and persecutions of their descendants and the calamity of their subjects and vassals.]44

Ixtlilxochitl's distinction, or lack thereof, between the scribes (*escritores, tlacuilo*) and wise men (*filósofo, sabio, tlamatini*) in other chronicles establishes an attractive analogy with the situation in the European Middle Ages. It is not obvious that both functions were part of the same social role, since there were, precisely, different names for those who had wisdom and those who had skill. It is not surprising, then, that Sahagún placed the *tlacuilo* among the craftsmen—although according to the sources, there seems to be a closer connection between the *tlacuilo, tlatoani* (skillful in speaking, but also governor) and *tlamatinime* (having the wisdom of the word) than between the *tlacuilo* and the expert in several crafts. In Ixtlilxochitl it is perhaps due in part to the process of transculturation and the changing patterns (as he himself noticed at the end of paragraph) that blurred the distinction between *tlatoani* and *tlamatini*. For the Spaniards, very much used to the idea of philosophers and wise men who were at the same time scribes, the distinctive and complementary functions of the *tlamatini* and the *tlacuilo* went almost unnoticed. The Spaniards erased the differences between the two cultures by using their description of themselves as a universal frame for understanding different cultural traditions. Venegas's definition of the book stands as a paradigmatic image of a cultural product that was at once a distinctive material object, written in alphabetic characters by a wise man, that had to be read by or explicated by intelligent people. From the perspective opened by Venegas's description, we can understand today part of the difficulties the Spaniard had in understanding the materiality of Amerindians' reading and writing culture, as well as the action they had taken, either by burning their "books" or slowly erasing them by teaching the Amerindian to change the material configuration of reading and writing and the format in which signs were inscribed and information graphically recorded so that it might be orally disseminated.

Talking about Graphic Signs, Sign Carriers, and Persons of Knowledge and Wisdom

Shortly after the first twelve Franciscans arrived in Mexico on their mission to convert the Amerindian to Christianity (see chap. 1), a historical dialogue took place between the Franciscans and representatives of the Mexica nobility and men of wisdom. The dialogue was apparently recorded at the time it took place, probably over several weeks in 1524. Alphabetic writing allows for the inscription of what is said but not for a description of the scene of speaking. Mexica writing allowed for the inscription of the scene but not for what was said. Near 1565, in the Colegio Santa Cruz de Tlatelolco, Sahagún found the scattered notes, probably left by one of the twelve Franciscans or by an Amerindian already familiar with alphabetic writing. He put the pieces together and provided a free and somewhat distorted translation of the Mexica noble and wise men. He gave the dialogue the form of a Christian doctrine, with the title of *Coloquios y doctrina christiana*. The manuscript was found in the Vatican's secret archives and was published for the first time in 1924.[45] The fact that it was found in Rome and not in Seville suggests once more that Christianization and Hispanization were two different programs, even during the period in which Charles I of Castile and Aragon and Charles V of the Holy Roman Empire joined both goals in one person.

In the 1560s it was still possible to believe that conversion was quick and easy and that the Mexican recognition of Christianity was so obvious that there was no room for doubt. But my interest here is to "listen" to the dialogue again at that particular moment in which the question of reading, writing, books, and knowledge came to the foreground. Let's first look at the transcription of the original in Nahuatl and the close Spanish translation provided by León-Portilla as well as the English translation by Klor de Alva.[46] The scene of speaking is roughly the following. The twelve Franciscan friars, in a meeting with the nobles and tlatoani (governors), explain to them their own mission, and their roles as agents of God and the emperor. The *tlatoani* respond to the Franciscans in the terms transcribed below, and end their speech at the moment in which they decide to consult with the *tlamatinime* (wise men):

761   Auh inhin, totecujyoane
      [Y, he aquí, señores nuestros,]
      [And these, oh our lords,]

      ca oncate in oc no techiacana,
      [están los que aún son nuestros guías]
      [indeed, they are there, they still guide us]

      in techitquj, in techamama
      [ellos nos llevan a cuestas, nos gobiernan,]
      [these who carry us, these who govern us,]

      yn jpampa in tlaiecultilo
      [en relación al servicio]
      [in relation to these being served]

ca in toteoua yn jntlacaceuhcava
[de los que son nuestros dioses, de los cuales es el
  merecimiento]
[indeed, these who are our gods, these who have their merit]

cujtlapillj ahtlapallj
[la cola, el ala (la gente del pueblo):]
[that of the tail, of the wing,]

In tlamacazque, in tlenamacaque,
[los sacerdotes ofrendadores, los que ofrendan el fuego,]
[the ones who offer things, the ones who offer incense,]

auh in quequetzcova mjtoa
[y también los que se llaman quequetzalcoa]
[and those named the feathered serpents,]

in tlatolmatinjme
[Sabios de la palabra,]
[these are knowers of the word,]

770   auh in jntequjuh in qujmocujtlauja
[su oficio, con el que se afanan,]
[and their charge, with which they trouble themselves,]

in ioalli in cemjlhuitl
[durante la noche y el día,]
[by night, by day,]

in copaltemaliztli
[la ofrenda de copal]
[is the act of burning copal,]

in tlenamaqujliztlj
[el ofrecimiento del fuego]
[the act of offering incense,]

in vitztlj, in acxoiatl,
[espinas, ramas de abeto]
thorns, *acxoyatl,*

775   in neçoliztli.
[la acción de sangrarse]
[the act of blood letting,]

in qujtta, in qujmocujtlauja
[los que miran, los que se afanan con]
[These see, these trouble themselves,]

yn johtlatoquiliz ini jnmatacacholizq in jlhuicatl
[el curso y el proceder ordenado del cielo]
[with the journey, the orderly course of the heavens,]

in iuh iovalli xelivi.
[cómo se divide la noche]
[according to how the night is divided.]

Auh in quitzticate,
[los que están mirando (leyendo),]
[And these continually look at it,]

780   in qujpouhticate,
[los que cuentan (o refieren lo que leen)]
[these continually relate it,]

in qujtlatlazticate in amoxtlj
[los que despliegan (las hojas de) los libros,]
[these continually cause the book to cackle,]

in tlilli, in tlapalli,
[la tinta negra, la tinta roja,]
[the black, the color,]

in tlacujlolli quitaqujticate
[los que tienen a su cargo las pinturas.]
[is in the painting they continually carry.]

Ca iehoantin techitqujticate,
[Ellos nos llevan,]
[Indeed, they are the ones who continually carry us,]

785   techiacana, techotlatoltia
[nos guían, nos dicen el camino.]
[they guide us, they cause the earth to speak to us,]

tehoantin qujtecpana
[Los que ordenan]
[They are the ones who put it in order,]

in iuh vetzi ce xivitl,
[cómo cae el año,]
[such as how a year falls,]

in iuh otlatoca in tonalpoallj,
[cómo siguen su camino la cuenta de los destinos y los días]
[such as how the count of the destinies-feasts follows its
    path,]

auh in cecempoallapoallj
[y cada una de las veintenas,]
[and each one of the complete counts,]

790   qujmocujtlauja,
[de esto se ocupan]
[they trouble themselves with it,]

iehoantin yntenjz, incocol,
[de ellos es el encargo, la encomienda,]
[they have their charge, their commission,]

y mamal in teutlatollj
[su carga: la palabra divina]
[their duty which is the divine word,]

Auh in tehoantin
[y nosotros,]
[and we are those]

ca ça ye iyo totequjuh
[sólo es nuestro oficio:]
[indeed, who but have as our sole task,]

795   (in mjtoa) teuatl tlachinollj.
[Lo que se llama el agua divina, el fuego (la guerra)]
[(what is called) divine water, fire.]

auh ça iehoatl ypan titlatoa,
[y también de esto tratamos,]
[And only we speak on it,]

tictocujtlauja yn jtequjuh
[nos encargamos de los tributos]
[we trouble ourselves with the tribute,]

yn cujtlapillj, yn atlapallj
[de la cola y el ala (del pueblo).]
of the tail, the wing.

. . . .

803   Ma oc tiqujnnechicocan
[Permitidnos que reunamos]
[Let us, for now, assemble them,]

yn tlamacazque, in quequetzalcoa
[a los sacerdotes, a los quequetzalcoa.]
[the ones who offer things, the feathered serpents.]

ma tiqujmacaca
[Que podamos darles]
[Let us give them.]

in jhyotzin, yn jtlatoltzin,
[su aliento, su palabra.]
[His precious breath, His precious word.]47

101

The
Materiality of
Reading and
Writing
Cultures

The dialogue continues with the meeting between the *tetecuchtin* (in charge of the military apparatus) and the *tlamatinime* (members of the noble class in charge of the religious apparatus), where they discuss the answer they will give to the twelve Franciscans. This scene is followed by the moment in which *tlatoani* and *tlamatinime* return to talk with the Franciscans and, this time, the word is in the mouth of the *tlamatinime*. Their answer is a respectful disagreement with the Christian doctrine presented by the Franciscans. One of the central points is the discourse about the Christian God and the Mexica *in Tloque in Nauaque* (the Owner of Nearby and Together). The *tlamatinime* refer to the Christian God as *in Tloque in Nauaque* and they express their admiration that the Spaniards have come "from the clouds, the fog, from the very inside of the immense water" in order to bring "his book, his painting, the celestial word, the divine word" [*yn jamux, yn jtlacujlol*, 990; *in ilhuicac tlatolli, in teotlatolli*, 991]. After listening to the *tlamatinime*, the twelve Franciscans begin their reply as follows:

1098   ca muchi tamechilhuizque
        [Todo os lo diremos]
        [Indeed, we will tell you everything,]

        tamechcaquitizque
        [os lo haremos escuchar,]
        [we will cause you to hear it,]

1100   intla anquinequ
        [y si es que vosotros queréis.]
        [if you desire it.]

        yoa uel tamchilpachiuitizque
        [Y os habremos de tranquilizar]
        [And we will be able to cause you to have a full heart,]

        iehica in tehoantin ticpia
        [porque nosotros guardamos]
        [because we guard it,]

in teuamuxtli in teutlatolli
[el libro divino, la palabra divina]
[the divine book, the divine word,]

in oncan neztoc ycuiliouthoc
[en donde se ve, está escrita]
[there, where it lies visible, it lies painted]

1105   tlatlamantitoc
[está debidamente dispuesta]
[it lies arranged,]

in ixquich ytlatoltzin
[toda la que es su palabra,]
[all that is His precious word,]

in tloque naoque
[del Dueño del cerca y del junto.]
[this one the Possessor of the Near, Possessor of the
    Surrounding.]

The scene of speaking shows various aspects relevant for understanding conflicting religious views that impinge on the ideas of writing, the book, and the social roles associated with reading and writing
practices. León-Portilla was inclined to offer alternative readings when
he translated the activities performed by *tlatolmatinjme* (those who
have the wisdom of the word) (line 769). The translation of line 779 is
"los que están mirando" [those who are looking at], and León-Portilla
adds "leyendo" [reading]. The following line is translated "los que
cuentan" [those who narrate], and the parenthesis specifies "those
who refer to what they read," which, following the logic introduced in
the previous paragraph, could be translated as "those who narrate
what they look at," instead of "read." The following line, 781, could
be read without parenthetical clarification as "those who unfold the
book," although in this case the parenthesis further specifies that it is
indeed "the pages of [the book]" that are being unfolded. At this
point it is necessary to introduce Sahagún's own free translation of
lines 761–803, which he summarizes in one paragraph, and more
specifically what corresponds to lines 761 to 781:

> Demás de esto sabed, Señores nuestros, que tenemos sacerdotes
> que nos rigen y adiestran en la cultura y servicio de nuestros dioses;
> ay también otros muchos que tienen civersos nombres, que en-
> tienden en el servicio de los templos de noche y de días, que son
> *sabios y ábiles, ansí cerca de la rebolución y curso de los cielos como*
> *cerca de nuestras costumbres antiguas, tienen los libros de nuestra*
> *antiguallas en que estudian y ojean de noche y de día.*[48]

103

*The
Materiality of
Reading and
Writing
Cultures*

[And furthermore may you know, good sirs, that we have priests who direct and train us in the culture and service of our gods; there are also many others who have diverse names, who understand the service of the temples by night and by day, who are as *wise and skillful in regard to the revolution and course of the heavens, as they are in regard to our ancient customs; they hold the books of our ancient lore, which they study and look upon, by night and day.*][49]

Sahagún distinguishes understanding the trajectory of the stars and the configuration of the sky from "looking upon" [*ojear*] the books day and night. As we shall see, such a distinction is less clearly made in the paleographic edition and in León-Portilla's and Klor de Alva's translations. Since Spanish orthography was not clearly established in the mid–sixteenth century, despite Nebrija's efforts, I was tempted to translate *ojear* (to look at) (Spanish: *echar los ojos, mirar con atención a determinada parte;* Latin: *oculos conjicere*) by "peruse" (to read through, to read with attention), which would be more akin to *hojear* (going through the pages of a book; Latin: *folia volvere*). This second option would be close to León-Portilla's clarification of his translation, in which "estan mirando" [they are looking at] replaces the verb *estan leyendo* (they are reading). Also notable in León-Portilla's translation and absent in Sahagún's version is the verb "despliegan" [they unfold], which once again corresponds to Bernal Díaz del Castillo's description of the Mexica *amoxtli:* "they unfold them like Castilian pieces of fabric." Sahagún could not have been aware, by 1565, of what a Mexica painted artifact was and what differences there were between "reading" in fifteenth- and sixteenth-century Spain and Mexico-Tenochtitlán.

While Sahagún places the accent on the book, the Nahuatl version (as well as León-Portilla's translation) emphasizes the spoken words and their agents, *tlatolmatinime* (those who have the wisdom of the word, *tlatol* + *tlamatinime*). Molina, in the sixteenth century, translated *tlatolli* as "word," while Simeon, toward the end of the nineteenth century, was more generous in his rendering and translated it as "speech, discourse, exhortation, history, story." He also rendered the derived expression *tlatollótl* as "history, process, life, biography."[50] More recently, León-Portilla interpreted the same word in the context of the Mexica conception of *toltecayótl,* which would be closer to what in late fifteenth- and sixteenth-century Europe was understood as cultural tradition and civility. In this context, *tlatollótl* was a word designating, at the same time, speech or discourse and, specifically, a discourse in which the memory of past events and deeds was preserved. León-Portilla rendered this second meaning by the expression "discourse-memory" (*palabra-recuerdo*).[51]

The discourse of the *principales* in charge of the military apparatus, but also skillful in speaking (*tlatoque*),[52] introduces a difference between two social roles: their own and that of the *tlamatinime*, and consequently two concepts of discourse: the first skillful in speaking, the second having the wisdom of the word. On top of the Aztec hierarchy, *tlatoani* and *tlamatinimi* (which, interestingly enough, is written *tlatolmatinime* in line 769 of the paleographic version) are the social roles in which the power of the spoken word is embodied.

What does it mean "to be in charge" of the paintings, to read the red and black ink? Does it mean that they are in charge of interpreting them or writing them? Is the *tlamatini* also a *tlacuilo*? Apparently not. Those who have the wisdom of the word are those who can "look" at the sky or at the painted books and interpret them to tell stories based on their discerning of the signs. The oral narrative of the wise men seems to have a social function as well as a rank superior to the *tlacuilo,* who was placed by Sahagún among those who were skilled craftsmen. A Spaniard's understanding of Amerindian writing practices and sign carriers was tinted by an emerging idea of progress that went hand in hand with the origin of comparative ethnology. The model organized the world and intercultural relations in terms of what Fabian expressed in the formula "the denial of coevalness."[53] Such a denial, certainly at work in the authors I have commented on in chapter 1, comes with particular force and clearness in Juan Bautista Pomar. Pomar was born in the same town as Ixtlilxochitl, around 1535. He was well informed about the Amerindian past and Texcoco (capital of Acoluhacan and one of the cities of the triple alliance, with Mexico-Tenochtitlán and Tlacopan) and was literate, probably educated in the schools founded by de Gante in the same city, a decade before he was born. It was from the perspective of an educated person that he described the education of the nobles in his native town. As was already pointed out, Pomar placed the power of knowledge in the letters and in the body, since without letters knowledge is limited. It seems that disregarding the difference in societies and memories, the lack of letters was an observation made in different times and different places. Martín de Murúa Perú makes observations about the Incas similar to those of Pomar about the Mexicas:

> Aunque al Ynga y a sus reinos les faltó el arte tan industriosa de saber leer y escribir, medio tan famoso y conveniente para comunicarse las gentes de unas provincias a otras, y para salir los hombres de las tinieblas de la ignorancia, y alcanzar el título tan

deseado de sabiosy, y trascender y alcanzar los secretos descono-
cidos, y aun casos sucedidos de tantos millares de años como tenemos, sabemos y gozamos mediante las letras.[54]

105

*The
Materiality of
Reading and
Writing
Cultures*

[Although the Inca and his kingdoms lacked the most industrious
art of knowing how to read and write, a most famous and conve-
nient means for people to communicate among different provinces,
and for men to sally forth from the shadows of ignorance and reach
the most desired title of wise men, and transcend and reach unknown secrets, and even events transpired over many thousands of
years, such as we possess, know and enjoy by means of letters.][55]

Both Pomar and Murúa recognize that Mexicas and Incas had their
ways of knowing, although the lack of letters put them in a position
lower than the Spaniards. Before introducing the letter as a warranty
of knowledge, Pomar mentions that in the education of the nobles
there is a particular branch in which "they specialize in the knowledge
of the star and the movement of the sky in order to predict the future"
(see lines 775–85, above).

The whole range of questions regarding the materiality of reading
and writing cultures seems to be summarized in these two examples.
The increasing relevance of alphabetic writing in Western culture contributed to the change in meaning of the Latin verb *legere* (to read).
One of its original meanings was "to discern." It changed when it
began to be applied to discerning the letters of the alphabet in a text
and acquired the modern sense of reading. One can surmise that *legere,* in the sense of looking at and discerning the meaning of whatever
one is looking at, is precisely what is implied in what Pomar reports
about the Mexicas' "knowledge of the stars and the movement of the
sky," and what the *tlatoque* who spoke to the twelve Franciscans had in
mind when they referred to those who have "the wisdom of the word"
as those who are "looking at" and why León-Portilla was inclined to
add *leyendo* (reading) next to "they are looking at". In the same way
the *tlamatinime* looked at the sky, they also looked at the inscriptions
in solid surfaces made out of the tree bark, which they unfolded, and
looked at.[56] Thus, the Spaniards and the Mexicas had not only
different material ways of encoding and transmitting knowledge but
also—as is natural—different concepts of the activities of reading and
writing. Mexicas put the accent on the act of observing and telling out
loud the stories of what they were looking at (movements of the sky or
the black and the red ink). Spaniards stressed reading the word rather
than reading the world, and made the letter the anchor of knowledge
and understanding. Contemplating and recounting what was on the

painting (*amoxtli*) were not enough, from the point of view of the Spaniard's concept of reading, writing, and the book, to ensure correct and reliable knowledge.

This conflicting view reached its peak in Sahagún's *Coloquios* at the moment in which the twelve Franciscans had to explain for the second time to the *tlamatinime* (those who have the wisdom of the word) what they have explained previously to the *tlatoque* (governor and skillful in speaking).

Sahagún provides his own interpretation of Mexica discourse (see lines 1098–1105, above) and furnishes it with the connotations surrounding the Spanish concept of writing and authority:

> todo esto os declararemos muy por extenso si lo queréis oyr y satis-
> fazeros emos en todo, *porque tenemos la sagrada escriptura donde se*
> *contiene todo lo que os diremos, que son palabras de aquel que da el ser*
> *y el vivir en todas las cosas.* Esta sagrada escriptura, de que muchas
> vezes os emos hecho mención, es cosa antiquísima; son palabras
> muy verdaderas, certíssimas, dignas de todo crédito.[57]

> [we shall explain all of this at great length if you wish to hear it, and
> we shall satisfy you with all our explanations, *because we have the*
> *sacred scripture wherein are contained all the things we shall tell you,*
> *for they are the words of He who gives being and life to all things. This*
> *sacred scripture,* of which we have spoken many times, is very an-
> cient, its words are most true, definite, and worthy of belief.]

It would have been difficult for the *tlamatinime* to understand the connections between human writing and the writing of God, or between the archetype book and the metagraph book, according to Venegas's distinction, which was naturally embedded in the answer provided by the twelve Franciscans (fig. 2.11). It would have been equally difficult for them to understand a concept of truth that presupposed both a philosophy of language that prioritized the letter and a religious belief that attributed the final truth to the written version of the spoken words pronounced by God.[58] At the same time, it was just as difficult for the twelve Franciscans to understand that the materiality of Mexica reading and writing culture drove them to a conceptualization of the word, the painted "books" and the relations between words and signs with the *in Tloque in Nauaque* (the Owner of the Near and the Together) that was not necessarily constructed around alphabetic writing.

God's metaphor of writing, according to which his words are dictated to men, is so well known that we need not press the idea further.[59] Less familiar to scholars dealing with similar topics are communicative situations across cultures in which agents are, so to speak, on different sides of the letter. The Mexicas had a set of concepts to outline their semiotic interactions, and their negotiations with the spoken words, written signs, the social roles and functions attached to such activities. They also had an articulation of the social and religious functions of spoken words and written signs that could hardly be translated to Western categories (e.g., philosopher, man of letters, scribe, or poet) without suppressing (and misunderstanding) their activities, given a context in which the conceptualization of semiotic interactions is based on a different material configuration of the reading and writing cultures. On one side of the dialogue, the agents were members of a learned culture in which the ideology of the letter and the book was equated with learning and wisdom. On the other side, the participants were members of a society in which wisdom and learning were deposited in the body of the elders (*huehue*), and looked at in

107

*The
Materiality of
Reading and
Writing
Cultures*

Fig. 2.11.   A contemporary perspective of young Sahagún surrounded with "books"

the sky and in the painting and transmitted in oral discourse (*tla-tolli*).[60] The image of the other that members of each group constructed changed with the changes in the personal pronoun designating the speaker and the listener, relating them to the context of a particular reading and writing culture. The mobility of the locus of enunciation was, in this case, loaded with the ideology of the book and *amoxtli,* with the spoken word and the diversity of graphic signs. The "other" depended on and changed with the change of speaker, which, in this case, belonged to two disparate discursive situations and cultural traditions.

How could the Mexicas understand that the sacred writings and the Divine Book were the proof of God's existence and the warranty of Truth when they were not only alien to such a configuration of book and God but also to the Western notion of truth?[61] Quite simply, the Mexicas were unable to understand because instead of reading the Letter of the Book, they were accustomed to listening to the Sages of the Word as well as looking, recounting, and displaying the painting of their *Amoxtli.* How could the Spaniards understand and accept the position expressed by the Sage of the Word if they believed that a lack of alphabetic writing was not only a sign of civil barbarism but also one of religious marginality? How could a group of lettered men whose very social role presupposed the concept of letter understand the Sages of the Word, whose very social role presupposed oral transmission of knowledge? "To read" meant unmatched activities for the Spaniards and for the Mexicas, as well as other Amerindian communities. The story of Atahualpa, in the episode of Cajamarca, in which he holds the Bible to his ears expecting to hear the Book talk, is as well known and revealing as the metaphor of the "talking book" in the autobiography of Frederick Douglass.[62] Mexicans described as "contemplating and recounting what is in the picture and on the sky" what Spaniards described as "reading the pages of a book" and, by extension, "reading" the universe as a book written by the hand of God. There is a double interpretation of this analogy. One interpretation would tell us that what Mexicas and Spaniards were doing with the artificial signs inscribed on solid surfaces and with the natural signs wandering around the universe was basically the same, since they were looking at and making sense of them. The second interpretation could be formulated as a question: why did the Spaniards, in their accounts, leave the impression that the Mexicas were doing well in reading and writing matters, although they were not yet at the level of Spaniard intelligence and cultural achievements? Chronicle after chronicle of the first encounters describe the materiality of the reading and writing cultures and show the difficulties the Spaniards had in understanding how the

Mexicas could have been satisfied with an oral description of what they saw in the paintings. On the other hand, there is scattered evidence that the Amerindians had difficulties in understanding how a book or a page can "talk," and how "painted signs" (the alphabet) could tell what could have been told by way of speaking. They were, so to speak, on opposing sides of the letter, the Mexicas not aware of its existence, the Spaniards perfectly aware and convinced lack of letters placed human communities in the realm of absences: among the unlettered. The Mexicas were aware of the significance of being skilled in the art of speaking and the meaning of having the wisdom of the word.

It was the speech of those who knew how to "look at the stars and the sky" and to "unfold the *pinturas*" that the Mexicas referred as authoritative, not to writing and the book. On the contrary, the Spaniards, if they were aware of the power of the spoken word, also accepted the warranty of the written word and the book. It is to writing and the book that the Franciscans referred in their dialogue with the *tlatoque* and the *tlamatinime* who underlined spoken discourse. The other experience of Anáhuac was that the veracity of one god and the falsity of others could be judged by invoking the graphic inscription of the letter in an object that did not look like their *amoxtli*. How could the *tlamatinime*, routinely contemplating the paintings drawn by the *tlacuilo* and telling stories, exercising at the same time the power of the spoken word, be reconciled with the idea that the true meaning was contained in the silent words of the Sacred Book? Conflicting ideas about speech and writing, about the materiality of reading and writing cultures, is what the process of colonization brought about during the first encounters between Spanish men of letters and Mexicas skilled in painting and speaking. The seed was planted for similar interpretations and behaviors during the colonization of other European nations during the nineteenth and twentieth centuries.[63]

When Just Speaking Well Was Not Good Enough

It is time, then, to push a little further our understanding of the social and cultural function of the Mexicas' learned spoken (or rhetorical, according to Sahagún) discourses and its relation to wisdom.

The Franciscan Bernardino de Sahagún paid more attention to the Mexicas' speech than to their writing. While Acosta was writing his *Historia* and inquiring about Mexica knowledge and uses of letters, Sahagún remained mute about Mexica manners and uses of writing. As I have mentioned, book 6 of the *Florentine Codex* was devoted, instead, to "Rhetoric and Moral Philosophy."[64] In it, Sahagún compiled those discourses in which the elders organized and transmitted their wisdom to future generations. It also contains examples of well-constructed and sophisticated speeches. Sahagún was aware of their cultural relevance, which he made explicit in the very first paragraph of the prologue to book 6:

> All nations, *however savage and decadent*[65] they have been, have set their eyes on the wise and strong in persuading, on men prominent for moral virtues, and on the skilled and the brave in warlike exercises, and more on those of their own generation than on those of others. There are so many examples of this among the Greeks, the Latin, the Spaniards, the French, and the Italians that books are full of this subject.[66] (italics mine]
>
> The same was practiced in this Indian nation, and especially among the Mexicans, among whom the wise, superior, and effective rhetoricians were held in high regard. And they elected these to be high priests, lords, leaders, and captains, no matter how humble their estate. These ruled the states, led the armies, and presided in the temples. . . . *I think that by means of these virtues they achieved dominion, although it lasted little time and now they have lost all, as one will clearly see who will compare that contained in this Book with the life they now lead. This being very clear, I do not tell the reason for it.* [italics mine]

It is not enough for Sahagún to compare the Mexicas with the Greeks, Italians, and Spaniards; he also compares their past glories with their present decay. In addition it was necessary to defend the credibility of the kind of speeches he was going to report to those who had taken the Indians to be barbarians because they were illiterates; and it was also necessary to make clear that the content of book 6 was not invented, that "all the informed Indians will assert that this language is characteristic of their ancestors and the works they produced" (*Florentine Codex,* 1:66). If Sahagún put so much emphasis on the Aztecs' formal speeches, he did it because the image of the barbarian, savage, and illiterate Indians that had been constructed during the process of conquest and colonization did not allow much room for well-thought-out speeches (as we have seen in the previous section). How could they do that without letters? Acosta honestly asked. Indeed, although oratory was a well-known kind of oral speech that had been codified since Aristotle's *Rhetoric* and, later on, by the great Roman rhetoricians (Cicero, Quintilian), the codification (rhetoric) of oral speech (oratory) was after all a written artifact.

Some thirty years later, another Franciscan, Juan de Torquemada, devoted several chapters of his *Monarquía indiana* (book 13) to the discourses (*pláticas*) used by parents to educate their children. He provides two examples: a discourse a mother addresses to her daughter, and one addressed by a peasant to his son, already married. Torquemada could not hide his admiration for the eloquence of such discourses and the difficulties he, like Andrés de Olmos and Bartolomé de las Casas, had in translating them into Castilian:

no las hemos sabido romancear con la dulzura y suavidad que en su lengua estos naturales las usaban, atendiendo más a decir lisa y distintamente la sentencia de la doctrina, que la elegancia del lenguaje con que entre ellos se platicaba; porque confieso que en el decir su razón estas gentes, así en contar con sus bienes como en referir sus males, son aventajadísimos retóricos, no porque ellos hayan oído ningún precepto retórico de los que enseña Quintiliano, ni de los que da Cicerón en sus particiones, sino por serlo ellos naturalmente y tan elocuentes que les es muy fácil decir cualquier cosa que quieren; . . . *Por las dichas pláticas y avisos dados podrán colegir los que con buenas entrañas quisieren considerarlo, que estas pobres gentes e indios naturales de México, Tetzcuco, Tlaxcalla y sus comarcas, alcanzaban y sentían, por natural razón y más unos que otros, como vemos entre otras gentes, que no todas tienen una misma habilidad y discreción.*[67] [italics mine]

[We have not been able to translate them into Spanish with the gentleness and mildness which these people used in their own language, and we have dwelt more on translating the meaning of the doctrine plainly and clearly, than the eloquence of the language they used themselves; for I confess that when these people express themselves, be it either to tell of their good or their bad fortune, they are outstanding rhetoricians, not because they have heard the rhetorical precepts of the type taught by Quintilian or Cicero in his divisions, but rather because they have a natural capacity, and they are so eloquent that they can talk about anything they desire with great ease. . . . *Any high-minded person who would wish to do so, would conclude, given the said conversations and notices, that these poor wretches, and native indians of Mexico, Tetzcuco, Tlaxcalla and its environs, were able to understand and sense things by dint of natural reason, some more so than others, as with any culture, for not all of them possess the same skill and wisdom.*][68]

Not every aspect of the Amerindian cultures attracted Spanish men of letters with the same intensity. They devoted, for instance, much more time to reconstructing Amerindian genealogy, religion, and customs than to exploring Amerindian conceptualizations of their discursive practices and means of recording the past. The authority of alphabetic writing and its "natural" links with history and rhetoric furnished sufficient proof for the Spaniards to look at other cultures as inferior. All of which illustrates, once more, the difficulties of understanding differences and using differences to construct power positions.

Sahagún's transcription of oral Mexican discourses and the subsequent compilation by Juan Bautista (1600) under the title of *Huehuetlatolli* (a Nahuatl expression meaning "ancient word" or "discourse of the elders")[69] are paradigmatic examples of the authority of the elders in a society in which oral transmission is more important than written communication, and wisdom is deposited in the living body rather than in the book. The Franciscans (Olmos, Sahagún, Juan Bautista) documented native discursive practices, but not their own categorization and evaluation of verbal behavior.[70] I am not implying that they should have, since I am well aware that this possibility was not within their scope of knowledge or expectations. It was a natural assumption for a man of letters in the sixteenth century to consider the Greco-Roman legacy to be the true categorization and evaluation of speech in matters of grammar and rhetoric, and not to worry about what the Amerindians might have thought about their own speaking and writing activities. The missionaries collected and transcribed what had been said but did not collect Amerindian conceptualizations, nor did they describe in (ethnographic) detail diverse acts of saying. The classical legacy in the field of rhetoric had stressed the description of acts of saying not necessarily for the understanding of them, but rather to teach and encourage good discursive performances. Missionaries had, therefore, some standards to recognize and evaluate a good speech as a good performance but did not have the tools to undertake a description of saying acts, taking into account communicative situations, social roles, and sex and gender in semiotic and verbal interactions. Speech and oral discursive genres were valued, although not enough to equate them with written discursive genres.

Let's take a closer look at the discourses collected by Sahagún as examples of Aztec rhetoric and moral philosophy. And let's examine critically the image of the Amerindian left by the Spanish missionaries and men of letters who judged and depicted them in relation to their lack of letters. A preliminary organization of discourse, compiled by Sahagún according to their content, follows.[71]

1. The first eight chapters are devoted to the monologues addressed to the gods by high religious and political officers, in which the gods are asked for help to solve the problems afflicting society.

2. Chapters 9 through 16 are illustrations of human communicative situations related to public affairs and civil government. Although there are also in this group discourses by the newly appointed leader directed to the gods, they are in the tone of thanking the gods for his new social status. What characterizes this group of discourses is their function in the political administration of the society. Thus, there are discourses that the leader addresses to the nobility or to the people, as well as discourses that the nobility address to the people in support of the newly appointed leader. Those who were in charge of pronouncing this kind of discourse were characterized as "skillful in speaking."

3. The third group comprises the discourses that the leaders addressed to their sons in order to train them in the administration of public affairs and as future leaders of their people; and the discourses addressed to their daughters, training and teaching them their role in society and in the preservation of the unblemished image of their lineage. It is also in this context that the mothers' discourse to their sons and daughters could be included, making the distinction between parental relations and social roles. This group seems to illustrate the discourse pronounced by social leaders and members of the nobility.

4. The fourth group embodies those discourses pronounced by the people for the education of their children. Most of them are oriented toward procreation, addressed by both the mother and the father (fig. 2.12).

One question that immediately comes to mind is related to the formal character of these discourses, their transmission and their pronunciation in different situations by members of different generations. Are these examples of one specific situation, or are they models of discourses pronounced and repeated in an indefinite number of similar situations? The amount of available *huehuetlatolli* as well as the lack of information about the social condition of their production and reception does not allow for an empirical description of the role this discursive genre played in Aztec society. However, a general description could be undertaken, based on both the contribution of specialists in Nahuatl culture who have studied the *huehuetlatolli*,[72] and on contemporary studies on the ethnography of communication that have shed light on the structure and function of discourse in societies in which oral communication is fundamental in politics, social relations, education, religion, and so on.[73]

The *huehuetlatolli* were transcribed in alphabetic writing by the Franciscan friars from 1546 (the date when Andrés de Olmos might have collected them) until 1600 (the date when Juan Bautista pub-

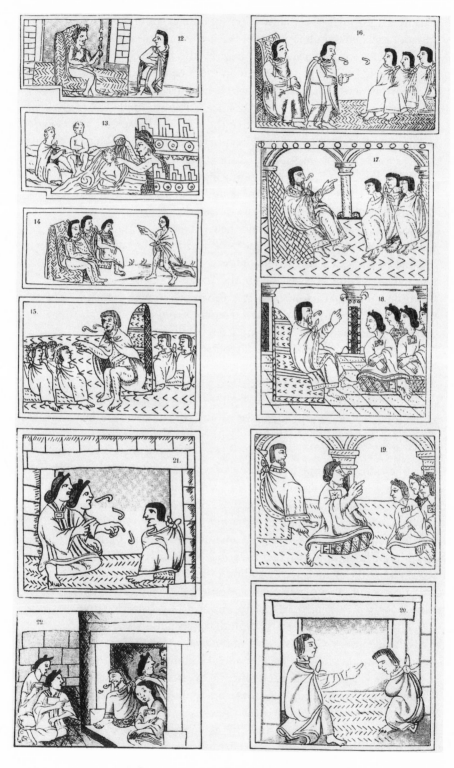

a

Fig. 2.12.   Graphic representations of speeches

maton mattinemj, maco
njc[ha]mjctinemj jnjnemja, inj
gujcaiatz, auh injuetzia a
uh maic oal chocas, maic
oal mellaguaoas jnoiquac
itla ipan choloto, in noma
lauh, innomotecuynj. A
motzontecotzin anelchi
qujuhtzin njqueoa : tlen
qujmoma chitia, ma amech
motlamatca tlalili into.° auh
maximotlacotilican, maxi
motequjttilican, maxicmo
nanamjqujlican intloq̄, in
naoaque, mioalli, inehecatl

¶ Capitulo dezisßiete,
del ra zanamjento, lleno
de muy buena doctrina
enlomoral, que el señor
hazia a sus hijos, quãdo
ya aujã llegado alosa
ños de disctecion : exor
tandolos àhuyr, los vi
cios, y a que se diesen,
alos exercicios de noble
3a, y de virtud.

¶ Ic cax tolli omome ca
pitulo, vncan moteneoa
cen tlamãtli œzca qualli, te
nonotzaliz tlatolli, nenemj
liztilonj : injc qujn nonotza
ia, ipilhoan tlatoanj : inj
quac ie ixtlamati, ie tlaca
quj, qujn tlaquauh ma
caia, injc qujtlalcahujz
que, injx qujch inaqualli,
in naiectli. Auh injc qujtla
quauhtzitz qujzque, im pilte
qujtl, intla tocategujtl : auh
injx qujch qualli iectli.

lished his own collection). Angel María Garibay has asked what the relation between Olmos's, Juan Bautista's, and Sahagún's collections might have been. His answer is the following.

> Examinando el problema con detención, no hallo más respuesta que la de la existencia de dos fondos documentales, ambos procedentes de Olmos. El primero sería de elementos recogidos de personas populares, o sea de la gente menor, y ese quedaría aprovechado tanto por el mismo Olmos en su Gramática, como por Juan Bautista en su edición. El segundo repertorio sería el que se tomó de labios de gente principal, perteneciente a la nobleza y el sacerdocio, única que pudo informar sobre estas materias. Y esta colección es la que tuvo y aprovechó Sahagún para su obra, incorporándola en su libro VI.[74]

> [Having examined the problem at length, I can find no other answer than the existence of two documentary resources, both of them originating in Olmos. The first was probably elements gathered from the people, that is from the common folk, and Olmos himself in his Grammar as well as Juan Bautista in his edition must have availed themselves of this resource. The second source probably came straight from the mouths of the principal people, the nobility and the clergy, the only ones who would be able to inform them of such matters. And this collection is the one that Sahagún had and used for his work, which he incorporated into book 6.][75]

Garibay's comments underline the relationships between social stratification and discursive production. The generic name of *huehuetlatolli,* identifying discursive genres that cut across distinct social strata, accentuates the age of the person authorized to pronounce them ("words or discourse of the elder") as well as the traditional value of the discourse itself ("ancient word"). It is well known that in societies in which knowledge is transmitted orally, the elders are the storehouse of wisdom.[76] It is also well known that the authority of the elder was still relevant during the European Middle Ages, when the social function of writing had not yet superseded the value attached to the living memory of the body as a treasure trove and the age of the person as depository for and authority on wisdom.[77] Thus, while a society that has writing and attributes to it a greater value than to oral discourse uses books for the organization and transmission of knowledge,[78] a society in which oral transmission is fundamental uses the elders as organizers of knowledge and as sign carriers.

Although it would be difficult to make any generalization about the cultural function of speech and its relevance in social life among the

Aztecs based on the corpus collected by Sahagún, it is nonetheless
interesting to look at two aspects related to the social function of
speech that emerge from this collection. The first is the use of speech
to train speaking behavior. Thus, be it the mother addressing her
daughter or the father addressing his son, or vice versa, speech behavior appears to be very important in the social formation of the
adolescent. What follows are recommendations given by the mother
to her adolescent daughter, following the father's recommendations
toward her general behavior in life:

> And thy speech is not to come forth hurriedly. As thou art to speak,
> thou art not to be brutish, not to rush, not to disquiet. Thy speech is
> to come forth in tranquility and with gentleness. Thou art not to lift
> up nor to lower much [thy voice]. As thou art to speak, as thou art
> to address one, as thou art to greet one, thou art not to squeak.
> Thou art not to murmur. Straight forward is thy speech to come
> forth; in medium voice is it to come forth; nor art thou to make it
> fanciful.[79]

It is interesting to observe that the mother's recommendations on
verbal behavior are given in the context of other bodily behavior.
Sahagún introduces the sequence of discourse in chapter 19, from
which the previous quotation is taken, recommending first "to place
well within her the words of her father" (which Sahagún transcribes in
chap. 18). Then, the mother "told her how to live well, how to present herself, how to speak, how to look at one, how to walk, and how
not to interfere in another's life and how not to abuse another." In-
sofar as speech, contrary to writing, presupposes the presence of the
body in the very act of speaking, it should surprise no one that the
counseling about speech refers to the context of body-related behavior: how to walk well, how to present oneself, how to look at
another. The father's advice to his son is also given in a context of
body-related behavior, although the kind of acts that are mentioned
mark the distinction between the social roles of male and female.
Public rather than domestic life comes across in the father's counsel to
his son. Prudence in public, continence in eating and drinking, mod-
eration in sleeping are some of the recommended behaviors next to
speech:

> thou art to speak very slowly, very deliberately; thou art not to speak
> hurriedly, not to pant, nor to squeak, lest it be said of thee that thou
> art a groaner, a growler, a squeaker. Also thou art not to cry out, lest
> thou be known as an imbecile, a shameless one, a rustic, very much

a rustic. Moderately, middlingly art thou to carry, to emit thy spirit, thy words. And thou art to improve, to soften thy words, the voice.[80]

This example illustrates that letters or a writing system that allows for the transcription of speech is not a necessary condition for civilization; illiterate people can have very sophisticated manners, be highly concerned with education and with social behavior. If, in the realm of technology, there are a number of things that cannot be done without writing, in the realm of human culture and behavior there seem to be no written achievements that cannot be equally attained by speech. If writing as well as speech distinguishes the human species from other organisms with nervous systems, it is speech that was developed—before writing—into an instrument of education, social organization, and coordinated human interactions.[81] And even when writing developed as an instrument of religious power, social organization, and human interaction, speech was not abandoned. I am not trying to defend, with this argument, the Western logocentric tradition that Derrida worked so hard to debunk.[82] I am only suggesting that the fact that contemporary linguistic science was founded on the experience of speech and suppressed writing from its field of inquiry does not necessarily mean that writing in the West was never preferred over speech; that it was a sign of a superior level of culture and a true measure of civilization. Renaissance philosophy of writing, prior to and during the colonization process, bears witness to the fact that the value of speech over writing in Plato and the subsidiary role attributed to writing in Aristotle and in Saussure were inverted during the late European Renaissance.[83]

A Book Is Not Necessarily a Book: The Materiality of Signs and Their Descriptions

Spaniards translated *amoxtli* as "book." The previous discussion suggested, I hope, the implications of such a translation, given the fact that the network of meaning Amerindians associated with the materiality of their reading and writing cultures was suppressed and supplanted by the network of meanings Spaniards created around similar kinds of cultural practices. While the translation of *amoxtli* as "book" or *libro* may be correct inasmuch as this rendering offers the best alternative in the English or Spanish lexicon, it is also misleading since it does not take into account the etymological meaning of words and the social function related to those translations in the respective lan-

guages. As a consequence, the ideas associated with the object designated by those words are suppressed and replaced by the ideas and the
body of knowledge associated with that word in the lexicon and the
expressions of the culture into which the original is translated. Thus,
the translation of *amoxtli* as "book" does not capture the differences
in the conceptualization of the activities related to the object, such as
"to write"/*tlacuiloliztli* and "to read"/*amoxitoa*. A partial description of the knowledge associated with the word *book* and the verbs *to
write* and *to read* in fourteenth- and fifteenth-century Spain, and a
comparison with their Nahuatl equivalents (*amoxtli, tlacuiloliztli,
amoxitoa*), would soon make it evident that the Aztecs could hardly
have had books in the same sense that Castilians understood that
word. They did, nevertheless, have books.[84]

The point I am trying to make here is the following: while it is
possible to generalize by saying that writing (in the sense of scratching
on solid surfaces or using any kind of material meant to codify meaning) is an activity common to cultures on this planet (and it is likely
that every culture with writing systems has expressions to designate
these activities), *the conceptualization* (i.e., the "meaning network")
associated with the word and the activity is *culture specific*. The same
statement could be made in relation to the materiality of sign carriers
and their conceptualization in different cultures. *Book* is neither the
universal name nor the universal concept associated with solid surfaces
in which graphic signs are inscribed, preserved, and transmitted. It is
only from the point of view of a culture capable of applying its regional
concept to similar practices and objects of other cultures that could
see ancient Middle East clay tablet and Egyptian papyrus as forerun-
ners of Western and Christian books.[85] If the hypothesis is that *book*
designates the object and implies its representation in a network of
semiotic interactions, then the question "What is a book?" should
be answered in the same way that the question "What is writing?" can
be answered: a book is not an object whose essential property can be
identified, but rather a cultural and regional interpretation of a specific
kind of object. Writing, although it refers to an activity rather than to
an object, follows the same logic. Mexicas referred to the red and black
ink to describe an activity similar to what Spaniards referred to as
writing.[86] The development of speech and the extension of hands to
scratch solid surfaces (originally "to write" came from the Anglo-
Saxon *writan* and meant "to scratch" marks with something sharp; in
Icelandic it was *rita*, "to scratch"; in Swedish *rita*, "to draw, to trace";
in Dutch, *rijten*, and in German *reissen*, "to tear") have increased the
complexity of semiotic behavior among the species homo and have
contributed to the consolidation of features we recognize as human.

119

*The
Materiality of
Reading and
Writing
Cultures*

Because in the West the concept of writing was associated with activities of scratching or drawing graphic signs on solid surfaces, Peruvian quipus presented a lot of difficulties to be interpreted and accepted as writing.

If the properties that make an object a book are neither in the object nor in the class of objects of which the book is one example (mainly because there is no such thing as an essential meaning supporting all different ideas of the book but, rather, changing conceptions of sign carriers), then we have to seek an answer to the question within the specific cultural descriptions of similar kinds of objects. The question now becomes "What kind of conception/description does a culture associate with a class of physical objects made of graphic marks on a solid surface or in visually knotted and colored strings?" Or something equivalent, such as: "For whom is a physical object with a given set of characteristics a 'book'? How much is the idea of the 'book' based on the alphabet and on literacy? What kind of 'books' do we find in societies with nonalphabetic writing systems?" One possible answer to this set of questions seems obvious: *amoxtli* and *vuh* were words coined to designate a class of objects within a society with picto-ideographic writing systems, while *book,* during the fifteenth century, was a word used to designate a class of objects within a society at a complex stage of alphabetic literacy. This answer, however, does not tell us much about the kind of representation associated, in each culture, with the words in question. To explore this issue, it is necessary to relativize the notion of the book that we all bring with us and become observers of our own cultural presuppositions. Let us explore first the question of writing and then the question of the book.

According to current estimates, the biological lines of hominids to which human beings belong is a lineage about fifteen million years old. The human features to which one is accustomed today were consolidated far more recently (about three million years ago). One of the crucial aspects of this consolidation was the emergence of a particular kind of semiotic interaction: speech. All species of animals characterize themselves by their ontogenetic, communicative, and semiotic behaviors. The first accounts for all the actions of the individual; the second for their tendency to live in "common union" with other individuals of the same species; the third for their ability to exchange signs. To live in common union implies communicative behavior and, therefore, the transmission and exchange of signs. If speech and writing distinguished the species Homo sapiens from other species, reading (from the Anglo-Saxon *raeden,* to discern) seems to be one aspect in the sphere of semiotic interactions shared by all species of animals: although not every species uses hands to write, they certainly are able to discern (i.e., to read) the semiotic behavior of other animals as well as the changes in nature.

If it is true that with speech a form of semiotic interaction was introduced that had a significant impact on biological configuration (enlargement of brain size) as well as on the organization of communal life (law, family life, planning, etc.),[87] with writing (from pictography to the alphabet) both a restructuring of thought and a reorganization of social life were attained.[88] Writing (in the general sense of the use of hands and the extension of hands with a sharp instrument, brush, pen, fabric, etc.), together with speech, distinguishes the network of semiotic interactions proper to humans from the more limited one found in other animal species. Writing, which is of interest here for its ties to the book, seems to be a universal of culture; the book, however, is not. The book could be conceived as a general object among communities with different writing systems only if there is agreement to call "book" any kind of material or solid surface on which graphic signs are inscribed (i.e., the book as mere object); it is culture specific if what a culture understands by "book" (e.g., Holy Book) transcends the object and it becomes a text: the idea of the object on which graphic signs are inscribed as conceived by the culture producing and using it.

Concluding Remarks

I hope to have avoided the dangers of placing an all-powerful colonizer in front of a submissive native by taking a mountain detour, in which the snakelike road I followed placed the reader in front of a vast scenic view. You may have perceived, in the distance, that colonial semiosis implies constant interactions where relations of domination cannot be avoided, adaptation by members of cultures in conflict take place, and opposition (from "inside") and resistance (from "outside") the official power is enacted in various forms. Speaking, writing, and sign carriers, as well as their conceptualization, was one set of relations in which colonization took place. Thus, the spread of Western literacy linked to the idea of the book was also linked to the appropriation and defense of cultural territories, of a physical space loaded with meaning. The Western book became a symbol of the letter, in such a way that writing was mainly conceived in terms of the sign carriers: paper and the book. Reading and writing practices were more and more conceived in terms of the sign carrier; reading the word became more and more detached from reading the world, as the *tlamatinime* would have preferred to say.

Paradoxically, modern technology has returned us to the "beginnings of the book" (*biblos*) in that microfilms, screens, disks, and tapes have become the new kind of surface on which writing is inscribed. The new forms of storage and retrieval of information are in the process of eliminating our bookish habits. Soon, we will not need to peruse pages to find the necessary pieces of information. We are already having access to alphabetical and thematic menus from which to obtain what we need. The metaphor of the Divine Book could be replaced, then, by the metaphor of the Electronic Book, an international data bank in which all knowledge will be contained. A professor of literature, teaching Borges's "The Library of Babel," will have to explain to his or her students what a "book" and a "library" were.

During the process of colonization, however, the book was conceived by Spaniards as a container in which knowledge from the New World could be deposited, as a carrier by means of which signs could be transmitted to the metropolis, and, finally, as a text in which truth could be discerned from falsehood, the law imposed over chaos. The book, furthermore, also played a very important role in the reverse process of sign transmission: from the metropolis to the colonial periphery. Printed books facilitated the dissemination and reproduction of knowledge and replaced, in the New World, the practice of the *tlacuilo* and the function of the *amoxtli* and contributed to the colonization of languages.

Part 2

The Colonization of Memory

Chapter 3

Record Keeping without Letters and Writing Histories of People without History

History, Literature, and Colonization

An animated debate on the interrelations between history, literature, and fiction about ten years ago awakened the interest of scholars in the humanities, who were beginning to look at other kinds of discourses beyond literature, and of those in the social sciences, who were turning their attention toward discursive phenomena. The works of Hayden White helped widen the scope of an issue very much discussed since the 1950s in historiography and the philosophy of science,[1] but very much ignored in the human sciences at large. The debate, illuminating in so many respects, remained, however, within the realm of the letter and the Western conceptualization of history, literature, and fiction. Two of the formulas popularized by White, "the fiction of factual representation" and "history as literary artifact," illustrate my point.[2] History and literature have in common an alphabetically written narrative. The idea that every narrative about facts and events is fictional was supported by the belief that an alphabetically written narrative does not capture the essence of the events but is a particular organization of the given. Certainly, the similarities between history and literature are not supported by belief in the fictional character of any kind of representation. While history is rhetorically grounded, literature is based on a logicophilosophical conception of discourse. The first belief is regulated by a set of conventions governing the construction of verbal narratives, the second by a set of conventions regulating the relations a discourse establishes with the world and in our conviction about its reliability regarding the events being reported.

125

A second feature of the debate was its chronological frame. With a few exceptions, its paradigmatic examples were taken from Western historiography since the eighteenth century—an interesting period indeed, since it is the period in which the very concept of literature replaced the Renaissance concept of poetry; human letters as a language-centered form of knowledge was replaced by belles lettres as a language-centered form of enjoyment. It is also a period in which the concept of fiction replaced the notion of mimesis and verisimilitude and became one of the distinctive features of literary narratives. In this chapter I will move back in time and space, to encounter alternate forms of writing, recording, and transmitting the past that allow for a reframing of the debate on fiction, literature, and history in the context of literacy, colonization, and writing histories of people without history.[3]

The discussions on history, literature, and fiction acquired a new dimension with the historiography introduced by the Indian group of subaltern studies. History began to be explored in its complicity with empires. Ranajit Guha expressed it succinctly by saying that the historiography of Indian nationalism has been dominated for a long time by colonialist and bourgeois-nationalist elitism and that both originated as "ideological product of British rule in India."[4] Gayatri Spivak has noticed that the concepts of territoriality and of woman are quite relevant in subaltern studies.[5] Territoriality in subaltern studies is anchored with kinship and community. In my own book, instead, territoriality is linked more with community and with the implementation of cognition by the group of people in power. But perhaps what is more important in the reframing of historiography by the group of subaltern studies is the complicity between the subject and object of investigation (as I attempted to develop it in the Introduction), between subaltern studies and subalternity. Or, to put it in other words, it is not just the conceptual reframing of history as narrative, literature, or fiction that matters but, rather, the ways in which understanding the past could impinge on speaking the present as political and epistemological intervention.

During the same years that the Indian subaltern studies group were dismantling the complicity between historiography and empire and building new links between scholarship and political intervention, Edouard Glissant was overturning the allegiances between history and literature and building new links between scholarship and political intervention, looking at history and literature once again from the perspective of the empire rather than from their epistemological underpinning. For Glissant history and literature were just instruments of the Western empire to suppress and subjugate other forms of re-

cording the past and of finding means of interaction for which literature became the paradigm:

> History is a highly functional fantasy of the West, originating at
> precisely the time when it alone "made" the history of the
> World. . . . At this stage, History is written with a capital H. It is a
> totality that excludes other histories that do not fit into that of the
> West. . . . Literature attains a metaexistence, the all-powerfulness
> of a sacred sign, which will allow people with writing to think it
> justified to dominate and rule peoples with an oral civilization. . . .
> It is again this double hegemony of a History with a capital H and a
> Literature consecrated by the absolute power of the written sign
> that the peoples who until now inhabited the hidden side of the
> earth fought, at the same time they were fighting for food and
> freedom.[6]

My own reading of Amerindians' and Spaniards' record keeping is
closer to Glissant's framing than to White's or Guha's. It attempts to
circumvent the universality of "history" and to conceive "historiography" as a regional Western invention (particularly in its post-Renais-
sance version); and to conceive record keeping of human memories as
a more general practice of which Western historiography is one of its
manifestations. The fact that this regional record-keeping maintains a
complicity with empire and imperial expansion gave it its universal
value and allowed imperial agencies to inscribe the idea that people
without writing were people without history and that people without
history were inferior human beings.

Literacy and the Colonization of Memory: Writing History of People without History

For more than a century, from Brother Ramón Pané (who remained in
the Caribbean and lived with the Amerindians between Colombus's
first and second voyages) to the Franciscan Juan de Torquemada
(who, toward 1615, finished a vast narrative in which he included the
origin of the Mexica, the conquest of Mexico, and the Franciscan
activities during the sixteenth century), a concern and a complaint
persisted.[7] The concern was the Amerindians' qualifications to have
history (because of their lack of letters) and their competence to tell
coherent narratives. Torquemada expressed his opinion in the following manner:

One of the things which causes the most confusion in a republic and which greatly perplexes those who wish to discuss its causes, is the lack of precision with which they consider their history; for if history is an account of events which are true and actually happened and those who witnessed them and learned about them neglected to preserve the memory of them, it will require an effort *to write* them down after they happened, and he who wishes to do so will grope in the dark when he tries, for he may spend his life collating the version which he is told only to find that at the end of it he still has not unravelled the truth. *This (or something like this) is what happens in this history of New Spain, for just as the ancient inhabitants did not have letters, or were even familiar with them, so they neither left records of their history.*[8]

The belief that only alphabetic literacy allowed for a reliable recording of the past was so authoritative among Spanish intellectuals of the sixteenth century that the society in which they lived translated the medieval *litteratus* by *letrados* (men of letters) and changed its meaning to designate the social roles involved in writing matters. The celebration of alphabetic writing analyzed in the previous chapters led Antonio de Nebrija not only to consider the letter the greatest invention of humankind but also to elaborate on the connections between alphabetic writing and history.

In his *Reglas de la ortografía en la lengua castellana* (1517), Nebrija repeated almost verbatim what he had said in his Castilian grammar twenty-five years before about the greatness of the letter. But in this case, he tied up the invention of letters with the glory of the prince and all those who, being in a position of power, need to be remembered:

> For Palimedes in the Trojan War did not win as much renown in organizing battles, giving the passwords, passing on his surname, assigning the watches and vigils, in discovering weights and measures, *as in the invention of four letters:* the Greek y, and three more aspirated letters: ch, ph, th.[9]

From the letter to the glory of the prince there is certainly a great gap and an indirect road, since it is the invention of letters rather than the strategies of war that established the glory of the prince. However, there is also an inherent connection between the letter and the glory of the prince that resurfaces in Torquemada's complaint about the lack of letters among the Mexica. Torquemada's concept of history (or historiography) implies the dominant Ciceronian definition of it, which was forged on the experience of alphabetically written narra-

tives accomplished by Greek and Roman historians, as well as the
rhetorical legacy of imperial Rome (mainly Ciceronian and Quintilian). It was the belief in the accurate preservation of memory and the
glorification of the past by means of alphabetic writing that resulted in
a powerful complicity between the power of the letter and the authority of history. So concerned was Nebrija in taming the voice that the
consequences of his effort went beyond the first-level connection between the oral and the written to reach a second level of cultural
literacy, in which taming the voice impinged upon the control of
memory.

From such a philosophy of language and writing, it should come as
no surprise that Spanish men of letters appointed themselves to write
down the history that Amerindians could not properly write because
of their lack of letters. This belief was so long-lived that even Bartolomé de las Casas, who fought all his life against the belief of his
compatriots and men of letters that Amerindians lacked intelligence
and humanity, had no choice but to admit that they belonged to the
class of barbarians identified with the illiterates:

> The second class of barbarians are those who lack a literary lan-
> guage [qui literali semone carent] which corresponds to their ma-
> ternal idiomatic language, as is Latin to us, and thus know how to
> express what they think.[10]

Since it was common belief at the time (clearly expressed in historiographical treatises)[11] that history was composed of words and
things, the "lack of history" Spaniards referred to should not be taken
as a lack of significant "things" (events, belief, ideas, memories) in the
Amerindian past, but just as the lack of written narratives accomplished by the agency of letters. For Spaniards did not question the
value of Mexica or Maya inscriptions, since they fell within the range
of documentation that Renaissance historians used to tell stories
about the past. Mexica or Mayan narratives of their own past were
taken by Spaniards as equivalent to the evidence provided by coins,
medals, and other kinds of inscriptions, but certainly not as equivalent
to a written narrative by Thucydides or Tacitus.

How did the Mexicas narrate their past? To what kind of evidence
were Spaniards looking when they complained or raised doubts about
the accuracy of Amerindian written memories? Mexica writing was
mainly picto-ideographic, with a few signs to represent sounds. Figure
3.1 is a condensed version of the *Tira de la peregrinación*, a narrative
that in its original form is folded as an accordion, about three meters
long and fifteen centimeters wide. The *Tira de la peregrinación* (which

bears the name of the Italian knight Bernardo Boturini Benaducci, who collected it among other Mexican antiquities around 1740) was probably painted circa 1550. Although painted under the Spanish rule, it was done by a *tlacuilo*, probably of the first generation after the conquest, who preserved very much the style of the ancient codices. The *tira* narrates the Mexica peregrination from Aztlán, place of origin, imagined to be some place between current Southern California and northern Mexico (state of Chihuahua), to their point of arrival, Chapultepec and Tenochtitlán (currently, Mexico City).

Let's look briefly at the first "chapter" (the episode in the upper left corner) of the peregrination narrative (fig. 3.2). The woman and man seated on the left are presented in the conventional Mexica postures

a

Fig. 3.1*a*. The *Codex Selden*, from the Mixtec region, painted around 1521. It tells the story of the beginning of a genealogy, starting at the lower right corner and moving up in Boustrophedon fashion. The birth of a princess is indicated by the umbilical cord.

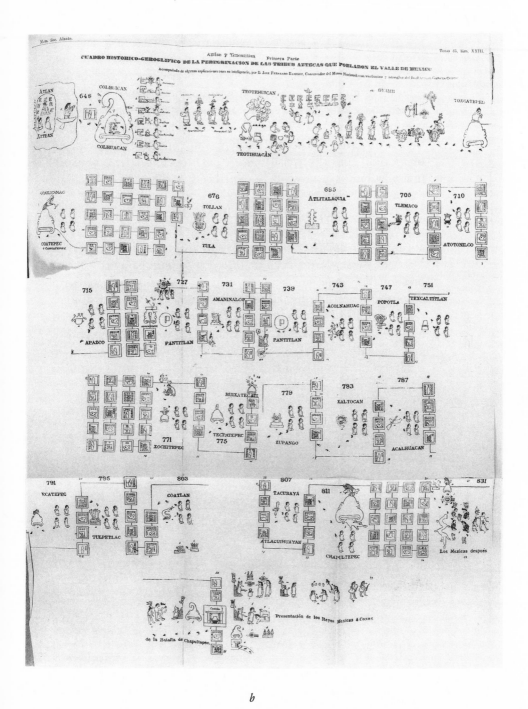

Fig. 3.1*b*. *Tira de la peregrinación:* from Aztlán (top left)
to Tenochtitlán (bottom center)

and costumes of their gender: she sits with her feet folded under her, covered by her long skirt and *quechquemitl;* he sits on his rump, with his bent legs covered in front by his cloak. If, as human figures, both are typical, they have also been singled out by their proper names: a round shield (*chimalli*) is attached by a line to her head, identifying her as the priestess Chimalma. Thus, her image conveys the meaning both of an individual and of a group. The next human figure, un-named and standing in his canoe, functions not as a participant but to convey the action of rowing across the lake. The other protagonist is the tribal patron (and god) Huitzilopochtli, conventionally indicated on the right side by the small human head helmeted with the head of a hummingbird. The protagonists are, therefore, Chimalma, the Mexi-cas, and Huitzilopochtli.[12]

Of course, changing the materiality of writing practices engenders alternative conceptions of reading activities. The verb *to read*—as has already been discussed in the previous chapter—did not exist in Nahuatl. *Amoxitoa* has been translated as "reading a book," an ex-pression that can be understood by a literate Western person, but such a translation does not render its full meaning. *Amoxitoa* is a com-pound word whose roots are *amoxtli,* a tree in the Valley of Mexico and, by extension, the bark of a tree in which writing was inscribed, and *toa,* which means "to narrate" or to tell a story. One can surmise that those who were trained to "read" the "books" (such as the *Tira de la peregrinación*) looked at the picture while telling the story. Cer-

Fig. 3.2.   Detail of *Tira de la peregrinación:* first scene, leaving Aztlán

tainly, the interpretation changed when the interpreter changed and,
mainly, when the ruler for whom the interpreter worked changed.
Torquemada was certainly bothered by what he perceived as erratic
narrative and unstable meaning as opposed to a steady control of
meaning through an alphabetically written narrative under the rule of
historical writing. He was unable to make a distinction between the
human need to record the past and the variety of forms the fulfillment
of that need might take. It was hard for him, as for any Spanish man of
letters, to understand that narratives recording the past could function
independently, outside speech and its control by alphabetic writing;
and that a visual language and spatial relations are perfectly understandable to those familiar with the pictorial conventions. If we compare Mexica painted narratives recording the past with Western written narratives recording the past, we are able to identify, in both, a
common matrix constituted by the participants, the events, the spatial
location, and temporal marker. We can also find that both kinds of
narrative have, among others, the important function of identity
building. For the Renaissance men of letters, that was not enough.
They decided that history should fulfill the conditions established on
the experience of alphabetically written historical narratives. Since
Amerindians did not fulfill that condition, the *letrados* appointed
themselves to write the history of this people "without history."[13]

The notion of history and of people without history, which, if not
hegemonic, was certainly substantial during the sixteenth century,
developed from a philosophy of language built on the experience of
alphabetic writing. A few decades before Torquemada, Father Acosta
(a Jesuit living in Peru) stepped forward to take a position in the
debate as to whether the Amerindians lacked intelligence. With persuasive arguments he supported the idea that Amerindians were intelligent human beings. What they lacked was not intelligence, but letters. In book 6 of his *Historia natural y moral de las Indias* (1590),
Acosta states that nobody had discovered that "the Indians make use
of letters," and from this assumption he develops a theory of writing
based on Aristotle and the experience of Chinese and Amerindian
writing systems. Acosta believed that letters were invented to signify
the words we pronounce and that words are immediate signals of the
concepts and thoughts of man (he was, of course, referring to human
beings). Both letters and voice were created in order to understand
things: the voice for those who could communicate directly in the
same space; letters for those who could not be present but would be
able to read what had been written. Acosta emphasized that signals or
signs that were produced to signify other than words could not truly
be called letters, even though they could be written: a painted image

of the sun is not a cluster of written letters depicting the sun, but a painting. Based on this assumption, Acosta made two inferences: (1) man (humankind) has three different ways of recording memories: by letters and writing (primary examples are the Greeks, Latin, and Hebrews); by painting (primary examples Acosta found in almost every known civilization); and by ciphers and characters; and (2) none of the civilizations of the Indies used letters, but they did employ both images and figures. It was only natural that Acosta was surprised by the report of Tovar, a Jesuit living in Mexico who informed Acosta about the Mexicas' culture, about the Mexicas' means of recording the past, and about their elegant and sophisticated way of speaking. How could they have history if they did not have writing, and how could they be so elegant in their speech if they did not have rhetoric? asked Acosta. Tovar, who was familiar with the Mexicas' art of memory, attempted an explanation of how both remembering the past and remembering long sentences could have worked without the help of letters. He agreed, however, with Acosta's concerns about the Mexicas' lack of letters and writing. In a letter to Acosta Tovar suggests that even if they have different types of figures and characters used to "write things" [escribir las cosas], "their figures and characters are not as sufficient as our writing."[14]

The theory of writing held by Spanish men of letters during the Renaissance should become clear from these examples. The complicity between alphabetical writing and history, applied to Amerindian cultures, elicited Acosta's typology of writing. He concluded that anybody can keep records of the past, but history can only be written with letters. What was the foundation for this conception of writing history? What was the philosophy of historiography that made such a connection with writing possible? It is common knowledge that within the legacy of imperial Rome, works such as the *Ad herennium*, *De oratore*, and *Institutione oratoria* were the basic rhetorical treatises for any humanistic education. They imposed and transmitted the idea that history is narration and narration is the central part of constructing a text (*dispositio*). It is also a well-known fact that Quintilian in the *Institutione oratoria* (book 2, chap. 5) distinguishes three kinds of narrations: *fabula*, the furthest removed from truth and applied to tragedy and epic; *argumentum*, a feigned narrative that applied to comedy; and finally, *historia*, which was considered the true narration of past events. The complicity between history and alphabetic literacy comes from a culture whose learned members were able to write sophisticated treatises (rhetoric) about oral performances (oratory) and written narratives (historia). They laid the groundwork for conceiving the writing of history in terms of the fundamentals of oratorial dis-

courses—all of this a by-product of the imposition and growing relevance of alphabetic writing as the main learning device. Later, as basic
treatises of humanistic education, the works of Cicero and Quintilian
shaped the minds of those who would write histories of the New
World and colonized Amerindian memories.

Describing What One Sees, Remembering Past Events, and Conceiving History

The concept of history in the Western world was born at the same time
as the alphabet. Herodotus (c. 480–425 B.C.) and Thucydides (c.
460–400 B.C.) were considered the fathers of history and Greece the
original place of alphabetic writing.[15] Although this picture could be
challenged from the perspective of new developments in the history of
writing,[16] I suspect that it is still widespread among language-
centered disciplines. The Greek noun ἰστορία meant inquiry or learning by inquiry as well as the narrative by means of which what was
learned by inquiring was also reported. The verb ἰστορέω indicates the
action of inquiring, rather than a specific kind of inquiry, and its report
was designated by *historia* in the Italian Renaissance. The writer of
ἰστορία could himself have been the eyewitness, or he could have used
the report of direct informants who had witnessed the events themselves. Temporality and the chronology of events were not necessary components of ἰστορία. The conjunction of ἰστορία and ἰστορέω
with a lasting chronology of the events reported took place many years
later, when Roman writers began to inquire into the past of Rome and
the beginning of the empire. Tacitus, writing the history of Rome
during the first century A.D., used the expression *anales* to refer to the
events that took place before the time of his own birth and *historia* to
refer to the events contemporary with his own biography. However,
Roman historians such as Livy (59 B.C.–A.D. 17) and Tacitus were
writing about a subject matter, Rome, that they were able to trace to
its beginning and through its development until their own days. One
important difference between Herodotus, on the one hand, and Livy
and Tacitus, on the other, was that the latter two writers were living in
a society in which alphabetic writing and graphic record keeping constituted part of the society itself. Herodotus and Thucydides, instead,
lived in a society in which records were still kept in the body's memory
and transmitted orally. Cicero's definition of history, based on the
Roman experience, became the standard definition during the European Renaissance and was often repeated by historians of the New
World: *esse testem temporum, vitae magistram, vitam memoriae, veri-*

tatis lucen et vetustatis nuntian (witness of time, model of life, life of memory, light of truth, and messenger of antiquity).

Toward the end of the fourteenth century Ibn Khaldun (1332–1406), one of the classical Arab historians, wrote a monumental *Muqaddimah*, an extensive overview or introduction to his *Kitab al-Ibar,* which Rosenthal translated as "World history."[17] The modern reader might wonder if "history" in Franz Rosenthal's translation should be understood in the sense the word had for Herodotus or rather it would be closer to the Latin meaning of *historia.* For the Roman historians the word had a meaning closer to "a narrative account of past events" than to "report on witnessed events." In fact, Ibn Khaldun's written narrative and report resembles more a compendium of human civilization with particular attention to the Arabic world than a *historia* à la Tacitus or Livy. Furthermore, Khaldun attaches great importance to philosophy. If, on the one hand, he grounded his work on the significance of the written (*kitab*), he was also aware of the importance of philosophy in understanding the past of human civilization and the present of Arabic societies. In Rosenthal's translation, Ibn Khaldun remarks,

> The inner meaning of history [*kitab*], on the other hand, involves speculation and an attempt to get at the truth, subtle explanation of the causes and origins of existing things, and deep knowledge of the how and why of events. [History (*kitab*),] therefore, is firmly rooted in philosophy. It deserves to be accounted a branch of [philosophy]. (1:6)

The complicity between writing about the past and a rational foundation of its understanding (philosophy) clearly distinguishes his conception of *kitab* from Livy's notion of *historia,* Biondo's notion of *istoria,* or las Casas's notion of *historia.*[18] In the West, there is a remarkable tendency to link history with rhetoric instead of philosophy, particularly after the powerful legacy of Cicero and the Roman historian. If by the eleventh century both the Muslim and the Western Christian world were inheritors of Greek philosophy, history seems to have taken different roots in these cultures.

In Italy, toward the end of the thirteenth and beginning of the fourteenth centuries, things began to take a new turn. Almost ten centuries after the fall of the Roman Empire, Italy was a conglomerate of city-states, and it became the locus of a new development in historiographical writing. Cochrane has described the conditions facilitating the development of a consciousness that influenced historiographical writing in the West until the seventeenth century.[19] Humanist historiography, according to Cochrane, blended a practice

of record keeping (*ricordanza*) found among wealthy families within
the thriving Italian city-states and the chronological organization of
facts and events cultivated by the medieval chronist with the rhetorical
experience and training inherited from the blossoming domain of
letters in the Roman world. Roman historians (such as Livy and Tacitus) and Italian humanist historians (such as Bruni and Biondo)
shared a deep sense of the past based on the storage of written records
that distinguishes them from Greek historians, for whom writing history was more related to the written report of the investigation of
current events than with the reconstruction of the past based on written records. Contrary to Roman historians, humanist historians had
an image of the rise and fall of the Roman Empire at the same time that
a perspective on the ten centuries elapsed from its fall to their present
days. New World historians were deprived of such a perspective on the
past. The stories they were telling and they knew well began in 1492. A
deep sense of the past, paradoxically, did not belong to them who
wrote history but to those who the Spanish doubted had history because they did not have writing. The tension between those who had
the memories and those who appointed themselves to write history
was not an easy problem to solve, even by a careful and relentless
person such as Bernardino de Sahagún. New World historians approached their subject matter with a concept of historiography inherited from the Roman and humanist traditions at the same time that
they found themselves in a situation more akin to Herodotus and
Thucydides than to Livy or Biondo.

Let's explore further this distinction, making a stop in the sixth
century A.D., a century considered to be one of the first stages in the
configuration of modern Europe.[20] In retrospect, three interrelated
factors played a substantial role in this process: the rise of Christianity,
the Greco-Roman legacy, and the immigration of Germanic communities. This century has also been characterized by contrasting Byzantium, in which an effort was being made to reconstitute the Roman
Empire, with the West, in which a plurality of newborn city-states
replaced the unity created by imperial Rome. Hispania or the Iberian
Peninsula was linked to Byzantium, and together with Africa and Italy
was one of the strategic points for a Byzantine reconstruction of the
orbis terrarum modeled on the Roman Empire. Hispania was the
place in which the Hispano-Romans resisted Byzantium. In Hispania,
Seville was the place that in the eighth century A.D. witnessed the
Muslim expansion. A century before, in 556, during the revival of the
Visigothic culture, Isidore was born in Seville. Isidore of Seville is a
good example of the Hispano-Roman intellectual of the sixth century
A.D. who contributed to a notion of history related to alphabetic writ-

ing that would prove crucial to the future expansion of the Christian West and the construction of a new idea of Europe. Conceiving and writing history was, no doubt, an important step in the direction of consolidating the classical legacy. History as a discipline or discursive practice became a substantial tool in such an enterprise. Let's explore Isidore of Seville's concept of *historia*.

Book I of his famous *Etimologiae*[21] begins with an exploration of the letter (chap. 3) and ends with a definition of writing history (chaps. 41–44). Naturally, this link came to Isidore from Varro's distinction, in high education, between the trivium and the quadrivium.[22] Writing history was a subcomponent of the trivium (grammar, rhetoric, and dialectic). In Isidore's view the letter had been invented to write down and maintain the "memories of things" [res memoria]. The letters, according to a telling image used by Isidore, enable us to "tie things up," thus keeping them from "flying away with all those things that are forgotten":

> El uso de las letras se introduce para conservar el recuerdo de las cosas, pues para que no huyan por el olvido, se atan con las letras; pues en tanta variedad de cosas, ni todas se podrian aprender de oidas, ni facilmente se retendrian en la memoria.[23]

> [The use of letters was begun in order to preserve the memory of things, for in order that they may not fall into oblivion, they are tethered by means of letters; for with such a variety of things, it would be impossible to learn them all by hearsay, and it would be no easy task to retain them in the memory.]

Isidore recalls, in this context, the notion of *literatio* (literacy) introduced by Varro to refer to "the knowledge of reading, writing, and counting." Numeracy (*numeratio*) is included in the concept of literacy. The connections between the letter (*litterae*) and the act of reading (*legere*) were taken for granted because, he said, the word *letter* comes from *legiterae,* which means "to open the way for those who read" [legenti iter]; as well as the fact that what is repeated is repeated in the act of reading (*in legendo iterantur*). This interpretation shows that by the turn of the sixth century, the original meaning of *legere*— "to discern"—had acquired a restricted meaning, that of "discerning the letters of the alphabet" or reading (*leer* in Spanish; *lire* in Italian).[24]

Isidore's concept of history was inferred from that of Cicero. History, said Isidore, is the narrative of past events, and it is also the way of knowing past events. He was not perturbed by his own translation of

the Greek *apo tu historein* (to see or to know) or by the fact that the
Greek expression he was translating did stress the act of seeing (the
present knowing and the agency of the eye or witnesses) as opposed to
remembering events past. Isidore did not perceive differences between Greek and Latin concepts of history. He was even less bothered
by the consequences of his own translation, when he says, for instance:

> Pues entre los antiguos, nadie escribia historia más que aquellos
> que eran testigos y habian visto las cosas que narraban, pues mejor
> conocemos lo que hemos visto que lo que sabemos de oidas.[25]

[For among the ancients, without exception only those who were
witnesses and who had seen the things they narrated wrote history,
for we understand what we have seen better than what we know by
hearsay.]

In other words, Isidore was not concerned with the distinction
between a narrative of witnessed events (which will become past
events from a future perspective) and a narrative of the narrative of
witnessed events. Because he was not interested in such a distinction,
he was able to blend a conception of history as a narrative of past
events with a conception of history as a narrative of witnessed events:

> Las cosas que se ven se refieren sin equivocación. Esta disciplina
> pertenece a la gramática, porque se escribia solo lo que era digno de
> ser tenido en memoria. Por tanto, las historias se llaman monu-
> mentos, porque perpetuan las cosas señaladas. Se les llamo *series*
> por traslacion, tomado este nombre *a sertis florum*, de guirnaldas de
> flores.

[Things that are seen are reported without any ambiguity. This
discipline pertains to grammar, for only the things deemed worthy
of memory were written down. Therefore, histories are called
monuments because they perpetuate notable events. Figuratively,
they were called *series* from the expression *sertis florum*, garlands of
flowers.]

The lack of distinction between history as report of present events
by an eyewitness and history as record of past events remains in Isidore
when he describes the "historical genres." On the one hand he distinguishes three genres according to methods of organizing time
(*efemerides*, counting by days; *calender*, counting by months; and
anales, counting by year). On the other hand, he distinguishes history

from annals on the assumption that the latter is a narrative of the ancient times and past events that the historian could not witness, whereas *historia* is a narrative of the events taking place during the historian's time.[26]

In Italy, nine centuries after Isidore of Seville, humanist historiography would begin to blur the distinction between annals and history. The understanding of "history" (*apo tu historein*) as an eyewitness account began to be conceived as the narrative of past events, which were saved from oblivion by written records and transmitted to future generations by alphabetic narratives. New World historians found themselves in a situation similar to Isidore of Seville and later the humanists: they were unable to accept that past events could have been recorded without necessarily having letters, and, unlike Isidore, they failed to recognize the distinction between annals and history. Thus, it is in the context of the discontinuity of the classical tradition that we might understand some of the tensions and dilemmas faced by New World historians as well as some of the peculiarities of New World historiography briefly discussed in the previous section.

Recording the Past without Written Words: Discursive Types beyond the Classical Tradition

A large and increasing number of studies in the ethnography of speaking and on folk taxonomy over the past forty years have convincingly demonstrated that the Western categories of genres, so powerfully codified during the European Renaissance and transmitted to the colonial periphery as part of the package of spreading alphabetic literacy, are, like the Western notion of history, a regional conceptualization of discursive types and not a universal category by which non-Western discursive typologies could be established.[27] Such studies are of great help in guessing what the Spaniards (as well as, later on, the English, French, or German colonizers) could have misunderstood by using Western categories as a model to understand non-Western discursive types, instead of thinking in a model of human categorization in order to understand the similarities and differences between Mexicas and Spaniards. Certainly, the Spaniards were in no position to do so. If they had done it, there would be no reason to write this book.

We have seen, in the previous chapters, some examples of the writing-related genres. One particularly clear illustration is provided by the Texcocan historian Fernando de Alva Ixtlilxochitl when he refers to the source-based knowledge (recorded in Aztec writing) in which his historical narrative, following Western historiographical conventions, is cast. Miguel León-Portilla offers a useful complement to Ixtlilxochitl's description by his reconstruction of a Nahuatl word family expressing the Mexica conceptualization of oral discourses as well as written records.[28] The concept of *toltecáyotl*, which León-Portilla translates as *toltequidad*, or the peculiarity of the Toltecs' cultural identity,[29] is the most inclusive one. As such, *toltecáyotl* was a word employed among the Toltecs (the civilization preceding the Mexicas, from whom they claimed their cultural legacy) to refer to the cultural tradition and identity of a human and social community preserved, among other forms, by means of oral and written transmissions: *Toltecáyotl,* adds León-Portilla,

> abarcaba la *tinta negra y la tinta roja*—la sabiduría—la escritura y el calendario, libros de pintura, conocimiento de los caminos que siguen los astros, las artes, entre ellas la música de las flautas, bondad y rectitud en el trato de los seres humanos, el arte del buen comer, la antigua palabra, el culto de los dioses, dialogar con ellos y con uno mismo.[30]

> [encompassed *black ink and red ink*—wisdom—writing and the calendar, books of paintings, knowledge of the course of the stars, the arts, including pipe music, goodness and honesty in the treatment of one's fellows, the art of good eating, the ancient word, the cult of the gods, of conversing with them and with oneself.]

The concept of *toltecáyotl* seems to have escaped the scrutiny of earlier chroniclers, missionaries, and men of letters, since they questioned the Amerindians' competence to tell coherent stories and never paid attention to Amerindian agencies for keeping the communities' ties and defining their cultural identity. Had the missionaries realized that *toltécatl,* from which *toltecáyotl* was itself derived from *tollán* (the city of the Toltecs) and that among its meanings were, first, the person who lives in a *tollán* or who belongs to the Toltec community and, second, the artisans and the wise men, they would have perceived that the Amerindians from the Valley of Mexico were not so much different from the Spaniards from the kingdom of Castile. From *toltécatl* came *toltecáyotl,* which means "everything that pertains to and that is characteristic of those who live in a *tollán,* or city" [el conjunto de todo aquello que pertenece y es característico de quienes viven en una *Tollan* o ciudad].[31] In the Latin West the equivalent concept would be *civilization,* derived from *civitas,* which meant, in particular, "the condition or privileges of (Roman) citizens, citizenship"; and, in general, "the citizens united in a community, the body-politic, the state."[32] The Mexica had their own set of terms to designate their own mode of preserving their own memories and tradition.[33]

If *toltecáyotl* was a key concept in the Toltec construction of their own identity, to which any kind of "history" is related, *tlatollótl* was a key word in the semantic field devoted to conceptualizing discursive configurations and discursive types. *Tlatollótl* is derived from *tlatolli,* whose basic meanings are, first, "word" or "discourse" and, second, "word-memory" or "discourse-memory," a discourse whose function is to preserve and transmit the memory of the past. In this second sense it could also be understood as "essential discourse." It is the discourse by means of which the community construed, enlarged, and transmitted the idea of itself and the traces of its own past.[34] While in the first sense *tlatollótl* refers to the speaking competence of every member of the community, the second is more restricted, and it is applied to a more limited kind of discourse, those requiring particular social roles to be delivered and those related to the fixation and preservation of the collective memory. What is interesting about the uses of *tlatollótl* is that it could be applied to both oral and written agencies:[35]

> Lo que al comienzo fue sólo objeto de *tradición oral* pasó a ser tema y contenido de los *libros indígenas,* cuya escritura comprendía representaciones estilizadas de distintos objetos, es decir, pictografías, asimismo ideogramas y, en menor grado, glifos de carácter fonético.[36]

> [That which in the beginning was merely the object of *oral tradition* became the theme and content of *indigenous books,* whose writing included stylized representations of different objects: that is, pictographs, as well as ideograms and, to a lesser degree, glyphs of a phonetic character.][37]

Thus, the distinction between oral and written signs to preserve and record the memories of the community contradicts, in one sense, the heavy Western emphasis on history related to writing and, in another, creates a landscape of discursive genres in which oral and written types are part of a discursive configuration referred to by *tlatollótl.* The discursive configuration that in the West, during the sixteenth century, is referred to as *history* accepted as members of its class only written discourses (historical narrative, biography, chronicle) and created—as a consequence—a landscape in which only written genres were part of the historiographical discursive configuration.[38] In the domain of oral genres it is worth mentioning, as an example, *huehue-*

nonotzaliztli, an expression used to refer to a narrative of past (ancient) events delivered by an elder person (*huehue*); *te-nonotzaliztli,* used to refer to the narrative about some events or person; and, finally, *huehuetlatolli* (the ancient discourse delivered also by the elders), used to refer to the wisdom (philosophy) upon which social behavior is regulated and the younger generation educated. While the first two are discursive types accounting for events and "person processes" (biographies), equivalent to Western history, the latter is equivalent to Western philosophy. In the realm of oral interactions, all these discursive types are distinguished from a different discursive configuration denoted by the word *cuicatl* (song), used to refer to rhythmic discourse, generally delivered in association with music, and whose equivalent in the Western tradition would be the dithyrambic species (which play a minor role in Aristotle's poetics and which became lyric poetry during the reorganization of genres in the European Renaissance).[39]

Types of written (picto-ideographic) narratives have been formed in connection with the material sign carriers. *Amátl* was the Nahuatl word to name the surface upon which graphic signs were inscribed (equivalent to *biblos,* in Greece, or papyrus, in Egypt, and the *scriptum codex,* in Latin); *amoxtli* was used to refer the ensemble of the sign carrier and the signs inscribed on it. Thus, by *cecemeilhui-amoxtli,* the Mexicans referred to a daily account of events and by *cexuiuh-amátl* to a yearly account. León-Portilla further specified that *xiuh-amátl* is the equivalent to the Western annals. The expression *in hucauh amoxtli* was employed to refer to the sign carriers of graphically fixed events of ancient times.[40] Perhaps it was a discursive type that could have been used as an example by Francesco Patrizi, had he been aware of its existence, almost contemporary to the years in which he was contesting the Ciceronian notion of history. But this story will be told in the next section.

The History of Writing and the Writing of History (Boturini and Vico)

The efforts of the Italian knight Bernardo Boturini Benaducci to collect and understand ancient Mexican manners of recording the past is an exemplary and forgotten case.[41] It is a curious one, also. Boturini was an Italian and a follower of Giambattista Vico. He wrote in Spanish about ancient Mexican history for a Creole community in the New World and for a Spanish intellectual audience not ready for innovative or challenging ideas. Boturini went to Mexico in 1735, after a per-

egrination that took him out of Italy in 1733 because of the war between Philip V and France against the Hapsburgs. Boturini spent a
few months in England and then moved to Lisbon, where he was well
received in the royal house. He did not stay long, however, and moved
to Madrid. Because of his religious devotion, he walked from Madrid
to Zaragoza to visit the temple of Nuestra Señora. It was in Zaragoza
as a result of this devotion that he learned about the cult of the Virgin
of Guadalupe, in Mexico, who had become almost a century earlier
the symbol of the Creole population and consciousness. Boturini did
not hesitate in deciding to visit Mexico. Once there, he divided his
time between the goal of his mission (the Virgin of Guadalupe) and
the "discovery" of Mexican ancient history. Before his death in 1555,
he was able to finish his *Idea de una nueva historia general de la
America Septentrional,* printed in 1746, the first volume of the *Historia general de la America Septentrional: De la cronologia de sus principales naciones,* printed in 1749 (fig. 3.3).[42] It would be an under-
statement to say that Boturini's work remained marginal in the history
of historiography, although he had during his time a few strong sup-
porters. None, however, supported Boturini for the same reasons we
are interested in today, that is, Boturini's new concept of history and
historiographical writing.

The few studies and comments on Boturini's work are mainly in
relation to his new idea of writing history. Boturini was an admirer of
Giambattista Vico, whose first edition of the *Sciencia nuova prima*
(*SNP*) (1730) he knew.[43] Following Vico's model of a universal history of humankind, Boturini experimented with the history of the
ancient Mexican and divided it in three ages: the age of gods, the age
of heroes, and the age of men (or human beings). This distinction,
which has been traced back to ancient Egypt and was known through
Varro, was expanded by Vico. To each age Vico attributed a particular
kind of language. During the age of the gods, the language was hieroglyphic; during the age of the heroes, the language was composed of
signs and of "empresas heroicas" [heroic enterprises]; and in the age
of men, the language was epistolary, and they were able to communicate across space. Vico came to the conclusion that a civil history was
possible because each nation was able to write its own history in the
characters corresponding to each period.

The theory of the three linguistic (or semiotic) stages in the evolution of humankind that Vico laid out in book 3, chapter 25 of *SNP*
should be understood in the context of the Christian history of language, whose origin was attributed to Adam. After Adam came the
plurality of languages prompted by the episode of Babel, to which we
briefly alluded in chapter 1. Finally, there was the long and obscure age

extending between Adam and Homer, of which Hesiod's *Theogony* ("che vise certamente innanzi d'Omero") provided a glossary of the first language of Greece. Vico's vocabulary to describe speech and writing is not altogether clear and is given on occasion to long and complex debates. Vico employs the word *lingua* (language) for both speech and writing, although he also resorts to *scribere, lettera,* and *carattere* when referring specifically to writing. Sometimes even a specific name is given to a *carattere,* for instance, *geroglifici* (hieroglyphic). Thus when Vico describes the language of the first age, he imagines that such divine language (*lingua*) was somewhat similar to the Egyptian hieroglyphics and implies a correlation between the three kinds of languages and the three kinds of characters.[44] The first of these languages "was a divine mental language by mute religious acts or divine ceremonies," the second "was by heroic blazonings,

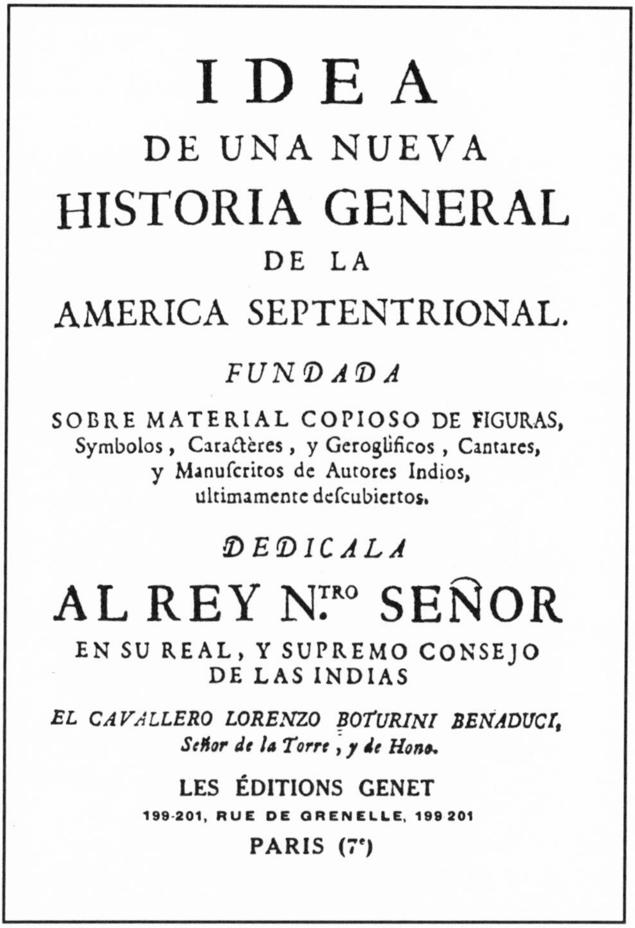

Fig. 3.3. Boturini Benaducci's first edition of his *Idea de una nueva historia de la America Septentrional*

IDEA
DE UNA NUEVA
HISTORIA GENERAL
DE LA
AMERICA SEPTENTRIONAL.

FUNDADA

SOBRE MATERIAL COPIOSO DE FIGURAS,
Symbolos , Caractères , y Geroglíficos , Cantares,
y Manuscritos de Autores Indios,
ultimamente descubiertos.

DEDICALA

AL REY N.ᵗʳᵒ SEÑOR
EN SU REAL, Y SUPREMO CONSEJO
DE LAS INDIAS

EL CAVALLERO LORENZO BOTURINI BENADUCI,
Señor de la Torre , y de Hono.

LES ÉDITIONS GENET
199-201, RUE DE GRENELLE, 199 201
PARIS (7ᵉ)

with which arms are made to speak," and the third is "articulate speech, which is used by all nations today."[45] The three kinds of characters are, first, the "divine, properly called hieroglyphics, used . . . by all nations in their beginnings. . . . And they were certain imaginative universals, dictated naturally by the human mind's innate property of delighting in the uniform." The second is "the heroic characters, which were also imaginative universals to which they reduced the various species of heroic things, as to Achilles all the deeds of valiant fighters and to Ulysses all the devices of clever men." And the third is the "vulgar characters which went along with the vulgar languages," or letters.[46]

For the second age, the language of arms, Vico does not offer an equivalent example, as he does for the first age. The language (*lingua*) of the third age is, according to Vico, speech and alphabetic writing, with Homer its paradigm. Thus, not only does Vico trace an evolutionary process from the age of gods to the age of man, but he also traces an evolutionary process of language according to which the last stage corresponds to "letteri volgari" [the alphabet].[47] Consequently, whatever culture has not reached such a stage remains somewhere between the first and the second age. However, Vico's theory is not as simple as this introductory paragraph suggests, and a second reading can problematize the first.

Vico's disagreement with those who maintained that the origin of speech preceded the origin of writing (*lettere*) and his well-known thesis that both have a common origin contested the Renaissance philosophy of language that celebrated the letter, paving the way for scholars such as Boturini, who was able to perceive what escaped sixteenth-century men of letters and missionaries. Vico states his thesis in a very obscure and problematic formula: "tute le nazione parlarono scrivendo" [every nation spoke by writing]. It was easy for Boturini to conclude, following this premise, that the Amerindians, prior to the arrival of the Europeans, had their own way of writing, by speaking and by hieroglyphics and the language of arms. Accordingly, and following Vico's second premise, by which every nation writes its history in the language corresponding to each age, Boturini concluded that the Mexicans had their own manner of writing history. Thus, he entitled his first report on his findings a "new idea of history," precisely because he realized that alphabetic writing was not a necessary condition for writing history, despite the fact that sixteenth-century scholars had difficulties in understanding this. Boturini's contribution was not so much his division of Mexica history in three ages, since he suppressed the fact that the Mexicas themselves divided their own chronology into four ages previous to the present.[48] His main contribution was his recognition of the Mexicas' own legitimate way of recording the past. Certainly, Boturini took this idea very far, and we should not necessarily expect what was impossible to deliver within the eighteenth-century horizon of knowledge. It was more than enough that Boturini understood that the Amerindians had their own valuable ways of preserving memories. By recognizing this he indirectly introduced a new philosophy of writing upon which to evaluate Amerindian manners of preserving memories. Boturini was able to solve much of the puzzle presented to sixteenth-century observers of the Amerindian history of writing and their writing of history: namely, that every human community had its own manner of recording the past and that the connivance between alphabetic writing and history was a regional invention of the West. He could not go far enough to recognize that the Mexicas' five ages were as desirable as Vico's three. His model was of one evolutionary world, not of alternates.

Vico's dictum "Every nation spoke by writing" deserves, at this point, further exploration. Vico, contrary to Nebrija, considered the alphabet just one form of writing. Writing to Vico meant any kind of visible sign somehow related to the world of ideas and not necessarily to speech. The distinction between writing and idea (and not between writing and speech) is crucial, for by *lettere* he refers to any visible sign (like thunder or storm, in the primal language of the first age [*SNP*, book 3, chap. 3, p. 897]), and by *lettere volgare* he alludes to alphabetic writing and the articulated language of the age of the men (or human beings). Vico uses *carattere* (character in the sense of script) in his analysis and depiction of the world of ideas. Following his distinction between the world of signs (*lettere* and *lettere volgare*) and the world of ideas (*carattere*), he proposes a division of labor between the philosopher, who deals with *carattere,* and the philologue, who deals with *lettere.*[49] The following charts Vico's concept of *lingua* and the relations between *lettere* and *carattere.*[50] *Lingua* comprises

Lettere: percept, visible signs
Carattere: concept, mental ideas
Parlari: percept, audible signs

The three-way distinction is useful for remapping Vico's concept of the three ages of the world and their corresponding languages, all of them in the realm of the *lettere* (not in *carattere* or *parlari*): the language of the gods (where the *lettere* are natural signs read or interpreted as hieroglyphs), the language of the heroes (where the *lettere* are man-made signs read as signs of war), and the language of human beings (where the *lettere* are *letteri volgari,* or alphabetic writing).

Thus, to say that every nation spoke by writing is to say that sign production (aural or visual) is a kind of speaking and any sign production (aural or visual) is at the same time a kind of writing. If Vico refused to accept that the *lettere* were invented by the Greeks (even if he takes Homer as the paradigmatic example of the language of the third age), it was because he did not accept that writing was invented after speech. He believed that semiotic processes from the beginning of human existence involved sound, body movement, ideas, and graphic signs by which some kind of coordinated behavior among living nervous systems was attempted. Vico's concept of *lingua* is a complex matrix composed of ideas, different kinds of visible signs, and sounds.

There was in Vico, however, a hesitation between the synchronic and the diachronic handling of his own model. He asserts that the three kinds of language (by sounds [*parlari*], by natural means [lightning and storm], and graphic signs [*lettere*]) were born at the same time, although he also suggests a hierarchical dominance based on chronological development. First was the language of gods, followed by the language of heroes, and, finally, the language of human beings. The hierarchical relation derives from the fact that while during the first and second ages the language of human beings was not yet in place, during the third age the language of gods and heroes survived. Thus, Vico perceived the Chinese and the Aztecs as equally "behind" in alphabetic writing (*letteri volgari*) because in both cultures people still wrote in hieroglyphics:

> "Nell'Indie occidentali i messicani furono ritruovati scriver per geroglifici, e Giovanni di Laet nella sua *Descriziene della Nuova India,* descrive i geroglifici degl'indiani essere diversi capi d'animali, piante, fiori, frutte, e per gli loro ceppi distinguere le famiglie; ch'e lo stesso uso appunto ch'hanno l'armi gentilizie *del mondo nostro.* Nell'Indie orientali i chinesi tuttavia scribono per geroglifici."[51]

> [In the West Indies the Mexicans were found to write in hieroglyphics, and Jan de Laet in his *Description of the New India* describes the hieroglyphics of the Indians as divers heads of animals, plants, flowers and fruits, and notes that they distinguish families by their cippi; which is the same use that is made of family coats-of-arms in our world. In the East Indies the Chinese still write in hieroglyphics.][52]

While Vico cannot be accused of utterly falling into the trap of the Renaissance celebration of alphabetic writing, as Acosta did, he could not, however, avoid its ideology. He perceives Aztecs and Chinese as having a system of writing which had not yet reached the pinnacle of the *letteri volgari*.

Vico introduced, nevertheless, a new way of looking at the history of writing and the writing of history. The happy coincidence that Boturini read Vico and went to Mexico allowed him to see in Mexican writing what missionaries of the first century failed to see: the Amerindians' magnificent and exemplary (to paraphrase his own expressions) ways of writing history, which could be positively compared—according to Boturini—with the most celebrated histories written anywhere in the world. Boturini gave two reasons to support his statement:

1. Lo primero, porque es la mas facunda de todas quantas hasta el presente se han descubierto, por tener quatro modos de encomendar a la publica memoria sus cosas notables: el primero, en Figuras, Symbolos, Caracteres y Geroglificos, que encierran en si un mar de erudicion, como se vera adelante: El segundo, en Nudos de varios colores, que en idioma de los Peruanos se llaman Quipu, y en el de nuestros Indios [he refers to central Mexico] Nepohualtzitzin: El tercero, en Cantares de exquisitas metaforas, y elevados conceptos: El quarto, y ultimo, despues de la Conquista Española, en Manuscritos de ambas lenguas Indiana, y Castellana; algunos en papel Nacional, y otros en el Europeo, por cuyo medio se viene en conocimiento de las particularidades de su Vida Civil.
2. Lo segundo, por hallarse adornada de una Chronologia tan exacta, que vence en primores a la de los Egipcios, y Caldeos; pues explica sus años con quatro caracteres, *Tecpatl, Calli, Tochtli, Acatl,* que quiere decir, *Pedernal, Casa, Conejo y Caña,* arcano de los quatro Elementos, y de muchas erudiciones Astronomicas, texiendolos en *Triadecateridas,* y formando con quatro de ellas 52 años, que son el *Cyclo Solar Indiano,* en el qual se demuestra un Systema perpetuo, e infalible, que es la más genuida propriedad de la verdadera ciencia (PLATE 3 and 4).[53]

[1. Firstly, because it is the most eloquent of all that have to date been discovered, since there are four ways of committing noteworthy matters to public memory: first by means of Figures, Symbols, Characters, and Hieroglyphs, each of which contains a sea of wisdom as we shall see shortly. Secondly, by means of multicolored knots, which are called quipu in the Peruvian language and *nepohualtzitzin* in the language of our Indians [i.e., those in central Mexico]. Thirdly, in poems full of exquisite metaphors and noble conceits. Fourthly and lastly, after the Spanish Conquest, in manuscripts written in Indian and Castilian; some on local paper, others on European, by which we have come to know about the peculiarities of their Civil Life.

2. Secondly, because they are blessed with such a precise Chronology, that it surpasses in its elegance that of the Egyptians and the Chaldeans; for the years are explained by four characters: _Tecpatl, Calli, Tochtli, Acatl,_ which mean _Flint, House, Rabbit,_ and _Reed,_ the mystery of the four elements, and much more astronomical scholarship, weaving them in _Triadecateridas_ so that four of them equal fifty-two years, that is, the _Indian Solar Cycle,_ which is a perpetual and infallible system, which is in turn the purest property of true science.]

Boturini, thus, accepts that history can be written without _letteri volgari_ (alphabetic writing); it can be written with just "letters" (any kind of sign). He then describes how Mexicans wrote their history in the age of gods and the age of heroes. He stops before the third age, which presumably created a theoretical problem that could not have been solved by following Vico. The conquest of Mexico interrupted the natural continuity of Mexican history and introduced a discontinuity in the history of writing that resulted in the coexistence of conflicting spoken languages and systems of writing. To account for what happened in the sixteenth century Boturini would have had to invent a fourth age, the age of colonial encounters, when people with _lettere volgari_ transmitted their system of writing to people with _lettere_ (nonalphabetic writing). He does mention, however, the existence of "manuscripts in both languages, Indian and Castilian." What is unusual in Boturini (even more so if we remember Acosta's doubts and Garcilaso's uncompromising tribulations by making his uncle talk about the Incas' manners of preserving the past) is the conviction and the enthusiasm with which he studied Amerindian histories:

> Aun mas admira la verdad, y sencillez con que los Historiadores antiguos, assi en las Pinturas, como en los Cantares, referian las cosas dignas de memoria. Si ganaban, o perdian las Batallas, pintaban el sucesso con las mayores puntualidades; y los Philologos componian unos Cantares de jubilo, o de lamentacion, celebrando, o llorando, al son de sus instrumentos musicos . . . las mas menudas circunstancias de su buena, o mala fortuna.[54]

[What is even more amazing is the truth and simplicity with which the ancient historians depicted things worthy of memory, as much in their paintings as their poems. If they won or lost a battle they would paint the event with precise attention to detail; and the Philologists composed poems of rejoicing or sorrow to celebrate or lament the slightest circumstances of their good or bad fortune to the sound of their musical instruments.]

Thus, Boturini's *Idea de una nueva historia* is, indeed, a history of Amerindian historiography, and more specifically, a history of the historiography of the two ages, the age of gods and the age of heroes.

Boturini not only wrote a history of America Septentrional (Mexico), he also collected and described a wealth of documents to show how the Mexicas themselves wrote their own history. In this particular aspect Boturini went further than his mentor. His personal experience with ancient Mexican sources in the very country in which such sources were produced gave him a perception of ancient Mexican manners of recording the past that Vico could not have had by reading Jean de Laet or other secondary descriptions. Where Boturini somewhat failed, as did many others born before and after him, was his inability to understand that the classical models he was using to organize the Mexica chronology conflicted with the chronology of the Mexica he himself described with such detail and admiration. He failed, however, to fully recognize that the Mexicas' model of the ages of the world (or of universal history) was as valid as the one Varro borrowed from the Egyptians and Vico borrowed from Varro.

It is well known that the Mexica divided time into five ages, or Suns, the Fifth Sun being the one indicating the present time, the time in which the cosmological locus of enunciation is situated (fig. 3.4). It is, in other words, those in the present who placed themselves under the Fifth Sun who were able to tell the story of the previous four. This implies that the previous Four Suns might not have existed, and that they were an invention of the present. Such an observation is not only valid for Mexica's ages of the world, but for Varro's and Vico's as well. Being both human inventions and being difficult to assess whether universal history *is* really divided in three or four ages, we should conclude that the one that prevails is the one that could be heard, rehearsed, and repeated. The Mexica Fifth Age remained as a proof of their rationality regarding chronology and calendaric organization, but not, unfortunately, one that could stand on its own next to Varro's and Vico's. Boturini, in other words, praised Mexica's own manners of writing history. He replaced it, however, with a Western chronological model. By commenting on these examples I should repeat, once again, that I am not interested in building on a critique of Boturini but on a learning experience. One of the lessons I am learning from Boturini is how easy it is to recognize others' values and how difficult it is to let them stand on their own.

A second aspect that deserves special attention is the fact that Mexica's five ages of the world were not characterized by the evolution of language and writing, but by an evolution of nourishment. During the first age, or Sun (Sun 4 Tigre) the main sustenance was *bellotas de encina* (holm oak acorn). During the second age (Sun 4 Wind) a transformation took place in basic nourishment and people ate a kind of water maize (*acecentli*). In the third age (Sun 4 Fire-Rain) a step forward was taken in food support and the *acecentli* was supplanted by *cincocopi*, a kind of root of maizelike plant. This change ended up in the fifth age (Sun 4 Movement) in which maize, the plant and edible encountered in almost every single narrative of origins of Amerindian people, becomes the principal nourishment. Thus, while Vico proposed a universal history divided in three ages with a particular

Fig. 3.4.   The Mexica fifty-two year cycle, divided in four parts of thirteen years each. Place and time are two sides of the same coin.

kind of language attached to each, Mexica believed in a universal history divided in five ages and with a particular kind of food attached to each. Vico's model survived, however, and it survived within a critical complicity with alphabetic writing. For even if Vico took a giant step in relation to Nebrija, both in his efforts to put alphabetic writing next to other writing forms and in his efforts to account for the simultaneity of the origin of speech invention and of the invention of writing, his own model remained within an ideology in which language (speech and writing) had the same privilege that food had in the Mexica model of universal history.

When Boturini's application of Varro's-Vico's model to organize Mexica history is looked at closely, one is astonished by the simultaneous superimposition and suppression of cultural models. For example, the Egyptians also divided universal history in three ages, but they could not have attached to each age a particular kind of language in the way that Varro, who lived in a period and culture in which the intellectual elites were in full possession of alphabetic writing, could have done.[55] Language, in other words, could be used as a distinctive feature in a model of universal history, but language is not necessarily a distinctive feature of universal history itself. Thus, Boturini stood at the crossroads between an Egyptian legacy transformed by Varro and incorporated it in the Western classical tradition. The Mexicas' own model of universal history was alien to both the Egyptian and the Western classical legacy, and the encounter between the Western and the Mexica models (or, better, people acting and interpreting according to different models of universal history) brought a new light into the practice and conceptualization of recording the past. Let's listen to what Boturini has to say about the issue:

> Siguiendo la idea de la celebre division de los tiempos, que enseñaron los Egypcios, he repartido la Historia Indiana en tres Edades: la primera, la de los Dioses: la segunda, la de los Heroes: La tercera, la de los Hombres, para baxar por grados succesivos hasta quando nuestros Indios se hallaron constituidos en sus Goviernos Humanos, y dilataron en la America sus Imperios, Reynos, y Señorios, y por fin conquistados por las Armas Españolas, se apartaron de sus antiguas Idolatrias, abrazando la Fe Catholica. . . . y desta suerte determine tratar de sus cosas en dichos tres tiempos, Divino, Heroyco, y Humano, que es lo mismo, que el doctisimo Varron explica en otros tres, Obscuro, Fabuloso, e Historico.[56]

[Following the idea of the famous division of time, as taught by the Egyptians, I have divided Indian History into three Ages; the first is the Age of the Gods; the Second, the Age of the Heroes; and third, the Age of Man. In this way there is a gradual descent to the point at which our Indians established their Humane Governments, and their Empires, Kingdoms, and Dominion spread throughout America until, vanquished by Spanish arms, they renounced their idolatrous ways and embraced the Catholic faith. . . . Thus I decided to describe their ways in the aforementioned three ages: Divine, Heroic, and Human, which are the same as those that the learned Varro explains as follows: Obscure, Mythical, and Historic.]

The tension between conflicting models naturally persisted—as I understand it—all along Boturini's book. The admiration for the Mexicas' exact chronology was not enough to accept it in its own right. Vico and Varro were authorities of Boturini's own cultural past that he could not avoid, while Mexican chronology was a remarkable construction that he could only admire. Thus, in chapter 3 of his _Nueva historia_ he followed Vico closely and attempted to characterize the ages of the world according to the language particular to it. He identified and described "the mute speech" ("hablar mudo," "parlari mutti") of the Divinity in the original time of Mexican civilization, applying Vico's lexicographic derivation and transformation of the Greek expression mythos into the Latin _mutus_ (mute, inarticulate).[57] Since Boturini did not have the philological background exhibited by his indirect mentor in developing his argument, he just stated the case in a form that could only be understood by someone familiar with Vico:

Mas creyeron en esta primera Edad, que todas las cosas necesarias, y utiles al sustento de la vida humana, eran verdaderas Deidades, y por esto las demostraron con Geroglificos Divinos mentales, que son unos Generos fingidos Divinos, que les enseño el entendimiento humano por aquella natural propensión de deleitarse de lo uniforme, y porque lo que no podían hacer con la abstracción de las formas por universales, lo hacian con los Retratos, y Semejanzas, las que iré explicando con una interpretación natural, clara, y evidente hasta el dia de hoy no sabida, y aun negada a los entendimientos Indianos. (_Idea,_ 9)[58]

[Yet in this first age they believed that all of the things that were necessary for sustaining human life were true deities, and consequently they depicted them intellectually with divine hieroglyphs, which are make-believe divine genres. These they learned through

human understanding and the natural tendency to take pleasure in
the uniform, and they did with portraits and likenesses what they
could not do with universally abstract forms, the likes of which I
shall explain with a natural, clear, and obvious interpretation, never
before seen, and withheld even from Indian understanding.]

Boturini solved the problems that Amerindian history presented to
someone making an effort to cast it in Vico's categories by listing and
describing thirteen major deities and explaining the meaning of each
of them in Aztec cosmology. For example, the first deity, Tezcatlipoca,
is described by Boturini as

Geroglifico de la Divina providencia, primera Deidad Indiana, da a
entender, como nuestros Gentiles confessaron se governaba el
Mundo por una Sabiduria Divina, que tenia su asiento en el Cielo, y
a su cuidado todas las cosas humanas. (*Idea,* 11)

[The hieroglyph of divine Providence, the first Indian deity, so to
speak, so our Gentiles acknowledged that the world was governed
by Divine Wisdom, whose throne was in heaven, and in whose care
were all human things.]

Moving from deity to deity, Boturini described the Mexicas' narrative of the origin and order of the world. His serial description was
preceded by an explanation of how the Mexicans wrote their histories:

Y porque no quedassen las primeras cosas con descuido olvidadas,
componían los Indios, y referian al pueblo la historia antigua con
una Fabulas Divinas, que separaré de las demas de otros tiempos,
llamandolas a su lugar adequado, y explicandolas en el propio sentido de sus Autores, que fueron Poetas Theologos, y baxo del sim-
ulacro de varias Deidades, pretendieron historiar las cosas de la
Religion, y costumbres de sus tiempos. (*Idea,* 10)

[And so that the first things would not be thoughtlessly forgotten,
the Indians composed the ancient history by dint of divine tales and
related them to the people, which separated them from all other
times, and they invoke them at the appropriate time, and deliver
them in the way their authors meant them to be, who were poet
theologians, and behind the image of various deities they sought
the histories of their religion and the customs of the times.]

Boturini closed his report of the first age by stating that since this
age was governed by the "mute language of the God" it must have

begun, of necessity, by simulating the divinities. At this point Boturini became aware of the difficulties of attuning the compatibility between the language (in the specific sense of Hebrew, Castilian, or Nahuatl) and language as "divine hieroglyph" of the first age. His account is very revealing of the difficulties he must have encountered. Boturini assumed that during the first age the "lengua muda de los Dioses" (the mute language of the gods) was prevailing. It was necessary, therefore, to have the simulacrum of the divinity since religion (or "providenza," according to Vico) was the very origin and foundation of all nations.[59] Thus,

> Y como era preciso, que en coordenar las lenguas (salvo la Hebrea, que empezó, y duró siempre lengua de un solo Dios) conviniessen los hombres en un comun pensamiento, assi les fue mas facil explicarse a los principios con Geroglificos Divinos, que como Generos mentales arrastraban tras de si en compendio dilatados conceptos, los que no podian estos primeros Fundadores dar a entender con la lengua articulada, la que fue en esta Edad muy escasa, y de palabras regularmente monosylabas, e imperativas, que discurso fueron, y son las raizes desta lengua Madre Indiana, Nahuatl, y con la que los primeros padres mandaban a sus hijos, y nietos las cosas, que debian executar, *pues me imagino que los subditos mas bien demostraban su obediencia con el silencio.*[60]

[And it was necessary that in coordinating the languages (with the exception of Hebrew, which was and ever shall be the language of one God) men agreed on a common mode of thought and so initially it was easier for them to express themselves with divine hieroglyphs, which they dragged behind them like intellectual genres in a compendium of vast concepts, and the first founders were unable to express such concepts articulately, for language in this age was limited, full of monosyllabic words, and imperatives, the basis of their speech, and the roots of the Indian mother tongue, Nahuatl, the language that the first fathers used to tell their children and grandchildren what to do, for I am sure that their subjects did nothing more than to obey in silence.]

It would be tempting here to accuse Boturini of having a generous imagination. It would be more beneficial, instead, to underline the foundations from which his imagination departs: a new concept of history and a new concept of the relations between history and writing come forth from the merging, in Boturini's persona, of Vico's theory and philosophy of writing and his own encounter with the records of

the ancient Mexicans. In this regard, no less interesting is Boturini's
interpretation of the historiography of the second age, in the light of
Vico's theory and philosophy of language and writing. The second
part, devoted to the age of heroes, was divided in two sections with a
transition chapter. In the first part, Boturini identifies the Symbols
Heroicos or symbols of the age of the heroes. He begins by describing
the signs of the sun and the moon and follows with a description of the
symbols of the days and the years. He clearly describes the interconnections between the four elements, the organization of space and
time, all represented by the same set of symbols (see figs. 3.4 and 3.5):

Tecpatl (Flint): South, Fire and one of the four seasons, depending
on sign dominating the year. For instance, when the year is domi-
nated by Actl, Tecpatl is Summer; but when Tecpatl dominates the
Year, Tecpatl is Spring.
Calli (House): East, Earth and same rotation of the four seasons
Tochtli (Rabbit): North, Air, and same rotation for the four seasons
Acatl (Reed): West, Water, and same rotation for the four seasons.

But he missed once again the opportunity to bring to the foreground that the Mexica magic number was four and not three (figs.
3.6, 3.7). The transition chapter is devoted to the transformation that
took place from the age of gods to the age of heroes. Boturini imag-
inatively concludes that a "Metamorphosis Indiana" could be written
as complement of the "Metamorphosis Ovidiana." Boturini clearly
agrees with Vico when he moves to the heroic and military symbols
and read arrows, bows, *escudos,* and so on as the language of the second age. Next to the heroic-military symbols, Boturini placed the
heroic-political symbols:

La misma Lengua Symbolica, que en el parrafo antecedente se
demostró ser Lengua de Armas, fue tambien lengua de Govierno,
con la qual nuestros Indios dieron razones de las tierras, que havian
habitado largos tiempos, llevandolas assimismo pintadas en sus escudos, y symbolizadas muy a lo vido, o por las peregrinas frutas, y
flores, que producian, o por algun particular esfuerzo, que hicieron
en desmontarlas, y reducirlas a la labor. (*Idea,* 77)

[The same symbolic language, which as previously stated is the
language of arms, was also the language of government, with which
our Indians gave accounts of their lands, which they had inhabited
for many years, and likewise they bore them painted on their
shields, and symbolized vividly, or by strange fruits and flowers that

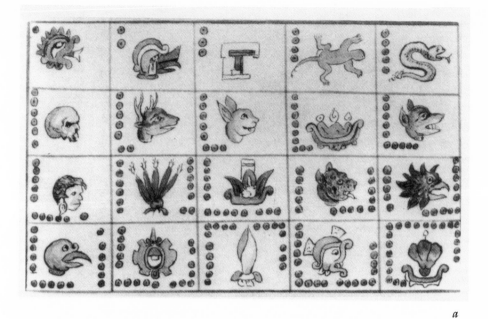

a

Eſta figura sellama. acatl ꝛ.
             caña

Eſta figura se dize tecpatl.

16

b

Fig. 3.5. *a,* The twenty days of the months. From left to right and top to bottom: alligator, wind, house, lizard, serpent; death, deer, rabbit, water, dog; monkey, wild grass, reed, jaguar, eagle; buzzard, motion, flint, rain, flower. From *Book of the Gods and Rites and the Ancient Calendar,* by Fray Diego Durán. Copyright © 1971 by the University of Oklahoma Press. *b,* Close up of two of the four signs of the thirteen-year cycle, reed and flint. The four signs of each thirteen-year cycle were also signs of the days.

they grew, or by some particular endeavor that they undertook to demolish them and reduce them to labor.]

Finally, he also placed, in the second age, the origin of a "raro modo de historiar" [a strange manner of writing history] by knots (what the Peruvians called quipu and the Mexicans *nepohualtzitzin*) and by oral songs, which Boturini considers to be either of historic or poetic value. It is worth quoting what Boturini has to say about the quipus as a manner of writing history, as an answer to Garcilaso's question to his uncle and Acosta's question to Tovar:

los Quipu llegaron a la mayor excelencia, y con tanta sublimidad de artificio, e ingenio duraron hasta la Conquista, que sirvieron a los Emperadores Incas para matricular sus innumerables Vassallos; dar

Fig. 3.6.   The shape of the world: space directions and time period, an example from the *Codex Féjérvary-Mayer*

razon de lo crecido de sus Exercitos, pues la situación de los Nudos subministraba una estraña Arithmetica de una como Columnas Decenarias, Centenarias, Miliarias, etc.; referir las Batallas, y Hazañas de sus Monarcas, y explicar todo aquello, que nosotros damos a entender con la escritura (alfabética, especificación mía, WM), y con la ayuda de estos Quipu, que fueron los monumentos mas antiguos de aquel Imperio, y se hallaron en los Archivos de la Imperial ciudad del Cuzco, y entre los Incas consanguíneos de los Emperadores, pudo el Nobilíssimo Historiador Garcilasso Inca de la Vega fundar la Historia, que escribió de su ilustre Patria. *Y porque, aun después de la Conquista, no podian tan facilmente los Indios peruanos entrar en el Alfabeto Europeo, y olvidar la antigua costumbre de sus Quipu, continuaron en usarlos algun tiempo en todos sus comercios, y necesidades de la vida; y el Padre Acosta refiere que vió una Muger llegar a la Iglesia con un manojo de cordones, y Nudos, con el qual abrió al Confessor las puertas de su conciencia.* (*Idea*, 85–86) (italics mine)

Fig. 3.7.   The shape of the world in Mesoamerica, from the *Codex Borgia*

[Quipus reached the utmost perfection, and with such sublime craftsmanship and ingenuity, that they lasted until the Conquest, for the Inca emperors used them to keep track of their many vassals; to take account of the extent of their armies, since the position of the knots furnished a strange arithmetic based, for example, on columns of tens, hundreds, and thousands, etc.; they were used to report battles, and the deeds of their rulers, and to explain all the things that we would explain with alphabetic writing, and, with the help of these quipus—which were the oldest testimonies of that empire, previously housed in the archives of the imperial city of Cuzco, as well as the blood relatives of the emperors themselves, the most noble historian Garcilaso Inca de la Vega was able to undertake the history of his illustrious homeland. And since, even after the conquest, the Peruvian Indians had some difficulty grasping the European alphabet and abandoning the ancient custom of the quipu, they carried on using them for some time in all their dealings and necessities of life; and according to Father Acosta, he saw a woman going to church with a handful of strings and knots, with which she opened the doors of her conscience to her confessor.]

Having recognized the proper way of recording the past in the age of gods and the age of heroes, Boturini moved to the age of human beings. At this point Boturini opened up a can of worms, perhaps without being fully aware of the implication of his move. It was also at this particular juncture that he began to dissociate himself from Vico, allowing for a critique of the Eurocentric perspective embedded in Vico's philosophy of language and history. Let's explore why.

The third age, which began in A.D. 660, is described in chapter 21. The year A.D. 660 is almost one thousand years before the "discovery" of the New World (1492) and the conquest of Mexico (1521). Consequently, the discovery and conquest themselves could not have been taken by the Mexica as a beginning of anything. What led Boturini to take the year A.D. 660 as the beginning of the third age was the fact that he was able to locate around those years the compilation of the first *teucamoxtli*, the written record par excellence, as distinguished from *amoxtli*, which referred to written records in general.[61] Boturini also made it clear that the history of the Amerindians had not yet been properly written by any European historian; this of course was true, but of relative importance. The history of the Europeans had not yet been written by any Amerindian either. The records Boturini had in his hands, along with Amerindian narratives written in alphabetic script by Amerindian historians such as Chimalpaín and Ixtlilxochitl, could have suggested to him that there were histories written by the other. And, in fact, Chimalpaín's inclusion in significant moments of the history of Spain, from 1479 to the conquest of Mexico and after, is a vivid example that a universal history could be written from different loci of enunciations within the same culture, which also means different cultural perspectives and models. Boturini naturally fell short once again and could not avoid the temptation of integrating the Amerindian past into a universal history written from a European perspective:

> En el dicho año 660 entró, rigorosamente hablando, en nuestros Indios la tercera Edad, ó sea el Tiempo Histórico, y assi se hace manifiesto, que mis trabajos Literarios, estendiendose desde la Confusion de las Lenguas, que fue el año de 2497, que calculé antes, fundado en la opinión de los LXX. hasta el de 660 de la Encarnacion, que fué el de 5859 de la Creacion del Mundo, segun dichos LXX. toman a su cargo la Historia de 3362 años, que por no haver entrado en poder de alguna otra Pluma, viene á ser privativamente mia, y de tanto gusto, y utilidad al Publico, que de balde la ignorancia se podrá ocupar en deslucirla. (*Idea,* 140)

> [Strictly speaking, that same year, 660, saw the arrival of the third age for our Indians, that is historical time, and so it becomes clear that my literary studies, which cover the time of the confusion of language, which took place in the year 2497, as I calculated previously, based on the opinion of the LXX, until the year 660 of the Incarnation, which was the year 5958, in the creation of the world, again according to the LXX, are dealing with the history of 3362, which, never having been written about before, is my exclusive privilege, and such an enjoyable one, and of such use to the public, that it would be foolish to claim otherwise.]

Perhaps because Boturini was following Vico, and Vico is not always easy to reduce into a single interpretation,[62] the integration of Amerindians to a European universal history could be interpreted following two lines of reasoning. One interpretation would have the Amerindians subordinated to universal history. The other would give priority to Amerindian history and perceive the conquest as part of an autonomous history (that of the Third Age) as well as a discontinuity of the regular flow of events and a "natural" way of recording them. In both cases, a diatopical (or pluritopic) hermeneutics is required, since Boturini makes evident that there is no reason to believe that one model of universal history is substantially more accurate than the other. Boturini's achievement, then, could be located in his subversion of one single principle held by previous Castilian and European

historians: that there is a natural and substantial complicity between
history and alphabetic writing, and that record keeping *without* letters
does not have the same authority as record keeping *with* letters.

163

*Record
Keeping
without
Letters*

Alternative Renaissance Legacies: Francesco Patrizi and Eguiara y Eguren

Boturini was not very successful in convincing people with his ideas.
He had on his side, however, a handful of Creole intellectuals in Mexico who, toward the mid–eighteenth century, were also reevaluating
the history of their country. As already mentioned in chapter 2, José de
Eguiara y Eguren wrote a monumental work known as *Bibliotheca
mexicana,* in five volumes, introduced by a prologue (or actually, a
series of twenty prologues [*anteloquia*]) in which he explained the
motivation of his enterprise and described, in general, the content of
the *Bibliotheca* (fig. 3.8). What makes Eguiara y Eguren's *Bibliotheca*
relevant to the previous discussion is the fact that, like Boturini, he
attributed great value to the documents and monuments of ancient
Mexico, but he did so under a different ideological program. It was the
growing national consciousness of Mexican intellectuals that drove
Eguiara y Eguren to a reevaluation of the "history" written by ancient
Mexicans rather than Vico's idea that oriented Boturini's perception.
Both coincided, however, in distinguishing the universality of record
keeping from the regionality of Renaissance historiographical conceptions that modeled the perceptions of missionaries and men of letters
during the sixteenth century. Eguiara y Eguren quoted a lengthy passage from Julián Garcés, first bishop of Tlaxcala, in a letter written in
1533 and addressed to Pope Paulo III:

> Pintaban, no escrivían: no usavan de letras, sino de pinturas. Si
> querían significar alguna cosa memorable, para que la supiesen los
> ausentes en tiempo o en lugar, usavan de pinturas, según aquello
> que insinuó Lucano, cuando dixo:

> Si avemo de dar crédito a <la> Fama
> Los de Faenicia fueron los primeros
> Que en toscos carateres se atrevieron
> a señalar las bozes duraderas.
> No avía sabido Memphis el secreto
> de escrivir en cortezas de los Biblios
> Solas las fieras, aves y animales
> Guardavan el lenguaje misterioso
> que estava en solas piedras esculpidos[63]

[They did not write, they painted: they did not use letters, but rather paintings. If they wanted to express something memorable, so that those absent in time or place would know of it, they used paintings, according to that which Lucan suggested, when he said:

If we are to give credit to Fame
Those of Phoenicia were the first
Who in rough characters ventured
to set lasting words.
Memphis had not known the secret
of writing on Biblios
Only the beasts, birds and animals
Guarded the mysterious language
that lay sculpted only in stone.[64]

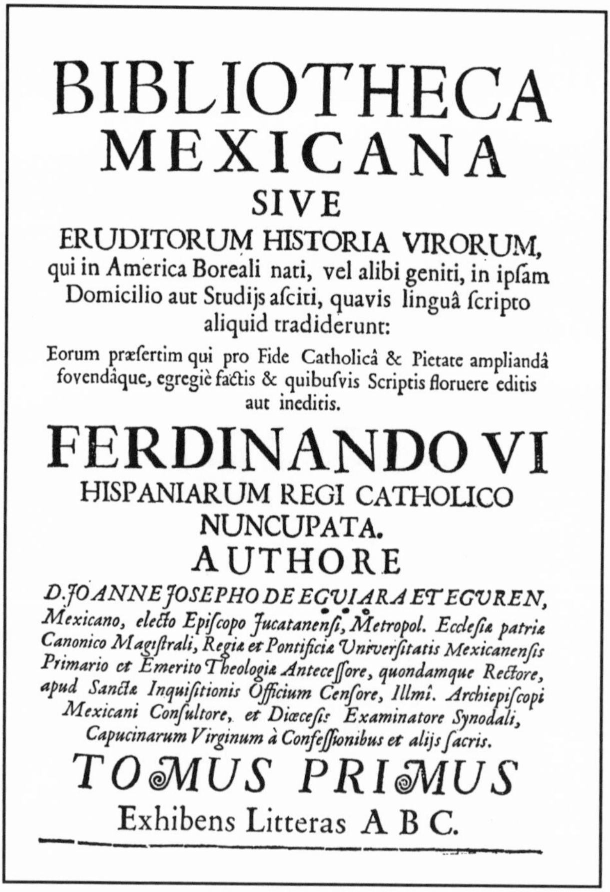

BIBLIOTHECA
MEXICANA
SIVE
ERUDITORUM HISTORIA VIRORUM,
qui in America Boreali nati, vel alibi geniti, in ipfam
Domicilio aut Studijs afciti, quavis linguâ fcripto
aliquid tradiderunt:

Eorum præfertim qui pro Fide Catholicâ & Pietate ampliandâ
fovendâque, egregiè factis & quibufvis Scriptis floruere editis
aut ineditis.

FERDINANDO VI
HISPANIARUM REGI CATHOLICO
NUNCUPATA.
AUTHORE
D. JOANNE JOSEPHO DE EGUIARA ET EGUREN,
Mexicano, electo Epifcopo Jucatanenfi, Metropol. Ecclefiæ patriæ
Canonico Magiftrali, Regiæ et Pontificiæ Univerfitatis Mexicanenfis
Primario et Emerito Theologiæ Antecefore, quondamque Rectore,
apud Sanctæ Inquifitionis Officium Cenfore, Illmi. Archiepifcopi
Mexicani Confultore, et Diæcefis Examinatore Synodali,
Capucinarum Virginum à Confefionibus et alijs facris.

TOMUS PRIMUS
Exhibens Litteras A B C.

Fig. 3.8. A *Bibliotheca mexicana*, describing ancient *amoxtli*

Eguiara y Eguren quoted this passage in order to defend the idea that although Mexicans were not familiar with alphabetic writing they, as many other civilized societies in the past, had their own writing system for recording the past. One can surmise, from the examples of Boturini and Eguiara y Eguren, that the Ciceronian concept of history was so attached to alphabetic writing that *res gestarum* became almost indistinguishable from *res gestae,* to the point that it was believed that history was made of words and things, and not that it was just one alternative among many of recording the past.[65]

A similar view was advanced during the sixteenth century by a dissident philosopher, Francesco Patrizi (fig. 3.9).[66] The celebration of the letter (as we have seen in chap. 1) and its complicity with history were so strong during the sixteenth century that an alternative perspective ran the risk of being condemned to oblivion. Francesco Patrizi

Fig. 3.9.   Rethinking what (in the West) history really is: frontispiece of Francesco Patrizi's *Della historia dieci dialoghi*

DELLA

HISTORIA

DIECE DIALOGHI

DI M. FRANCESCO PATRITIO

NE' QVALI SI RAGIONA DI TVTTE LE CO-
se appartenenti all'historia, & allo scriuerla, & all'osseruarla.

Con gratia, & Priuilegio per anni X.

IN VENETIA, APPRESSO ANDREA
ARRIVABENE,   M D L X.

was near both possibilities. The second half of the sixteenth century was, in Italy, the period in which historiographical treatises flourished. The Ciceronian tradition was the most relevant, although alternative views began to emerge in the voices of Bodin and Patrizi. The more political and law-oriented view of history defended by Bodin saw its days of glory during the eighteenth century, when the influence of rhetoric was declining.[67] The more eccentric view defended by Patrizi had less chances of survival in a society in which alphabetic literacy was one of the yardsticks used to measure civilizations, to consolidate the images of the self-same and its distinction from otherness.[68] Curiously enough, Patrizi's view also indirectly flourished in the eighteenth century in Vico's work, although the Italian philologue and philosopher did not make a concerted effort to rescue Patrizi's ideas from oblivion.

To better understand Patrizi's oppositional conception of history, let's remember the legacy of the rhetoricians of imperial Rome.[69] As we mentioned in the previous section, in sixteenth-century European universities rhetorical treatises such as *Ad herennium, De oratore,* and *Institutio oratoria* were on every reading list for a serious humanistic education. These treatises both constructed and conveyed the idea that history was narrative and that narrative was the "body" of history. Thus narrative was not only important in writing history, but also history was the true narrative itself. That is to say, history was both what happened and what was narrated, history and historiography. Consequently, there was not much difference in saying that history was narrative than in saying that history was the memory of past events in narrative form.

Patrizi was not really convinced that the Roman rhetorical legacy was the most satisfactory way of conceiving history. In his *De historia dieci dialoghi* (1560), he devotes book 1 to a dialogue in which he expects to arrive at a definition of history ("cosa l'historia sia"). Bidernuccio, one of the three participants in the dialogue, responds to Patrizi's question "what is history?" with the canonical Ciceronian definition: "L' historia e cosa fatta, remota dalla memoria de nostri tempi" [history is what happened in the past, removed from present memories]. Patrizi's answer was simple: he claimed that he did not understand what history was. He argued that he had found several contradictions in the definition of history provided by "external books" [*libri di fuori*]. And one of those contradictory definitions was the one sustained by Cicero: that history is the memory of past events, and the true narrative of those events. After a long debate in which Patrizi argued that history cannot only be conceived as a narrative of past events, but that it should also be considered as a narrative of *present and future events,* he concluded by stating that he finally grasped the idea of how history is made, but he insisted that he was not clear yet as to what history was. At this point Compte Giorgio, the third participant, intervenes by asking a seemingly rhetorical question: what else could history be but writing? Patrizi replied with another question: what if history was also *painting* (*pintura*)? If we consider this answer from the perspective presented by Acosta some twenty-five years later, it is, frankly, surprising. After questioning that history was just the narrative of the past, he questioned that historical narrative be considered only in terms of writing (implying, of course, alphabetic writing). One of the examples he provided was the history of Alexander III, painted in the hall of the Venetian Council. But certainly the dissident Patrizi was not content with just presenting the idea that a painting was as valid as (alphabetic) writing in relation to history: he pushed the issue further and defended the idea that sculpted and painted record keeping are more properly history than written ones, because they reveal the events to the eyes without need of mediation by words. At this point, and after questioning that history be considered nothing more than a narrative of past events and a written narrative, he moved to question whether history be narrative at all! He introduced his argument by asking a question to Bidernuccio: would you consider history sculptures and painting that include a narrative ("lettere narranti alcuna cosa")? Bidernuccio's answer is certainly affirmative, and the justification is that the words attached to sculptures or painting are true narratives of some kind of events. Patrizi consistently dissented and argued that history was not narration but memory. Memory is what counts—according to Patrizi—in a definition of what is history, and not the kind of signs employed to keep a record of past events. Since the example provided by Patrizi on this occasion was Egyptian history, which developed, according to him, from their manner of keeping records of the Nile's floods, I surmise that natural signs were also in Patrizi's view authorized means to preserve the memory of past events. It is at this point that Patrizi's concept of external books plays an important role in his argument.

The definition of history proposed by Patrizi implied a philosophy of language that diverged radically from the philosophy of language presupposed in the treatises by Roman rhetoricians. On the one hand, he had first enlarged record keeping to include nonalphabetic writing. Second, he introduced the distinction between *libri scritti di fuori* and *libri del alma*. And third, he introduced the distinction between *visible signs*, in which external books are written, as opposed to *mental images*, which are written in the "books of the soul."

Despite the efforts made by Boturini to restore some credit to the Amerindians' means of record keeping and the effort of his predecessor, Francesco Patrizi, to contest a restricted view of history dependent on the letter, individual struggles make their mark in the academic history of ideas, although not necessarily in the belief system attached to institutional power and the transmission of knowledge to future generations. Amerindian agencies to record and transmit their past have been silenced for several centuries. If they are resurfacing today, they are as interesting objects of study, and as oppositional voices of colonized subjects during and after the conquest and colonization began, but seldom as alternatives to Western modes of thought (previous to the sixteenth century). The past is a set of possible worlds that cannot be changed and voices that cannot be restored, but we could certainly change our current perception of the past by constructing new images of how things might have been if they were not what missionaries and men of letters told us they were. And certainly we have several ways of achieving our goals: one will be the adventure of reconstructing what might have happened; a second will be to reread the signs of the past in the context of our present concerns; a third will be to say that there is no choice and that reconstructing the past is not a concern *from* the past but *of* the present. The latter is the option I have chosen in this book.

Boturini's enthusiasm for Vico's concept of historical development as a way of correcting the legacy of previous chronists and historians regarding the Amerindians' lack of history prevented him from paying attention to their own concepts of chronological development, instead of imposing the model that Vico engineered based mainly on his experience of the classical tradition. Although Vico was aware of non-Western legacies, Greece is too strong a reference point of his thought not to be suspicious. In other words, Vico struggled between the legacy of the cultural tradition (Greco-Roman) of which he was a member and the knowledge he acquired about cultural traditions of which he was an outsider. Boturini celebrated Vico's new and challenging ideas with enthusiasm, yet he did not (and could not) take the model a step further and recognize that the "idea of a new history" was not just a new Western idea, but the uncovering of a new way of keeping historical records, both in the memory saved in the body of the elder as well as in the graphic inscriptions common to the great civilization of Mesoamerica and the weaving and knotting of the great Andean civilizations.

A large and increasing number of studies in the ethnography of speaking and on folk taxonomy over the past forty years have convincingly demonstrated that the Western categories of genres, so powerfully codified during the Renaissance and transmitted to the colonial periphery as part of the package of spreading alphabetic literacy, are, like Western concepts of history, a regional conceptualization of discursive types and not a theoretical construction that accurately describes and analyzes non-Western discursive typologies.

Concluding Remarks

I hope to have convinced the reader that the relations between history, fiction, and literature show a different configuration when we move back to the sixteenth century and look at the issue from a cross-cultural perspective and in colonial situations. There are, indeed, two different aspects deserving further considerations. One is the relationship between literature, history, fiction, and truth before the eighteenth century in the Western tradition. The other is the relationship between Western notions of literature, history, truth, and fiction and non-Western conceptualizations of record-keeping practices, oral and visual means of social interaction, systems of belief attached to different kinds of record keeping, as well as to oral and visual means of social interactions. These two aspects came together, comparatively, during the first stage of the massive spread of Western literacy that began with the expansion of the Spanish and Portuguese empires and Christianity.

In the following chapter I will explore certain aspects of Renaissance codification of knowledge throughout discursive practices. If history and literature (in Glissant's terms) became complicitous in imperial expansion after the eighteenth century, during the late Renaissance they had the encyclopedia and letter writing as companions. However, alphabetic writing (in connivance with Christianity) was the foundation not only of the massive transmission of information but also, and mainly, of its organization and evaluation. China, Islam, and the New World were all evaluated (in their organization and transmission of knowledge) with the yardstick of Renaissance discursive genres and their implicit epistemology.

Chapter 4

Genres as Social Practices: Histories, *Enkyclopaideias,* and the Limits of Knowledge and Understanding

Letter Writing, Human Communication, and Historiography

Peter Martyr (Pietro Martire d'Anghiera) was an Italian humanist who, around 1480, joined the court of Isabella and Ferdinand and became part of the intellectual movement that put Castile above all others in the Spanish kingdom. He was concerned with the political situation between Spain and Italy and shared Isabella's preoccupation with Castile as well as Ferdinand's interest in the Spanish domain in Europe. Since 1492, Peter Martyr had been attentive to the ramifications of Columbus's voyages and of Spanish explorations. His preferred means of expression and communication was letter writing, which, as he clearly articulated in a letter to his younger addressees, was a natural activity of a man of learning. In his letter to Gilberto, son of Count Borromeo, dated January 5, 1493, Peter Martyr stated:

> Tu padre, que me escribe con mucha frecuencia, me envía alguna vez que otra tus saludos, pero hasta ahora ninguna carta tuya. Por tanto, que voy a responder, si no me han llamado? Solo puedo decirte una cosa: hermosa tarea es en la juventud la de provocar a los mayores de edad: de ellos pueden, en cierto modo, robar lo que han de escribir por su cuenta. Si por verguenza—aunque esto no sea propio de gente honrada—no se atreven a hacerlo, adquirirán menos cultura y serán de menos utilidad.[1]

[Your father, who often corresponds with me, occasionally sends me your regards, but as yet I have not received a single letter from you. Therefore, what am I to reply, if I have not been called upon to answer? I can tell you one thing only: provoking one's elders is a beautiful task in one's youth; to a certain extent you can steal from them what you have to write yourself. If out of modesty—although this is unbecoming for honorable folk—you dare not do this, you will be less cultured and of less use.]

Letter writing as a mean of communication was a common practice toward the end of the fifteenth century among the humanists.[2] During the sixteenth century it also became a fundamental instrument of administrative control and government.[3] Alphabetic writing and letter writing (*epistola*) as a genre had at the time a long history in the West and during the process of colonization generated numerous communicative situations that were narrated in hundreds of anecdotes ranging from colonial Peru to colonial Nouvelle France (Canada).

Garcilaso de la Vega told a story that transcends the specific Andean context in which he situated it. An overseer in Lima sent ten melons to the landowner Antonio Solar, loaded on the back of two Indians. He also gave the Indians a letter to carry; at the same time he warned them not to eat the melons because if they did the letter would report their actions. During a pause in their travels, the Indians decided to taste the melons, but, aware that the letter could bear witness, they made sure it could not "see" them eating the melons.[4] The anecdote clearly depicts the cultural effect of a system of writing that can convey the saying of speech. In the West, particularly during and after the Renaissance, the purpose of writing was perceived as making the reader hear the spoken word behind it. According to this conception, the written word itself contained no information but merely transmitted information that was stored elsewhere. Thus, alphabetic writing, together with a conception of what it was, introduced a substantial modification in sending messages across space and time, since it provided a graphic form for replacing the spoken. The Indians reported by Garcilaso did not understand it. As is always the case, a tool and the discourse describing and justifying its uses grow and diversify themselves. One learns not only that *epistola* is, during the European Middle Ages, a means of communication across time and space but a sophisticated discourse about different kinds of *epistola* and how to write them. For instance, a distinction was made between *epistolis familiares* and *epistolis negotiales*.[5] The latter became a basic instrument in the expansion of the Spanish and Portuguese empire and in the organization of their overseas possessions. A new domain of letter

writing flourished during the Renaissance in which the *epistola* became not only a manner of family and business communication but
mainly of intellectual exchanges.[6] It is in this context that Peter Martyr joined letter writing with historiography at a time in which both
were heavily dependent on rhetoric.[7]

Kristeller has discussed letter writing and historiography as two
major genres of humanist literary production:

> The private letter was not merely a vehicle of personal communica-
> tion; it was intended from the beginning as a literary composition
> to be copied and read. The humanist letter-writers consciously imi-
> tated the classical example of Cicero or Seneca, and they wrote and
> collected and published their letters with the purpose of having
> them serve as models for their pupils and successors. Moreover, the
> letter served some of the functions of the newspaper at a time when
> there was no press and when communication was slow and uncer-
> tain.[8]

If the letter was, as Kristeller pointed out, a "substitute for a short
treatise of scholarly or literary or philosophical content," it was also—
particularly in the early years of explorations and conquest—strictly
linked to historiography, which in the writing of Peter Martyr and
Gonzalo Fernández de Oviedo y Valdés played the role of today's
newspaper. If the letter to Borromeo illustrates the first aspect of letter
writing underlined by Kristeller (models for their pupils, an educational method), the second aspect could be illustrated by the letters in
which Peter Martyr begins to write about Columbus:

> Desde el primer origen y designio reciente de acometer Colón esta
> empresa del Océano, amigos y príncipes me estimulaban con cartas
> desde Roma a que escribiera lo que había sucedido pues estaban
> llenos de suma admiración al saber que se habían descubierto
> nuevos territorios y nuevas gentes, que vivían desnuda y a lo natu-
> ral, y asi tenían ardiente deseo de saber estas cosas.[9]

> [From the earliest beginnings of Columbus's oceanic enterprise to
> his more recent plans, friends and princes incited me with letters
> from Rome to write about what had happened, since they were
> filled with utmost admiration upon knowing that [he] had discov-
> ered new territories and peoples, who lived naked and in a natural
> state, such that they possessed an ardent desire to know of these
> things.][10]

Reading Peter Martyr's epistolary during the early years of the
"discovery" is an experience quite different from reading his *De orbe*

novo decades. While the latter is an epistolary narrative in which most contemporary events indirectly related to Columbus's enterprise have been eliminated, the epistolary (as a daily paper) moves freely from news reported from a "certain Columbus, from Liguria," to the events in Spain as well as in Italy and France. The meaning of Columbus's voyage, as seen in the epistolary of Peter Martyr, could be compared with the way in which, one century later, Muñón Chimalpaín in Mexico inserted the information about Columbus into his chronicles of the ancient Mexican. In Peter Martyr's epistolary, Columbus barely makes the news, he was so busy keeping track of the political situation in Castile and Italy. In Chimalpaín's *relación*, Columbus barely makes the news, busy as he is in keeping track of the history of ancient Mexicans. Peter Martyr introduces a short paragraph about Columbus in a letter addressed to Juan Borromeo (Golden Knight), between one paragraph devoted to an attempt to assassinate the king and another on the French invasion of Italy, a series of events that, around 1540, will be used by Guicciardini to write his history of Italy. Between those two paragraphs, Peter Martyr introduces the following:

> Hace pocos días volvió de los antípodas occidentales cierto Colón, de Liguria, quien a duras penas consiguió de mis Reyes tres naves, porque creían quiméricas las cosas que decía. Ha regresado trayendo como pruebas muchas cosas preciosas, pero principalmente oro que, naturalmente, se produce en aquellas regiones. *Pero demos de lado a las cosas ajenas, ilustre Conde, pasémoslas por alto.*[11]

> [A few days ago, there returned from the Western antipodes a certain Columbus, from Liguria, who had with great difficulty acquired three ships from my king and queen, for they believed the things he said to be chimerical. He has returned, bringing as proof many precious things; but principally gold which, naturally, is produced in those regions. But let us leave aside these irrelevant matters, illustrious count, let us pass over them.]

The event that was perceived by Columbus himself, and by López de Gómara (1511–64) sixty years after the fact in *Hispania vitrix,* as a milestone after the creation of the world had no consequences for Peter Martyr in comparison with the political crisis the Italians were enduring. Unlike Peter Martyr, Muñón Chimalpaín wrote his *Relaciones originales de Chalco-Amaquemecan* in Nahuatl instead of Latin. And he wrote them toward the beginning of the seventeenth century in Mexico instead of at the end of the fifteenth century in Barcelona, in the court of Castile and Aragon. Chimalpaín's *Relaciones,* written in a chroniclelike form, has two entries for the year 1493 (or 13 Pedernal in Mexica chronology). The first is devoted to a sun eclipse, to the battle of Acatlán and to the birth of Cacamatzin Teohuateuhctli, lord of Amaquemecan, and so on. The second entry is devoted to Columbus. It begins at the moment in which Columbus is given three ships and 120 men. Chimalpaín narrates the "discovery of America" in the following manner:

> Pero el viernes 12 del mes de octubre del mismo año de 1492, dos de los vigías vieron aparecer tierra hacia la hora del alba. Con la señal de tierra todos se regocijaron y gran descanso experimentaron sus corazones. Cuando llegaron *allá* observaron que estaba habitada *aquella* tierra, y directamente dirigieron sus barcas a una playa baja. *Aquel* lugar donde tocaron era el llamado Guanahamí.[12]

> [But on Friday the twelfth, in the month of October in that same year of 1492, two of the lookouts saw land appear around the hour of dawn. With the sighting of land, all of them rejoiced and their hearts felt great relief. When they arrived there, they observed that the land was inhabited, and at once steered their boats toward a low beach. That place where they landed was known as Guanahani.][13]

Contemporary to the writing of Peter Martyr, Columbus's voyage was also alien to an Italian in the court of Castile. A century after the "discovery," Columbus's voyage was also alien to a Mexican for whom the events of Spanish history were marginal to the history of his people, both because Spain was different territory and because Columbus arrived at a place that was not his own, as is clearly shown by the demonstratives Chimalpaín uses: "allá" [over there]; "aquella tierra" [that land over there]; "aquel lugar" [that place over there].

Reporting Foreign Events and Writing Ethnic Histories

Peter Martyr's coexistence with the discovery and conquest of Tenochtitlán should not be the only reason to distinguish his *De orbe novo decades* from other genres of historiographical writings. Also important is the fact that Peter Martyr wrote a history twice removed from his own personal story: first because, as he clearly stated in the letter in which he informed Borromeo about "someone named Columbus, from Liguria," such events were alien to him; second, because he was in an even less adequate position to talk about the Amerindians. Briefly, neither the Spaniards' deeds nor the Amerindians' customs, society, and religion were part of the memory of his people. A comparison with Guicciardini's history of Italy could be helpful here. The periods covered by Peter Martyr's *Decades* and Guicciardini's history are very similar. The former moves from 1492 to 1530, the latter from 1490 to 1534. Guicciardini, contrary to Martyr, wrote the history of his own people, in a moment of historical distress for his country. Guicciardini, who was born in 1483 and died in 1540, was also a contemporary of the events he narrated, although he was some thirty years younger than Peter Martyr.

> I have determined to write about those events which have occurred in Italy within our memory, even since French Troops, summoned by our own princes, began to stir up very great dissensions here: a most memorable subject in view of its scope and variety, and full of the most terrible happenings; since for so many years Italy suffered all those calamities with which miserable mortals are usually afflicted, sometimes because of the just anger of God, and sometimes because of the impiety and wickedness of other men.[14]

During the same years that the "Italian calamities" were beginning, Peter Martyr was celebrating the end of the "Castilian calamities":

> Este es el fin de las calamidades de España, este es el término de los felices hados de esta gente bárbara que hace—segun dicen—unos ochocientos años, al mando del conde Julian, vino de Mauritania—de donde siempre conservaron el nombre de Moros—y oprimió cruel y arrogantemente a la vencida España. Oh dolor! cuanto fue hasta ahora su crueldad, su fiereza e inhumanidad para con los cautivos cristianos. Al fin, mis Reyes, adeptos a Dios, derivan por tierra aquella cruel tiranía, quebrantada por los descalabros de años enteros.[15]

> [This is the end of the calamities of Spain, this is the turning point of the good fortune of this barbarous people who—as they say—some eight hundred years ago, under the command of Count Julian, came from Mauritania, from whose name they are called Moors, and they oppressed and vanquished Spain with arrogance and cruelty. Oh woe! Their cruelty, their ferocity, and inhumanity against the Christian captives is unsurpassed. Finally, your Majesties, under God's auspices, you are bringing down that cruel tyranny, which has been broken by years of constant defeat.]

Peter Martyr's celebration of Castilian success did not restrain him from forewarning of the events that would soon take place in Italy. He

anticipated them in a consolatory letter he addressed to Cardinal Asca-
nio Visconti on the death of Cardinal Arcimboldi. Peter Martyr sus-
pected, in a letter dated June 2, 1492, that a war between Italy and
France was imminent. But while Peter Martyr was conversing with his
Italian peers about the Italian events, he was also informing the archbishop of Granada as well as Castilian noblemen about the Italian
political climate. In a letter dated September 1, 1492, and addressed to
the count of Tendilla:

> Atencion!, ilustre Conde, que circula el rumor de que Alfonso,
> futuro sucesor del Rey Fernando en el reino de Napoles, ha arra-
> strado a su padre a que trate con el Rey Carlos de Francia de arro-
> jarle del gobierno del ducado de Milán a Ludovico Sforza, porque
> se opone a entregar las riendas del ducado al joven Juan Galezzo,
> yerno de Alfonso.[16]

> [Beware, illustrious Count! For rumor has it that Alfonso, future
> successor of King Fernando in the kingdom of Naples, has put it
> into his father's head to negotiate with King Charles of France with
> the aim of ousting Ludovico Sforza from the government of the
> duchy of Milan, because he refuses to relinquish control of the
> duchy to Juan Galezzo the younger, Alfonso's son-in-law.]

Peter Martyr was becoming increasingly concerned with the Italian
situation toward the end of 1492 and the beginning of 1493. The very
days in which Columbus approached the Indies, Peter Martyr was
writing about the "presagios" and "pronósticos" of the Italian crisis.
He observed in a letter addressed to Scanio Sforza, viscount, cardinal,
and vice-chancellor that

> Noto, ilustrísimo Príncipe, que se está preparando un nuevo es-
> trépito de armas y escucho con avidez los nuevos y perniciosos
> planes que se barajan para llamar a los franceses a Italia. . . . Yo, que
> me duelo de las cosas de mi patria—de la cual siempre fueron los
> franceses enemigos encarnizados—opino que no debe meterse en
> el propio lecho una víbora o un escorpión para que con su veneno
> inficione el del vecino.[17]

> [I observe, illustrious Prince, that a new clash of arms is being
> prepared, and hear with piqued interest the new and pernicious
> plans being laid to call the French to Italy. . . . I, who am pained by
> the affairs of my country—of which the French were always bitter
> enemies—hold that one should not admit a viper or scorpion into

one's own bed, so that with its poison it may infect that of its neighbor.]

It was the "Italian calamities" that required the attention of a historian such as Guicciardini, and those were the events being witnessed with a dramatic intensity by Italians in Italy and abroad. In Spain, Nebrija was devoting his energy to teaching Latin and the humanities in an Iberian Peninsula that he perceived, after his years of study in Rome, as dominated by the barbarians, and to normalizing Castilian orthography. Thus, the intensity of the events was perceived differently by persons involved in, influenced by, or observing them while writing their "histories" in letter form (e.g., Martyr as an anchorman in TV reports) or in a proper historiographical narrative (e.g., Guicciardini writing, circa 1540, the history of Italy from 1494 to 1535). All in all, while Guicciardini, by writing the history of Italy, joined the voices of previous Italian historians of the city-states (like Bruni or Biondo) and contributed to the imaginary construction of Italy after the fall of the Roman Empire, Martyr reported about events that were happening, so to speak, in front of his eyes and about people (Amerindians) he had only the slightest idea about.

Telling What Happened and Constructing Historical Events

The distance between the events narrated, the acts of narration, and the evaluation of the past are all intervening factors in the way social interactions began to be construed as historical events. The organization, evaluation, and transmission of a *set* of events as *historical* events are in large scale dependent on the rhetorical restrictions of narrative genres as well as on the skill of the person narrating them, in oral or graphic form. I am concerned, however, with the personal positioning of the writer or storyteller in the narration of events and how a person carves his or her locus of enunciation at the intersection of the events narrated, personal stories, and the communicative situation he or she put her- or himself in by writing or narrating an event. In this chapter I am more interested in genre restrictions than in personal skills for the construction (organization, evaluation, and transmission) of knowledge. Discursive frames (or genres) are a necessary condition for constructing knowledge, as they depend both on regional cultural traditions as well as on the means of communication (e.g., oral or graphic).

Peter Martyr is, thus, a telling example of the crossroads between the genre legacy of Italian humanism, a personal story of the witness in exile who deplored the situation in his own country and celebrated the

consolidation of the kingdom of Castile and the excitement of transoceanic navigations. As an Italian and a humanist, he was concerned
with the political situation of his country, which he discussed with his
peers in epistolary writing. As an Italian in Spain, he was not concerned with the construction of Castilian territoriality along the lines
of peninsular historiography since Alfonso el Sabio (1221–84) and El
Gerundense (1421–84).[18] Further, an Italian in Spain, Peter Martyr
was not involved in the exploration and colonization of the Indies but
was a witness and an informant from whom his Italian peers requested
information. His *locus enunciationis* was constructed, among other
features, by the voice of a humanist well versed in languages (in the
studia humanitatis), well acquainted with the Greco-Roman tradition, and well connected with the intellectuals and public figures of his
time. His discourse about the New World, therefore, was the discourse of a humanist interested in understanding and disseminating
information rather than the discourse of the humanist interested in
the pragmatic and legal aspect of the conquest, or a historian interested in the construction of Castilian territoriality, such as Florian de
Ocampo (Charles V's historian) or Ambrosio de Morales (Philip II's
historian).[19] If, as a humanist, he believed in epistolary communication, as a historian he arranged the letters in another discursive genre,
the *Decades,* a narrative form strictly related to the book (as sign carrier) and alphabetic writing (as fixation of oral discourse). The *Decades*
cannot be conceived without the inscription of the letter and the
format of the book. From epistolography to historical writing there
was not much difference: assembling, organizing, and transmitting
information in the form of historiographical narrative confronted the
New World historian with problems radically different from those faced
by his Italian or Spanish fellows, who dealt with a subject matter deeply
engraved in the historian's (own as well as the people's) memory.

O'Gorman has pointed out the interfaces between epistolography
and historiography in Peter Martyr. He has also critically examined the
common opinion that Peter Martyr has the distinction of being the
earliest historian of the New World, by asking "in what sense are Peter
Martyr's *Decades* history?"[20] O'Gorman's answer to his own question
points toward the links between New World histories, Renaissance
historiography, and literacy:

Podemos decir, en conclusión, que las *Décadas* seguramente cons-
tituyen por su intención primaria una obra de índole historiográfica
del tipo formal renacentista; pero como, al mismo tiempo, exhiben
rasgos de una cierta fresca ingenuidad que recuerda el arcaísmo de
un Herodoto, es preciso matizar esa clasificación para vincular tam-

bién las *Décadas* a la gran corriente tradicional de los libros de viaje,
por más que su autor no haya pasado a las regiones en que tan
difusamente se ocupa. Se trata de un fenómeno en extremo intere-
sante, merecedor de más atención de la que ha recibido; *es algo así
como un salto atrás dentro del desarrollo ideológico del proceso de la
historiografía.* Pero no un salto atrás debido a un reaccionarismo
impuesto por las exigencias de nuevos temas, de nuevos problemas
que no encontraban facil cabida dentro de los moldes forjados por
la erudición y el gusto profesionales de la época. *En apariencia,
pues, es una especie de marcha atrás, pero su verdadero sentido estriba
en que se inicia así la renovación de la problemática del conocimiento
histórico que languidecía en la ya estéril prisión de los cartabones
tradicionales* y, en efecto, es de notarse a este respecto que la gran
revolución que en ese campo representa el pensamiento del siblo
XVIII, no pudo haberse realizado sin la extraordinaria apertura de
los horizontes temáticos debida, precisamente, a los cronistas indianos, y que duda cabe, que a Pedro Martyr le corresponde un sitio
preeminente en esa empresa.[21]

[In conclusion, we can say with all certainty that, given its primary
intention, the *Decades* constituted a sort of historiographical work
of the formal type found in the Renaissance; but since, at the same
time, there are characteristics of a fresh candor that recall the archa-
ism of Herodotus, it is necessary to sharpen this classification so as
to link the *Decades* to the great traditional trend of travel literature,
since the author has not been to the regions upon which he vari-
ously expounds. We are dealing with an extremely interesting phenomenon, worthy of more attention than it has previously received;
*it is something of a leap backward within the ideological development
of the process of historiography.* Yes, it is not a leap backward due to its
reactionary nature, a nature imposed upon it by the demands of
new themes, new problems that could not easily be accommodated
within the established erudite molds and the professional tastes of
the age. *In appearance, then, it is a sort of step backward, but its true
meaning stems from the fact that it forces us to reconsider problems of
historical knowledge, problems that languished in the sterile prison of
traditional bevels* and, in fact, it is worth pointing out in this respect
that the great revolution that eighteenth-century thought represents in this field could not have taken place without the extraordinary opening of thematic horizons due precisely to the Indian
chroniclers, and there is little doubt that Peter Martyr plays a pre-
eminent part in this enterprise.]

If we disregard O'Gorman's rhetoric and place the accent on the organization of knowledge rather than on its content, the intuition that Peter Martyr's *Decades* is a step back in the history of historiography should be emphasized. New World histories of the sixteenth century, beginning with Peter Martyr's, resembled Herodotus's *istoria* rather than the *historia* of the Romans and humanists, for at least three reasons. The most obvious, which I have already mentioned, is the synchrony between the events reported and the life span of the historians reporting them. The investigation of the historian based on the report of eyewitnesses (like Peter Martyr) or a combination of eyewitnesses and direct experience (like Oviedo y Valdés, las Casas, or Acosta) are the most obvious characteristics of sixteenth-century historiography. A second reason is the historian's contact with unknown lands and unknown people, which parallels much of Herodotus's investigation rather than Roman or humanist historians narrating the past of their own empire or city-states. A third peculiarity is the encounter between a person who is able to organize knowledge in alphabetic writing and in book form with people without alphabetic writing whose concept of the past and whose manner of recording and telling stories about the past were totally alien to Western narrative rationality.

Since I have already discussed the first reason in the previous paragraphs, let's explore further the second and third. What distinguished Roman historians from Herodotus was the fact that while Herodotus worked in the boundaries between Greek and foreign worlds and cultures, Roman historians were mainly concerned with constructing the space and memories of Roman territoriality. The experiences of humanist historians were closer to the latter than to the former.[22] Cities like Florence were former colonies of the Roman Empire that developed into powerful city-states, powerful enough to have originators and executors of historiographical writing. Cities like Rome, formerly the center of a political and economic empire, became the center of the Christian world and, therefore, powerful enough to justify the writing of their history. Consequently, when Bruni wrote the history of Florence and Biondo the history of Rome, they were looking back to ten centuries of history in the Italian peninsula. Their experience was quite different from a peripatetic historian like Herodotus reporting what he saw or heard, or of a sedentary one like Peter Martyr who received written information from eyewitnesses about distant lands and peoples, when alphabetic writing was already established in a wide range of the population.

If in historiographical writing (as well as in other discursive genres) we can identify and distinguish three kinds of agents (the originator, the executor or historian, and the source of information [or informant]) and a set of discursive genres (or frames), then Peter Martyr not only has the distinction of having written a history in letter-writing form but also of having been informed by means of letters. There is then a mirrorlike image between the date the event materialized and was reported in epistolary form by an eyewitness agent, on the one hand, and the moment when Peter Martyr received a bundle of letters from the New World and wrote further letters in which he reported to his Italian confreres the events that materialized a few months earlier. Peter Martyr's rapport with this source-based knowledge was quite different from the negotiations of humanist historians with their sources. Cochrane has distinguished in Bruni's (1369–1444) history of Florence the informant- or source-based knowledge (medieval chronicles and *ricordanzas* or memory books written by members of wealthy Florentine families) and the non-source-based knowledge or discursive genres, mainly the Roman historians.[23] Peter Martyr could not have delved into the past of the subject matter he was writing about, for the discursive genre that provided him with the source-based knowledge was the same genre in which he had to organize and transmit knowledge.

Letter writing is, in the first place, the closest substitute to oral conversation. When the interlocutors are not sharing the same physical space (and there are no voice carriers such as the telephone or tape recorder), alphabetic writing allows the transmission of knowledge across space. Historiography, which toward the end of the fifteenth century occupied a particular place next to poetry in the context of the trivium (grammar, rhetoric, and logic), rested—as the trivium itself indicates—on alphabetic writing and on graphic records (coins, medals, architecture, as well as all sorts of written records). Historiographical writing was not a mirror image of source-based knowledge, as it was for Peter Martyr, who offered a formidable example of the connivance between the letter (i.e., alphabet), letter writing, and historiography in the acquisition, organization, and transmission of knowledge. It is helpful to remember, also, that while *istoria* in Greek meant report of an eyewitness, letter writing (in English) refers to a form of communication that "carries" the voice that cannot be heard in a graphic record that could be read. The Spanish translation of letter writing is *carta*. The *Diccionario de autoridades* (the eighteenth-century dictionary of the Academy of Spanish Language) reports that *carta* comes from the Latin *charta*, which means the skin of an animal or the bark of a tree in which a message to be immediately carried out to his/her receiver was written down (see chap. 2). *Epistola*, in Latin, was used to refer to a written and direct communication between people and was semantically and culturally related to a messenger (*epistularis*) of Jupiter—very much used, also, in the context of government as a social practice performed by the *epistulares* (or secretaries of the state).

Genres, Audiences, and Packaging Information

So far I have described the relationship between two of the agents involved (the executor, letter writer, or historian) and the informant. Let's explore further the relationship between the executor (letter writer or historian) and the originators of the letters and the *Decades*. The last seven *Decades* were dated 1524, thirty years after the first, when the author was about seventy years old. They were dedicated to Francisco Mario Sforza, duke of Milan. Peter Martyr opens the last *Decade* by tracing the history of their originators:

> La primera de mis *Décadas* acerca del Nuevo Mundo dediquela al tío paterno de Su Excelencia, el vicecanciller Ascanio, Príncipe Ilustrísimo que fue entre los cardenales, y por ninguno aventajado, *porque con reiteradas instancias me mandaba comunicar a su Excelencia lo que aconteciera en esas regiones occidentales.* Como insigne testimonio de lo que digo te ofrezco Marino Caracciolo, hombre dotado de todas las virtudes y experiencias, protonotario Apostólico electo de Catania, y al presente embajador junto a tu persona, el cual era secretario de Ascanio cuando el Oceano comenzaba a abrirnos sus puertas, cerradas desde el principio del mundo hasta nuestros días. El era—y así lo declara—quien recibía mis escritos en nombre de su señor y redactaba sus respuestas, según se las dictaba.[24]

> [I dedicated the first book of my *Decades* about the New World to Your Excellency's paternal uncle, Vice-Chancellor Ascanio, Illustrious Prince, who surpassed cardinals and all others in excellence, *for by persistent demand he ordered me to send report to your Excellency of what was happening in these western regions.* As distinguished testimony of what I say I present Marino Caracciolo, a man endowed with all virtues and experiences, Apostolic notary elect of Catania, at present your personal ambassador, who was Ascanio's secretary when the ocean first opened its doors to us, which had been closed since the earth's creation until our time. It was he as he himself declares—who received my writings in your lord's name and wrote the replies, as they were dictated to him.]

The events of the New World were a theme of conversation and a curiosity that Peter Martyr is in a position to satisfy. Whatever he said, based on the information he gathered and his learned judgment, had as much to do with the content of the letters he received from the Indies as it did with what he imagined were the expectations of his readers, which he construed on the basis of his familiarity with the Italian cultural and historical context. One of the differences between letter writing and writing history is that in the first case the personal knowledge of the addressee shapes to a certain extent the presentation of the material. However, because the humanists considered letter writing a genre that deserved to reach the printed press and the book form, when Peter Martyr moved from writing letters to writing history in epistolary form, he managed to keep the personal tone characteristic of personal letters and to reach—at the same time—a larger and more impersonal audience.

The reasons Peter Martyr offered for writing the *De orbe novo decades* were related to the mixed genres, letter writing and historical narrative, he had selected. Thus, if according to the historiographical principles of the time he stated that one of the reasons for writing the *De orbe novo decades* was "salvar del olvido tan grandiosos acontecimientos" [to rescue from oblivion such magnificent events], there were also important reasons not necessarily related to the historical dimension of the events that played an important role in Peter Martyr's decision-making process, since it would have been hard for him to have a "historical perspective" on events that were happening in his own present.

> Fallecido Ascanio, y caído yo en la desidia por falta de estímulos, fue el Rey Federico, antes de que la fortuna se le tornara de madre cariñosa, en dura madrastra, quien recibió seguidas ediciones de mi libro por medio del cardenal de Aragón, su primo. Estimulado más tarde por el Pontífice Máximo León X y sucesor Adriano VI, quienes me aconsejaron salvar del olvido tan grandiosos acontecimientos, les dediqué el conjunto de las *Décadas* que andan impresas. A tí, Príncipe Ilustrísmo, que naciste tarde, y subiste tarde al trono de tus mayores, quiero referirte los acontecimientos sobrevenidos.[25]

> [After the death of Ascanio, when I had fallen into idleness through lack of incentive, it was King Frederick, before fortune took him from his loving mother to his harsh stepmother, who received consecutive editions of my book from the cardinal of Aragon, his cousin. Inspired at a later date by Pope Maximus Leon X and his successor Adrian VI, both of whom advised me to rescue such great events from oblivion, I dedicated the entire printed version of the

Decades to them. I would like, Illustrious Prince, who was born too late and came too late to the throne of your elders, to recount to you the events that took place.]

The *Decades*, very much like the letters he began to write about Columbus's voyages, were motivated by the curiosity of his Italian acquaintances rather than the Crown of Castile or his own desire to use his writing about the New World as self-promotion. Peter Martyr looked much like Vespucci. Both were Italians working for the Castilian Crown. Both had intellectuals and friends among the Italian nobility. Their writing, therefore, distinguished them from the writing of Columbus (in the case of Vespucci) and of Oviedo y Valdés (in the case of Martyr) not so much in terms of nationality (Columbus was also Italian, after all), but in terms of the addressees of their writings. Columbus's addressees were the queen and king or served as official administrators of the Crown (e.g., Santander). Instead, Vespucci and Peter Martyr wrote their letters to friends and acquaintances in Italy. Oviedo y Valdés, who lived in Santo Domingo from 1514 to 1557 and served as official chronicler after 1532, made of his writing an instrument of service to the Crown and to his own self-promotion.[26]

The difficulties of finding a niche among generic categories that Peter Martyr's *Decades* presents could be attenuated if instead of making it fit into one category (letter writing or history), an effort is made to describe the mobility and the flexibility of its organization and to explain why it is so. Peter Martyr wrote under the guidance of well-established conventions and norms. The norms of letter writing and of organizing a long and detailed narrative about a given subject were well established. *De orbe novo decades,* then, singled out from the outset a topic, a referent and an organization of the material. The question remains, however: why then have a history in which historiographical principle has been invoked? Was there a necessary connection between "decades" and "history"? Were they equivalents? Did only historical narratives conform to the "decades" format? The reader must forgive me for recalling the meaning of "decade": a discursive type for the organization and transmission of knowledge according to which each unit (decade) is comprised of ten subunits (chapters), and the entire book also comprises ten units or decades. It is a systematic and symmetric way of organizing knowledge that fits the taste for order, equilibrium, and harmony of the Renaissance humanists and their public. While letter writing allowed Peter Martyr to correspond continually with his Italian confreres, the *Decades* allowed him to fit a chaotic amount of contemporary information into a well-ordered and harmonious whole. Finally, the invocation of history placed his writing in the context of memory against oblivion, one of the functions that Cicero attributed to history writing. There is nothing wrong then in accepting *De orbe novo decades* at the same time as decades (the organization of knowledge at the level of the *dispositio*) and letter writing (organization of knowledge at the level of the *appelatio*), modeling it according to the specific person being addressed. The difficulties exist only if our goal is to fit every possible text into one and only one discursive type, instead of understanding the complexities of a text in the context of the discursive types available to the writer and the audience, as well as the interaction of norms and conventions.

The Truth Is Also Relative to the Locus of Enunciation and the Norms of the Genre: Histories, Encyclopedias, and *Calepinos*

I have compared Peter Martyr with Guicciardini and have mentioned Leonardo Bruni a couple of times. A comparison between an Italian from Areto who wrote about Florence toward 1440 and an Italian from Milan, who studied in Rome from 1477 to 1487, then moved to Spain to fight against the Moors, finally became a priest and *un hombre de la corte* (a gentleman of the court) and ultimately spent thirty years of his life writing about the New World to his Italian friends, might sound somewhat far-fetched. It is not, however, once we recall that the comparison is being made in order to pin down the differences between humanist historiography and New World histories. The set of questions summarized under who is writing what, for whom, and why, acquires in the comparison a new meaning. New World histories, even in the form they take in the work of Peter Martyr (a man of letters writing in Latin to his fellow Italians about the New World) opened up the gates toward an understanding of the darker side of the Renaissance and of humanist historiography. The archive (e.g., the *ricordanza* used by Bruni) and the classical authors are replaced by daily information; letter writing is, on the one hand, the document equivalent to the *ricordanza* but without the temporal distance between the moment in which the events took place and the moment they are organized, interpreted, and transmitted; on the other hand, letter writing is not only the document but also the genre of the scholarly discourse. Letter writing became, in Peter Martyr, the substitute of Bruni's well-organized narrative based on the source-based knowledge provided by *ricordanza* and medieval chronicles and of the non-source-based knowledge furnished by previous Greco-Roman histo-

rians. If Leonardo Bruni has the distinction of marking the beginning
of humanist historiography,[27] Peter Martyr, a humanist himself, has
the distinction of inaugurating the kind of writing that will be a distinctive feature of the darker side of European Renaissance and humanist historiography: the hybrid cultural products generated by and
in colonial situations.

Bernardino de Sahagún, whom we have already encountered in the
previous chapters, was a Franciscan who, contrary to Peter Martyr,
went to Mexico in 1529 and lived and wrote there the rest of his life.
He divided his work into twelve parts instead of ten, wrote in Castilian
and Nahuatl instead of Latin. The form of gathering and organizing
information considerably changed from one work to the other. But
there are also other factors worthy of consideration. Around 1561,
when Sahagún began to work on the organization of the massive
amount of information he had collected about Amerindian culture
and history, Sir Francis Bacon was born in England. By the second half
of the sixteenth century Sahagún was an already mature and seasoned
Franciscan working on the organization of knowledge from cultures
alien to him, while young Bacon was rethinking the Western epistemological tradition and reorganization of knowledge.[28] The end results in both cases were quite disparate, indeed, as they illustrate alternative conceptions of knowledge. Nevertheless, both drew from the
encyclopedic tradition. Bacon was concerned with reshaping and su-
perseding his own ethnic tradition, the Western organization of
knowledge. Sahagún, instead, was concerned with shaping the knowledge of a tradition to which he did not belong and had to deal with the
conflict between his own ethnic tradition and the one he was trying to
understand. One of the main differences between Sahagún and Bacon
is the role they played in the history of the encyclopedia: first, despite
Sahagún's efforts and achievements, his *Florentine Codex* has not been
included in the standard history of encyclopedias;[29] second, Sahagún
used the encyclopedic model to organize information while Bacon
critically examined it. Bacon was placed at the crest of Western construction of knowledge; Sahagún in the periphery of Western expansion. The fact that Sahagún has often been compared with what anthropological knowledge would be in the nineteenth century, a
forerunner of anthropology before anthropology was born, could be
reexamined in this context. However, while Bacon was having a decisive impact on the mainstream of Western intellectual life, Sahagún
was being silenced in the periphery of an increasingly religious, economic, and intellectual consolidation of Europe and its domination all
over the world.

While Peter Martyr collected all his information from letters he received from the Indies, Sahagún's basic information came from oral contact with Amerindian people (fig. 4.1). Beyond the conversations across linguistic and cultural boundaries entertained by Sahagún and his informants, there was also an interesting cross-play in the uses of languages and writing systems. Not only Spanish and Nahuatl, but also alphabetic and picture writing systems were part of the dialogue (fig. 4.2):

> All the things we discussed they gave to me by means of *paintings*, for that was the writing they had used, the grammarians saying them in their language and writing the statement beneath the painting.[30]

In gathering information, Sahagún confronted difficulties that were not even dreamed of by Peter Martyr, who moved freely and

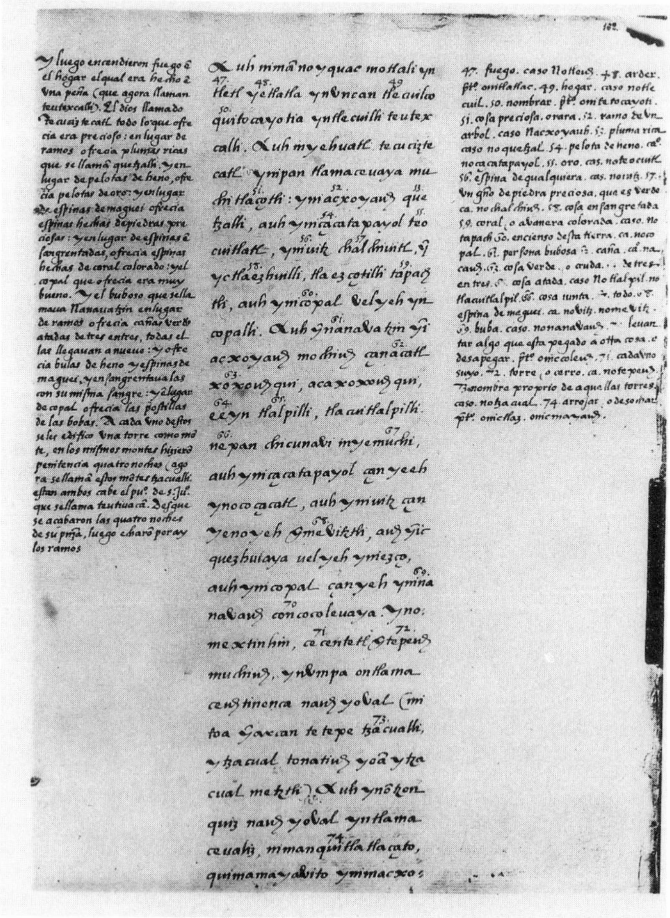

Fig. 4.1. Writing other cultures in sixteenth-century Mexico: *a*, Sahagún's *Memoriales con escolios*; *b*, Sahagún's *Primeros memoriales* (toward 1560)

easily between letters in Spanish coming from the Indies and letters in Latin he was sending to his friends in Italy and in Spain. What in the previous two chapters were abstract considerations about writing, the book and the notion of history during the sixteenth century, acquired concrete dimensions and presented daily difficulties for Sahagún:

> These people had no letters nor any characters, nor did they know how to read or write; they communicated by means of images and paintings, and all their antiquities and the books they had about them were painted with figures and images in such a way that they knew and had memory of the things their ancestors had done and had left in their annals, more than a thousand years back before the arrival of the Spanish in this land. Most of these books and writings were burned at the time of the destruction of the other idolatries,

Fig. 4.2. Mixing writing with drawing in late medieval Europe: a page from *Chroniques,* by Bernard de Tuy

but many hidden ones which we have now seen did survive and are still kept, from which we have understood their antiquities. (2:165; italics mine)

Sahagún left explicit descriptions of his working method. They are very often quoted and are well known by those familiar with sixteenth-century Mexico. I would like to repeat them, however, in this context. It should be mentioned, also, that Sahagún had specific questions prepared in advance in order to fulfill the main purposes of his inquiry: to know the ancient religion, to create or inspire texts from which a rich vocabulary could be obtained (*Calepino*), and to record the

Nahuatl's great cultural possessions.[31] First, then, in the village of Tepepulco Sahagún reported that

> In the said village I had all the leaders assembled, together with the lord of the village, Don Diego de Mendoza, an old man of great distinction and ability, very experienced in civil, military, and political and even idolatrous matters. Having met with them, I proposed what I intended to do and I asked that they give me qualified and experienced persons with whom I could talk and who would be able to answer what I asked. They answered that they would discuss the proposition and give me an answer another day, and thus they took leave of me. Another day the lord and the leaders came and, having made a solemn speech, as they used to do then, they pointed out to me ten or twelve leading elders and told me I could speak with them and that they would truly answer everything that might be asked of them. There were also four latinists, to whom I had taught grammar a few years earlier in the College of the Holy Cross in Tlatelolco.
>
> With these leaders and grammarians who were also leaders I conversed many days, nearly two years, following the order of the draft outline I had made.[32]

Toward 1560, Sahagún moved from Tepepulco to Tlatelolco, already with a significant amount of written material, where he repeated what he had done in Tepepulco when he began to collect information orally: "assembling all the leaders [in Tlatelolco], I proposed to them the business of my writings and asked them to designate for me several able leaders with whom I could examine and discuss the writings I had brought from Tepepulco." The significance of this second stage lies in the fact that it was devoted to work with Amerindians in order to work on the first written draft, rather than in collecting more information transmitted orally or in Mexican writing:

> The governor and the mayor pointed out to me eight or ten leaders chosen from among all of them, very skillful in their language and in the things of their antiquities, with whom (*in addition to four or five collegiates, all of whom were trilingual*), while closed off in the college for a period of more than a year, everything I had brought from Tepepulco was corrected and expanded, all of which had to be rewritten from a terrible copy because it had been written hurriedly. (1:106–7)

Finally, Sahagún moved from Tlatelolco to Mexico-Tenochtitlán, where he stayed in the Franciscan convent for a period of three years, still working on his writing, but at this point doing it by himself.[33] He was reaching the point of the final organization where the discursive genres and patterns of his own cultures would begin to take over the discursive genres and cultural patterns of his informants:

> for a period of three years I read and reread these writings of mine by myself, went back and corrected them, and _divided them into books, into twelve books, and each book into chapters and some books into chapters_ and paragraphs . . . and the Mexicans added and corrected many things in the twelve books while they were being put into smooth copy, so that the first strainers through which my works were sifted were those of Tepepulco, the second those of Tlatelolco, the third those of Mexico; and in all these scrutinies there were college-trained grammarians.[34]

Although there is still a long story of Sahagún's manuscript between 1564 or 1565 and 1578, when he wrote the version of _Florentine Codex_ known today (fig. 4.3), the basic organization in books, in chapters, and in paragraphs was basically decided in those three years in Saint Francis, in Mexico.[35] But such organization belongs to a culture in which alphabetic writing and the idea of the book merged to create a visual and cognitive pattern for the organization and transmission of knowledge. It is to this organization that I will devote the following pages, now that a general idea about how Sahagún gathered and assembled his information has been related.

It is not without a certain humor that Sahagún reported about people's queries on the _Calepino_ he was writing. It was not without surprise that Sahagún replied to his friends, telling them that he was not writing a dictionary, like Calepino did. Sahagún understood very well that even if such a work would be useful, he was not in a position to do for the Nahuatl what Calepino did for Latin. Dictionaries need a tradition of written words to become realities. What the missionaries could do was to write _vocabularios_ (see chap. 1) or, as Sahagún saw his project, to do the necessary groundwork to allow others to write dictionaries. Here are Sahagún's reflections on his and Calepino's projects:

> It would certainly be highly advantageous to prepare such a useful work [a dictionary] for those who want to learn this Mexican language, as Ambrosio Calepino did for those wanting to learn Latin and the meanings of its words, but there has certainly been no

Fig. 4.3. Informing the Crown, but not reaching the printing press: a page of the manuscript *Florentine Codex*, by Bernardino de Sahagún (1578)

opportunity *because Calepino took the words and their meanings, their errors, and their metaphors from the reading of the poets and orators and Latin authors, substantiating everything he said with the authors' sayings, a foundation that I have not had due to the lack of letters and writing among this people;* but whoever would want to do it could do so with facility, because by my labor twelve books have been written in the proper and natural language of his Mexican tongue, which besides being an entertaining and profitable composition presents all the ways of speaking and all the words this language uses, just as well substantiated and sure as those written by Virgil, Cicero, and the other Latin authors.[36]

What should hold our attention for the next few pages is the taken-for-granted belief that it was perfectly natural to organize all the information he gathered over the years into twelve books, without asking how the Mexicas themselves organized and transmitted their knowledge. Besides the coincidental or symbolic implications of the twelve books, the fact remains that organizing knowledge in units called "books" has strong implications for the complicity between writing and knowledge, as it has been analyzed in chapters 2 and 3. It also assumes that the organization of knowledge should be in book form, as was stated in the description provided by Venegas. So the *Florentine Codex,* thus named because of the place where it was found (Florence) and the name used to refer to bound artifacts in which writing was collected and preserved (codex), is a unit in twelve books, but what those twelve books amount to is not clear. It has been assumed, however, that it is part history and part encyclopedia.

Among the many considerations leading to the final version of the *Florentine Codex,* finished toward 1578, there are then one cognitive and one pragmatic. The cognitive one is related to genre as cognitive patterns for organizing information. Thus, books, history, encyclopedia would all be indications, during Sahagún's time as well as in subsequent reading of his works, of the genres invoked by the words and by the form. The pragmatic one is related to the intervention of Juan de Ovando, in charge of the Council of the Indies and the request to translate into Spanish all the writings that Sahagún had compiled and written in Nahuatl thus far. The *Florentine Codex* owes a great deal of its final form to Ovando's program for gathering and organizing information from the Indies, since 1570, under Philip II.[37] Let's explore these two aspects one at a time.

It has been pointed out that Sahagún's general plan for the organization of the information in written form, and in twelve books, came from several sources.[38] Pliny the Elder and Bartholomaeus Anglicus (or Bartholomew de Glanville) have been singled out, nevertheless, as the most likely and possible sources. But since Bartholomaeus Anglicus based his own writing on Pliny and Isidore of Seville, it can be concluded that one of the primary main cognitive models for organizing information came to Sahagún from these sources through Bartholomaeus Anglicus, an English Franciscan who became a lecturer at Magdeburg in 1230. His *De proprietatibus rerum* (1220–40) was widely read and consulted for over three centuries. It occupied also a distinguished place in the history of European encyclopedias of the Middle Ages, once *encyclopedia* was accepted as a word to designate a general collection and organization of knowledge. Bartholomaeus Anglicus's compilation is organized as follows:

1–2	God and the angels
3	The soul
4–7	The body and its anatomy, diseases, etc.
8–9	Astrology, astronomy, time
10–11	Matter, form, air
12	Birds and insects
13	Water and fishes
14–15	Geography
16	Geology
17	Trees and herbs
18	Animals
19	Colors, scents, flavors, liquors
20	Weights and measures, numbers, sounds

For comparative purposes it will be useful to remark that a Dominican friar, Thomas of Cantimpre, compiled a similar work around the same time as Bartholomaeus Anglicus, although it was not as influential. His *De natura rerum* was written in France between 1228 and 1244 and, like the work by Anglicus, had the object of preserving and explaining the Christian faiths. Cantimpre arranged his encyclopedia in the following manner:

Books

1–3	Man (anatomy, soul, monsters)
4–9	Animals (quadrupeds), birds, ocean monsters, freshwater and saltwater fish, snakes, worms
10–12	Botany (trees, aromatic trees, aromatic herbs)
13	Sources of water
14–15	Metals and precious stones
16	The atmosphere
17–18	The seven planets; the motion of the spheres
19	The four elements

The form of Sahagún's compilation thus had a previous model in the Christian world to be followed. His purposes, however, were not exactly the same as those that might have motivated Anglicus or Cantimpre. Sahagún referred continually to his writing as "this work" (*esta obra*), implying "written work," and in the opening paragraph of his prologue, he compared his own work with that of the medical doctor. In the same way that the doctor has to diagnose his or her patient in order to reestablish the order in the body, the missionaries had to diagnose theirs in order to restore order to their soul. The analogy is certainly illuminating because of its consequences. While one can assume the similarities of the physical bodies across cultures, one cannot assume the same regarding the souls (using Sahagún's vocabulary). It is at this specific juncture that ethnic and gender differences acquire a significance larger perhaps than class differences. In fact, Sahagún was not trying to "cure" only people who belonged to his own culture but people from quite different ones. The diagnosis of souls from cultures alien to the one to which the doctor belongs (following Sahagún's analogy) implies dialogue and mediation. Sahagún's informants, however, were not properly mediators but just that, informants. Sahagún was trying to know their souls in order to be more successful in their conversion. He was not engaged in a cross-cultural dialogue between people equally rational and equally correct in their belief and values. There was not much negotiation in the domain of the organization of knowledge and its significance in both communities. Sahagún was in possession of the Truth warranted by the Divine Book as well as of the metagraph book: the "written work" in "twelve chapters"; a packaging of the wisdom of one culture from the perspective of the wisdom of another alien to it. From this inter-cultural tension emerged some of the basic differences between Sahagún's "work" and the Western encyclopedia that he took as his model. Sahagún's distribution of the twelve books, as given by the titles of the books, was as follows:

Books

1   The Gods worshiped by the Natives of this Land of New Spain
2   Calendar, Fiestas and Ceremonies, Sacrifices, and Solemnities which these natives of New Spain performed in Honor of their Gods
3   The Beginning of the Gods
4   On Judicial Astrology or The Art of Divining used by these Mexicans to know which days Were Fortunate and Which Were Unfortunate
5   Omens and Forecasts
6   Rhetoric and Moral Philosophy
7   Natural Astrology
8   Kings and Lords; Governments and Kingdoms
9   Merchants and Artisans
10 Vices and Virtues of Indian People; parts of the body, Health and Medicine
11 Animals, Birds, Fish, Trees, Grass, Flowers, Metals
12 The Conquest of Mexico

Sahagún, like Bartholomaeus Anglicus, began his classification of knowledge with heaven and gods and then descended to the natural world. Some of the differences can be detected in the places attributed to astrology and health in both works. But the most important one lay elsewhere. First, Sahagún accounted and organized the knowledge coming from a pagan society and, second, he included a chapter on rhetoric and moral philosophy, whereas language and ethics were contemplated by neither Anglicus nor Cantimpre. Regarding the first aspect, it is obvious that Sahagún's experience was quite out of the ordinary and as such he did not have models to follow from his predecessors. The second aspect, the fact that Sahagún's alleged sources did not include either ethics or language, should not be a cause of dismay. There were other examples, whether or not available or known to Sahagún, which did place a great emphasis on language and ethics. A good example in vernacular languages was Brunetto Latini, born in Italy around 1220 and exiled to France toward 1263. He wrote *Le livres dou tresor*, which was divided into three books (book 1: theology, universal history, physical sciences, geography, agriculture, and natural history; book 2: ethics, the virtues, and sins; book 3: secular rhetoric and politics). Long before Latini, leading directly toward Isidore of Seville, was the Roman Marcus Terentius Varro (116–127 B.C.) who wrote his *Disciplinarum libri IX,* organized according to the trivium (grammar, logic, rhetoric) and the quadrivium (geometry, arithmetic, astronomy, and music).[39] He added medicine and architecture, and thus reached the nine books of his disciplines. Thus, the attention that Sahagún paid to Mexica oratory (see chap. 2, in this book) was not coming from the organization of the known (as was the case in Pliny and Bartholomaeus Anglicus) but from the organization of the form of knowledge (as was the case in Varro and in the first book of Isidore of Seville's *Etimologiae*). All of which take us back to the question of the encyclopedia.

Scholars have viewed Sahagún's work as an encyclopedia based on its similarities with models that have been already mentioned previously. Chiefly, Gaius Plinius Secundus (A.D. 23–79), better known as Pliny the Elder, wrote one of the first models of encyclopedic writing in the West. His influence on New World writers is very well known. Oviedo y Valdés wrote his *General y natural historia de las Indias* (1537–48) both by following and detaching himself explicitly from Pliny. Oviedo accepted the model of a general compilation and of natural history, but he rejected Pliny's written sources and replaced them with his own direct experience.[40] A few decades later under Philip II a medical doctor was sent to the New World to write a report on natural resources and the potential for the exploration and improvement of medications. When Francisco Hernández went to the New World, he had already translated thirty out of the thirty-seven books of Pliny's *Natural History,* from Latin into Spanish.[41] Now, how is it that a "natural" history became a model for the encyclopedia?

According to the *Oxford English Dictionary* the modern word *encyclopedia* comes from the Greek *enkyklios paideia. Paideia,* in the sense of education, seems to have entered (or at least, become more relevant in) Greek cultivated vocabulary after its expansion under Alexander the Great (324–323 B.C.). *Paideia* has been used to denote this particular age of Greek civilization, and the better-known meaning of *paideia* as education seems to have been a derivation from the first meaning: for a person to fulfill all the requirements of a given stage in a society, education is required. Thus, the expression *enkyklios* (general) *paideia* (education) or, as another translator suggested, "a well-rounded education," was originally associated to education and the organization of the curriculum. A well-rounded education comprised different kinds of knowledge and skill, both in the realm of *sophia* and of *techné.* During the European Middle Ages the foundation of Greek education became the trivium (introduced toward the ninth century) and the quadrivium (introduced toward the sixth century). Thus, a well-rounded education (or a liberal arts education in our day) was derived from *enkyklios paideia* and later on took the form of the seven liberal arts (grammar, rhetoric, and dialectic, the trivium; arithmetic, geometry, astronomy, and music, the quadrivium). How, then, did Pliny's *Natural History* (*Historia naturalis*) become the model for the encyclopedia?

To judge by the title, Pliny wrote a *historia* that was, in many respects, in keeping with the pattern of collecting, reporting, and classifying inherited from the Greeks, and mainly from Aristotle's *De caelo* and *Historia animalium,* that he included in his work on natural philosophy. In Rome, philosophy was not held in as high esteem as it was in Greece, and Pliny's *Natural History* is more descriptive, less philosophical, than Aristotle's *Historia animalium.* If Aristotle wrote a history of animals, it was not, supposedly, because he believed that animals, like humans, had memories to preserve, but because he did not think that one writes history only when one has something to say about the past of human beings, human deeds, or human societies. Which is another way to say what I was saying in the previous chapter: "history" in the ancient world not only had a meaning quite different from what it became during the European Renaissance, but it was altogether a different genre and kind of writing practice. It seems possible, consequently, to believe that Pliny became a model of encyclopedic writing and the encyclopedia became a genre due, perhaps, to a mistake made by a copyist who transformed by a stroke of the pen the Greek expression *enkyklios paideia* into one word, *enkykliopaideia,* which was translated into Latin as *encyclopaedia*. However, the idea of a roll or scroll containing all available knowledge and named encyclopedia seems to be completely alien to the ancient Greek and Roman worlds.

Now, if one looks back to the examples upon which the history of an encyclopedia as a genre has been constructed, one can distinguish between two models: an encyclopedia in which ways of knowing are organized, and an encyclopedia that organizes the known. Two sources of these legacies are Pliny and Varro. Pliny offered a chaotic organization of the known; Varro offered a systematic organization of the ways of knowing.[42] In the context of such legacies, Sahagún introduced (perhaps without knowing it) a third alternative: the reconfiguration of the known coming from patterns of cultures alien to the knower's tradition, resulting in the repression of native categories to perform the same classificatory operations. Such a move could have had at least two possible interpretations. The first is that in order to make the alien familiar, it has to be translated into the categories of one's own culture. The second is that by doing so, the risk of suppressing alternative organizations of knowledge is difficult to avoid. Sahagún's *Florentine Codex* helped to save the known in Mexica culture from oblivion, at the same time that it repressed (although not suppressed) Mexica ways of knowing.

Let's explore the pragmatic aspect of Sahagún's work as related to Juan de Ovando's (president of the Council of the Indies) request to translate into Spanish what he had written so far in Nahuatl. The fact that the *Florentine Codex* was finished in 1578, and the date corresponds to the years in which the first systematic effort to collect and organize information from the Indies was being made (engineered largely by Juan de Ovando; see chap. 6 for more details), is a clear indication that Sahagún's work (which began under the Franciscan project to convert the Amerindians) finished as a report requested by the Council of the Indies. As such, Sahagún's work followed the paths of thousands of official reports that were used and published or used and filed, according to the interests or dangers implied. If the artifact was considered a curiosity or a valuable object, it ended up in the hands of some members of the Royal House or its beneficiaries. If it was not, it landed in the archives of the council. It has been suggested that the bilingual version of Sahagún's *Florentine Codex,* with color as well as black and white illustrations, ended up in Florence because Philip II offered it as a present to his daughter when she married Lorenzo el Magnífico.

Sahagún's final years and the completion of his masterwork coincided with the years in which Sir Francis Bacon, in England, was conceiving a radical transformation in the encyclopedia as a way of knowing. He did not call his work encyclopedia but *Novum Organum* (1620). He came up with a clear reconceptualization of human learning and an organization of knowledge that was intended to solve many problems and inconsistencies he encountered in his predecessors. His *Novum Organum* was an encyclopedia properly speaking, in the sense that his classification of knowledge was intended to change the ways in which knowledge was organized and transmitted. Bacon's project was to influence education and curricular organization and to change the medieval legacy embodied in the trivium and the quadrivium. A simplified version, which encompassed all forms of knowledge, is summarized in the following paragraph:

> The best division of human learning is that derived from the three faculties of the rational soul, which is the need of learning. *History* has reference to the *Memory, Poesy* to the *Imagination,* and *Philosophy* to the *Reason. . . .* Wherefore from these three fountains, *Memory, Imagination,* and *Reason,* flow these three emanations, *History, Poesy,* and *Philosophy;* and there can be no others.[43]

Bacon's effort was based in the Greco-Roman legacy. The difficulties, for instance, that Sahagún might have encountered in organizing the knowledge he gathered from the ancient Mexicans was unknown to Bacon, even when Philip II of Spain married Mary Tudor and became the King of Wales, Ireland, and England. But even if Sahagún's works had been available to Bacon, he might not have changed his perspective on the organization of knowledge based on the Greco-Roman tradition. Bacon's main goal was the organization of knowledge within the classical tradition as constructed by European humanists; Sahagún's main goal was the organization of knowledge of people and societies hitherto unknown to the knowing subject proposing the organization of knowledge. Bacon laid out the foundations for science and epistemology in the modern period. Sahagún, negotiating the tensions between an encyclopedic and Christian tradition for the organization of knowledge, laid out the foundations for human sciences and hermeneutics in the modern period. Vico did not know of Sahagún, either. But, as the example of Boturini suggests,

Vico would have been receptive to Sahagún's efforts to understand the intellectual edifice of people and societies beyond the horizon of European knowledge.

Organizing the known in a way that encompasses memory and current knowledge was neither a distinguishing feature of the West nor of cultures with a long history of writing practices. Toward the eleventh century both the Islamic and Christian worlds as inheritors of the Greek legacy were strong religions of the book and had also developed sophisticated written tools to systematize the known as well as the way of knowing. In the same way that Isidore of Seville (in the sixth and seventh centuries) made an effort from the Christian point of view, one century later Ibn Qutayba (or Kutaiba, A.D. 828–89) authored a work called *Kitab 'Uyun al-Akhbar,* normally translated as *The Book of the Best Traditions.*[44] Those translating *kitab* faced the same kind of problems encountered when translating *amoxtli.* *Kitab* would be better translated, in this context, as "the writing" or "the written records" of the best traditions. Beyond the conceptual differences in the Christian and Islamic worlds regarding writing/*kitab* and book/*al-Kitab,* there is also a significant difference in the way the known is organized.[45] God and the heavens are not at the beginning of Ibn Kutaiba's work. His thematic sequence was the following: power, war, nobility, character, learning and eloquence, asceticism, friendship, prayers, food, omen. During the ninth century Islam was at the beginning of its imperial expansion, as was Christianity when Bartholomaeus Anglicus was influential in Europe as well as during the sixteenth century, when Sahagún was outlining Mexica's knowledge. Unfortunately, no equivalent to Ibn Kutaiba has survived from pre-Columbian Mexico, and the examples one can find during the colonial period (see the next section in this chapter) are hybrids, the result of the survival of ancient wisdom and the spread of Western cultural literacy.

One century after Ibn Kutaiba, a Persian scholar by the name of Al-Khwarizmi (ca. A.D. 975–97) wrote a work devoted to organizing ways of knowing rather than assembling the known. His work was entitled *Mafatih al-'Ulum* and was translated as *Key to the Science,* although I would prefer *wisdom* to *science,* given the years in which the work was written, unless it is specified that science is understood as a collection of knowledge from oral and written sources. What is relevant to my discussion, however, is that Al-Khwarizmi divided his work in native (or indigenous) and foreign wisdom in the following manner:

Quranic law
theological philosophy
Arabic grammar
Secretarial duties
Writing the past

/

Wisdom {
The indigenous wisdom

The foreign wisdom

\

philosophy, logic
medicine, arithmetic
geometry, astronomy
music, mechanics
alchemy

Al-Khwarizmi, contrary to Bacon, whom he preceded by several centuries, used the Greek legacy in a different context of knowledge and understanding. He suggested that the organization of knowledge is not universal but culture dependent and had the wisdom to bring that to the foreground. Bacon's silence about alternative forms of knowledge and his universalization of the regional concept of history, philosophy, and poetry as *the* form of knowing make one forget that alternatives existed and that the regional could hardly be accepted universally. Ibn Kutaiba, several centuries before and contrary to Sahagún, organized the known according to the needs of an expanding Islamic empire. Thus, he began by power, war, and nobility. Education came after, and it was related to the shaping of the youngster's character. If encyclopedias (because of their complex story) are both grouping the known and organizing ways of knowing, Sahagún's encyclopedia offers the wonderful spectacle of Mexica civilization as known by a Spanish Franciscan at the same time that it hides from us the Mexica's own organization of their own ways of knowing. A glimpse at the silence behind the noise of the *Florentine Codex* allows one to perceive the hybrid cultural production by Amerindians who learned the alphabet and, by writing, constructed a locus of enunciation different from the one carved by an Italian humanist in the court of Ferdinand and Isabella, as Peter Martyr, or a Spanish Franciscan who began his work under Charles I and finished it under Philip II.

The Discontinuity of the Classical Tradition: Genres
and Amerindian Organization of Knowledge in the
Colonial Period

203

*Genres as
Social
Practices*

Encyclopedia, then, brings us back to education and, consequently, to genres in the organization and transmission of knowledge. A secondary meaning of *enkyklios paideia* was "teaching in circle," applied to the physical setting in which the transmission of knowledge was performed rather than to the "well-rounded education" contemplated in the curriculum. One can surmise that the expression was coined when education was mainly an oral affair and the written organization of the known as well as the way of knowing was not yet in place. One can further speculate that teaching in circle became a secondary meaning once a well-rounded education became a practice related to writing and *enkyklios paideia* accentuated the written aspect in the codification and transmission of knowledge.

Education among the Aztecs is not as well documented as among the Greeks and is certainly less explored. It would be difficult at this point to determine whether the Mexica had a concept to refer to the form and content of the curriculum (well-rounded education) or the physical setting in which education was imparted (teaching in circle). There is enough evidence, however, to know which term they used to cast the concept of an educated person (*in ixtli, in yollotl* [the face, the heart]), which corresponded, of course, to the ideal of *toltecayótl*: all that a person living in the community (or city, *tollán*) should know and what they should be. If we move from the goals of education (to shape the "face and the heart" of the young and future citizens), we will soon find that the means by which education was transmitted involved different genres, oral and painted, in which knowledge was organized. And knowledge was organized, stored, and transmitted in both oral and painted repertories of genres.

A turning point took place after the conquest, when the native goals and forms of education suffered a breakdown and the foreign began to be implanted. Together with the spread of basic Western literacy (learning to read and write) went the spread of higher Western literacy (learning to read and write certain kinds of texts in a certain way). The history of education in the New World shows the paths followed by the colonization of languages at the level of cultural literacy.[46] The few Amerindians educated in Spanish colleges, such as the well-known and prestigious Santa Cruz de Tlatelolco, founded by the Franciscans, "integrated" the Renaissance philosophy of writing and historiographical conceptions in their writing of Amerindian history. Mexican historians of the colonial period such as Ixtlilxochitl,

Tezozómoc, and Muñón Chimalpaín had (toward the end of the sixteenth and beginning of the seventeenth centuries) begun to negotiate the conflict between the forces of their own traditions (both in the
content of their memories as well as in the way of remembering and
transmitting them) with the rhetorical education they received in
Castilian institutions. The tension of the past, which Amerindian historians needed to remember, fix, and transmit, conflicted with the
models of writing history from a tradition that was not their own.
These tensions were manifested in the conflicts between the physical
location in which the act of writing took place and the language in
which the history was written: Chimalpaín or Tezozómoc wrote in
Nahuatl, in colonial Mexico; Ixtlilxochitl wrote also in colonial Mexico, but in Spanish. Garcilaso de la Vega wrote in Spanish and in Spain,
after leaving Peru when he was still an adolescent; Guaman Poma de
Ayala wrote in broken Spanish and used drawings more than alphabetic writing to address Philip III from the viceroyalty of Peru.[47] The
variations between the language in which writing was performed and
the place of the performance sketched the scene of writing for those
few Amerindians who could use pen and ink and whose written pieces
would, eventually, reach the printing press. Of all the names just mentioned, only Garcilaso de la Vega actually saw the writing under his
name in printed form. The rest had a limited circulation in manuscript
form and were printed between the latter years of the nineteenth and
early years of the twentieth centuries.[48]

The effort to colonize Amerindian languages and memories required, I have submitted, the introduction of a tool (alphabetic writing) and of discursive frames (Renaissance system of genres).[49] However, the spread of Western literacy did not develop as smoothly as the
first educators tended to believe. Western systems of writing and
discursive genres were actually adapted and used by the Amerindians
in order to sustain their own cultural traditions. Alternative "histories," either collective enterprises such as the *Popol Vuh* and the *Books
of Chilam Balam* from the Yucatán peninsula (both recorded in alphabetic script toward the mid-sixteenth century) or individual, such as
Muñón Chimalpaín or Ixtlilxochitl in Mexico (both written in the first
decades of the seventeenth century), punctuate, on the one hand, the
plurilingual and multicultural character of colonial situations and, on
the other, illustrate how such written practices collided with the Renaissance philosophy of language and writing held by missionaries and
men of letters. It is at this intersection where the discontinuity of the
classical tradition can be located and the fractured symbolic world of
colonial situations be analyzed.[50]

Native "books" from the Yucatán peninsula, such as the several

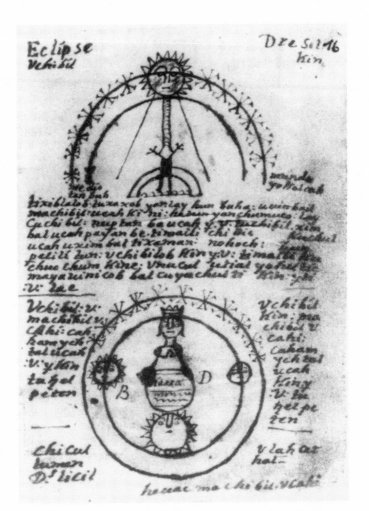

Fig. 4.4. The solar and lunar eclipse in the manuscript known as *Book of Chilam Balam of Chumayel*

Books of Chilam Balam or the *Popol Vuh* from the highlands of Guatemala, among others, offer good examples of the survival and adaptation of indigenous generic categories during the colonial period.[51] There are several extant manuscripts of the *Books of Chilam Balam* that also take the name of the town to which they belonged; for instance, the *Book of Chilam Balam of Chumayel* (fig. 4.4) or of *Tizimin*.[52] Roys, who studied and translated into English the *Chilam Balam of Chumayel* in the early 1930s (fig. 4.5), suggested that a possible translation could be the *Book of the Prophet Balam*, since *chilam* was the title of the latest great "prophet" of the Maya civilization (who Roys supposed had lived during the late fifteenth and early sixteenth centuries).[53] He also suggested that each book "is a small library in itself and contains a considerable variety of subject material. Beside the prophecies we find brief chronicles, fragmentary historical narratives, rituals, native catechism, mythological accounts of the creation of the world, almanacs and medical treatises."[54] One is surprised that Roys did not use the word *encyclopedia* to describe such a collection of knowledge.

Since the *Books of Chilam Balam* as we know them today have been fixed in alphabetic script that transformed the oral tradition and the hieroglyphic way of recording, organizing, and transmitting knowledge in ancient Maya civilization, it is possible to surmise that Renaissance genre categories went together with alphabetic writing. And in fact, Arzápalo Marín has suggested that the actual form of the *Books of Chilam Balam* responded very much to the so-called *repertorios* (or *reportorios*) *de los tiempos,* a Renaissance genre characterized by the

Fig. 4.5. Course of the sun and solar system as redrawn in the Roys edition of the *Chilam Balam of Chumayel*

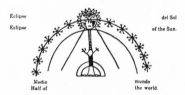

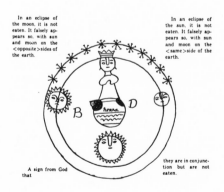

compilation of miscellaneous knowledge.[55] What is most interesting is the fact that the Spanish *reportorio de los tiempos* refers to knowledge-organizing devices related to the calendaric computation and prognosis. It seems the Spaniards did not recognize the similarities between their own prognoses and what they called the "art of divination" in Amerindian cultures. The Maya, however, might have perceived the similarities when they recorded their ancient wisdom in what came to be known as the colonial *Books of Chilam Balam*. López Piñeiro has described the Spanish *reportorio de los tiempos* as a very popular genre of astrologic literature in which prognoses associated with health, agriculture, and navigation were associated with the civil and ecclesiastical calendar. Interestingly enough, they were initially called *lunario* (from *luna,* moon) and then became established as *reportorio*.[56] The fact that the "books" of *Chilam Balam* also contain European material is indicative of their hybrid character and of the use and transformation (for reasons that should be studied in particular cases) of European script and genres by native people of the Yucatán peninsula. As has been discussed in chapter 2, genres and the organization of knowledge in the *Books of Chilam Balam* go back to the spread of Western literacy; that is, to education, to teaching how to read and write and to organizing and transmitting knowledge. The Maya (as well as the Mexica) had their own ways of doing these things, which were, in part, transformed by the encounter with Spanish missionaries and men of letters.

One should keep in mind, however, that the kind of "encyclopedia" or mixture of genres that we encounter in the colonial *Books of Chilam Balam* presumably existed, before they were compiled in a single unit, as a diversity of genres common to pictographic writing (bookkeeping, time reckoning) without parallel in oral genres. The colonization of genres in this case was not successful. As time went on, the European script that the friars were so eager to transmit in order to be more effective in the Christianization of the natives was used *by* Amerindians to stabilize their past, to adapt themselves to the present, to transmit their own traditions to future generations and, in summary, to resist the colonization of language. Arzápalo Marín advanced the hypothesis that the *Books of Chilam Balam* are an adaptation and transformation of the *reportorio de los tiempos,* a general and encyclopedic compilation of miscellaneous knowledge, very popular in the European Renaissance and well known in the viceroyalty of New Spain.[57] If the hypothesis could be supported, it would be possible to see in greater detail examples of how the European tradition of assembling knowledge in one book was transformed and used by the Amerindians while at the same time seeing how the Amerindians' own system of genres was transformed by the introduction of Western literacy into their education.

Letter writing, history, and encyclopedias are all genres attached to alphabetic writing as practiced and conceptualized in the Greco-Roman tradition. Even rhetoric, as was pointed out previously, is a sophisticated set of written instructions for the production of oral discourse. It was rhetoric, oratory, and ethics that Sahagún had in mind when collecting and organizing the material that became book 6 of his *Florentine Codex,* entitled "Rhetoric and Moral Philosophy." By taking a closer look at this chapter, we will have a better sense of what education, organization, and transmission of knowledge might have been like in ancient Mexico. During the years that Peter Martyr was encouraging and supporting letter writing in the education of the young, practicing what he was preaching by writing letters to his friends and intellectual peers, and pondering the significance of letter writing and writing history, the Mexicas had a different approach to perhaps similar goals. Mendieta puts it in a very interesting and revealing way. He collected, toward the end of the sixteenth century, enough information to be convinced that "These indians raised their children following the doctrine of the philosopher (Aristotle) without having read his books."[58] Mendieta described Mexica education with admiration, although he could not overcome his need for a written source of reference and authority. One can imagine that it would have been difficult for Mendieta to believe that ancient Mexicas and ancient Greeks, as human beings, had similar experiences of life (i.e., people are born, grow up, and die; people train their children for survival and improvement; and people think about their existence in the world without "reading the philosopher," as Mendieta puts it); and further that the Greeks, although deserving admiration for great human achievements (like the Chinese, the Egyptians or later the Islamic civilizations), should not necessarily be taken as the model.

Sahagún held the speeches of the Mexica in high esteem both for their delivery as well as for their moral content. As a result, he called the book in which he collected a sample of their speeches "Rhetoric and Moral Philosophy." Sahagún was rather silent about Mexican writing systems and organization of knowledge in written (or painted) form. He might not have been interested in revealing the fact that the Mexica were accomplishing, by means of oral discourses, what the Spaniards (as well as other European states during the sixteenth century) were accomplishing by means of writing. Since rhetoric was the discourse in which the rules and examples for the production of oral and public discourses (oratory) were established, it could be concluded that Sahagún did not collect rhetorical discourses (with the exception of the two examples just quoted) but oratorial (formal) discourses used in public affairs and in education. And even if he recognized the beauty and sophisticated value of the speeches (the rhetorical *elocutio*), he was mute regarding their pragmatic values and functions (the rhetorical action in public or *actio*). The *actio*, however, is implied in Sahagún's description of the situation in which the discourse was pronounced, but nothing was said about the significance of oral discourse in Aztec culture. The discourses collected by Sahagún can be seen, from the point of view of the rhetorical *actio* and the social function of oratory, as forms of control and socialization.

As forms of social control, the discourses established a direct and privileged form of communication between the Mexica leaders and their gods, one that was not open to all members of the community. Formalized speech was used when the leaders addressed the people. In a society in which literacy was not widespread and written records were in the hands of the leaders, massive communication was performed by speech, which became the main vehicle of social control. Formalized speech was also one of the main instruments of socialization. Where no textbooks exist, education has to be achieved through oral discourse. Thus, it should be clear now why *huehuetlatolli* was used by the Amerindians to name a formal discursive genre in which knowledge was transmitted and education accomplished and why the elders were respected as the repository of knowledge and source of wisdom. Although the cult of the elder was still practiced in the European Middle Ages,[59] during the Renaissance alphabetic writing and the cult of the book took the place of the "men of wisdom." It was perhaps difficult for an educated Spaniard during the sixteenth century to draw a parallel between *el hombre sabio* (the man of wisdom) and *huehuetlatolli* (those who have the wisdom of the word; *huehue* = elder, *tlatolli* = word or discourse). Moreover, socialization and social control emerged not only in what was being said but in the manner of saying it. Thus, the emphasis placed in the previously quoted discourses, the father to his son and from the mother to her daughter, on the manners in which speech should be delivered and its relation to the position of the body are not only rhetorical advice but also social norms (fig. 4.6).

The Spanish missionaries and men of letters who studied or described Amerindian cultures had a disadvantage in relation to a present-day observer. It would have been difficult, if not impossible, for the missionaries to detach themselves from their own system of beliefs and to observe themselves describing the Amerindians. The distance between the missionaries' own descriptions of the Amerindians in the sixteenth century and the descriptions humanists or social

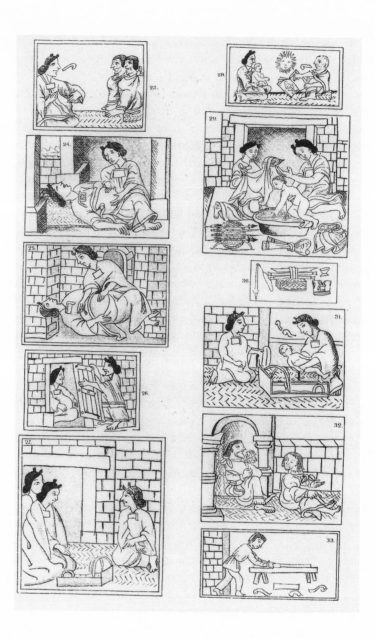

Fig. 4.6. Oral genres in ancient Mexico: Mexica forms of verbal behavior as depicted in the *Florentine Codex*

scientists provide nowadays of the missionaries describing the Amerindians during the sixteenth century facilitates the understanding of
the missionaries in a way that they could have not understood them- *Genres as*
selves. It would have been impossible for Sahagún, for instance, to *Social*
think that Greco-Latin oratorial examples and rhetorical treatises *Practices*
were not the appropriate yardsticks to measure Mexican discourse
against and to praise them as far as they approached the model, but
rather that Mexican discourses were equivalent examples to what had
been the experience of the Greek sophists or of Aristotle when he
attempted a written formalization of oral discourses in his *Rhetorica*.
In other words, Sahagún was not in a position to examine the Greco-
Roman tradition critically from the experience of the formalized oral
discourse among the Mexican leaders, parents, and elders. He had no
other choice than to evaluate Mexica discourses from the perspective
of the Greco-Roman tradition.[60]

There is, finally, the question of genre as it relates to speech. Initially, the question of genre was related to the lack of (alphabetic)
writing. But in fact, how could someone manage to understand genres
in oral communication when that person had been educated in a literate tradition in which, by the late fifteenth and early sixteenth century,
the question of genre in rhetoric and poetics was so well developed,
and all its development was based on written practices? Beyond the
repeated mention of the lack of history during the sixteenth century,
but with the recognition that the Amerindians had their way of recording the past, the true question of genre remained implicit. It came
to the foreground quite recently, when Angel María Garibay published his *Historia de la literatura Náhuatl* and confronted the difficulties of organizing Nahuatl literature following the classification of
genres in the Western tradition. Historians and missionaries during
the sixteenth century had more important worries than the question of
genres. As a consequence, the documentation about Amerindian
categories of discourse classification was not easy to find in sixteenth-
and early-seventeenth-century source material. At any rate, there are
three aspects in particular that should draw our attention in relation to
the topic under consideration.

First is discourse classification when speech is the main source of
preservation, organization, and transmission of knowledge, ethics,
and education, and when speech is also used in the sphere of pleasure
and entertainment (a sphere of human communication that could be
compared with Western poetry or literature). Although I will limit
myself to historiography, poetry, and rhetoric (three of the major
discursive categories during the Renaissance) and their equivalents in
Amerindian cultures, the whole sphere of linguistic interactions in

both traditions could be examined from the same perspective. León-Portilla has provided, in the domain of the Aztec culture, a reconstruction of Nahuatl vocabulary for genre classification both in the domain of conservation and transmission of the past as well as in the domain of rhythmic discourse related to music and narrative prose.[61] Such a reconstruction, seen in the context of research done on folklore genres and the ethnography of speaking, shows that sophisticated discourse classification and generic categories do not depend on writing to be organized, nor is writing a necessary condition for lasting discursive patterns. When a graphic system is not in place to fix discourses whose form has become an example of a given genre, human memory fulfills the function of ink and paper. Based on the premise of the recursive capacity of humans, which allows us to be at once participants and observers of our own actions and interactions, it is possible to assume that the members of any human community will participate in social (labor, family relations, religious organization, etc.) and semiotic (all forms of communication about labor, family relations, religious organization, etc.) interactions at the same time that they will become observers of their social and semiotic interactions. At this second level, every member of a community needs a vocabulary to describe his or her own social and semiotic practices.[62] Intellectual leaders, in Amerindian as well as in European societies, are those able to conceptualize and articulate in convincing ways the form and content of social and semiotic interactions. The difficulty at this level, however, is to avoid falling into the trap of the distinction between literature and folklore, one of the consequences related to the celebration of the letter and to the downgrading of speech as a valid form of education, verbal creativity (Western literature), knowledge (Western science), and wisdom (Western philosophy). If we accept that human discursive practice presupposes human observations and descriptions of our own semiotic interactions (or verbal behavior, to use a different jargon), then oral interactions would be inconceivable without a conceptualization (description and observation) by those who engage in them (practitioners, participants). Both oral interactions and their conceptualizations constitute what I call orality. The same principle applies to written interactions and their conceptualization by those who engage in them. Both alphabetic written interactions and their conceptualizations constitute what I call literacy.[63]

Second is discourse classification when the introduction of the alphabet made it possible either to fix preconquest oral composition or allowed Amerindians to adapt the alphabet to their own oral and written traditions, as we have seen in the previous section. Furthermore, once the alphabet had been adapted by Amerindian communities, it did not necessarily mean that they would value writing in the same way that Western culture did. Tedlock has shown, in the case of the *Popol* *Vuh,* that oral transmission is still the preferred performance among the literate Maya-Quiche of Guatemala.[64] The hybrid cultural pro- duction emerging from the blending of the endurance of preconquest Amerindian with Western discursive practices illustrates what I have called colonial semiosis. Based on what has been said in the previous paragraph, the foundation of colonial semiosis could be outlined in a simplified version of the well-known semiotic square (fig. 4.7).[65]

The sixteenth-century philosophy of writing celebrating the letter provided the foundation for a philosophy of written discourse that reemerged (in the twentieth century) in the "consequences of liter-acy" and the "grand divide" theses depicting oral and literate cul-tures.[66] The belief in the power of writing to transform (and implicitly upgrade) consciousness was responsible for the image of the grand divide, and it was, in the twentieth century, a rational articulation of the implicit judgment made by sixteenth-century missionaries and men of letters when they were confronted with societies whose mem-bers were deprived of letters.[67] The ethnographic works done on the genres of speech in non-Western communities have shown that orality is an equivalent to, rather than an outdated precursor of, literacy.[68]

Third, the endurance of oral discourse for pleasure, entertainment, or transmission of knowledge nowadays in Amerindian communities has made it possible to study the contexts of verbal interaction and understand the sophistication in verbal behavior without the help of writing; and to realize that discourse categorization is not only possi-

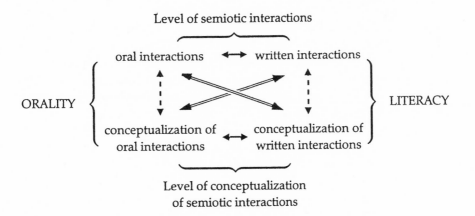

Fig. 4.7.   The semiotic square

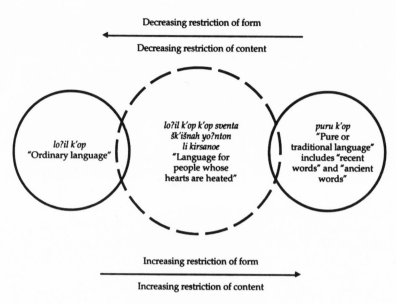

Fig. 4.8.   A simplified version of Chamula's discursive genres

ble but also necessary. Bricker has analyzed the ethnography of some traditional Mayan speech genres and disclosed a complex system of discourse classification, which she divides between formal and informal speech (perhaps the primary and secondary systems, in Bakhtin's genres);[69] Gossen did similar work among the Chamulas, analyzing their own taxonomy of verbal behavior and evaluating of their own discursive genres.[70] The result of his analysis reveals three large areas of linguistic behavior represented in figure 4.8.

Each discursive configuration (like the formal and informal categories in Bricker's reconstruction of Mayan speech genres) is comprised of a large number of discursive types. "Pure or true speech," for example, comprises types such as new or recent words, and ancient words, true recent narratives (tales, genealogies), ancient narratives (accounts of the distant past), games, ritual speech, and frivolous languages. Furthermore, discursive configurations and discursive types are bound to the cosmological pattern. Thus, while the ancient word belongs to the first, second, and third creation according to the four ages of the world, the new or recent word belongs to the fourth creation, which is the one in which the Chamulas are living. Gossen has surmised that there is a correlation between linguistic behavior, style, and cosmological order and has found that heat is a basic metaphor that functions as the canon of Chamula criticism in all their speech performances:

Controlled heat symbolizes order in both a diachronic and synchronic sense. Language is but one of several symbolic domains
which Chamulas think and talk about in terms of heat metaphors.[71]

The heat metaphor (as in "to speak with a heated heart") applies
not only to language but to other domains of social interactions, as
well as thoughts, religion, ethics, and cosmology. In Gossen's words,
this

> brings us to the fact that oral tradition is primarily concerned with
> norms and limits of permitted variation within them. In this sense,
> Chamula oral tradition is a more or less invariant expressive system
> that provides information which helps people to deal with more or
> less invariant aspects of the social system. It therefore is fitting and
> consistent that the primary invariable aspect of Chamula cosmos—
> the sun deity—should provide a native metalanguage for talking
> about some of the invariable canons of language use.[72]

Since the term *metalanguage* was discredited in academic circles
after 1974, it would be preferable to talk about how language is used to
describe and evaluate the uses of language; or what descriptions and
evaluations speakers make of their own verbal behavior (or semiotic
interactions, to use another jargon, which take us beyond speech and
alphabetic writing). The point I am trying to make is that if this complexity of linguistic behavior and its categorization and evaluation
could be perceived and understood today among the Chamulas, it is
conceivable that the oratorial pieces collected by Sahagún under the
name of "Rhetoric and Moral Philosophy" were pieces of a larger
puzzle that the Franciscans, who worked closely with the first generation of Mexicas after the conquest (the Jesuits arrived as late as 1572),
were unable to understand. And it could also be surmised that if a
marginal community, like the Chamulas, survived and maintained
their own patterns of verbal behavior, the Aztecs in Mexico-Tenochtitlán, at the height of their economic and political power, most likely
had a complex system of categorization and evaluation of their speech
whose understanding might still escape humanists and social scientists
for whom the letter is a necessary condition for cultural development.
If this might be the case for today's humanists, it was certainly true for
many of the Spaniards (as well as those educated in the ideology of the
letter) who were devoted to understanding people without letters.

Concluding Remarks

During the years in which Peter Martyr was writing his *De orbe novo
decades* and spreading the ideal of European humanism, the Mexica

intelligentsia was performing similar tasks with alternate means and goals. Both Peter Martyr and the anonymous Mexica coincided, however, in their respect and love for human intelligence and wisdom, and for the acquisition and transmission of knowledge to the young. During the years in which Bernardino de Sahagún was collecting information and organizing it into what would become the *Florentine Codex*, members of the Maya intellectual elite were writing the *Books of Chilam Balam*, using a new tool (alphabetic literacy) to preserve and transmit ancient wisdom. Bernardino de Sahagún and the anonymous Maya coincided, however, in their love and desire to acquire, organize, and transmit knowledge to members of their own respective communities. All four cases, as disparate as they might seem, were part and parcel of the colonial situation under the Spanish empire. Modern and contemporary organization of knowledge has insisted on dividing them. Thus, Peter Martyr—because he was Italian and wrote in Latin—had a marginal role in the history of Spanish and Latin American culture; Bernardino de Sahagún, perhaps because of his mixture of Nahuatl and Spanish, seldom occupied the same role as Las Casas, Gómara, or Acosta in the intellectual history of the New World colonization. The Mexica *huehuetlatolli* and the Maya *Books of Chilam Balam* were certainly the delight of specialists in Mesoamerican culture but were seldom considered in the history of colonial ideas and cultural practices. All four cases, however, had two interrelated aspects in common that allow me to bring them together in this chapter: they are related to education and to genres as tools to organize and transmit knowledge. My intention is to highlight a fruitful network, beyond the causal connections between events, persons, or object to be compared.

There is also an important difference. Peter Martyr and Sahagún (even if his work was not published during his lifetime) were on the side of power and social control and on the brighter side of the Renaissance. The Maya *Books of Chilam Balam* and the Mexica *huehuetlatolli* were on the side of the socially controlled. In the first case, genres as social practices worked toward the spread of Western literacy and the reconfiguration of the classical tradition. In the second case, genres as social practices worked toward the preservation of Amerindian memories and the discontinuity of the classical tradition. In a colonial situation the conflict of interpretations is played out at the basic level of cultural conversion, on the one hand, and the transformation of cultural traditions that give rise to new and emergent identities (in this case, both European and Amerindian), on the other.

Part 3

The Colonization of Space

Chapter 5

The Movable Center: Ethnicity, Geometric Projections, and Coexisting Territorialities

Father Ricci's Move: Negotiating Ethnic Centers and Geometric Projections

Around 1584, according to the story told by Father Ricci himself,[1] the Chinese Mandarins visited the first Jesuit mission established at Shao-xing. The Chinese saw, on a wall of the mission-room, what was for them an astonishing depiction of the earth. Although it is not certain which map Father Ricci took with him to China, it is presumed that it was a printing of Abraham Ortelius's *Tipus orbis terrarum* (1570) (fig. 5.1). The Chinese Mandarins seemed to be astonished by the fact that the earth looked like a sphere mostly covered by water; and they were still more astonished when they realized that the Chinese empire, which up to then they believed was not only at the center of the earth but also occupied almost its entire surface, was reduced to a small portion of land in the upper-right-hand corner of the map. D'Elia reconstructed this crucial moment in the following narrative:

> Ricci had observed that his guests, before looking at the world map in the European language, displayed on the wall of his residence in Shao-King, complained when they saw their China on the right-hand side, at the end of the known world, and near the corner, instead of at the center of the world as until then they had believed it was, in the belief that the world was square.[2]

> Ricci thought it inopportune to be angry at the pride of the Chinese and afterwards, without getting any closer to the geographical

truth, he saw no other alternative than merely to change the layout adopted by the European cartographers. This in fact undermined their world map from that time on by putting the two Americas on the left of the observer, Europe and Africa in the center and Asia on the right; naturally China and Japan were represented at the extreme right of the map. Ricci, wishing to have a legitimate account of the susceptibility of his guests, placed Europe and Africa on his world map on the observer's left, with Asia in the center and the two Americas on the right.[3]

According to scholars of Chinese culture and civilization,[4] the Chinese conceptualization of space was based on a confederation of five directions: north, south, west, east, and middle, with China as the Middle Kingdom. The Chinese universe was sometimes (perhaps more for political than for cosmological reasons) diagrammed as a grid of nested rectangles. In figure 5.2 (a "map" dated around the fifth century B.C.), the center stands for the imperial palace and the next rectangle—reading outward—represents the imperial domains. The

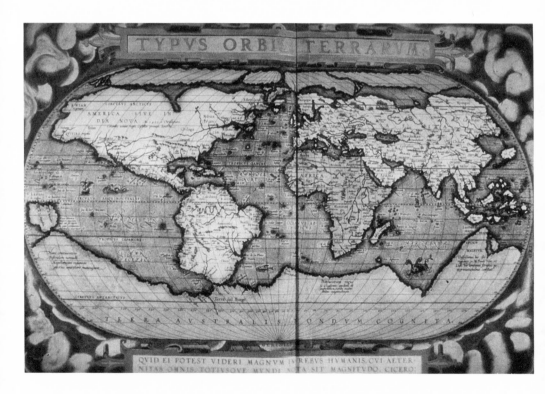

Fig. 5.1. A late-sixteenth-century European perspective of the world: Ortelius, *Tipus orbis terrarum* (1570)

lands of the tributary nobles are surrounded by the zone of pacification where border peoples were adjusting to Chinese customs. The land of friendly barbarians follows and, finally, the outermost rectangle separates Chinese civilization from the lands of savages who have no culture at all.[5]

Although Father Ricci was in China almost two thousand years after this diagram of the world was drawn, it could be assumed that the surprise expressed by the gentry of the Ming dynasty when they saw the Ortelius-like map on the wall of the mission-room was due to the fact that their conceptualization of space as well as of the place assigned to China in the configuration of the earth remained attached to the rectangular matrix with China in the center. It may be difficult to believe that the conceptualization of space conveyed by the diagram from the fifth century B.C. was still relevant in China toward the end of the sixteenth century. However, the Italian traveler Gemelli Carreri claimed to have seen, circa 1700, a Chinese "map" very similar to the center-oriented representation in rectangular form shown in figure 5.2.[6] But it is precisely this long tradition that makes special the moment Ricci showed the world map to his Chinese guests. The encounter between two different configurations of the earth looks very

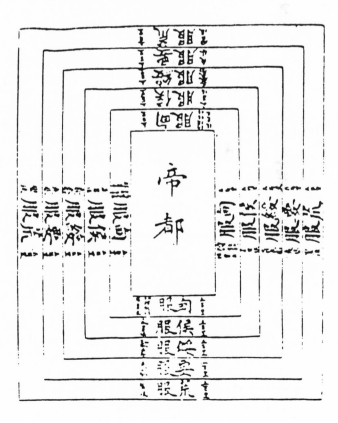

Fig. 5.2. An example of Chinese concentric geographic description, a kind of "map" merging cosmographical patterns and territorial control

similar to the encounter between two different conceptions of writing and the book, as we explored in chapter 2, a propos of Sahagún's *Coloquios y doctrina Christiana.*[7] Ricci's move toward the Chinese was not the same as the Franciscan's move toward the Mexica. Ricci was able to concede and change the geographical center, although he may never have doubted that the ethnic center remained in Rome. But Ricci was dealing with maps, and not with the Holy Book, as was the case with the Franciscans. Geometric projections seem to have allowed the introduction of a double perspective: first, a dissociation between a center determined ethnically (Rome, Jerusalem, or China) and a center determined geometrically, which does not replace but complements the ethnic one; second, the assumption (so well illustrated by Ricci) that the locus of observation (geometric center) does not disrupt or interfere with the locus of enunciation (ethnic center). It seems obvious to me that, for Ricci, the ethnic center remained in Rome, although geometrically he was able to place the Pacific and China in the center of the map, as if geometry were the warranty of a nonethnic and neutral ordering of the shape of the earth.

By redrawing the world map and placing the Pacific instead of the Atlantic at the center of the world (fig. 5.3), Ricci was able to detach the ethnic from the geometric rationalization of space.[8] From the geometric perspective, the surface of the earth could be drawn from equally valid (and movable) centers of observation. However, the Chinese Mandarins were not yet in a position to accept such a move, and their first reaction was to wonder how their ethnic center could

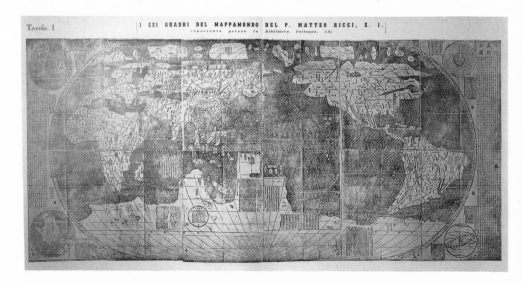

Fig. 5.3. A late-sixteenth-century alternative perspective of the world: Ricci's *mappamondo*

have been decentered. The Mandarins' astonishment, as perceived by Ricci himself, showed that the power of the center does not depend necessarily on geometric rationalization but, on the contrary, that geometric rationalizations are enacted around the power of the ethnic center. Once the ethnic perspective is detached from the geometric one, the authoritative center becomes a matter of political power rather than of ethnic subjectivity. That is, in my understanding, the crucial dimension of Ricci's move and the power of cartographic revolution in the West since the early fifteenth century.[9]

Although the history of Father Ricci's map in the cartographic history of the East is beyond the scope of this chapter,[10] a glimpse at it will help in understanding the struggle between coexisting territorial representations during the economic and religious expansion of the West. Ricci's map encountered strong opposition and resistance in China, although it was more readily accepted in Japan. Current world maps printed in Japan (fig. 5.4) show the location of lands and water

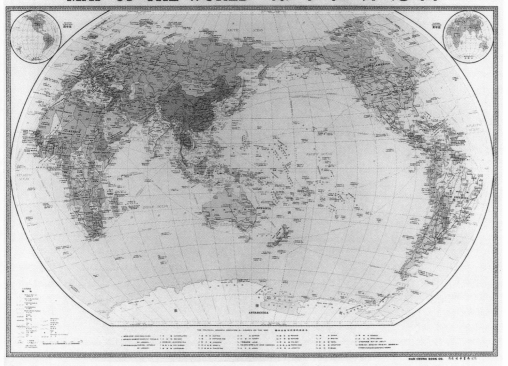

Fig. 5.4. A twentieth-century Japanese perspective: a world map printed in Hong Kong in 1988

introduced by Ricci's redrawing of Western world maps, as does the Japanese map shown in figure 5.5, from the eighteenth century. The Japanese cartographic tradition based on Ricci's world map began with the Shoho world map of 1645.[11] In China, instead, the situation was not as smooth as Ricci and the Jesuits pretended it was. Ch'en has shown that some of the people who reportedly met Ricci did not make a distinction between the traditional "western regions" in Chinese cartography and Europe.[12] The official history of the Ming dynasty, written while Ricci was still in China, does not follow Ricci's map. In some cases, criticism of Ricci has been quite harsh, as can be appreciated in the following evaluation:

> Lately Mateo Ricci utilized some false teachings to fool people, and scholars unanimously believed him. . . . The map of the world which he made contains elements of the fabulous and mysterious,

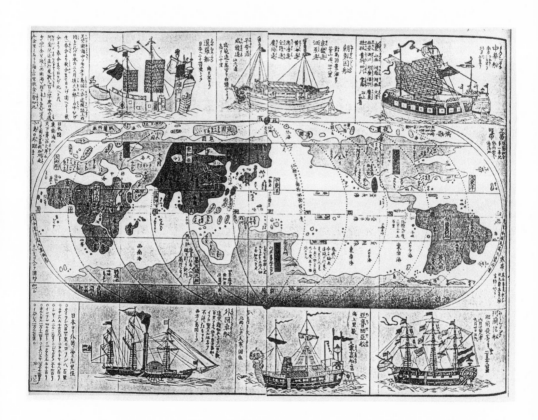

Fig. 5.5. An eighteenth-century Japanese perspective of the world: Ricci's perspective recast in a different graphic tradition

and is a downright attempt to deceive people on things which they personally can not go to verify for themselves. It is really like the trick of a painter who draws ghosts in his pictures. We need not discuss other points, but just take for example the position of China on the map. He puts it not in the center but slightly to the west and inclined to the north. This is altogether far from truth, for China should be in the center of the world, which we can prove by the single fact that we can see the North Star resting at the zenith of the heaven at midnight. How can China be treated like a small unimportant country, and placed slightly to the north as in this map? This really shows how dogmatic his ideas are. Those who trust him say that the people in his country are fond of travelling afar, but such an error as this would certainly not be made by a widely-travelled man.[13]

It is tempting (at least in my case) to read the preceding paragraph as a complaint from someone who defends his position although he is utterly in the wrong. The temptation comes from the natural tendency to judge colonial situations from the point of view of what Fabian calls the "denial of coevalness."[14] The impression the reader gets from Ricci's account is that the Chinese cartographers and intellectuals were "behind" in time, not yet quite as developed as their European counterparts.[15] Such an impression stems from the dictum of serious and outstanding modern scholars who are able to say, when describing Ricci's contribution to Chinese cartography, that "it gave the Chinese a true picture of the world as it was then known." Such generalizations are based on a denotative concept of the sign and on the correspondence theory of truth, which disregards the locus and the subject of enunciation as well as the needs and functions of territorial descriptions. Instead, a universal knowing subject is presupposed and identified with the regional European cartographic perspective. If the dictum "a true picture of the world as it was then known" is replaced by "the true picture of the world as it was then known by Europeans and Chinese," the statement would do justice to colonial situations in which at least two perspectives on the world coexist. The attribution of true value depends on the perspective taken by the speaking subject, as can be seen in Ricci's as well as in Chinese scholars' respective accounts. We know today that the Jesuits toward the end of the sixteenth century were either not aware of or ignored the changes in the image of the cosmos introduced by Copernicus. They lived in a universe whose center was the earth and not the sun. There was a difference between the Jesuit and the Chinese scholars, nonetheless, and the difference was relevant not at the level of true correspondence between maps and the world but at the level of power.[16] Ricci's territorial representation was more powerful than that of the Chinese on two accounts: first, because it went together with an economic and religious expansion that allowed Ricci to promote the European conception of the world in China while the Chinese were not in a position to promote their own territorial view to the Europeans; and second, because it produced the effect that the ethnic center was transcended and replaced by a geometric one when, indeed, geometric projections during the sixteenth century became a new model of a Eurocentric conception of the world.

Cortés, Durán, and Sahagún's Move: The Human Body, the Sacred Place, the City, and the Shape of the Cosmos

The Spanish experience in Mexico regarding the conceptualization of space was different—as should be expected—from Ricci's experience in China. Cortés (a man of arms), Durán (a Dominican), and Sahagún (a Franciscan) were involved—in one way or another—in (re)drawing the shape of the city, the earth, and the cosmos. Contrary to Ricci's experience in China, Mexica intellectuals did not have a chance of expressing their own opinion about the ways in which the Spanish described their own territory. Their silence does not mean, however, that they readily accepted either what was proposed to them or the manner in which they were introduced and described to the European audience to which Cortés's, Durán's, and Sahagún's writing were addressed. The aim of this section, consequently, is bringing to the foreground coexisting territorialities that have been repressed by Spanish (and European) mapping of the city, the earth, and the cosmos. The section will journey—comparatively—first, through similar foundations for the ordering of space and time in different civilizations before the sixteenth century and, second, will show the survival and coexistence of premodern cosmologies with modern cartography. One fundamental premise of this part of the book (as well as of the chapter) is the increasing fissure in the emerging Western civilization between, on the one hand, a concept of time attached to cosmology and religion and a concept of time attached to business and administration and, on the other, a concept of space attached to the body, the community, and the place and a concept of space attached to geometric projection and arithmetic calculus.[17]

When I began to read about the history of cartography in order to

understand the implications of Ricci's move for the colonization and
reconfiguration of space, I soon learned that the omphalos syndrome
governing territorial descriptions, both in its spatial aspects (people
believing that they are at the center of the world) as well as its religious
ones (people believing that they have been divinely appointed), was
not peculiar to the Chinese but was actually quite widespread. I
learned also that generally the omphalos syndrome is related to the
body as the model of the cosmos and the *axis mundi* is related to a
sacred place as the center of the world. It became apparent in both
cases that the ethnic center had to be grounded on some basic experience other than the body and the sacred place, such as the east-west
movement of the sun and the moon (as one of the most fundamental
features of spatial orientation),[18] the perception of space from a personal rather than a collective perspective in which the human body is
located as fundamental reference for territorial representation, or a
combination of these factors. Arnheim's assumptions that some fundamental principles of spatial description are deeply rooted in human
nature[19] and that particular manifestations take place in specific historic conditions and under the rules of enduring traditions support my
intuitions.[20] Lumsden and Wilson's plea for a new human science
deserves to be reconsidered from the perspective of the shape human
beings attributed and continue to attribute to the earth and the cosmos. It is not toward a biological determinism that I am heading, but
to the recursive capacity that places all human beings and human
cultures at the same level of intellectual achievements, at the same
time that it shows their diversity and coevolutionary transformations.[21] The distinction between the materiality of nature and culture,
on the one hand, and the human description of it in their constant
transformation and adaptation to the natural and social environment,
on the other, is one way of solving the old philosophical problem cast
in terms of realism versus idealism or the conflict between the world
and the word. The dichotomy vanishes when a distinction is made
between *existence* (or the materiality of what there is) and *the description of what there is*. A description of the world is what makes it relevant to us, not its mere existence. The domains that human beings can
perceive or *describe* are much more limited than what *there is*. Expanding knowledge is, precisely, the human capacity of expanding the
range of descriptions without exhausting the ontological domains.

In the particular case of the body and the shape of the cosmos, the
correlation between micro- and macrocosmos was a shared belief
among certain intellectuals of the European Middle Ages. Such a correlation was very influential in depicting the earth and the universe.[22]

The micro-macrocosm theory believes that humanity is a little world, and that the world had the form of a great man (or human being). The Christian version of this theory is exemplified by the body of Christ,[23] as illustrated in figure 5.6. The *Ebstorf* map (fig. 5.7) provides a paradigmatic illustration of territorial representation in Christian cosmology. While the human body in general suggests the four horizontal directions (head and feet indicating east and west and extended arms north and south) and the movement of the sun and the moon mark the east-west orientation, Christian cosmology located the east (sunrise) next to Christ's head, where Paradise was also placed. Jerusalem and Christ's navel coincide, which justifies the metaphor "the navel of the world" given to a place that is at the same time the center of the human body and the center of the cosmos. The power of the center is very similar in conception to the rectangular

Fig. 5.6.   The body, the earth, the cosmos: graphic versions of the micro-macrocosm theory

Chinese "world map" shown in figure 5.2, in which the Middle Kingdom has a function similar to Jerusalem in Christian iconography. If
this "map" complies with a political rather than with a religious or
philosophical organization of the territory, the description provided in
The Book of Lieh-tzu (about 125 B.C.)[24] places the Middle Kingdom in
the center of four oceans and between the southernmost corner of the
west pole and the northernmost corner of the east pole:

> *In the southernmost corner of the western pole* lies a land that extends
> no one knows how far. It is called the Ku-mang land. There the
> forces of *Yin* and *Yang* do not meet, and therefore the contrast
> between cold and warm does not exist. . . . The people do not eat,

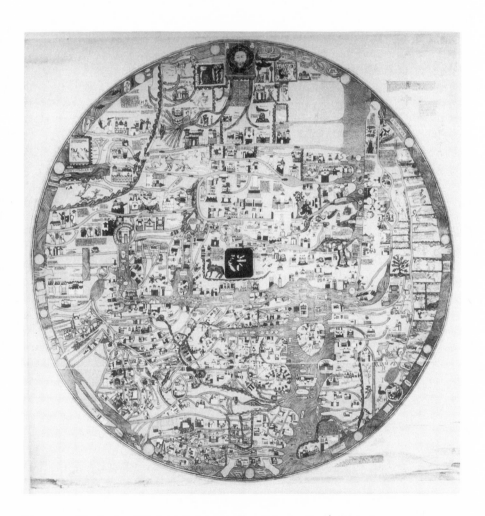

Fig. 5.7.   The body of Christ and the ordering of the earth: the *Ebstorf* map

and do not wear garments, but sleep almost all the time. . . . *The Middle Kingdom lies amidst the Four Oceans,* to the north and south of the Yellow River and to the east and west of the Great Mountain (*t'ai-shan*) in an area far greater than a thousand square miles. Dark and light are separated. . . . Nature thrives, the arts and the crafts are highly developed. . . . *In the northernmost corner of the east pole* lies a land called Fu-lo. It is always hot there, sun and moon shine constantly with a glaring light. . . . They do not eat cooked food. They are hard and cruel by nature.[25]

Thus, the geographical center appeared to be correlated in some cases to the human body, sometimes to the four directions, and other times to both (see infra, the discussion of ancient Cuzco). There are cases, I submit, in which the ordering of space takes the human body as model and its navel as the center of the cosmos; in others, the body is taken as a reference point positioned at the center of the four horizontal and two vertical directions. Space, religious belief, and ethical order come together in an ethnic rationalization of space where the center is determined by a semantic configuration originating in the human body and extending to the space and life of the community as a center.[26]

There is no reason to think that in pre-Columbian civilizations a similar configuration of the cosmos did not exist. Alfredo López Austin has devoted an extensive and well-documented study to tracing the network between the description of the body, the configuration of the cosmos, and the system of ideas among the Mexicas.[27] He suggested a connection between the three vertical levels of the cosmos (sky, surface of the earth, and underworld) and the three spiritual or energetic centers. The brain (*tonalli*) corresponded to the higher sky; the heart (*toyolia*) to the lower sky, and the kidney (*uhiyotl*) to the earth's surface and the underground. Since the sun was placed in the lower sky, it was related to the human heart, and the head, or the brain, also received the name of *ilhuicatl* (or sky). Through the cosmos, the energetic centers were related to the nuclear family: the celestial Father, the earthly Mother, and, in between, the place of the Children. The body was also related to the calendar. Each sign of the twenty-day unit-cycle (equivalent to Western months) corresponded to a part of the body. It was related to medicine in the sense that the disorders of the body and their diagnosis were based on the correspondence between the ill part of the body and the corresponding day in the unit-cycle.

Within an ethnic rationalization of space (be it medieval T/O maps or Mexica four corners of the world), the sacred place establishes the

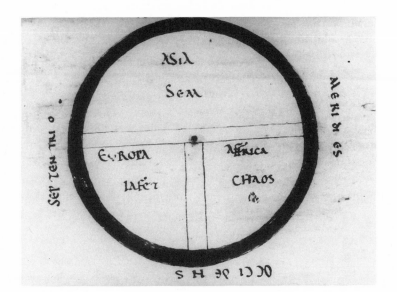

Fig. 5.8.   The earth divided in three and the three sons of Noah: Asia-Shem, Europe-Japheth, and Africa (Lybia)-Ham

axis mundi, where space and time meet; where the vertical and the horizontal join forces with the movement of the skies and the changes of season. When Bernardino de Sahagún in the final copy of the *Florentine Codex* had to account for the direction of winds in Mexica astrology, he requested a *tlacuilo* to depict—within a rectangle—the earth round and divided in three parts (fig. 5.8), as it was usually described in Christian cosmology (fig. 5.9), and then placed the wind directions in the four corners of the rectangle. It certainly did not escape Sahagún that the Mexica divided time in four and that to each cycle in time there was a corresponding place in space (see, e.g., fig. 3.7), which missionaries associated with the four cardinal points. But in any event, Sahagún did not stress the mixing of space and time in Mexica cosmology, and he used a T/O map (in which the meeting point of the crossbar and stem of the *T* within the *O* mark Jerusalem as the center of the world; see chap. 6) to account for the configuration of the heavens and a circle divided in four to account for the organization of time.

As was pointed out in the previous chapter, one of the models followed by Sahagún was Bartholomaeus Anglicus's *De proprietatibus rerum*. The 1492 edition of this text included a description of the world modeled on T/O shape. There was certainly a long, strong tradition of the cosmos divided in three parts, so strong that in 1578 when he was finishing the *Florentine Codex* Sahagún overlooked that a fourth part of the earth had been added almost a century earlier. The name of Cosmas Indicopleustes is seldom mentioned during the period, although he stands at the very foundation of such a tradition. His *Christian Topography* is one of the first descriptions of a tripartite and Christian conception of the earth.[28] In his description Cosmas placed Asia in the Orient, Lybia (and not Africa) in the southwest, and Europe in the northwest. The west, it is worthwhile to remember, was at the time divided between Lybia (which would become Africa) and Europe (which would be identified more and more with the Christian West during and after the sixteenth century).[29] It should come as no

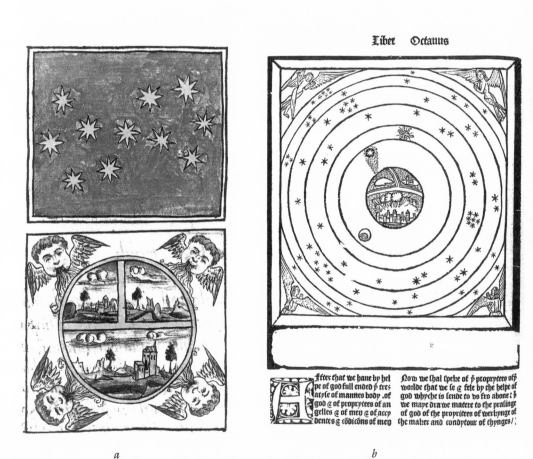

a   *b*

Fig. 5.9.   Circling the square and reducing the four corners of the world to the three sections of the T/O maps: *a,* Sahagún's depiction of the wind against the background of an (inverted) T/O map; *b,* a possible model, Bartholomaeus Anglicus, *De proprietatibus rerum,* in the edition of 1492

surprise, then, that the well-known medieval T/O maps systemat-   233
ically placed Jerusalem at the center. The map shown in figure 5.8 was   ———————
used to illustrate Isidore of Seville's (A.D. 560–636) *Etimologiae*.[30]   *The Movable*
Oriented with the East at the top, the map contains the names of the
three continents and identifies each with one of Noah's sons: Asia with
Shem, Europe with Japheth, and Africa with Ham.[31]

Between Ricci's move (at the end of the sixteenth century) and the
Christian T/O maps (during the European Middle Ages) came the
updating of the Ptolomaic tradition and the ordering of space according to a geometric center. By showing that the geometric center is
movable and that the observer could be removed from the position
established by his/her body, community, or center of power, Ricci
showed that the ethnic centers (e.g., Christian Europe, Rome) could
coexist without conflict with geometric ones (e.g., China, the Pacific).
Ricci's move has at least two readings. One reading focuses on the
paradigmatic changes taking place in sixteenth-century Europe: the
position of the earth in the universe was being displaced from
the center to a peripheral orbit. The second reading focuses on the
belief that the ethnic *axis mundi* was being replaced by an objective
and geometrically calculated *mapamundi*. Both readings unravel two
sides of the same coin: ethnic centers remained, as always, attached to
an observer placed at the center of a community or of a locus of power;
geometric calculus created the illusion that a universal, objective, and
nonethnic observer was possible. The modern idea of science is part
and parcel of the dissociation, in the Western tradition, between an
ethnic center (which became subjective, political, and ideological)
and a geometric one (which became objective, neutral, and scientific)
and produces the illusion that geometry is not attached also to a basic
ethnic perspective.

The Dominican friar Diego Durán, also working in Mexico around
the time that Sahagún was writing his *Florentine Codex,* had a slightly
different version of the Mexicas' four dimensions of time (fig. 5.10).
And their attitudes toward the Mexica were also quite different than
the attitude Ricci had vis-à-vis the Chinese. Durán accounted for the
fusion of space and time in the Mexica cosmology and described the
counting of the years in relation to the division of the earth:

> The round circle was divided into four parts, each part containing
> thirteen years. The first part belonged to the East, the second to the
> North, the third to the West, and the fourth to the South. The first
> part, belonging to the East, was called the Thirteen Years of the
> Reeds, and so it was that each square of the thirteen contained a
> picture of a reed and the number of the year in the same way that we

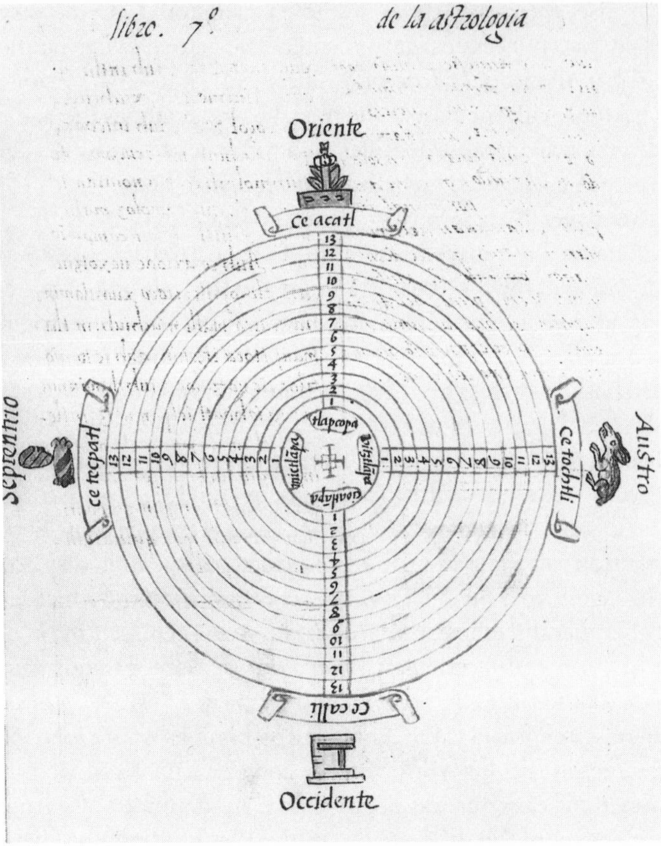

Fig. 5.10a. Sahagún's rendition of Aztec cosmology (1578): The circle overtaking the square, and the four corners of the world

Fig. 5.10b. A pre-Copernican diagram of the universe (from Peter Apianus's *Cosmographia*, 1539)

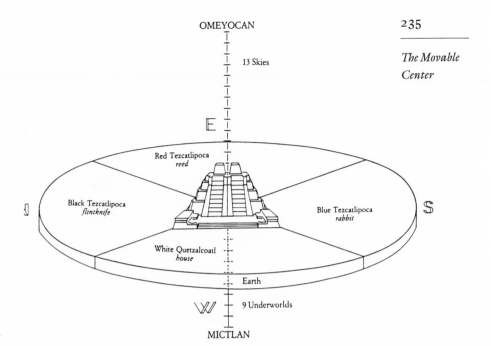

Fig. 5.II.   The temple, the city, the universe: the Temple of the Sun and the structure of Tenochtitlán

reckon the day on this present year, as in December, 1579, we say, "Such and such a thing happened in this year."[32]

Since the Mexica themselves divided the world in four parts, Durán and Sahagún did them justice not only in modeling the fourth corner of the world but also in linking space and time. There remained, however, two dimensions in which the Christian model served to colonize Mexica cosmology by turning it into Western concepts of space and time. In paintings found in Amerindian codices in which their own cosmography and cosmology are depicted, the shape of a square or a rectangle is preferred to that of the circle. The design in the *Codex Féjérvary-Mayer* (see fig. 3.6) shows the four directions of the universe in time and space and is the manner in which the Mexica described to themselves what Sahagún and Durán describe to and for a European reader. Here, the four directions of space and time stemmed from the Temple of the Sun (or Templo Mayor) (fig. 5.II), which was at the same time a sacred place and the navel of the world: it was the center of the four horizontal directions; the center of the horizontal organization of the universe in thirteen places above (heavens) and nine below, and, finally, the center of the Fifth Age, or the age of the sun in which the Aztec were living.[33]

Beside the sacred places, geopolitical centers had a more limited function, in the sense that, contrary to the "navel of the world" or *axis mundi*, they organize the earthly world without cosmological implications. Let's move to the Muslim world of the thirteenth century. Six or seven centuries after Cosmas and Saint Isidore established the foundations for the Christian conceptualization of space, which had a serious effect on the colonization of Amerindian space well into the sixteenth century, the Muslim Ibn Khaldun was reading the Greek historians, philosophers, and geographers (Ptolemy) of the Hellenistic era and writing his famous prolegomen (*muqaddimah*) to a description (history) of the Arab people placed in a universal context.[34] It was customary in the European as well as in the Muslim Middle Ages to include a chapter describing the shape of the cosmos and the form of the earth, and Ibn Khaldun did not change the tradition. He included a map of the earth (fig. 5.12) by Al-Idrisi, following Ptolemy. Since he was born and lived in northern Africa, he placed the Arabic world at the center of the planet (nos. 30, 33, 37).

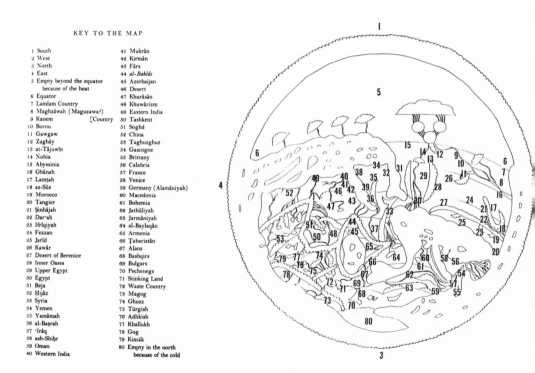

KEY TO THE MAP

1	South	41	Mukrân
2	West	42	Kirmân
3	North	43	Fârs
4	East	44	al-Bahlûs
5	Empty beyond the equator because of the heat	45	Azerbaijan
		46	Desert
6	Equator	47	Khurâsân
7	Lamlam Country	48	Khuwârizm
8	Maghzâwah (Maguzawa?)	49	Eastern India
9	Kanem [Country	50	Tashkent
10	Bornu	51	Soghd
11	Gawgaw	52	China
12	Zaghây	53	Tughuzghuz
13	at-Tâjuwîn	54	Gascogne
14	Nubia	55	Brittany
15	Abyssinia	56	Calabria
16	Ghânah	57	France
17	Lamṭah	58	Venice
18	as-Sûs	59	Germany (Alamâniyah)
19	Morocco	60	Macedonia
20	Tangier	61	Bohemia
21	Ṣinhâjah	62	Jathûliyah
22	Dar'ah	63	Jarmâniyah
23	Ifrîqiyah	64	al-Baylaqân
24	Fezzan	65	Armenia
25	Jarîd	66	Ṭabaristân
26	Kawâr	67	Alans
27	Desert of Berenice	68	Bashqirs
28	Inner Oases	69	Bulgars
29	Upper Egypt	70	Pechenegs
30	Egypt	71	Stinking Land
31	Beja	72	Waste Country
32	Ḥijâz	73	Magog
33	Syria	74	Ghuzz
34	Yemen	75	Türgish
35	Yamâmah	76	Adhkish
36	al-Baṣrah	77	Khallukh
37	'Irâq	78	Gog
38	ash-Shiḥr	79	Kimâk
39	Oman	80	Empty in the north because of the cold
40	Western India		

Fig. 5.12.   Where the world was not divided in three: Al-Idrisi's map

Or perhaps better, the center of the world this time was not Jerusalem, but the Mediterranean (e.g., the middle of the earth),[35] a geopolitical center around which the main places of the Arab world are located (Syria, Iran, Egypt). As was customary only in Muslim cartography, South is at the top and North at the bottom, with empty spaces beyond the equator (no. 6) and toward the south (no. 5) and north pole (no. 80). Ibn Khaldun provided a native point of view of the earth in which the center of space and memory is the Arabic world. The appropriation of Ptolemy in the West, since the fifteenth century, constitutes in itself an interesting story, for the Arabic cartographic tradition founded in Ptolemy will be marginalized by the expansion of Europe and European cartography. Europe, as a unit well distinguished in the T/O map tradition, was not recognized as such in Ibn Khaldun's map, in which northern cities are mentioned (for instance, in no. 54, Gascogne; no. 57, France; no. 58, Venice; etc.) but not as part of a unit called Europe. Even less distinct was a unit called Asia, although Ibn Khaldun listed a large number of cities east of the Arab world (e.g., western India, no. 40, and eastern India, no. 49). Bernard Lewis reports that until the nineteenth century "Muslim writers on history and geography knew nothing of the names which Europeans had given the continents. Asia was unknown, and ill-defined Europe—spelled Urufa—received no more than a passing mention, while Africa, Arabicized into Ifriqiya, appeared only as the name of the eastern Maghrib, consisting of Tunisia and the adjoining areas."[36] Imaginary constructions take on, over time, ontological dimensions; descriptions of an object become the object itself. The Christian partition of the world into three units, according the mental frame of their sacred narrative as described in the T/O maps, was indeed a Christian invention and not a natural division of the earth supposedly known and accepted in different cultures. Ibn Khaldun drew a geopolitical map and wrote a political-economic history of the world from the Arab perspective.[37] What Idrisi's map and Ibn Khaldun's comments teach us is precisely that maps are and are not the territory. They are not, because they do not reflect any essential reality of the shape of the earth or of the cosmos. They are because, once they are accepted, they become a powerful tool for controlling territories, colonizing the mind and imposing themselves on the members of the community using the map as the real territory. If it were a one-to-one correspondence between maps and territories, the world would have been naturally divided in three parts according to the natural Christian partition of it. However, Islam intellectuals did not see the world divided in three parts, and if a Muslim navigator had "discovered America" instead of a Christian one, the "fourth part" of the world would not have been

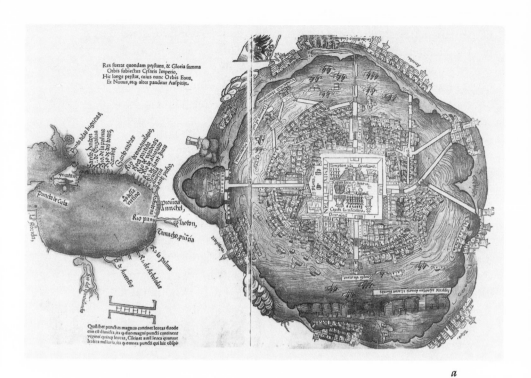

Res fuerat quondam prestans, & Gloria summa
Orbis subiectus Cesaris Imperio,
Hic longe prestat, cuius nunc Orbis Eous,
Et Nouus, atq; alter panditur Auspitiis.

Quælibet punctus magnus continet leucas duode
cim est dimidia, ita q; duo magni puncti continent
viginti quinq; leucas, Cōtinet autē leuca quatuor
Italica milearia, ita q; omnes puncti qui hic cōspi

a

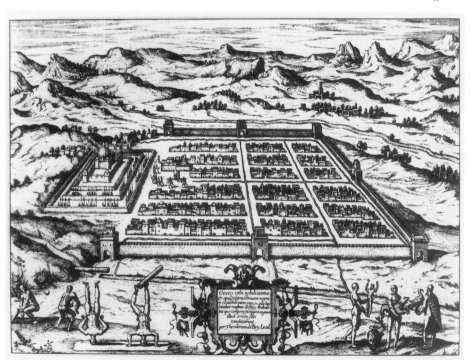

b

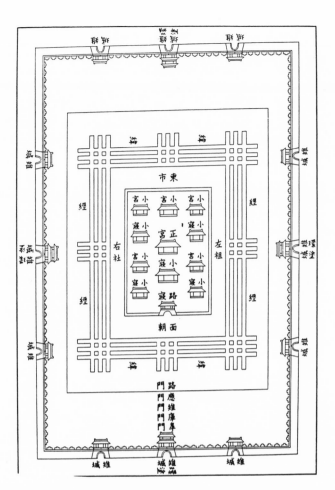

c

Fig. 5.13. European descriptions of non-European cities: *a,* Cortés's map
of Tenochtitlán; *b,* Cuzco imagined toward the end of the fifteenth century;
c, a Chinese walled city

conceived as such, nor would it have been a problem to accommodate
this part to the three previous parts because, simply, the idea of the
earth divided in three did not exist in the Islamic world.

And finally there were the cities, which could be either designed
and conceived in terms of sacred places or geopolitical centers. Hernán Cortés, for instance, recognized Tenochtitlán only as a geopolitical unit and erased the sacred connotations in the Mexica organization
of life. The well-known map of Mexico-Tenochtitlán that Cortés sent
to Charles V (fig. 5.13*a*)[38] was also described in his first letter:

> This vast city of Tenochtitlán rises out of this saltwater lagoon, and
> on whichever side one wishes to enter the central part of the city

from the mainland, one must travel two leagues. *There are four
roads into the city, each one two short lances in breadth and entirely
paved by hand.* The city is as large as Seville and Córdoba. Its
streets, the main ones that is, are most wide, and some of these and
all the rest are half earth and half water and the natives travel up and
down them in their canoes; here and there, the streets are interrupted where the water passes from one canal to another, and at
each opening (some of which are very wide) there is a downbridge
made out of stout, well-fashioned and robust wooden beams,
bound together, some of them wide enough to bear ten horses
passing side-by-side.[39]

There is no reason to expect Cortés to know about the religious
implications of city structures. When Cortés describes the four roads
leading toward the center of the city, he probably did not remember
that Alexandria (fourth century B.C.) had a similar structure. He was
certainly more familiar with the structure introduced by the Roman
land and urban surveyors,[40] and with the *forma urbis romae* spread
through the Roman colonies. He looked at the city from a military
perspective (perhaps learned from the complicity between city structure and colonial control in the Roman Empire) and not at its cosmographic dimensions.[41] It might not have occurred to him that
when the Mexicas entered the city they were approaching the center
of their world.

A comparison between ancient China and ancient Mexico is fruitful
at this point. There is a double meaning in the Chinese logogram for
"wall," which could also be interpreted as "city."[42] The center, surrounded by the four quarters, was conceived as the homeland with the
Middle Kingdom having the city of Peking as its sacred center.[43] Like
the map of nested rectangles in figure 5.2, there was an inner city
within walls; within the Imperial City was the emperor's residence and
the empire's administration. And within that, the Forbidden City, into
which only members of the imperial household were admitted. And
finally, the Hall of Divine Harmony, the center of the world, where the
emperor had his Sacred Throne Room. Tenochtitlán followed a similar pattern. The Lake Texcoco, in the Valley of Mexico, was described
in Mexica narratives about their origins as the place designated by
Huitzilopochtli, the supreme deity who indicated the road to the
Aztecs and moved them from Aztlán to Mexico-Tenochtitlán. In the
center, the calendar stone was placed from which armies were dispatched to the four quarters of the empire, following an inverse direction from that of Cortés's army and justified with a different rationale.
Cortés entered the city at the moment in which geometric rationaliza-

Fig. 5.14.   The structure of the city and the grid of the cosmos: frontispiece of the *Mendoza Codex*

tion of space was replacing ethnic ones, both in their Christian and Amerindian versions.

The parallel structures of the cosmos and the city are illustrated in the frontispiece of the *Mendoza Codex* (fig. 5.14). The frontispiece of the *Codex* is a matrix similar to the matrix of the city Tenochtitlán.[44] Contrary to Durán's organization of space, the lines dividing the four quarters are not perpendicular to each other but diagonal. Each quarter is dominated by a god-creator and is linked to an element of allegorical significance and to a color: rain god, fertility, red, on top where the sun rises; wind god, knowledge, white, where the sun sets; earth god, death, black, to the left-hand side of someone facing the sunrise; and fire god, uncertainty, blue, to the right of someone facing sunrise.[45] Also, contrary to the Mexica calendar as depicted by Durán and Sahagún, in which time has been detached from space, the Mexicas' own depiction in the *Mendoza Codex* blends time with space. Tenochtitlán, in the center, is surrounded by the four quarters of the world and by the count of the years. Durán, instead, has placed the sun in the center, which should not be interpreted necessarily according to the heliocentric concept of the universe but as his misunderstanding of Mexica cosmology. The city is also surrounded by water, as indicated by the blue borders of the picture. At the center, the city is indicated by the classical image of the blooming cactus growing from a stylized rock with an eagle landing on it, fulfilling the prophecy of their gods announcing the place in which their peregrination from Aztlán (place of origin) would end. Territoriality, within a context of ethnic rationalization of space, is a complex calculus of time, space, memory, and semiotic codes. Wheatley summarizes the ethnic calculus in ancient Chinese cosmology by saying that the *axis mundi* is "the place where earth and sky meet, where the four seasons merge, where wind and rain are gathered in, and where *ying* and *yang* are in harmony."[46] Similar patterns have been followed in Mesoamerica and the Andes, as Wheatley himself notices, and this has also been analyzed with regard to both the structure of Tenochtitlán and the Mexicas' thoughts.[47] The map or plan of Mexico-Tenochtitlán printed in the Nuremberg edition of Cortés's letters delineates, at the level of the city, how the colonization of space functions not only at the cognitive but also at the pragmatic level. At the cognitive level, Cortés's map disguises the Mexica concept of the world and the links between the city and the cosmos under the look of a European guided by the legacy of Roman city planners and urban surveyors. At the pragmatic level, the possibilities of the printing press to convey and instill verbal descriptions and visual images overpowered the hand-painted codices that remained in the possession of a few administrators or persons of the royal house. Durán and Sahagún helped to disseminate an image of the Mexica cosmovision in which the four essential components were reduced to three (in Sahagún's T/O map) or space detached from time (as in Durán's and Sahagún's calendar).

Let's move now from an ethnic rationalization of space built upon the idea of the center to an ethnic rationalization construed upon geometrical progression detached from the physical location of the individual or the community. Let's go back, in other words, to the significance of Ricci's move remapping the East Indies to López de Velasco mapping the West Indies.

López de Velasco's Move: Blowing Up Geometric Centers and Disguising Ethnic Ones

While Ricci in China as well as Durán and Sahagún in Mexico were dealing with conflicting cosmographic and territorial conceptions, López de Velasco, cosmographer of the Council of the Indies since 1571, was figuring out how to map the new territories rather than to understand how the Amerindians did it themselves. López de Velasco belonged to a practical tradition in the foundation of mapping, related to colonial expansion, in which Roman lands and urban surveyors left a lasting legacy.[48] Furthermore, at the turn of the sixteenth century Ptolemy became the paradigm of the geometric rationalization of space, gaining ground among intellectuals and educated persons, and slowly discrediting ethnic rationalizations, such as Christian T/O maps or Chinese nested squares. While in the first part of this chapter I looked at Ricci's adventure with his world map and then to the body as a model of territorial description and justification of the omphalos syndrome, I would like to focus in this next section on the need of geometric projections to manage the increasing amount of information and the mobility of the center as a need of territorial control and spatial colonization. While geometric projections in mapmaking allowed for the mobility of the geometric centers, ethnic concerns dominated the economic, political, and religious expansion of Christendom, and of the Spanish and Portuguese empires. Thus, while the ethnic center of cultures in expansion (like the Spanish or Christians) remained and was strengthened by its complicity with the geometric rationalization of space, the ethnic centers and rationalizations of space of colonized cultures were suppressed (like Chinese, Mexica, or Andean). The expansion of the Spanish empire coincided with the historical moment, in the West, when Christianity, after losing its religious center (Jerusalem), created another from which the campaign to Christianize the world began. Paradoxically enough, the mobility of the religious centers seemed to have had some indirect consequences in the transformation of geographical discourse and territorial descriptions. Let's explore López de Velasco's move from this perspective.

Toward 1574 López de Velasco, who was appointed cosmographer

of the Council of the Indies in 1571, was fulfilling his duties by writing
the *Descripción y demarcación de las Indias Occidentales* (1574), a
detailed account of the Spanish possessions from what are now called
the Caribbean Islands to the Philippines (fig. 5.15).[49] He divided the
Spanish territories into three parts: Indias Septentrionales (northern
Indies) which comprised the area from Florida to the Straits of Panama; Indias Meridionales (southern Indies), from the Straits of Panama to Patagonia; and Indias del Poniente (western Indies), which
included the Philippines, Moluccas, and so on (fig. 5.16). López de
Velasco's report came as one of the consequences of an evaluation (*vi-
sita*) to the Council of the Indies ordered by Philip II and was based on
the recommendation of Juan de Ovando, in charge of such an evaluation, to have a systematic way of collecting information about the
colonial possessions.[50] If López de Velasco's verbal description and
the fourteen maps attached were the first step toward a systematic
collecting of information about the New World, the second step was
the *Instrucción y memoria* (Instruction and memorandum; hereafter
referred to as the *Memorandum*), a list of fifty questions distributed to

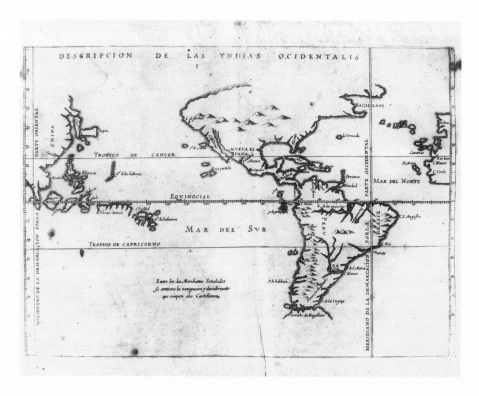

Fig. 5.15. Mapping the Spanish possessions: the *Descripción y demarcación
de las Indias Occidentales*

every corner of the Indies in which an alcalde or a public notary was available to collect information and answer each of the questions.[51] One specific question asked for a *pintura* of the location being surveyed. As a consequence of this request, several *pinturas* were attached to the *Relaciones geográficas,* which were the written report and the reply to the *Memorandum.* Thus, like the reaction of the Chinese mandarin to Ricci, some maps drawn by the "indios viejos" [older Indians] are the remaining testimony of coexisting and conflicting territorial descriptions in the colonial period. Resistance among Amerindian intellectuals, however, did not have the visible force Ricci encountered in China, and the preservation of Amerindian traditions suffered under the impact of Spanish and Christian colonization of space.

The map shown in figure 5.15 was complemented by a verbal description:

The Indies, the islands and terra firma in the Ocean which are commonly called the New World, are the lands and seas which lie within the boundaries of the kingdom of Castile, which is a hemi-

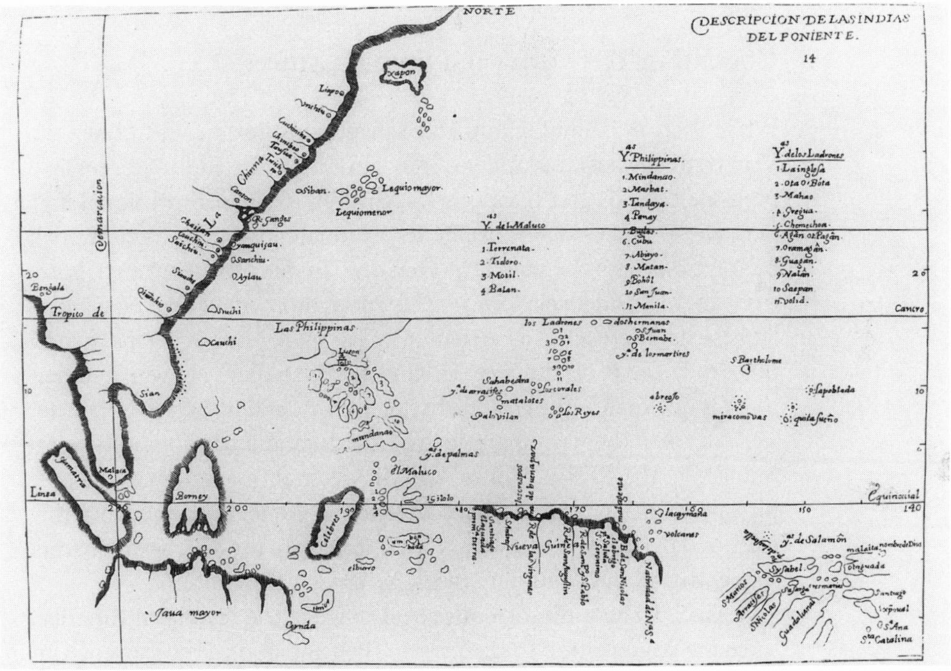

Fig. 5.16. Mapping the Spanish possessions beyond the "New World": the *Indias del Poniente*

sphere, or half of the world, beginning at 180 degrees west from a meridian circle which passes through 39 degrees longitude west of the meridian of Toledo.[52]

However, while in his own geographical discourse López de Velasco concealed native territorialities, in his massive plan to gather information implemented through the *Memorandum*, he opened the doors—unintentionally, of course—to a discourse (the *Relaciones geográficas de Indias*), which allowed for a reading of native alternative conceptualization of space. Native territorialities, which had been disregarded in López de Velasco's report as well as in the subsequent history written by Herrera y Tordesillas and printed in several editions between 1601 and 1730,[53] emerged, however, in the *Relaciones geográficas*. Although it—like many other colonial writings—did not reach the printing press until the end of the nineteenth century (during the colonial period they did not have any particular force or effect other than providing information for the official chronist or historians),[54] they allowed—in retrospect—for the mobility of the center, which had been fixed in López de Velasco's *Descripción* and reproduced and transmitted in Herrera y Tordesillas's official *Historia*.

Coexisting Territories and Empty Centers

While Ricci in China, Durán and Sahagún in Mexico, and López de Velasco as the cosmographer of the Council of the Indies were mapping the cosmos and the earth—according to their institutional imperatives—Amerindians began to negotiate their own traditional conceptions with the new, imported one. In one way or another, seen from an Amerindian perspective the world, more often than not, looks like coexisting territories within the same space. Such a perspective is quite different from the Spanish (and European) one, in which either there is not such a thing as coexisting territorialities (like in López de Velasco) or, if there is, Amerindian cosmology and cosmography were reduced to the Christian ones. We will see, in the paradigmatic example of Guaman Poma de Ayala, how the world is described from the fractured perspective of a subaltern Amerindian, toward the end of the sixteenth and the beginning of the seventeenth centuries.

Coexisting here means both coexistence in the history of America since the colonization to the present days and also the coexistence in the same graphic space of two territorial descriptions. The first refers to the physical usurpation of territories as well as to graphic alternatives to Amerindian conceptualization of space implemented by the

Spanish administration and spread by the printing press. The second
refers to a practice perceived during the colonial period, mainly during
the first hundred years, whereby territorial descriptions (or mapping)
on the part of the Amerindians cohabit on the same piece of paper or
flat surface on which the territory has been described.[55] We have seen,
in the case of the colonization of language and of memory, that mil-
lions of Amerindians live today guided by the belief system of their
ancestors.[56] More than eradication of previous belief systems, colonization implied, first, that whoever does not embrace the hegemonic
values is marginalized and, second, that whoever is spatially marginal
with respect to the values of the metropolitan centers is also behind in
time (see chaps. 3 and 4). Integration by conversion meant, precisely,
moving people from the savage margins to the civilized centers, and
the idea of identifying the margin with the past began to emerge. The
denial of coevalness that Fabian identified in the philosophical foundation of anthropology in the nineteenth century was already at work
in the sixteenth, when religious, intellectual, and economic expansion
blended comparative ethnology with values and established a hierarchy of human beings and human cultures.[57]

Indeed, the sixteenth century witnessed several displacements of
the center. The earth gained a fourth continent in the view of the
Europeans, who had divided it previously in three, at the same time
that it was removed, by the Copernican revolution, from a central
position in the universe to the more modest one of turning around the
sun along with the other planets. It could be concluded from this
transformation that placing the sun at the center of the universe and
dividing the earth into four *continents* instead of into four *corners* not
only helped identify differences between cultural traditions, but also
implied that one was right and the other was wrong. Differences, once
again, were translated into values. But, of course, not all sixteenth-
century European men of letters accepted the idea that the sun, rather
than the earth, was the center of the universe. For a learned man like
Acosta, writing at the end of the sixteenth century, the earth still occupied the center. This was true as well for Garcilaso de la Vega, who
was writing a few decades later. The basic similarities in the way the
cosmos and the earth were divided and organized escaped the missionaries and men of letters, who only had eyes for superficial variations, which they interpreted as radical disparities. Once the New
Continent was added, European, Mesoamerican, and Andean civilizations had in common a quatripartite organization of the earth. There
were, of course, differences, such as the separation of time and space
and the coexistence of an ethnic fixed and a geometric mobile center
in European rationalization of space.

In Mesoamerican and Andean cosmologies, as we have already seen, the center of the four corners of the world coincided also with the present time, or the fifth age succeeding the previous four times when the world was destroyed. Still, it would be erroneous to retain a homogeneous picture of pre-Columbian cosmologies. It is important, nevertheless, to remember that, despite the differences, the quatripartite division of space and time was common to all of them,[58] from which Amerindian people inferred both the order of the cosmos and the count of the year.[59] The configuration of space in Mesoamerican and Andean civilization was largely abstract, in contrast to European T/O maps, which were based on knowledge of land configuration on three continents (Europe, Africa, and Asia) and unconnected with time.[60] Furthermore—and as we have already seen—the quatripartite division is valid not only for the organization of space and time, but also for the entire organization of urbanity and social life. León-Portilla provides the following description of urban organization based on the magic number four:

> Estas cuatro entradas se consideran "las cuatro esquinas" del pueblo. En ella se instalan al llegar la noche cuatro seres sobrenaturales llamados Balamanes, los cuales tienen por funcion cuidar el cuadrilatero que forma el pueblo, impidiendo que entre a el espiritus nocivos que alteren el bienestar de sus pobladores. En el centro de la aldea se instala un quinto Balam, conocido como thrup el que, no obstante su tamaño diminuto, se le considera el de mas poder.[61]

> [These four entrances were considered the four town corners. At dawn four supernatural beings called Balamanes occupy each of the corners and have as their task to watch the square, that is, the town, keeping the bad spirits away from the townspeople. The center of the village is occupied by a fifth Balam known as *thrup*, who, despite being very small, is nonetheless the more powerful.]

The symbolism here also empowers the center as the privileged place of space (here) and time (now). Among the Aztecs (or Mexica, as they called themselves), one function of the center was to symbolize the fifth sun, the present age. It was not the center of the horizontal quatripartite division, but the center of the vertical division between the upper world, the earth, and the underworld. Elzey has summarized the Aztec cosmology as follows:

> Time and space are homologized . . . at the abstract level of the structure of the world and the structure of its history. Cosmology

becomes a model for telling of the history and destiny of the universe; conversely, the birth of the gods and the establishment of their proper realms provides a paradigm for organizing the world into vertical tiers and horizontal quadrants.[62]

But the center was also the reference point to organize the past and to tell their own histories. Elzey continues:

> The Aztec kingdom is described by one source as "the root, the navel and the heart of this whole earthly mechanism." At the "center" of the world the Aztecs constructed a temple of the tribal god Huitzilopochtli. The god commanded the priests to "divide the men, each with his relations, friends and relatives, into four principal wards (barrios), placing at the center the house which you have built for my rest." Huitzilopochtli's order, in effect, is to construct Tenochtitlan on the model of the horizontal cosmos of the four quadrants and the four directions, held together in harmony by the power and authority which issues from the "center."[63]

It should not come as a surprise that the Incas, in the Andes, organized space and time along similar lines. They named their territory Tahuantinsuyu, which could be translated as "the land of the four parts or corners," and its geographical center Cuzco, which Garcilaso de la Vega rendered as "the navel of the world."[64] Urton, following the pathbreaking work of Tom Zuidema, has studied the organization of terrestrial space in the community of Misminay, in the Andes.[65] What this very detailed study of the organization of terrestrial and celestial space in a living community shows is that the quatripartite organization is a fundamental cognitive structure that has remained despite the spread of Western cultural literacy (fig. 2.17). Urton begins his book with this wonderful story:

> Late one afternoon while doing fieldwork in the community of Misminay, Peru, a thirteen-year-old boy with whom I was pasturing sheep volunteered the information that, in preparation for planting, everyone in the community was watching the stars called Collca ("storehouse") very closely each night. I was aware that the early part of the rainy season had been extremely dry that year (1976) and only a few people had been adventurous enough to plant their crop of potatoes. There was much discussion about how desperate the situation would be if planting did not begin soon. Following up on the young man's statement, I asked why everyone was watching Collca. His answer, accompanied by a sharp glance, was simple: porque queremos vivir ("because we want to live").[66]

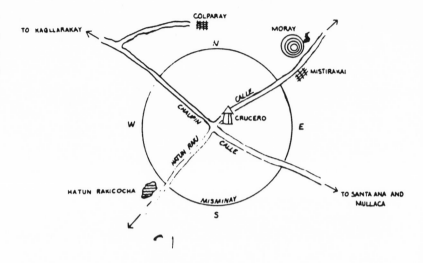

Fig. 5.17. Surviving cosmologies: the center path of Misminay
in today's Peru

The anecdote is one more example of intelligent interpretation,
ethnic rationalization, and social behavior that have been marginalized by other equally intelligent interpretation and social behavior
from people in control of economic, political, and technological
power. What is relevant for my argument is that, today, the community of Misminay bases the organization of terrestrial and celestial
space on the ancient Inca cosmology of the four quarters of the world.
Coexisting cosmographies in late-twentieth-century Latin America
might not be the same socially as they were during the sixteenth century, but it shows that the denial of coevalness is an ideological depiction of intercultural relations. The example of present-day Misminay
would make Guaman Poma de Ayala's *mapamundi* more relevant to
our discussion, for it allows us to understand the impact of Spanish
cartography in replacing Aztecan ethnic rationalizations of space by
geometric ones and using them to suppress the coexistence of parallel
histories and cosmographical conceptions in the colonized areas.

Underneath the surface of what looks, at first glance, pretty much
like a sixteenth-century European map, the four corners of the world
sketched by the two diagonals (fig. 5.18) of the rectangle in which the
mapamundi is inserted, the deep cognitive structure is what gives the
mapamundi its Andean-like rationalization of space. Contrary to
other similar cosmologies, in the Andes the division of the four quarters (*Tahuantinsuyu*) was at its turn subdivided into "upper" and

"lower" halves, although the basic matrix, similar to that of ancient
Mesoamerica and ancient China, shows that the center as navel of the
world (when the body is used as model or metaphor) or as the *axis*
mundi (when a temple, a city, or a mountain is used as model or
metaphor) is common to apparently unrelated cosmologies. The tripartite, instead of the quatripartite, division of T/O maps in Christian
cosmologies responds in my view to the same ethnic logic in the rationalization of space. The magic number three, instead of four, was
related to the Christian narrative of the origin of the world and the
post facto division of the earth based on the magic number three of the
sacred Trinity and Noah's three sons. For all these reasons, it certainly
would be an inaccurate and unfair evolutionary judgment to state that
pre-Columbian cultures discovered the power of the center after they
met Christian cosmology. It would be more accurate to say that Christian cosmology was built on an ethnic rationalization of the cosmos
and of the earth that was complemented by the Ptolemaic cartographic projections during the religious and economic expansion of

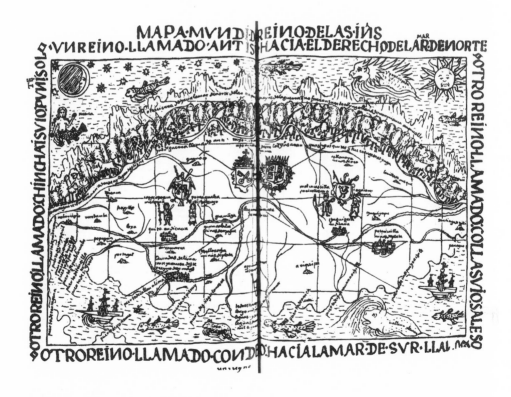

Fig. 5.18. Alternative colonial models to Western cosmographies:
the *mapamundi* of Guaman Poma de Ayala

the sixteenth and seventeenth centuries. As Ricci's move has shown, the mobility of the center in a cartographic projection and geometric rationalization of space does not conflict with a second-order ethnic rationalization, which kept Rome as the center of the Christian world even when the center of the geographical world could be placed in China and the Pacific.

Let's go back to Guaman Poma's map. There are clearly two readings of the map from the perspective I am suggesting. One is marked by the deep cognitive structure of the four corners and the center, the other by the surface structure of European cartography. Following the works of Zuidema, Watchel has summarized the double spatial structure of the "high" and the "low" (high: Chinchaysuyu [1] + Antisuyu [3]; low: Collasuyu [2] + Cuntinsuyu [4]), the four quarters of the world, and the correlation between spatial distribution and social organization.[67] Chinchaysuyu is the privileged quarter for Guaman Poma, to which he attributes nobility, strength, and dominance. The other pole of the "higher" division is the Antisuyu, and its people are the opposite to the Chinchaysuyu: hostile barbarians who eat human flesh. The inhabitants of the Collasuyu, the quarter of the lower part, opposite to Chinchaysuyu, like their counterpart of the higher part, the Antisuyu, are amoral, lazy, and corrupt, although they are also rich. Finally, the Cuntinsuyu is the exact opposite of the Collasuyu in terms of economical values: the inhabitants of the Cuntinsuyu are extremely poor. In modern terminology, civilization and barbarism distinguished the inhabitants of the two upper quarters; while riches and poverty characterized the people living in the lower quarters. On the other hand, the poor but virtuous and the civilized are opposed to the rich and the barbarians. In a world divided in four parts, subdivided in two, binary oppositions are replaced by a combinatorial game that organizes the cosmos and the society.

Furthermore, Guaman Poma's title reveals a tension between the two: by entitling it *Mapamundo del Reino de las Indias,* Guaman Poma identifies the superimposition of *tahuantinsuyu* and the Indies with the world. At a deeper level, the "map" is governed by a cognitive structure that could be interpreted as a transformed memory of the Inca Tahuantinsuyu, a native cognitive structure, corresponding with the view of the universe in Andean cosmology.[68] At the level of surface structure, the land surrounded by forest and water in the upper part and by water in the lower part, the map is a simulacrum of current world maps widely printed during Guaman Poma's time.[69] Whatever interpretation can be provided to better understand the complexities of Guaman Poma's world map, I am interested in the coexistence of conflictive territorial conceptions that renders a fractured perception of the world.[70]

Guaman Poma applied the same logic to the organization of space to the *Pontifical mundo* (fig. 5.19). Spain, in the lower part, has been depicted as a space with four corners and a center. The text reads, "Castilla below the Indies." On the upper part, the text reads, "The Indies of Peru on the top of Spain." The center is occupied by Cuzco. Castilla, the kingdom, and Spain, the country, are lumped together. The "Indies of Peru," an ambiguous expression from the point of view of the Spaniards, are the clear and well-defined regions of the West Indies in López de Velasco's *Descripción*. The *Pontifical mundo* does the job as well, however. For, if López de Velasco had the right to ignore the Amerindians' conceptualization of space, there is no special reason why an Amerindian like Guaman Poma had to get the picture as López de Velasco would have liked him to have it. However, the problem was (and still is) that López de Velasco was closer to the "real" shape of the New World than Guaman Poma, and his demarca-

Fig. 5.19. Colonial models alternative to Western cosmographies: the *Pontifical mundo* of Guaman Poma de Ayala.

tion became the reality of the Indies under Spanish rule, while Guaman Poma's demarcation remained in the archives as a curious cultural product for those who knew of its existence.

Finally, the center has been emptied. Although Cuzco and the Indies of Peru had been distinguished with a place next to the sun, there is still no such coexistence in maps drawn by the colonizer. Ortelius as well as López de Velasco proceeds as if no conceptualization of space had existed before they were able to map the "new" land. On the contrary, for Guaman Poma as well as for many *tlacuilo* who had the chance to paint or describe their town, they felt that their own territory remained but was occupied by someone else. There is a difference, however, in the work of the *tlacuilo* responsible for many of the *pinturas* (see chap. 6) in the *Relaciones geográficas de Indias* and Guaman Poma's *mapamundi* and *Pontifical mundo*. The difference is of scale and of cosmographical and cosmological awareness. The *tlacuilo* who painted the maps or the *Relaciones geográficas* limited himself to what the *relación* (and the public notary who enacted it) requested: a description of a town where the traces of the connection between city and cosmos have been erased. What remains is the coalescence of two worldviews in the same place. In Guaman Poma's *Pontifical mundo* the coalescence of two worlds, instead, has been projected into a cosmological diagram linking geography with a transcendent design of the cosmos.

Coexistence, Coevolution, and the Denial of the Denial of Coevalness

López de Velasco, contrary to Ricci, was not a Jesuit with the mission of converting the Chinese to Christianity, but the cosmographer of the Council of the Indies with the charge of gathering and organizing all relevant information about the Spanish territory in the West Indies. Although I am comparing López de Velasco with Father Ricci because both were active during the same years and dealt with the mobility of the center, their cases per se are quite dissimilar. Velasco, as cosmographer of the Council of the Indies, was mapping the Spanish possessions or West Indies, not making a world map; Ricci was transforming Ortelius to carry on the Jesuit mission in China. Furthermore, López de Velasco was not on a mission of conversion but simply in charge of mapping the territories and gathering information about the native population. Because the dialogue entertained between the missionaries and the natives was of a different nature than the dialogue entertained by the geographers and public notaries (*letrados, juristas*), reading the experience of *Descripción y demarcación de las Indias Occidentales* as well as of the *Relaciones geográficas de Indias* is quite interesting. López de Velasco's report was written with the conviction that the lands and coasts being mapped were just lumps to which no human conceptualization had been applied before the arrival of the Spaniards. He contributed to the knowledge of the periphery and to its incorporation into the ethnic center invented by those who were in a position to carry on the expansion of imperial Spain and Western Christendom. This is why we can conclude that while Father Ricci—with his world map—disdained Chinese cartography and space conceptualization, López de Velasco—with his map of the Indias Occidentales—repressed Amerindian territorial representations. However, the stronger tradition in Chinese cartography and narrative of the past allowed for a stronger (or at least more visible) resistance to Western territorial representations. The liquidation of Amerindian nobility and intellectual, however, left few traces of Amerindian resistance to Western territorial conceptualization.

Although by the last quarter of the sixteenth century Western cartographers had displaced the geographic and ethnic center from the Mediterranean to the Atlantic, and Rome began to be more centrally located than Jerusalem, Ricci's move consisted of disjoining the geographic from the ethnic rationalization of space.[71] Certainly this move did not convince the Chinese, who preferred the way their own cartographic tradition had solved the problems and satisfied the needs of territorial representations. It did convince Japanese scholars, however, as they saw in it the possibility of displacing the geographic and ethnic center from the Atlantic to the Pacific. The situation was different in the European expansion to the New World. López de Velasco's map of the West Indies presupposed the Atlantic as the geographic and ethnic center. Its successful reprinting in Herrera y Tordesillas's *Historia general de los hechos de los castellanos en las islas y tierra firme del mar océano* (1601) also indicates that López de Velasco's map was highly satisfactory to those who charted and controlled the administration of the Indies. The Amerindian *pinturas,* contrary to the Chinese reaction, suggest that, toward the end of the sixteenth century, the native population was losing its own patterns of territorial representation.

Durán and Sahagún, contrary to Ricci, did not entertain a dialogue with the Mexicas regarding the shape of the earth and the cosmos. They certainly talked to them, but apparently they did not listen in the same way that Ricci did. Durán and Sahagún rounded the square, so to speak, projecting both the figure of the circle and the tripartite division of the earth upon a cosmology conceived on the bases of the square and the world divided in four. It is in this context that Guaman Poma, in Peru, remains a paradigmatic example to illustrate alternative performances in conceiving and describing territories. He also allows us to understand that the colonization of language, memory, and space taking place at the same time in the administration controlled by the Council of the Indies and in the intellectual life of the court, monasteries, colleges, and universities does not necessarily imply the automatic removal of Amerindian (implicit) grammars, memories, and spatial ordering. Colonization of language, memory, and space implies that conflicting concepts, values, and actions directed toward language, memory, and space begin to coexist, although social and political power is not equally distributed.

Ricci's move illustrates how ethnic centers could be divided in sacred (or ideological) and geometric ones. His attitude not only reveals the differences between the two but also suggests that one is preferable to the other. The colonization of space (as well as of language and memory) took, during the sixteenth century, the form of an evolutionary process in which certain kinds of territorial representations (languages and ways of recording the past) were considered preferable to others. Differences were translated into values. What Pagden described as the origin of comparative ethnology could be recast in terms of what Fabian elaborated as a denial of coevalness.[72] During the sixteenth century a transition took place, in Europe, in the organization of space that impinged on the conception and evaluation of time. Fabian has suggested this transition, as shown in figures 5.20a and 5.20b. He has left, however, two centuries unaccounted for. Indeed, what happened between the time in which Mandeville wondered about the conflict between two different concepts of space and late-eighteenth- and early-nineteenth-century England, which is Fabian's paradigmatic example?

What happened was a long intellectual process that Maravall beautifully reconstructed as the emergence of the idea of "progress" in the European Renaissance.[73] Maravall stressed the importance of the "discoveries" for the consolidation of the differences and the need to integrate a fourth part of the world into a European consciousness. Thus, not only did the concept of experience become crucial in the vocabulary of the time, but the idea of progress also began to emerge in the comparison between the ancient and the modern and occupied a large part of the intellectual life and energy of the late Renaissance. Colonization of space (of language, of memory) was signaled by the belief that differences could be measured in values and values measured in a chronological evolution. Alphabetic writing, Western historiography, and cartography became part and parcel of a larger frame of

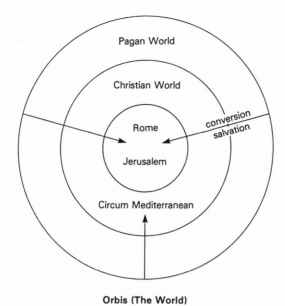

Orbis (The World)

Fig. 5.20*a*.　Premodern time-space

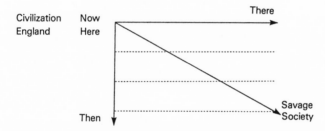

mind in which the regional could be universalized and taken as a yardstick to evaluate the degree of development of the rest of the human race. The supposedly progressive point of view taken by missionaries and men of letters in the sixteenth century manifested itself in terms of spreading the right religion, the right customs, and the right ways of learning. This point of view was supplemented by the concept of evolution, which continued to influence the humanities and the social sciences into the nineteenth century.

Concluding Remarks

I argued, in this chapter, that human transformation does not necessarily move *from* ethnic *to* geometric rationalization of space; that cartography does not suddenly emerge as a rational enterprise from previous irrational organization of space; and that history does not emerge from myth. I made an effort to show that alternative territorial orderings coexist in different forms and intensities. The geometric rationalization of space that took place during the sixteenth century, in the context of a much larger epistemic transformation in Western Europe, did not replace the ethnic ones. It redistributed them in significant ways: first, by retaining an ethnic center (Spain, Rome) at the same time decentralizing it (that was Ricci's move); second, by leaving out as nonexistent alternative territorial conceptualizations (that was López de Velasco's move). However, resistance and opposition brought to the foreground what had been left out by showing that alternative cosmographies and cosmologies had not been suppressed or substituted for by Western cartography (and those were the Chinese and Amerindian moves). Comparative approaches and a pluritopic hermeneutics could offer, then, an alternative to the success enjoyed by the Darwinian model (which explained the functioning of the natural system as well as the changes of life) in the social sciences and the humanities. Fabian's expression "denial of coevalness," which he used to describe this process, needs a change of perspective in the politics of intellectual inquiry and a move toward a "denial of the denial of coevalness." I explicitly argued, in this chapter and the previous ones, in favor of such a move and will reiterate it in the following and final chapter.

Chapter 6

Putting the Americas on the Map: Cartography and the Colonization of Space

Fixing the Center Again

That lands and peoples unknown to a European observer should be called "New World" simply because the observer had no prior knowledge of them brings to the foreground the larger issue of the arrogance and ethnocentrism of observers for whom what is unknown does not exist. Misunderstanding went together with colonization. Once something was declared new, and the printing press consolidated the idea among the literates, the descriptions of people for whom nothing was new about the place they were inhabiting, except for the arrival of a people strange to them, were suppressed. Space and place followed patterns similar to time and memory, already discussed in chapters 3 and 4. The presupposition that history was recorded alphabetically and that *res gestarum* was indistinguishable from *res gestae* complemented the idea that space was not mapped among the Amerindians. There were dissidents, of course, among the Spanish missionaries, but they were not strong enough to replace the more accepted and powerful versions of what history was and what visual descriptions (*tabula, descriptio,* later on called "maps") of the earth implied. Putting the Americas on the map and administrating the West Indies are good examples of coexisting territorialities and power relations.

The previous chapter focused on epistemological transformations that occurred when the rise of Christianity and mercantilism introduced new territorial dimensions over previous and coexisting territorialities of highly developed civilizations (China, Mesoamerica, the Andes, medieval Christian Europe). Transformation does not mean suppression of what was there before, but a redistribution of power relations. It has been suggested that among the most important changes introduced with the rise of capitalism were in territorial conceptions emptying spaces (of which López de Velasco offers a good example) and in obscuring sources of power by multiplying the bureaucratic apparatus (of which the Crown, the Council of the Indies, and the House of Trade are a good example; see below).[1] Thus, these new territorial dimensions did not conceal other alternatives but overpowered them in the international arena. The first part of this chapter is devoted to the efforts made by European men of letters and geographers to put the Americas on the map. The second part is devoted to mapping, naming, and administering the Indies, one of the main responsibilities of the Council of the Indies. And the third brings to the foreground territorial conception and "mapping" from the Amerindian perspective, a repressed locus of observation (perspective) that is at the same time a locus of enunciation (speech, writing, painting). From the Amerindian perspective, territoriality consisted of emptying the center rather than of emptying the space. The memory that might have survived among Amerindians of territoriality as a way of governing, defining social relationships, and organizing populations had to negotiate the new reality of complex bureaucracies, of having their space emptied or negated, and of figuring out the new and disguised sources of power.

The image of the earth that an educated European living toward the end of the fifteenth century might have had is illustrated by Henricus Martellus's map, composed circa 1490 (fig. 6.1). The map invites us to imagine that a hypothetical person, living about five hundred years ago, could have guessed that the distance from the extreme West (the Iberian Peninsula) to the extreme East (Japan and the coasts of China) was the same on both the front and the back of the map. Thus, our hypothetical person might have surmised that the East could be reached by navigating West and that the distance between West and East on the unknown side would be similar to the distance between West and East on the known side of the map. According to such a calculus, that hypothetical person would have thought that the center of the known part of the earth was a hypothetical point halfway between West and East, and between North and South.

The center of the world had not always been determined that way. About seven centuries before Henricus Martellus's world map, an educated Christian might have had a different picture of the world and its center, as illustrated by the T/O maps discussed in the previous chapter.[2] In T/O maps, the crossbar of the T represents the Don, the

Nile, the sea of Azov, and other bodies of water. These water masses separate Asia from Africa and Europe while the stem of the T represents the Mediterranean Sea partitioning Africa from Europe. The crossbar and the stem meet at the center of the circle, where Jerusalem is located. These maps were not drawn necessarily with the purpose of conveying geographical knowledge, for the center of the world was not determined geographically but ideologically.

It would certainly be wrong to think that Martellus's map at the end of the fifteenth century had the same convincing power that a world map has for us today. It would be more accurate to believe that it was one of many ways of representing the world, one with no particular significance for members of non-European cultures. That is to say, it was *only* in Europe where the Martellus world map was meaningful. Certainly, our hypothetical educated European had the right to believe that Martellus's map depicted the world as it was, just as the Chinese had the right to believe that the world took the shape of a cluster of nested rectangles or, later on, was centered on the Pacific instead of the Atlantic, as we have also seen in the previous chapter.

But none of this was known to the hypothetical European observer, living with the images provided by Martellus or the Christian T/O

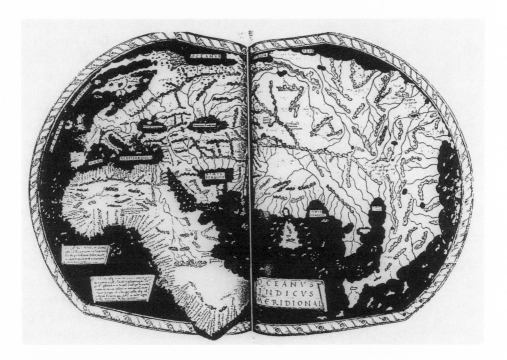

Fig. 6.1.   A European perspective of the world before the Atlantic explorations: Martellus's world map

maps. For a person coexisting with such geocosmography, China existed in the way it had been conceptualized by Europeans, and Anáhuac or Tahuantinsuyu Amerindians did not exist at all because they were not in the European's horizon. The Chinese seem to have had more vague ideas about Europe than Europeans had about China, which should not necessarily be interpreted as less knowledge but, rather, as having no need to know. Amerindians, on the other hand, were as ignorant about the existence of Europe as Europeans were about the existence of Anáhuac or Tahuantinsuyu. The world, however, existed in its diversity despite the mutual ignorance among members of different cultures. It is important to remember that each culture puts itself at the center of the world, and whoever belonged to that culture "naturally" believed that this was so. Our hypothetical European observer was just one observer among many, with a different knowledge of the parts of the world and their configurations than known in other cultures.

The European Invention of an *Orbis novus* Begins

Around 1493, about three years after the publication of Martellus's map, the image that an educated European might have had of the back of a map could be illustrated by the drawing that has been attributed to Columbus (fig. 6.2).[3] For those who were closely related to the Columbian adventure and were able to see the drawing, this was the moment a new image of the other side of the map began to emerge in the consciousness of our hypothetical European observer. The inverse process was also true, although it has not been as well documented as the European perspective. How did the idea and the image of unknown people and lands emerge in the consciousness of the Amerindians? How would they fit the "New World" (Europe, Asia, Africa) into their old cosmographic and cosmological representations? We do not know. Because this viewpoint is largely ignored, it is easy to believe that there simply was not one. One of the reasons, perhaps, for such an occurrence was that the Amerindians did not have much of a chance to figure it all out. Amerindian intellectuals, rulers, and educated persons of Mesoamerica and the Andes did not have the opportunity or the time to adapt their view of the universe when new information began to flow into their cultural domains. Europeans were much better prepared to register, organize, and disseminate new information. One example of that process was adding a fourth part of the earth.

The Mexican historian and philosopher Edmundo O'Gorman should be credited with the fundamental idea that the Americas (or

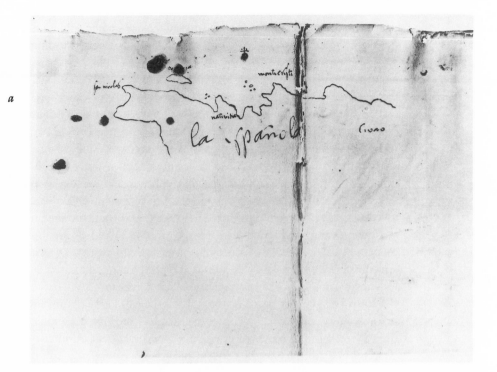

a

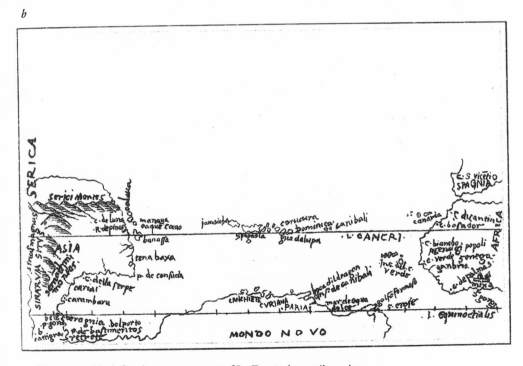

b

Fig. 6.2.   Undefined spaces: *a,* coast of La Española, attributed to Columbus (1492); *b,* illustrations of Columbus's letters, translated into Italian (ca. 1506)

America) were not discovered but invented. The cogent argument he developed to support his theory offers a counterpart to our hypothetical European observer. O'Gorman carved a new niche in which an alternative observer could be located and a new perspective developed. While the hypothetical European observer assumed that one's own point of view corresponded with *the* point of view or what the world really looked like, O'Gorman made the European perspective relative. His main contribution was to make us think along the lines we have been following from the beginning of this chapter and this book: that America was not an existing entity in the middle of an unknown ocean, waiting to be discovered, but that it was a European invention. Certainly, the mass of land existed, and the Amerindians and their own conceptual territorial and cosmological representations existed, but they were not "Americans" because America, as a way of conceiving the four parts of the world, did not exist.

The growing European awareness of a previously unknown part of the earth became a decisive factor in the process of integrating the unknown to the known, which also transformed the configuration of the known. In the process of describing otherness, our hypothetical observer helped redefine the concept of the self-same, that is to say, helped to construct the idea of Europe in the process of inventing a New World. Thus, rather than a hypothetical observer placing himself or herself in a well-defined Europe and discovering an unknown America, we had a long process in which the invention of America forced a redefinition of Europe and its place on the globe. Putting the Americas on the map also meant redefining Europe and the three continental configurations shown in T/O maps. Let's now take a closer look at some aspects of this dual process of inventing the Americas and redefining Europe.

Around 1507 or 1508 (about seventeen or eighteen years after Martellus's map), Johannes Ruysch (born in Antwerp, but of German parentage) published his *Universalior cogniti orbis tabula ex recentibus confecta observationi* in Rome (fig. 6.3). This map was published only four years after Amerigo Vespucci's letter, known today as *Mundus novus* (1503), in which he introduced the idea that the mass of land extending south of Cuba and Santo Domingo was not the coast of Asia but an unknown part of the planet. He referred to it as "novus" instead of "unknown" world. Once again our hypothetical European observer showed his unconscious arrogance and deep belief that what for him was not known had to be, of necessity, new; that whatever was not known to him, naturally did not exist. Ruysch's *Tabula,* or world map, was constructed under the same presuppositions.

Looking at the map now and thinking about how much new infor-

mation a European observer had at the beginning of the sixteenth
century to change his image of the world, one can notice, first, that in
Ruysch's *Tabula* only modern-day South America, which lies below
Santo Domingo and Cuba, or Hispaniola and Isabela, is depicted.
Second, it could be observed that the land has been identified as
"Terra sancte crucis sive Mundus novus." The fact that this map was
printed in Rome, and that the lands being explored were identified as
"Holy lands, hence New World," shows it was far from being geo-
graphically neutral and politically unmarked. Geographically we
should notice, however, how close the Caribbean and the "New
World" were to the coast of Asia.

Between 1503 and 1520, Martin Waldseemüller, a man of letters
who suggested the name America in honor of Vespucci, published his
Tabula terre nove, in Strasbourg (fig. 6.4). Below Hispaniola and Isabela (Santo Domingo and Cuba) we can see what is today northern
Colombia and Venezuela, emerging as if in a dream. Waldseemüller
also used the name of Terra Nova (*terra* being less presumptuous than
mundus) and showed in more detail what we have seen in the previous

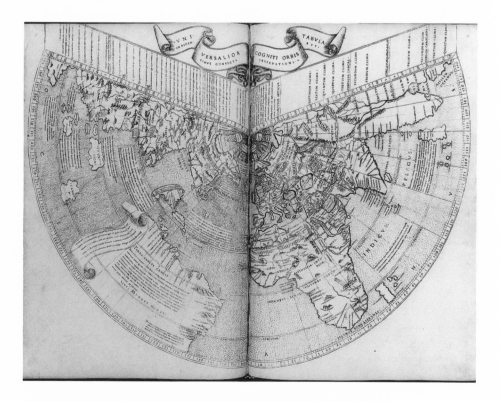

Fig. 6.3.   Imagining space and places: Ruysch's *Universalior cogniti orbis*

map (fig. 6.3). However, Waldseemüller is more specific in making a distinction between the South and Central America of today. That is not all, however, for *terra nova* has not only been geographically placed on the map, but also culturally and conceptually integrated into the imagination of our hypothetical observer: wild animals and naked people living in the wilderness were shown as distinctive features of the *terra nova*, which only a few decades earlier was unknown to European observers.

In 1520, Petrus Apianus published his *Tipus orbis universalis,* following a Ptolemaic projection but in a heart-shaped form (fig. 6.5). This time the chosen name was America instead of Mundus Novus or Terra Nova. Changing names shows, once more, that America was not something essentially determined and waiting to be discovered. The process of naming hints at that of invention: the integration of the unknown to the known in the expansion and consolidation of the European mind. It should be remembered that at the time Waldseemüller and Apianus printed their maps, Mexico had not yet been conquered by Cortés. His letters had not been published and no infor-

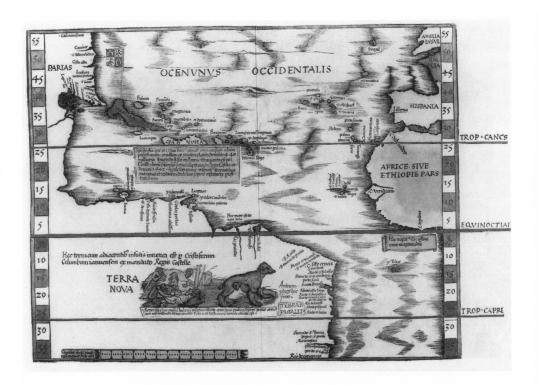

Fig. 6.4.   Waldseemüller's *Tabula terre nove* (1513)

mation about the Aztecs was circulating among learned and literate Europeans.

In 1540 one of the first detailed maps depicting the Americas as a mass of land extending from the North to the South Poles was published. It was named *Novus orbis,* and its author was the well-known cartographer Sebastian Münster (fig. 6.6). The distance from the Asiatic coast was either not yet known or not considered relevant, since Japan (Zipangus) was placed extremely near the Mexican coastline. The name Novus Orbis was attached only to the southern part. The land of the cannibals we saw in Waldseemüller's map was located in the same area of wild animals and people living in the wilderness. A leg and a head, hanging from the branches, have been neatly arranged to start a fire.

It was toward 1555 that the world began to look to our hypothetical European observer very much as it does today for many people on this planet. For theoretical as well as for practical purposes, it is interesting to remember that Charles V of Spain gave the Agnese map shown in figure 6.7 to his son, Philip II, who was to control the destiny

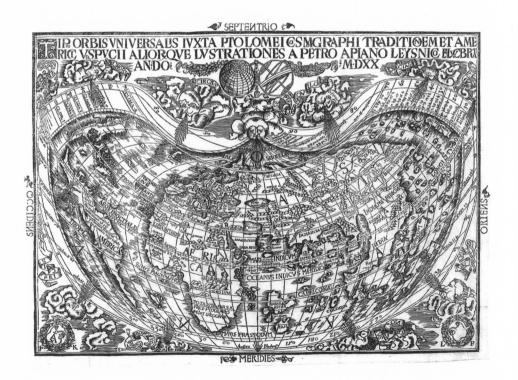

Fig. 6.5. Apianus's *Tipus orbis universalis*

of Spain and its domains for the rest of the century. However, I am most interested in underlining the scope of this image of the world and in clarifying why I said that for many people on this planet, the world today looks as it did in the seventeenth century.

For an educated person in Japan and probably a large part of Asia, the world today looks as it did for a person educated in the sixteenth or seventeenth century. Certainly, there is not much difference between Agnese's map and the Japanese world map shown previously (fig. 5.5) with the exception that the Americas are not in the extreme West, where they have since been situated, but in the extreme East. From such a perspective, Asia is not the Orient, as has been constructed by European intellectuals since the eighteenth century,[4] but the center of the world. It is still placed to the east of Europe, although it can hardly be construed as the Orient only when there is still an enormous mass of land further east of Asia. The Orient, consequently, is the Orient from the perspective of our hypothetical European observer, but not necessarily from the point of view of people living in China and Japan, who would perceive the Americas as the Orient. The case of the Ori-

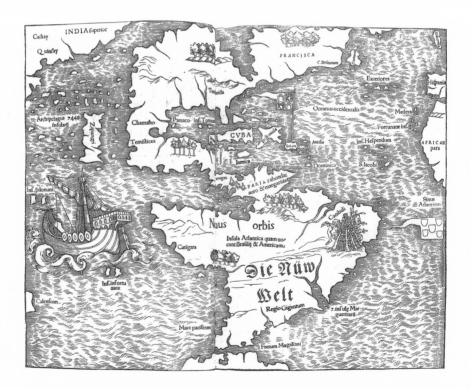

Fig. 6.6.   Münster's *Novus orbis* (1540)

ent and Orientalism is quite different from the idea of the Western Hemisphere, created and enacted by intellectuals from both Americas in order to distinguish themselves and their territory from what Europe invented and construed as the New World. As was already suggested, it was not only geographically that the Americas began to be put on the map. In the process, there was also the politics of naming and representing the barbarians, briefly touched on in the example of Novus Orbis, Terra Nova, and America on the one hand, and with the example of the cannibals on the other. Let's then go back to the end of the fifteenth century and trace some of these steps.

Populating the Borders with Imaginary Worlds

The name Harmann Schedel is perhaps less familiar to a contemporary reader than the title of the book he edited, *The Nuremberg Chronicle*, a compendium widely read in his own time. The text has been described as an amalgam of legend, fancy, and tradition interspersed with occa-

Fig. 6.7. Agnese's world map (1546)

sional scientific facts or authentic pieces of modern learning. A world map could not be lacking in a chronicle of such a type and time (fig. 6.8). His world map, drawn approximately three years after Martellus's, shows a different shape and proportion of land and water masses, although the land distributions are similar in both maps. Spain and the Atlantic coast of Africa were placed in the extreme left, while India and China were in the extreme right. However, the interest the map holds for us today does not lie so much in the shape in which the world was depicted, as in the curious inhabitants of its confines. In the left-hand border the map shows outlandish creatures and beings that were believed to inhabit the furthermost part of the earth: a six-armed man; a six-fingered furry human being, male or female; a centaur; a four-eyed man; and a hermaphrodite. In late-fifteenth-century Europe, as in China, the outermost corners of the world were supposed to be inhabited by such creatures or by ferocious barbarians. Nor was it surprising that Columbus was reported to have heard of dog-headed and pig-tailed people.

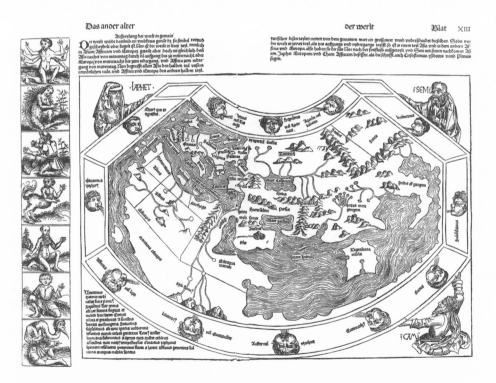

Fig. 6.8. Inventing the other: world map illustrating *The Nuremberg Chronicle*

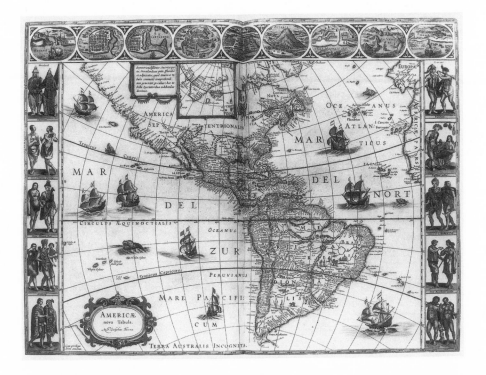

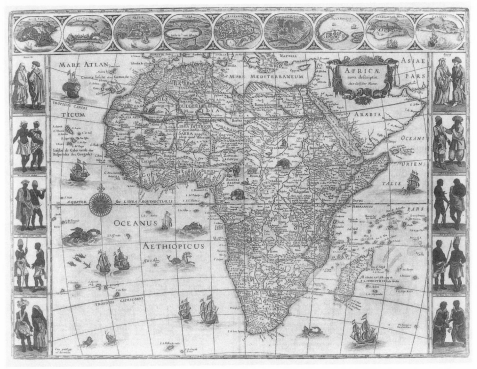

Fig. 6.9.   Imagining the other and defining the self-same: Blaeu's
Americae nova tabula

During the first half of the seventeenth century the French-German
cartographer Willen Blaeu published his *Americae nova tabula* (1630)
as part of his well-known atlas (fig. 6.9). A significant change of name
can be noticed in this map. The northern and southern parts have been
named America Septentrionalis and America Meridionalis, respectively. Furthermore, the image of the cannibals and dog-headed people has given way to a more humane perspective of the inhabitants of
the unknown lands, although the less civilized image has not been
changed. The borders of the map are illustrated with people and cities
of the Americas. Once the outermost unknown parts of the earth were
explored, there was no longer reason to believe that outlandish creatures inhabited them. By that time our hypothetical European observer had a more concrete idea of the habitants of the Americas and
was also able to represent them more "realistically." Between 1626 and
1676 in London, John Speed published his *America with those known
parts in that unknown world—both people and manner of building* (fig.
6.10). Speed supposedly took the idea of illustrating the borders from

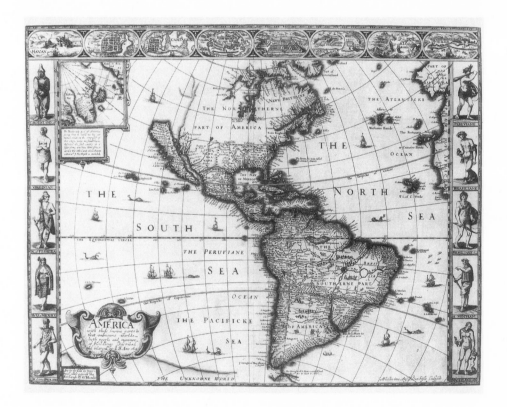

Fig. 6.10.   Speed's *America with those knowne parts in that unknowne
worlde* (1627)

Willen Blaeu and showed costumed figures, whom he took from trav-
elogue narratives and illustrations published previously. The tradition
continued in Amsterdam in 1639, when Janszoon Visscher published
his world map, in which the border acquired a new and significant
dimension in the European process of putting the Americas on the
map (fig. 6.11).

Let's first take a look at the four corners of the map. Europe and
Asia are represented by well-dressed ladies, while Africa and America
are represented by seminaked women. Comparing the representation
of Europe with that of Asia, a difference emerges in position. Europe is
sitting on the ground, while Asia is sitting on a camel. Thus, while Asia
is similar to Europe in that both are well-dressed ladies, they differ in
the surface on which they are sitting. However, Asia is similar to America and Africa, since both these seminaked women are sitting on animals, the armadillo and the crocodile, respectively. Asia, because she is
well dressed, resembles Europe, while she also resembles Africa and
America because she is sitting on an animal.

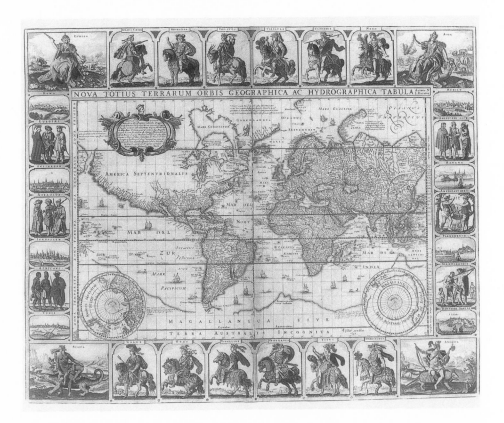

Fig. 6.11.   Visscher's *Nova totus terrarum orbis geographica* (1639)

America, depicted as a naked or seminaked woman with bow and arrows and sometimes with a decapitated head in her arms, was part of the late-sixteenth- and seventeenth-century iconology accounting for the fourth part of the world. The drawing shown in figure 6.12 was signed by Cornelis Visscher, a Dutch painter from the first half of the seventeenth century. The inscription under the portrait refers to America as the most strange of all the known continents and states that people in the Americas live in the wilderness without laws. Why the armadillo becomes the emblem (or at least one of the most distinctive ones) is a story that deserves to be retold, because it impinges on the process of putting the Americas on the map. Roger Barlow described the armadillo in his *Brief Summe of Geographie* (1540), a translation of Martín Fernández de Enciso's *Suma de geografía* (1519), as follows:

> There is a kinde of small beastes no bigter than a pigges of a moneth olde, and the fete, the hede and the eares be *like a horse*, and his bodi and his head is all covered saving his eares with a shell moche

Fig. 6.12.   Riding the armadillo: Cornelis Visscher's *America* (ca. 1555)

like the shell of a tortuga, but it is the very proportion of *an armed*   275
horse for this shelle hangeth downe by his sides and afore his brest   ———
moving as it were hanged by gynowes hinges, or moche like the   *Putting the*
lappes of a complete harneis. It is an admiration to behold it. Hit   *Americas on*
fedeth like a horse and his taile is like a pigges taile, saving it is   *the Map*
straight.[5]

This quotation shed new light about the use of animals on maps, on
the status of the armadillo as a New World emblem, and on the relations between the armadillo, the *tortuga* (turtle), and the horse. Saying that the armadillo is like a horse, and that America rides him
instead of a horse, illuminates the northern European imagination
when it came to invent the New World. Much before Visscher's illustration and some twenty years after Barlow's translation, Francisco
Hernández—who was appointed by Philip II to write the natural
history of New Spain—identified the armadillo by its Nahuatl name
(*ayotochtli*) and by a Spanish synonym (*o conejo cucubirtino*).[6] Hernández's analogy between the armadillo and the rabbit certainly de-
tracts from the analogies with the horse proposed by Barlow and challenged the ideological underpinnings of the imagery used to depict
America as the fourth part of the world. It was certainly a challenge
whose effects in the European population went unnoticed.

In fact, Hernández's manuscripts, as many others from the New
World, remained unpublished. Instead, Théodore de Bry's *Grand
Voyages* (1590–1634) circulated widely at the beginning of the seventeenth century, putting the Americas on the map in a very particular
way. America, instead of New World, became the preferred designa-
tion for Protestant countries eager to oppose the cruelties of Catholic
ones, Spain and Portugal.[7] Among the many attractions of Bry's collections are two aspects relevant to the process of putting the Americas
on the map. The first is that several world maps and maps of the
Americas are included.[8] Most interesting for our purpose are the ones
shown in figures 6.14 and 6.15. The caption of figure 6.14 reads
"America sive Novus Orbis respectu Europaeorum inferior globi ter-
restris pars" (America or the New World, *inferior* [lower?] part of the
terrestrial globe with respect to the Europeans nations). "Inferior"
could be interpreted as "placed in a lower part according to such and
such geographical orientation" or as "less developed, or of lesser qual-
ity." In the context of Bry's pictorial narrative, it clearly is both. Once
the Americas have been placed in the context of the world (fig. 6.14), a
detailed map is reproduced four plates later (fig. 6.15). This new map
of America, in which America Septentrionalis is distinguished from

America Meridionalis, is contemporary to the maps printed by Blaeu and Speed.

The second aspect is the emphasis on the depiction of cannibalistic scenes, on the nudity of the inhabitants of the New World, and on the survival of monsters and outlandish creatures populating it. The inclusion of monsters in Bry's illustrations should not come as a surprise if one remembers that in the sixteenth century such creatures were still alive and well. What is surprising is that when Bry published the first volume in 1590, enough explorations had been achieved to know quite well that no one saw such creatures. But, of course, such a reading will presuppose a correspondence theory of truth, instead of a performative one, applied to iconographic representation.[9] The question, then, is what was Bry trying to achieve by spreading such images

Fig. 6.13.   Placing the Americas in the "lower part of the world": Bry's *America sive Novus Orbis* (second part, 1590)

and putting the Americas on the map in such a way? Spaniards and
Portuguese were neither accountable for the presumably cannibalistic
practices among Amerindians, nor for the supposedly (in the eyes of
Bry, certainly) outlandish citizens of the New World. The explanation
might have to do with the connections between degraded human
nature as the result of degraded human behavior. This connection
between ethics and nature was described in detail, in the sixteenth
century, in Ambroise Paré's *Des monstres et prodiges* (1573),[10] and Juan
Maldonado's *Des Anges et des demons* (1603) and, above all, the publication in 1575 of Andre Thevet's *Cosmographie universelle*, from
which both Paré and Jean Léry (1585) borrowed several examples.
There are at least two universes of meaning cutting across the discussion of monsters, prodigies, angels, and demons. One is ethical and

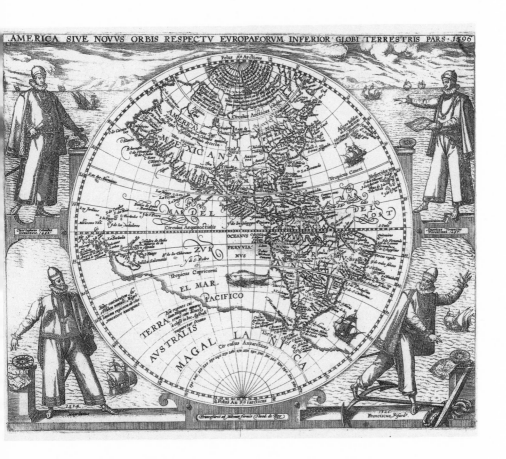

Fig. 6.14.   Correcting the drawing, keeping the place: de Bry's *America
noviter delineata* (third part, frontispiece)

has to do with the control of sexual behavior, and the other is ethnographic and has to do with the conceptualization of the New
World. The monsters, together with the cannibals and naked people,
offer a strong complement to the geographical place that America
occupies in the map: inferior with respect to Europe and the Europeans.[11]

Let's now go back to figures 6.11 and 6.12 and look at the two sides
and the top and bottom borders. Asians, Africans, and Americans—
men and women—are standing on their feet, while Europeans are
represented by males mounted on beautiful, aggressive horses. One
should notice, also, that the men are actually riding the horses while
the women are just sitting on top of the animals. And one could
further observe that the horse was, at that time, a highly valued animal,
very much a part of civilized life, related to war, conquest, and
power.[12] Finally, it should be noticed that males mounted on horses
are not anonymous male types, but well-identified heroes in the history of the West. The map is not only making a statement about
gender and ethnic differences but about historic and cultural distinctions as well. The contrast between women sitting on wild animals and
men riding highly valued horses, in addition to the contrast between
men riding horseback and people standing on their feet, creates another set of important distinctions in the process of putting the Americas on the map and constructing the image of the other by defining
the self-same.

Janszoon Visscher's map was chronologically preceded by the first
known map with elaborate borders, printed in Linschoten's "voyages" in 1594 (fig. 6.15).[13] This map introduced a change in the process of naming the lands and people that had already been emerging in
Ruysch's, Waldseemüller's, and Apianus's maps, as if in a dream.
America Mexicana and America Peruana are the names used to distinguish southern from northern lands. Magallanica (or the South Pole)
appears here as the fifth part of the world. The representation of the
four continents, however, is the same as the one we saw in Janzsoon
Visscher's map, to which Magallanica has been added, at the bottom
between America and Africa. The lady representing Europe is surrounded by fruits and has one of her feet on top of a T/O map, thus
suggesting that Europe dominates the world. Asia and Magallanica
are dressed but sit on wild animals. America and Africa are also sitting
on wild animals, but seminaked. The America Peruana and Mexicana
have their feet on a box full of gold. Two seemingly idyllic scenes are
depicted, although I would not be surprised if what is being cooked
are parts of human bodies, turning the *locus amoenus* into a cannibalistic feast. Of course, Bry's *Grand Voyages* was already making its pres-

ence felt in mapmaking, and the cannibalistic feast one can see under Mexicana and Peruana (bottom left corner of the map) had been inspired by one of Bry's designs, of which three of the thirteen parts had already been published by 1594 (fig. 6.16).

Finally, it should be noted that all these maps have something in common: in a culture with alphabetic writing, where conventions have established that reading proceeds from left to right and from top to bottom, a hierarchy for a meaningful distribution of objects on the space of the page has also been established. The places where the four continents located are highly significant, reinforcing the meaning already expressed by clothing and sitting positions. Europe, of course, is at the upper left corner. Following in hierarchical order, we see well-dressed Asia in the upper right corner. Africa and Asia seem to have been given equal weight in the hierarchy of the four corners, for America appears on the left in Linschoten's voyages, while it is on the right on Janszoon Visscher's map. Africa, of course, has been placed in an inverted position suggesting that both America and Africa were in

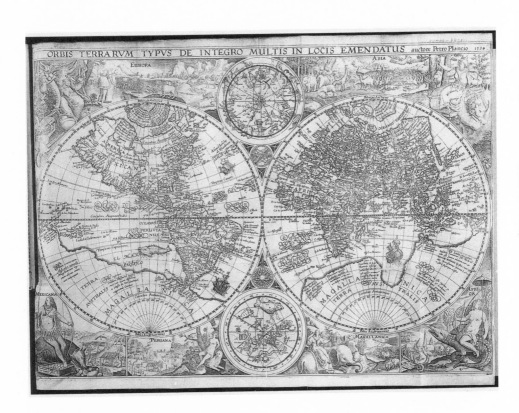

Fig. 6.15.   The influence of Bry in cartographic imagination: Linschoten's *Orbis terrarum tipus* (1594)

equally exchangeable places at the bottom of the map, while Europe and Asia remained in fixed positions, with Europe occupying the most significant one.

Maps are not territories, as the dictum goes. We could follow the chronology of this process up to the eighteenth and nineteenth centuries, looking at the changes in cartographic representations when mapping was not only in the hands of European cartographers but also those who became engaged in the process of nation building, in North, Central, and South America as well as in the Caribbean. But this process would take us too far afield and would require a change of topic. The focus would no longer be the emergence of the "Americas" in the European consciousness, but the emergence of the idea of the Western Hemisphere, and the replacement of the ideas associated

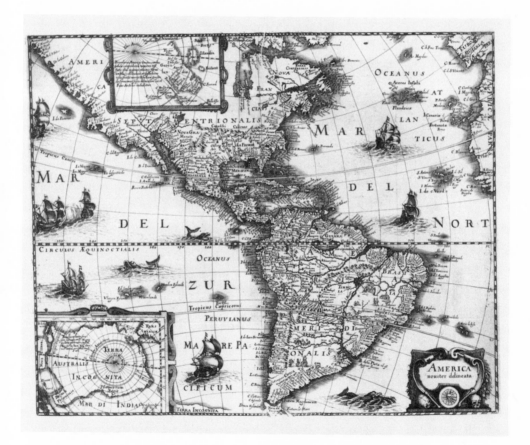

Fig. 6.16.   An example of the model: Bry's *Outinae milites ut caesis hostibus utantur* (How the soldiers of Outina handle their enemies)

with the name of New World in the consciousness of American intellectuals, both from the North and the South. My hypothetical European observer would have to be complemented with a hypothetical
American observer. Neither the American nor the European is a
monolithic entity but complex agencies divided by language, religion,
and economical projects. Although I will not pursue this development
further, I will return to it at the close of this chapter.

Mapping by Mandate and by Questionnaires: Putting the Indies on the Map

Putting the Americas on the map from the European perspective was
not necessarily a task devoted to finding the true shape of the earth; it
was also related to controlling territories and colonizing the imagination of people on both sides of the Atlantic: Amerindians and Europeans. The spread of European literacy in the New World colonies
transmitted a conception of the world projected in European cartography. The spread of cultural literacy in Europe showed the educated European the nature of an unknown continent. Economic
expansion, technology, and power, rather than truth, is what characterized European cartography early on, as well as the national cartography of the Americas at a later date.

From the perspective of the Council of the Indies (founded in
1524) and the House of Trade (founded in 1503), their need to put the
Indies on the map was quite different from that of northern European
cartographers and men of letters. So far I have primarily paid attention
to the process of integrating the fourth part of the world with the three
already known. I did not emphasize the process of mapping the details
of larger totalities, a distinction made by Ptolemy in his *Cosmography*
and followed by Renaissance cartographers. Ptolemy distinguished
geography, concerned with the entire known world, from chorography, concerned with particular places.[14] Ptolemy suggested that geography was like depicting the head, chorography like depicting one
of its parts (the eyes, the ears, the nose). When Petrus Apianus published his *Cosmographia,* he took Ptolemy's metaphor *at pedem litterae* and explained the distinction between the two with parallel
designs in which a world map was printed next to a human head and
the map of a city next to a design of the human ear (fig. 6.17). But
when it comes to maps and mapmaking, the question remains
whether chorography should be applied to the mapping of a country
within a continent or a city or place within a country. In what follows I
will use Ptolemy's distinction as parallel to the distinction between

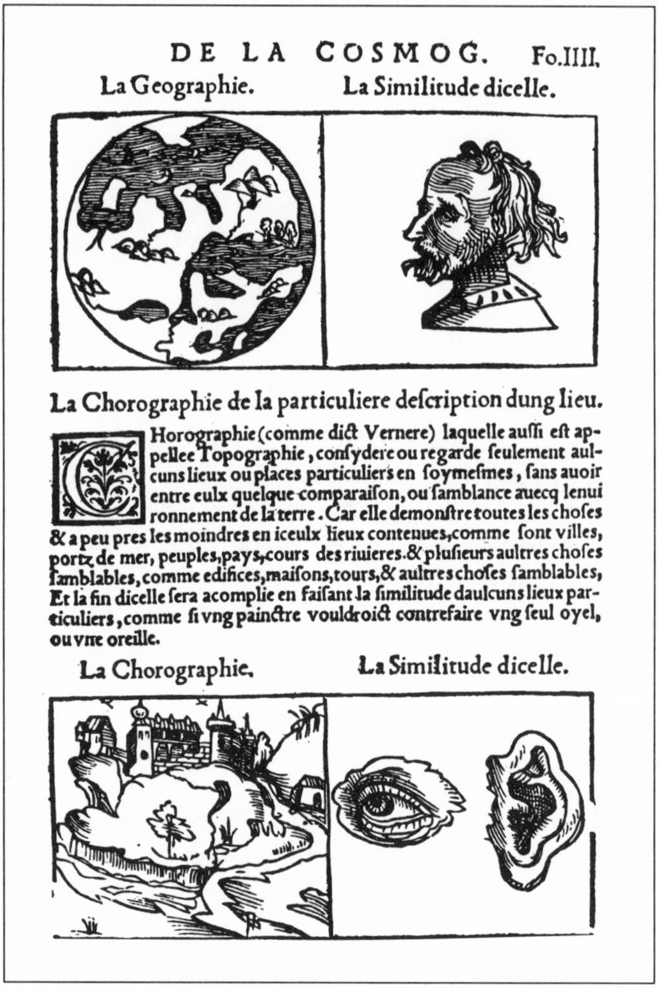

DE LA COSMOG. Fo.IIII.
La Geographie.   La Similitude dicelle.

La Chorographie de la particuliere defcription dung lieu.

Horographie (comme dict Vernere) laquelle auffi eft ap-
pellee Topographie, confydere ou regarde feulement aul-
cuns lieux ou places particuliers en foymefmes, fans auoir
entre eulx quelque comparaifon, ou famblance auecq lenui
ronnement de la terre. Car elle demonftre toutes les chofes
& a peu pres les moindres en iceulx lieux contenues, comme font villes,
portz de mer, peuples, pays, cours des riuieres. & plufieurs aultres chofes
famblables, comme edifices, maifons, tours, & aultres chofes famblables,
Et la fin dicelle fera acomplie en faifant la fimilitude daulcuns lieux particuliers, comme fi vng painctre vouldroict contrefaire vng feul oyel,
ou vne oreille.

La Chorographie.   La Similitude dicelle.

Fig. 6.17.   The human body as model for geographic discourse: Petrus
Apianus's *Cosmographia* (1539) (see chapter 1 for more on the human body
and the letter)

space (geography) and *place* (chorography), and chorography will be
applied to the mapping of towns or particular regions within a larger
whole. Consequently, López de Velasco's *Descripción* would remain
within the realm of geography (mapping the West Indies and its administrative units, audiencias, while the chorographic aspects were
not mapped by him but by those ("Indios viejos" as well as Spaniards
living in the area) who responded to the questionnaire and had the
chance of drawing a *pintura*. Relying on the distinction between geography and chorography I would like to examine two attempts to put
the Indies on the map, between 1570 and 1630, approximately, when

Philip II was replaced by Philip III. The official version depended on the Council of the Indies. The other was an individual and opposi- tional act of mapping that remained unknown to the general public until the twentieth century. The first belongs to the name of López de Velasco and the *Relaciones geográficas*, the second to Guaman Poma de Ayala and his *Nueva coronica y buen gobierno*.

Sometime around 1570 Philip II requested a visitation to the Council of the Indies and appointed Juan de Ovando, from the Gen- eral Council of the Inquisition, to be in charge of the evaluation. Ovando appointed López de Velasco as his assistant. As a result of the visitation, Ovando made two basic recommendations: (1) to create a systematic way of collecting and organizing all relevant information about the "matter" of the Indies, and (2) to make a systematic com- pilation of laws, edicts, and orders promulgated since the early years of the discovery and colonization of the Indies.

While the second recommendation produced the *Recopilación de las Leyes de Indias* (published under Philip II), the first was responsible for the *Descripción y demarcación de las Indias Occidentales* (1574) and the *Instrucción y memoria* (Instruction and memorandum), a set of fifty questions printed and distributed to all administrative centers and Spanish towns. The *Relaciones geográficas* are properly, as we shall soon see, the written replies to the fifty questions. This set of interre- lated activities was orchestrated by López de Velasco after the visita- tion to the council was finished. He was appointed *chronista mayor* (official chronist) of the Council of the Indies in 1571, and this proved to be one of the most significant moves for Spain's territorial control of its colonies. In fact, it was one of the most impressive moves in the colonization of space. It was heavily founded in alphabetic literacy and illustrates the distinctive role that writing and mapping played in the colonization of space. It implied at the same time a configuration of a new genre directly related to territorial control (the *relaciones*) and the transformation of humanist men of letters into notaries public and men of laws. Let's look first at López de Velasco's corpus (his *Descrip- ción*, the *Memorandum*, and the *relaciones*) and then at the transfor- mation of the social role.

In 1574 López de Velasco, wrote his *Descripción y demarcación de las Indias Occidentales*, in which he included fourteen watercolor maps of the Spanish possessions of the Indias Septentrionales (from Florida to the Straits of Panama), New Spain, Indias Meridionales (from the Straits of Panama to Patagonia), and Indias del Poniente (Philippines, Moluccas, etc.) (see figs. 5.15 and 5.16).[15] This report was a natural outcome of the visitation to the Council of the Indies ordered by Philip II and part of Ovando's recommendation to have a system to collect and organize information about the "things" of the Indies. Amerindians who had the chance to draw a *pintura* to be attached to the *relaciones* did not have the chance, however, to offer their own territorial perspectives. Thus, when the entire corpus of López de Velasco's geographic description is looked at, we have indeed a very interesting perspective on the process of putting the Indies (instead of the New World or America) on the map. Let's then take a closer look at this process.

The first step toward the description and demarcation of the Indies was a published set of *Ordenanzas reales* (Royal orders) in which a notary (*escribano de Cámara*) of each province or state was responsible for collecting and writing down in the *Book of Descriptions* (*Libro de las descripciones*) all relevant information concerning the Indias Occidentales, which would later be passed to the *chronista mayor*.[16] The official chronist was expected to organize and check the information of the book with a view to writing an encyclopedia of the geography, history, ethnography, and natural history of the Indies, thus complying with Ovando's recommendation to make a "systematic account about the 'things' of the Indies." López de Velasco's *Descripcion* was, then, the first systematic account after Ovando's recommendation and the first systematic chart of the Spanish transatlantic possessions. Printing did not directly favor López de Velasco's accomplishments until the second half of the nineteenth century. However, his verbal description was expanded and his maps were redrawn for a printed edition, published by Herrera y Tordesillas in one of the volumes (usually the end of the second) of his *Historia general de los hechos de los castellanos en las islas y tierra firme del mar océano* (1601). Herrera y Tordesillas was appointed *chronista mayor* in 1596, and his *Historia* was reprinted and translated several times until well into the eighteenth century. For all practical purposes, Herrera y Tordesillas's version of the *Descripción* became the reference for mapping the Spanish possessions from Florida to the Philippines. The successive reprinting of the work during the colonial period bears witness to its authoritative import. The 1730 Madrid edition, printed to amend the Antwerp edition, in which twelve of the fourteen maps were omitted, bears witness to the continuing significance and actuality of the maps.[17]

The premise that the lands were "new" and in need of being mapped is obvious in the way López de Velasco approached his description. What did López de Velasco (geographically) conceive and how did he describe the land he charted in fourteen maps? Allow me to repeat, in this context, a few words already quoted in the previous chapter:

The Indies, the islands and terra firma in the Ocean which are commonly called the New World, are the lands and seas which lie within the boundaries of the Kingdom of Castile, which is a hemisphere, or half of the world, beginning at 180 degrees west from a meridian circle which passes through 39 degrees longitude west of the meridian of Toledo.[18]

At a first glance, the distinction between "the Indies, the islands and terra firma . . . commonly called the New World" seems a simple question of synonymy. There is more to it, however, than a philosophical question of meaning and reference (e.g., the "morning" and the "evening" stars refer to the same planet, Venus). Let's first devote our attention to the "Indies, the islands and terra firma" (which is the expression used, and adapted, in Herrera y Tordesillas's *Historia*).[19] The northern and southern Indies were naturally divided, according to López de Velasco, by the Panama straits. The reading of a geographical sign (Panama straits) in terms of a "natural" division is an example of the blending of natural and geographical discourse that warrants the truth-value of the map: López de Velasco assumed that it was not the map that created the division but nature itself. But it is also an example of the underlying assumptions of the understander (in this case López de Velasco) reading "natural" signs (the Panama straits) in the context of a "natural" tradition (nonnatural signs). The eastern Indies presents a different kind of problem to the geographer and mapmaker of the Council of the Indies, for "naturally" these islands belonged to Asia rather than to the "commonly called New World." The criteria in this case were no longer geographic and "natural" but political: the island belonged to the transatlantic possessions of the Spanish kingdom. López de Velasco did not seem besieged by the contradiction when he described the third part of the Indies:

The West Indies are all the islands and terra firma which lie within the boundaries of the kingdom of Castile, to the westernmost point, whose frontiers, as I have said, extend to the other side of the world, to the city of Maluca, whence to the East and New Spain; there is a large gulf consisting of many islands, big and small, and many coastlines and much dry land, which form the Spice Islands (also called the Malucan Islands), the Philippines, the Coast of China, the Lequias and Japanese Islands, the Coast of New Guinea, the Solomon Islands and the Thieves Islands.[20]

The Indies, as the official name adopted by López de Velasco instead of New World, began to make sense. *New World* could not have referred to the Eastern Indies since they were not altogether "new." We are faced here with a process of mapping, naming, and silencing that is not strictly related to a reconceptualization of the earth, to which the expression New World was commonly associated, but with the mapping of the Spanish possessions. However, mapping the Spanish possessions or conceptualizing a "New World" has a specific locus of enunciation. Hence, the locus of enunciation, indicated in this case by the social role of *chronista mayor* and the institutional functions of the Council of the Indies is not the same as the locus of enunciation of Castilian and non-Castilian cartographers (Italian, French, German, etc.) concerned with the shape and location of the New World, or the locus of enunciation defined by the House of Trade, whose cartographers were concerned with the directions of the winds, coastal shapes, and port locations for charting navigations.

The House of Trades was created in 1503, twenty-one years before the Council of the Indies, and prior to the last voyages of Columbus and Vespucci. The House of Trade was in charge of all maritime affairs, including the regulation of overseas trade and commercial relations. Above all, it was in charge of charting new regions based on geographical records. A key figure in the House of Trade was the *piloto mayor* (chief pilot), and Amerigo Vespucci was the first appointed to that position. Thus, the maps of both the House of Trade and the Council of the Indies have a common root in the Columbus and Vespucci voyages. These maps do not conceptualize the Indies so much as the coastlines hitherto unknown to western Europe. From Columbus's first sketch of Hispaniola (1492; fig. 6.2) to the work of López de Velasco's predecessor in the Council of the Indies, Alonso de Santa Cruz, the coastlines were constantly being mapped.[21] And mapping was finding its locus in the house of geography as a well-defined disciplinary activity. Alonso de Santa Cruz, who, as the royal cosmographer, was affiliated with both the House of Trade and the Council of the Indies, wrote an *Islario general* (General view of the islands, 1560), preceded by a *Treatise on the Sphere*. This treatise, which was an adaptation of Sacrobosco's classic *Sphaera* (originally printed in the fifteenth century and reprinted well into the sixteenth century), is a clear example of the categories already in place in geographical discourse and the organization of geographic knowledge. Santa Cruz writes in the prologue:

> Geografía vale tanto como *descripción* o *pintura* de la tierra, porque *geos* quiere decir tierra y *grafía descripción* o *pintura*, porque en ella se trata de la correspondencia que tienen las partes del cielo a las de

la tierra, poniendo los grados de altura y mayor y menor día con otras muchas particularidades.[22] (italics mine)

[Geography means *description* or *painting* of the land, because *geos* means land and *grafía* means *description* or *painting*, since geography deals with the correspondence between the parts of the sky and those of the land, adding degrees of latitude, time differences, as well as many other important matters.]

The maps attached to his *Islario general*, together with the written discourse, are part of the "description or painting of the earth," and, in this case, charting navigations was the main goal (e.g., his *Libro de las longitudes*). His maps (fig. 6.18) focus on the coastline and wind directions rather than on the possessions of the Spanish empire, as is the case of the "description and painting" of López de Velasco.

The voyages of Columbus and Vespucci (who would later become director of the House of Trade) and the letters written about them could be seen as precursors of mapmaking related to the House of

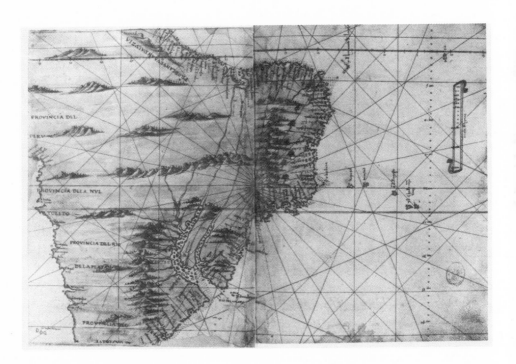

Fig. 6.18. Mapmaking and way-finding: Alonso de Santa Cruz's coastal designs of South America (1540)

Trade.[23] On the other hand, Columbus (but not Vespucci) may also be seen in the context of mapping associated with the Council of the Indies. Following the second voyage, in which Ferdinand and Isabella explicitly ordered Columbus to make "entera relación de lo que vieres" [a whole report of what you might see], we can see the effects the questionnaire attached to the memorandum had on mapmaking and geographical descriptions in the context of European Atlantic explorations. Mapping and geographical descriptions associated with the House of Trade showed less concern with similar activities by the Council of the Indies or by professional cartographers and men of letters. In the context of learning, the main question was to conceptualize, in writing and in mapping, the lands unknown to them. Thus, Orbis Novus, Nuevo Mundo, and America were the names most commonly used in the context of learning. The report written by Peter Martyr was named *De orbe novo decades* (see chap. 4) and was clearly written in a humanist context, while the first "history" of Oviedo y Valdés, written within the Crown's political and economic context, was called *General y natural historia de las Indias* (1537–48).

But this is not all. Maps and words have a distinctive graphic configuration today just as they did for an educated European of the sixteenth century. This was certainly the case when the process of putting the Americas on the map, by drawing coastlines and naming places, was at stake. Columbus's rage of naming reveals the commercial and political dimensions of his enterprise, subsequently pursued by the House of Trade and the Council of the Indies. This may have been beyond Columbus's original motivation, but not that of the kingdom of Castile, as expressed in the Capitulations of April 1492.[24] To reread Columbus in the context of his dialogue (oral and written) with the Crown is not farfetched, since he wrote what he did with a specific audience in mind and not in order to express his personal thoughts and feelings. Columbus's problem was to communicate not only with the Indians, but more importantly with the Crown. His act of naming was, on the one hand, a gift to his benefactors and, on the other, an inscription of new places in Castilian and Christian old memory. Semantic appropriation is not exactly the same as political and administrative appropriation. The different strategies involved in both cases should not prevent us from looking at them as two sides of the same coin. Like mapping, naming is also a semantic move attached to the political and economic strategies of the Crown, as well as the religious crusade engineered by Rome. Columbus appealed—at different times and with different intensities—to both contexts. Instead, Vespucci's letter to his Italian learned friends reveals what subsequently would become a very well defined (non-Spanish) mapping activity with which his name was associated.

289

Putting the Americas on the Map

The Transformation of Social Roles and the Administration of the Indies

Letrado (man of letters), a word of common use in sixteenth-century Castilian, summarized a network of meaning derived from the name of the alphabetic unit: *letra* (letter), as we have already insisted in chapter 1. Toward the sixteenth century *letrado* had two basic meanings in the *Diccionario de autoridades,* compiled in the eighteenth century: (*a*) *letrado* was applied to those who possessed scientific knowledge, for the idea of scientific knowledge was matched to the written word or letters ("*letrado* es el docto en las ciencias que porque estas se llamaron letras, se le dio este nombre. Viene del latino *litteratus,* que significa lo mismo"); and (*b*) *letrado* was also applied to those expert in law (scribes, notaries, lawyers) rather than in sciences ("*letrado* se llama comunmente al abogado. Lat. *Jurisperitus, Causidicus*").

Although it seems obvious that *letrado* comes from the Latin *litteratus,* what is not obvious is that the meaning of *litteratus* was the same as the meaning attributed to *letrado.* Parkes observes that in the Middle Ages *litteratus* was only applied to those who possessed knowledge of Latin, and it was sometimes related to learning (fig. 6.19). Maravall in a work published twenty years before complemented this observation by noting that learning was conceived in terms of the Greco-Roman tradition. Clanchy has reported that while toward the twelfth century *clericus* also meant *litteratus* and *laicus* meant *illitteratus,* the synonymy was due to a semantic change by means of which *litteratus* and *clericus* became interchangeable with terms meaning "learned" or "scholarly."[25] He has also suggested that while the antithesis *clericus/laicus* was a medieval creation, *litteratus/ illitteratus* had a Roman origin. Thus, the description we find in the eighteenth-century Spanish *Diccionario de autoridades* comes from the Roman rather than from the medieval background.

The second meaning of the word *letrado* can be better understood against the background of the first. Toward the second half of the fifteenth century, the semantic changes attached to the word *letrado* were signs of the social changes taking place in the domain of knowledge and administration. In fact, while a *letrado* in the sense of "a learned and scholarly person" may seem at first glance to have a more prominent social role than a *letrado* as "a person schooled in law and legal matters," certain differences may be perceived upon close inspection. Gil Fernández has expanded on the classic study by Maravall,[26] devoted to the idea of knowledge in the Middle Ages and the corresponding symbolic representation of social roles related to it, by describing the distribution of social roles and functions of grammarians, men of letters (*letrados*), and humanists during the sixteenth century. While in the Middle Ages—according to Gil Fernández—the hierarchy of knowledge had the theologians as a superior caste in relation to the grammarians, lawyers, and notaries, the situation began to change in Spain toward the end of the fifteenth century. Experts in legal matters began to hold positions of increasing importance.[27] As they gained in social status so the meaning of the word *letrado* shifted. They became a caste that detached itself from both the medieval *clericus* and the Renaissance humanist. In the context of the colonization of the New World the *letrados* (men of letters) were in charge of the intellectual legitimation of the conquest, whereas the *letrados* (experts

Fig. 6.19. How a humanist may have looked: Sebastiano del Piombo's *Portrait of a Humanist* (ca. 1520), National Gallery, Washington

in law and legal matters) took over everything concerning policymaking and administration. Parts 1 and 2 of this book have been devoted, partially, to the task of men of letters. Let's now devote some time to explore the significance of the men of law. The *letrados*-jurists and some of their work, such as the Ordenanzas de Indias and the *Relaciones geográficas de Indias,* are paradigmatic examples of the social roles in charge of the organization of the New World and the complicity between alphabetic writing, territoriality, and colonization.

I have already mentioned that in the sixteenth century the *letrado*-jurist began to play a role equal to or even more important than the *letrado*-humanist; the bureaucrat took over the organization of society and left the discussion of ideas to the intellectual. The Council of the Indies, which was the supreme institution for affairs concerning the Indies and the administration of the New World, had executive, judicial, and legislative functions. It consisted of cloak-and-dagger councillors on one side and robed councillors on the other. Men of arms and men of letters. The latter dominated the council through sheer force of numbers and through their experience in the affairs of the Indies, since many of them had been judges in high courts or had filled government posts in the New World. All facets of life were subject to the jurisdiction of the council, from high politics to detailed information on geography, political history, natural history, and so on.[28] The Ordenanzas de Indias are good examples of this situation and, also, of the increasing role played by literacy in the colonization of the New World. *Ordenanza* 1, for example, contains a philosophy for the administration, and it is made clear that if the members of the Council of the Indies were honest persons of noble stock and reputable lineage ("personas aprobadas en costumbres, nobleza, y limpieza de linajes"), it was because they were selected according to their knowledge (letters) and prudence ("escogidos en letras y prudencia"). It was also specified in the constitution of the Council of the Indies that the president would be advised by eight *consejeros letrados,* who were men of letters related not to science but to law. *Ordenanza* 27 was entirely devoted to underlining the significance of reading and writing letters as a regular affair of the council. Colonial administrators were aware that the technology of writing provided by the alphabet made it possible to effectively conduct business (like the telephone and electronic mail of today) and take control of the people and the land by compiling a huge set of regulations (*ordenanzas*) and a questionnaire (the *Memorandum*), which generated a massive amount of information (the *Relaciones geográficas de Indias*). *Letrados* and cosmographers joined forces to trace the boundaries (in words and maps) of newly acquired domains (fig. 6.20).

The Council of the Indies, of which López de Velasco was the first official cosmographer, was the main institutional locus for the organization, planning, and implementing of the massive information-gathering operation.[29] There was, however, an asymmetric relation to technology between the *Memorandum,* on the one hand, and the *relación,* on the other. While the *Memorandum* enjoyed the benefits of the printing press (which was "naturally" related to the power exercised by the council), the *memorias* were handwritten and never printed in their time. The first edition was that of Jiménez de la Espada, in the spirit of publishing documentation for the understanding of the past rather than printing as a transmission of information or opinion influential at the time that it was produced. The *relaciones,* thus, were handwritten and hand drawn. However, for those in control of the administration of the Spanish empire in the New World, the *relaciones* represented an important source of information for chroniclers and cosmographers of the council in order to write histories and chart new territories.

The fifty questions listed in the *Memorandum* generally ended up

Fig. 6.20. The complicity between letter writing, mapping, and the business of the state: Sebastiano del Piombo's *Cardinal Bandinello and His Secretary and Two Cosmographers* (1516), National Gallery, Washington

on the desk of a notary public, who would gather a representative number of Spanish and native people who, at their turn, would provide the answer to each question orally, while the notary public would fix them in writing and send them to his superior.[30] After passing through several steps of the administrative hierarchy, the *relación* ended up in the hands of some *letrado* in the council.[31] The tenor of the letter sent by the king to his governors was as follows:

THE KING:
Know ye, our Governor of . . .

Those of our Council of the Indies having at various times discussed the procedure that should be established in order that within it there can be certain and detailed information about the things of the said Indies, so that the council can attend to their good government, it has seemed a proper thing to decree that a general description be made of the whole condition of our Indies, islands, and their provinces, the most accurate and certain possible.

In order that you properly aid in forming such description, you will comply with the Instructions that have been drawn up for it, in printed form. They are herewith being sent to you. Because it is our will that such descriptions be made specifically in each province, we command you to make a description of that city in which you reside and of the places within its jurisdiction as soon as you receive this, our Cedula.

You shall send to each of the governors, corregidors, and alcaldes of the districts within your jurisdiction the number of the said Instructions which you deem necessary for them to distribute among the towns of Spaniards and of Indians within the scope of their district, town, or mayoralty. You shall dispatch them under command that as promptly as possible they shall comply and do what they are ordered to do by the said Instructions.

You shall collect the reports that may be made in each place. You shall send them, together with those you yourself have prepared, as promptly as possible to our Council of the Indies, for review. It will advise us if there are faults in them, and for what cause, and make appropriate recommendations.

Signed, San Lorenzo el Real, 25 May 1577

I, THE KING.[32]

What is relevant in this process is the fact that the oral report given by those who were invited to participate was written down by a *letrado* (notary public) who transformed an oral discourse into a written (alphabetic) report with administrative purposes. When compared with the picto-ideographic writing system and mapping in pre-Columbian central Mexico, for instance, the *Relaciones geográficas* also served to illustrate the intervention of alphabetic literacy in picto-ideographic literacy. Alphabetic writing had not only made it possible to inscribe what had been said in a communicative situation (losing forever the act of saying and hearing in which the notary and the informant were involved) and to develop its own communicative strategies, but also allowed the detachment of alphabetic writing and mapping in a way that is difficult to imagine in picto-ideographic writing and mapping.[33] In fact, when we look at the alphabetic written reports and the map of the *relaciones,* we perceive a distance between the two much greater than that between native writing systems and mapping: preconquest as well as postconquest, native maps were all more than an organization of space, a localization of places, and an indication of distances. They were mainly territorial configurations created by the record-keeping and spatial boundaries. The four maps of Cuauhtinchán (fig. 6.21), associated with the *Historia tolteca-chichemeca,*[34] are one of the most clear examples of territorial organization in a society in which history and geography had not been defined as two different disciplines.

While mapping the new territories was systematically handled by the Council of the Indies by means of the *Memorandum,* the oral reports and the maps provided by the Amerindians were absorbed and controlled by the administrative network and the fifty questions listed on it. Three of the questions requested a map or *pintura.* Thus, the "Indios viejos" who drew the *pinturas* of several of the *relaciones* toward 1580 (and who presumably were born toward 1530–40, ten to fifteen years after the arrival of the twelve Franciscans who began the spread of Western literacy in Mexico), were already between a tradition in which mapping and writing were both detached from speech and a new learning experience in which writing "reproduced" and fixed speech and mapping remained independent of it. The transformation was twofold: on the one hand was the process of learning new conventions for territorial ordering and, on the other, the process of social transformation by which, toward the end of the sixteenth century, the *tlacuilo* ceased having the crucial function he had had in preconquest time and that had survived through the first half of the sixteenth century, judging by the numbers of postconquest codices that have been dated around that time. It is hard to say, because of lack of information, whether the "Indios viejos" referred to by the Spanish notary in the written report of the *relaciones* embodied the survival of

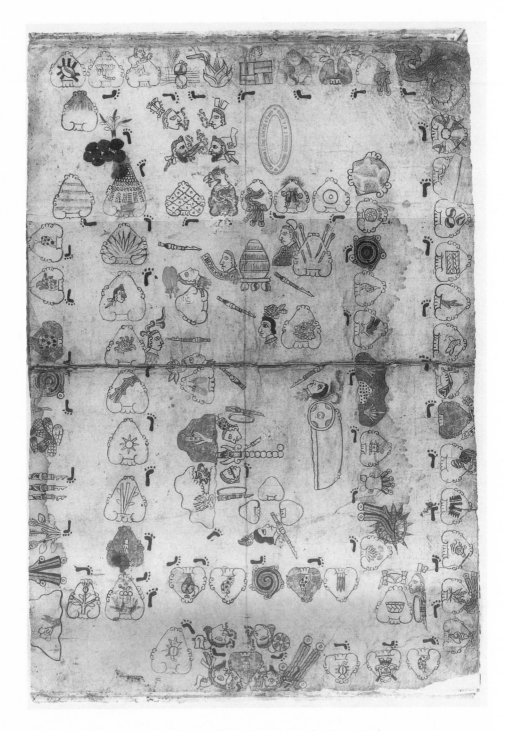

Fig. 6.21. Alternative territorialities: *Map of Cuauhtinchán 2* (ca. 1550), space and time among the Toltecs-Chichimecs

the *tlacuilo* or were just regular members of the society with basic knowledge of the Mexica pictographic tradition. In any event, whatever the social role of the "Indio viejo," he was at a remarkable disadvantage in relation to the Spanish *letrado* (notary public) and the official cartographer, not only because of social roles in a colonial situation, but also because the *tlacuilo* mastered a code in which writing and mapping were not as clearly distinguished as they were in sixteenth-century Spain. It would be difficult to imagine a Mexica painting with Montezuma sitting in front of his secretaries and cosmographers, as we can see in several paintings from fifteenth- and sixteenth-century Europe (see fig. 6.20).

The Other Side of the Mountain: Geography and Chorography from the Amerindian Point of View

In colonial situations, mapping and naming (i.e., geographical discourse) are to territoriality what grammars are to Amerindian speech and historical narratives to Amerindian memories. Once recognized, the dialectic between what is common in the perspective and diversity of the colonizer's semiotic moves and what is common in the perspective and diversity of the colonized semiotic moves requires a type of understanding that can no longer be based on a linear conception of history and a continuity of the classical tradition. This dialectic required a type of understanding that focuses on discontinuities and the counterpart of maps, grammars, and histories: the existence and persistence of speech over grammars, of memories over histories, of territorial orderings over maps. However, while writing the grammars of Amerindian languages and the histories of their memories challenged both the grammarian and the historian, verbal geographical descriptions and maps overpowered, so to speak, Amerindian *pinturas* and territoriality. The next section will be devoted to exploring the "noise" made by maps and geographical descriptions and the "silence" to which Amerindian territorial representations were reduced.

While all these activities, and more, kept European administrators and cartographers busy, Amerindians in Mexico and elsewhere were also concerned with territorial description, although not on the same scale as their European counterparts. Comparisons have to be made, therefore, at two different levels: the level of the absence (e.g., the Amerindian "lack" of world-scale geometric projections); and the level of the difference (e.g., how López de Velasco described New Spain and the Mexicans Anáhuac). Additionally, Amerindian "maps" are not as well documented as Spanish and European ones partly due to the fact that most of them were destroyed in the process of colonization.[35] Here we are confronted with another example in the cultural process when anything that is not recognized or mentioned by those who control the transmission and circulation of information does not exist. Power asserts itself by suppressing and negating both what is not considered relevant or is considered dangerous. The control of the cultural sphere is similar in many ways to maps. It gives the impression that it covers the territory, disguised under a set of principles that allowed for certain expressions to be ignored because they did not fulfill the basic requirement or because they were disturbing. Even Spanish historians and missionaries of the sixteenth century were silent about Amerindian territorial representations. For López de Velasco, as we have seen, the question never came up. Franciscan friars, like Sahagún, who were so careful in documenting all possible aspects of native lifestyles and their memories of the past, were also mute in matters of territorial conceptualizations.

Thus Amerindian "maps" painted during the colonial period that have come down to us are shrouded with uncertainties. Who painted them, when, and for whom are questions that cannot be readily answered, as is the case with Spanish and European maps. There are enough examples, however, to become acquainted with Amerindian cognitive patterns of territorial organization. These examples are from three different periods and pragmatic contexts. From the first period (between 1540 and 1560) come those "maps" which, although already showing Spanish influence, are predominantly Amerindian both in their graphic conceptualization of the territory as well as in the integration of narrative memories. Examples from this period are the *Mapa Sigüenza*, the *Tira de la peregrinación* (or *Tira del museo*), and the *Maps of Cuauhtinchán*.[36] The first two examples are spatial narratives of the Aztec peregrination from Aztlán to the Valley of Mexico. The *pinturas* of the third example are spatial narratives of the Toltecs-Chichimecs, from the Valley of Puebla. From the second period (approximately 1579–86) are the *pinturas* from the *relaciones,* although not all of them were painted by Amerindians. Enough examples can be found among those painted by Amerindians to show an increasing hybridization of cultural products not only in the mixture of elements included in the "maps" and the design of objects and events but, mainly, in the way space itself is conceptualized. Similar features are seen in the *pinturas* from the third period (1600–1750), all of them related to land possessions (*concesion de mercedes*) and land litigations.[37] All of these *pinturas* were produced under the specific conditions of colonial situations, and they are all examples of colonial semiosis, although traces of the preconquest painting style are still evident.

Thus, it should be kept in mind that the acts of describing, mapping, or painting the space depicted (or invented) and the way of depicting (or inventing) it are interrelated, although at clearly distinguished levels. The first corresponds to the level of action; the second to the relations between signs and their content; the third complies with a given way of doing things with signs and cognitive patterns.

The well-known *Mapa Sigüenza* (fig. 6.22) is a fine example of Amerindian *pinturas* from the mid–sixteenth century. Although the events and space described and the patterns of descriptions supposedly survived from preconquest times, the act of painting itself is a colonial one and, therefore, a case of colonial semiosis. The *Mapa Sigüenza* traces the territory in its spatial as well as temporal boundaries: the chart of the space from the legendary Aztlán to the Valley of Mexico and the chart of the peregrination of time from the point of origin (Aztlán) to the point of arrival (Chapultepec).[38] When compared with the *Tira de la peregrinación* (fig. 3.1) one would tend to believe that the former is colonial while the latter came to us as a

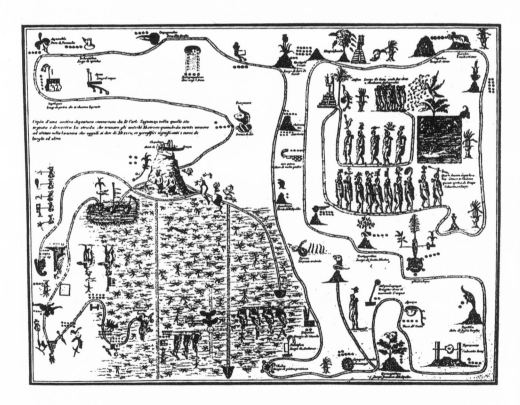

Fig. 6.22.   Alternative territorialities: *Mapa Sigüenza* (ca. 1550), origin and peregrination of the Aztecs

preconquest artifact. While both trace the peregrination from a place of origin to the actual habitat, there are obvious differences between the two. Human figures in the *Mapa Sigüenza* respond less to indigenous patterns than the *Tira de la peregrinación*. In the latter the counting of the years is clearly indicated and the signs are similar to the numerical signs encountered in other codices from the Valley of Mexico. In the *Mapa Sigüenza* the years have not been indicated. The years shown in figure 3.1b, in arabic numerals, have been added and represent a scholarly reconstruction rather than an original colonial chronological listing. We know, however, as seen in chapter 3, that the pre-Columbian ruling class had developed sophisticated means of time reckoning that they applied to place social events in time and to keep record of the past.

When compared with European maps, the *Mapa Sigüenza* is very imprecise as far as location (longitude and latitude) is concerned. This kind of geographical "imprecision" has been interpreted in negative (e.g., what the Amerindians did not have) rather than positive (e.g., what the Amerindians did have) terms. Territorial conceptions among the Aztecs were, of course, dissimilar to those of the Spanish. García Martínez reports that the territoriality of the *altepetl* (*alt,* water; *tepetl,* hill) encompassed both the natural resources as well as the memory of human history.[39] Contrary to European maps, the *altepetl* did not imply a precise delimitation of geographic boundaries. Geographic limits were fuzzy and variable and it was often the case that between two *altepetl* there were disputed lands as well as empty spaces. García Martínez concluded that it was during the process of colonization that a more defined sense of space, law, and history was projected onto the *altepetl*. I am not sure whether we should conclude that what the Spaniards perceived as a "lack" was due to the fact that the Mexica were simply unable to match the Spaniards' territorial conceptualization or rather that they really did not "lack" anything because they had different ways of fulfilling similar needs. The fact remains that locations are determined by the historical and sociological significance of an event in the collective memory "inventing" the peregrination and charting of the Nahuatl world. To place the point of origin (Aztlán) and the point of arrival (Chapultepec) in two opposite corners is an indication not only of a peregrination in time but also of a conscientious use of graphic signs to indicate that the two points, of departure and arrival (e.g., *Tira de la peregrinación,* my addition), are the most distant in space. In the words of Radin, "It is not an annual account set down year for year, but, like the Tira Boturini, shows unmistakable evidence of systematization."[40] On the other hand, Aztlán and Chapultepec are the sites to which more space is devoted in the *pin-*

tura: they are not only points of departure and arrival; of all the places indicated by the peregrination, they are the most significant. Duverger suggests that the peregrination of Aztlán was an "invention" after the arrival at the Valley of Mexico.[41] An obvious statement, perhaps, although a necessary one for the understanding of colonial semiosis and Amerindian "mapping" during the precolonial as well as colonial period. If during the expansion of the Mexica empire maps like these satisfied peoples' need to reassure themselves and their own tradition in front of rival communities, it is no less relevant that the ruling class of Amerindian civilizations moves from being in power to being disempowered. Construction of ethnic (*ethnos,* we) identities, however, is not limited to power. On the contrary, acts of opposition and resistance and the will to survive require a strong sense of individual and communal identity.

In our next example, the four *pinturas* of Cuauhtinchán[42] have a more complex history than the previous two, not only because there are four maps but also because of their obscure connections with the *Historia tolteca-chichemeca,* a narrative account of Amerindian communities from the Valley of Puebla.[43] Map no. 2 (fig. 6.21) is one more example of the "migration theme" (the Toltec's peregrination from Chicomoztoc to Cholula), of which the *Mapa Sigüenza* and *Tira de la peregrinación* are good Aztec examples. All three maps are pictographic registers of events, of persons participating in the events, of spatial boundaries and locations of legendary origin, as well as the actual habitat.

The fact that space and time are combined in the same *pinturas* might appear strange to a Western educated person of the twentieth century accustomed to a straightforward distinction between geography and history, between maps and narratives. To an educated person living in eleventh-century Europe, these *pinturas* would have been rather familiar. At least one type of medieval map was a combination of spatial boundaries with narrative elements.[44] The fact that one of the major sources of medieval *mappaemundi* was Orosius's *History against the Pagans* is already a telling example of the complicity between geography and history, of tracing boundaries and telling stories. It was not until the sixteenth century that geographers and historians would be clearly distinguished. When López de Velasco, for instance, was appointed *chronista oficial* of the Council of the Indies in 1571, the position implied both tasks, geographer as well as chronicler. In 1596, however, the post was divided in two, one for a geographer and the other for a chronicler or historian. Herrera y Tordesillas became the chronicler-historian, while his forerunner, López de Velasco, was a geographer-chronicler. Thus, the mixing of space and time in territorial ordering parallels the mixing of social roles associated with

writing and painting: the *tlacuilo* was a more versatile social role than
the geographer and the historian.

There is one more important element in Amerindian territorial
conceptualization and depiction that is not obvious in the previous
three peregrination examples. This single important element is the
"four corners of the world" discussed in chapter 5. We have seen that
this aspect transcends specific legacy and traditions and is found in
Mesoamerica, in the Andes, among the Navajos, in ancient China, and
in Jewish and Christian cosmologies.[45] It organized the world and the
communication between earth and heaven when information about
distant places on earth and techniques for calculating those distances
were neither available nor necessary. The connection between the
cosmos and the earth, instead of space and time, is what manifests
itself in territorial depiction in pre- or noncapitalist civilizations. The
four corners of the world is a fundamental cognitive pattern, which
becomes blurred once ethnic centers in the West are disguised under
geometric projections (see chap. 5). One remarkable example of the
connection between cosmos, earth, and human territoriality is provided by the Texcocan historian Fernando de Alva Ixtlilxochitl, at the
beginning of the seventeenth century, in a narrative account of how
the four-corner pattern offered to his ancestors a model for territorial
ordering and control. Ixtlilxochitl, a member of the Texcocan nobility, devoted a great deal of his life to tracing the genealogy and
history of his people. What follows is his narration of how Xólotl (a
leader of the Toltec-Chichimec people) took possession of the land
five years after the decline and fall of the Toltec empire:

> When Xólotl was building his new city of Tenayuca, in the same
> year of 1015, he decided to take possession of the entire land, from
> one sea to the other, and for this purpose he gathered together . . .
> his vassals . . . and he told them . . . that he wished to take posses-
> sion of the land, placing his boundary markers on the highest
> peaks; and gathering bundles of long grass which grew in the
> mountains . . . he set light to them, for without any opposition he
> considered the land his own, without having to take it from any-
> one, now without breaking the word of Icauhtzin, his great-
> grandfather, for the Toltecs had long since come to an end, and if
> any did remain, they were few and were left land which was to their
> liking, where they and their descendants might settle; establishing
> and distributing villages and towns, provinces and cities, with the
> formalities and rites and ceremonies which befit this task, and in
> order to subsist they created common land and forests for all sorts
> of hunting.
>
> Xólotl's resolution and mandate was accepted by his lords and

vassals, and then he personally, with his son, prince Nopaltzin and some others, nobles as well as commoners, went forth from the city and went straight to a mountain called Yocotl, which lies to the west of that city and is very high. They climbed to the top of the mountain and they were the first party who performed the rites which they would use: a Chichimeca lord shot four arrows with all his might into the four corners of the earth, east and west, north and south; and then, tying the bundle of grass at its tip and setting fire to it, and other rites and ceremonies of possession which they used, they descended the mountain, which is in the town of Xocotitlan . . . and they went to another mountain of great height which is called Chihnauhtecatl, whence to Malinalco, where they performed the same ceremonies, and before descending the first mountain, which was called Xólotl, four lords were dispatched to the four corners of the world, and in keeping with the custom they fired the arrows as a sign that they had taken possession of the entire land, which had belonged to the great Topiltzin, from one sea to the other. . . .

After having marked the boundary limits determined by Xólotl, and having sent the four lords to take possession of all the remaining land from one sea to the other, and having arrived by this time at his city, Xólotl ordered that all the land which fell within the first boundary be distributed among his vassals, giving each noble his share of people, and a town which he might found with them, and he fixed this first demarcation in order to settle it first with the people he had, and to the second demarcation, which extended across the entire land from one sea to the other, he sent the four lords so that they might multiply, and so that those who might come would gradually adapt and settle the entire land, as afterwards his descendants settled there, naming each town after the noble who founded it, and in the places marked by the Toltecs, such as the cities, no new names were given, and this is what was done, as can be seen in the demarcation of the city of Azcaputzalco, which went to a nobleman by the name of Izputzal.[46]

Because the four "wings" or "corners" of the world are also found in the Bible,[47] it is tempting to say that the Christian influence had made its way into the Ixtlilxochitl narrative. I would prefer to say (as I suggested in the previous chapter) that the four-corner cosmology is common to both ancient Mexicans and ancient Hebrews and that this basic human way of organizing the territory had different developments in unrelated cultural traditions. In any event, all the examples commented on in this section not only suggest Amerindian cognitive territorial patterns before the conquest but they also illustrate their survival during the first century after the conquest. The increasing repression of Amerindian communities since then has gone hand in hand with the suppression of native graphic traditions and modes of communication.[48] But suppressing written and graphic modes of territorial ordering does not necessarily result in the suppression of cognitive patterns rooted in the collective memory, beyond what graphic signs can preserve and transmit. Several examples of surviving Amerindian communities and cultures that have maintained the ancient Amerindian model of territoriality could be mentioned.[49] The New World, when it was not yet "new," was mapped before European navigators and cosmographers devoted themselves to the task of charting what they took as a lump without meaning. It is now time to move toward the second kind of Amerindian territorial representation during the colonial period and to the paradigmatic example of colonial semiosis: the coexistence in the same graphic space of two concepts of territoriality (e.g., tributary and capitalist) and a reversal of dependency relations (e.g., the Amerindian rulers and nobles moved from being in command to being commanded).

Fractured Territorial Ordering: Displacing the Locus of Enunciation

While the previous examples are associated with the survival of native nobility and the ruling class, and with acts of territorial depiction designed to maintain and protect their material possessions as well as the memories of their ancestors, the *pinturas* associated with the *relaciones* and with land litigations have a different pedigree. First, these *pinturas* could have been drawn by either Amerindians or Spaniards. Second, they contained either information requested in the *Memorandum* or claims (land litigations) provoked by Spanish authorities. And third, because of both the increasing implementation of European writing systems and the existence of a new generation of Amerindians who, by 1580, in places like Mexico, were at least two generations removed from the early years of the colonization process. The end result was that the *pinturas* of the second and third period (from 1577 to 1615, roughly) were more than Amerindian territorial descriptions with Spanish influence. They were properly hybrid cultural products which, from the Amerindian point of view, illustrated the coexistence of territories while, from the Spanish point of view, such coexistence was suppressed by geographical description and mapmaking.

First, let's approach the *pinturas* attached to the *relaciones,* and then the *pinturas* attached to settlements and land litigations. The *relaciones,* as it has been mentioned in the previous chapter, were a report by mandate, guided by the fifty questions prepared by the Council of the Indies, and eventually printed and distributed among the administrators of the Spanish possessions in the West and East Indies. A great deal of the answers were provided by these "indios" although the final written version was the responsibility of a notary public. The *pinturas* attached, according to question 10, were quite often drawn by "indios viejos y principales." Question 10 of the *Memorandum* (in which the fifty questions are laid out as well as instructions for completing the questionnaire) requested, specifically, a *pintura:*

> Describe the site and state the situation of said town, if it lies high or low or in a plain, and give a plan or colored painting showing the streets, squares, and other places; mark the monasteries. This can be easily sketched on paper, and shall be done as well as possible. It is to be noted which part of the town faces North and which South.[50]

From the beginning, the question itself imposes a cosmological orientation that is not aligned with what can be considered Amerindian orientations. While in Mesoamerican (as well as early Christian) cosmology spatial orientation was determined by the sunrise and sunset, European cartography of the late Renaissance preferred North and South. The direction of the sun's movement and the sacred place (Paradise) were replaced by modern technology and the compass.[51] A deeply rooted pattern for spatial orientation, based on cosmological experience and religious connotations, had been replaced by a more concrete need for charting navigation and measuring distance with the Arctic and Antarctic poles as reference points. On the other hand, when the *pinturas* were drawn by the Amerindians, they showed a distribution of space that is not found in the *pinturas* shown in *Tira de la peregrinación, Mapa Sigüenza,* or *Mapas de Cuauhtinchán.* I suspect that the differences could be read both in a chronological and a communicative context. Chronologically, the *pinturas* of the *relaciones* were produced at the end of the sixteenth century when the Castilian conquest of the territory was well advanced, while the *Mapa Sigüenza, Tira de la peregrinación,* and *Mapas de Cuauhtinchán* are all from the first half of the century. Whether these three *pinturas* were drawn for the internal use of the community (as seems to be the case in the *Historia tolteca-chichemeca*), or drawn to inform Spanish missionaries about their past (as seems to be the case of the *Mapa Sigüenza*),

the fact is that the represented territory remains a homogeneous space
bounded to the story of the community (Aztec or Toltec-Chichimec).
This is not the case in several of the *pinturas* from the *relaciones* and
from land settlement documentation.

Let's take the example of the *Relación de Chimalhuacán Atoyac,* a
town in the state of Mexico, and introduce question 16, which complements question 10 by requesting a verbal description of the place:

> Describe all towns, of Spaniards or of Indians, whether the town is
> situated in a mountain, valley or open plain, and the names of the
> mountains or valleys and district in which it lies. Record the native
> meaning of each of these names.

The answer to this question, in the written version of the notary
public, reads as follows:

> Como està dicho, el asiento deste pueblo es a la falda del dicho *cerro
> de Chimalhuacan,* y está asentado en la derecera del poniente; no
> está trazado en pueblo formado. Hay en él un monasterio de re-
> ligiosos de la *Orden del señor Santo Domingo,* como se verá por la
> pintura que está hecho, que está al cabo y fin desta relación.[52]

> [As has been said, this town is located at the foot of the said *Hill of
> Chimalhuacán,* and it is located in the direction of the west; it is
> laid out in a town already formed. In the town there is a monastery
> of monks of the *order of Saint Dominic,* as can be seen in the
> painting.]

The *pintura* attached to this *relación* (fig. 6.23) shows much more
than the verbal description suggests. The deep structure of territorial
depiction is not hinted at in the verbal report. Reading the painting
instead of the verbal description, we perceive, first, two clearly delin-
eated spaces facing each other. The two main objects, the hill and the
monastery, have been drawn in inverted top-bottom positions. At the
top of the hill (inverted position) we see the "casa de idolatria," indicated also by the design of an Aztec temple. The hill is represented by a
glyph very common in Aztec pictographic writing that is generally
found in the extant codices. Although it is not always a religious place,
it is often so. In this particular case the religious dimension is marked
by the temple. Facing the sacred Amerindian space we see the sacred
Spanish space, occupied by the monastery. Both hill and monastery
compete in size and relevance and occupy spaces clearly divided by
roads. The roads are indicated by footsteps, which usually distinguish

roads from rivers and are commonly found in other "maps" to indicate the direction of migrations. At first glance, it is possible to conclude that although the spaces are well delimited, the monastery occupies a more prominent position in the *pintura* than the hill. This conclusion may be due to our Western reading habits (left to right and top to bottom). From the direction in which some of the ancient genealogical codices were drawn and interpreted, however, this first impression could be proven wrong. A "boustrophedon" reading has been suggested for the understanding of several genealogical codices, in which

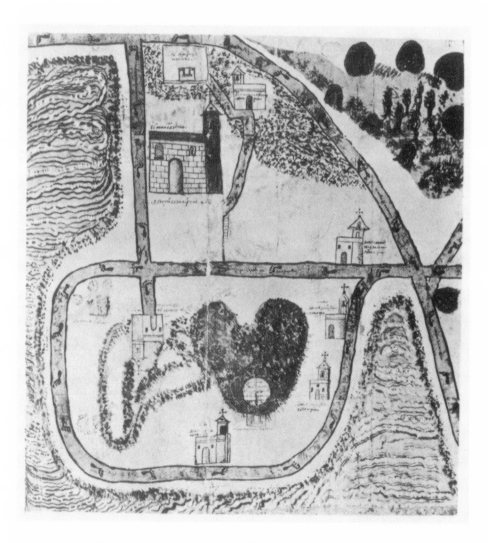

Fig. 6.23.   Fractured territorialities: the *pintura* of Chimalhuacán-Atoyac

case the relevant objects could be placed toward the bottom left instead of the upper right. But, in any case, what is striking in the overall organization of the space is the conflicting coexistence of the Amerindian and Spanish ethnic spaces, a telling example of a hybrid territorial representation in the context of colonial semiosis.

The *pintura* of Chimalhuacán is not an isolated case. Although more examples could be extracted from the *relaciones,* I am more interested in suggesting the general dimension of the phenomenon that could be also illustrated in maps found attached to land litigations. In the *pintura* of Huastepec (fig. 6.24) the positions occupied by the houses of Christian and Amerindian religious practices have been inverted (the temple on the top left and the monastery on the bottom right). The center of the map is left empty, either as no man's land or as the place in which Amerindian and Castilian spaces interact. The *pintura* was drawn toward the end of the sixteenth century in the state of Oaxaca. Although the context of the *relaciones* and of the land settlements and litigations are different, the cognitive patterns of spatial conceptualization from the Amerindian perspective, toward the

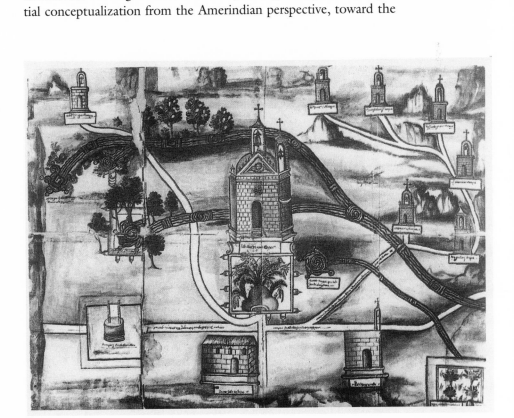

Fig. 6.24.   Fractured territorialities: the *pintura* of Huastepec

end of the sixteenth century, make it clear that the *pinturas* in which a still properly Amerindian territory was depicted was being replaced by *pinturas* in which the territory is divided and the center either emptied or shared.[53]

Finally, there is the fact that the center has been emptied. Ortelius as well as López de Velasco proceeded as if no conceptualization of space had existed before they were able to map the "new" land. On the contrary, for Guaman Poma as well as for many *tlacuilo* who had the chance to paint or describe their town, they felt that their own territory remained but was occupied by someone else. There is a difference, however, in the work of the *tlacuilo* responsible for many of the *pinturas* in the *Relaciones geográficas de Indias* and Guaman Poma's *Pontifical mundo*. The difference is of scale and of cosmographical and cosmological awareness mainly. The *tlacuilo* who painted the map of Chimalhuacán-Atoyac limited himself to what the *relación* (and the notary public who enacted it) requested: a description of the town where the traces of the complicity between city and cosmos have been erased. What remains is the coalescence of two worldviews in the same place. In Guaman Poma's *Pontifical mundo* the coalescence of two worlds, instead, has been projected into a cosmological diagram linking geography with a transcendent design of the cosmos. However, the *pintura* of the anonymous *tlacuilo* and Guaman Poma's *Pontifical mundo* are complementary indeed. While the first is grounded on the conflicting merger of the *altepetl* (Amerindian organization and administration of land, space, and memory) with the encomienda (Spanish organization and administration of land possession and production), the second is grounded on the conflicting merging between the four corners and the center, on the one hand, and the coexistence of the Indias del Peru with Castile, on the other.

What is more impressive, however, is the sustained effort of Guaman Poma de Ayala to map the world and contest the *Relaciones geográficas* from an Amerindian perspective. Let me expand on these two aspects one at a time. And allow me to refer again the drawing of the *Pontifical mundo* (fig. 5.19), which has already been analyzed from a different perspective in the previous chapter. The depiction of *Pontifical mundo* shows an organization very much like the one seen in the *pinturas* of Chimalhuacán-Atoyac and Huastepec (figs. 6.23 and 6.24). The space between the two worlds has been left empty in order to describe their coexistence. Much like the temple and the monasteries in the previous examples, the Indies (Las Indias) at the top of the picture emphasizes the East where the Sun (the Inca God) rises; below the empty space dividing the two worlds is placed Castilla. The symbolic richness of this *pintura* also lies in the fact that López de Velas-

co's map has not only been inverted, but has been redrawn from a
four-pillar cosmology according to which the Indies and Castile are
both at the center of the world.[54]

The existence of two centers is the best example I can provide of the
coexistence of territorial representation from the Amerindian point of
view. It is also a paradigmatic example of colonial semiosis and hybrid
cultural products: while López de Velasco as well as other European
mapmakers *emptied the space* in order to chart the Spanish possessions
(West Indies) or a New World, Amerindians *emptied the center* in
order to accommodate their sense of invaded territoriality, coexisting
with foreign ones. And emptying the center also means, in this context
of description, changing the locus of enunciation. While the *Pontifical
mundo* is placed at the beginning of the *Nueva coronica y buen
gobierno*, the *mapamundi* is placed toward the end and followed by
about sixty drawings of Peruvian towns, some of them quite similar to
pinturas from the *Relaciones geográfica* (fig. 6.25). If one takes into
account this section, it looks similar—although inverted—to López
de Velasco's general map of the Indias Occidentales, followed by thirteen detailed maps of different audiencias. In both cases, a general
picture of the Spanish domains or the world is shown, and then followed up by the parts of the totality (e.g., the eyes and the head).
When one reads the *mapamundi* and the sixty town drawings together with the *Pontifical mundo*, the sense that a new locus of enunciation is being carved by putting the Indies of Peru (instead of the
Americas or the Indias Occidentales) is reinforced. But alternative loci
of enunciation without the support of institutional power often are
not heard when they speak their present, although they are frequently
reclaimed as forgotten or suppressed examples to understand the past.

One Space, Several Territories, Many Actual Worlds

Putting the Americas on the map from the European perspective was
not necessarily a task devoted to finding the true shape of the earth; it
was also related to controlling territories, diminishing non-European
conceptualization of space, and spreading European cartographic literacy; thus colonizing the imagination of people on both sides of the
Atlantic: Amerindians and Europeans. This is not to say that the efforts
to expand Western cultures did not engender opposition and resistance. It is simply to recognize that the power of the economic and
religious expansion and the force of the printing technology have
been the most persuasive among all possible imaginable alternatives.
The spread of European literacy in the New World colonies transmit-

a

Fig. 6.25. *a,* One of the many
pinturas of towns attached to
Relaciones geográficas; b, one of
the sixty towns drawn by
Guaman Poma, placed after the
mapamundi

CIVDAD
LA VILLA DE RIOBAMBA

b

ted to educated Amerindians and Creoles their own territorial awareness and the idea that America was the fourth part of the world. Certainly, such a perspective was neither necessarily shared by everyone, *Putting the*
nor the only possible alternative, but obviously by those who had the *Americas on*
power and controlled chains of communication and programs of edu- *the Map*
cation. Had Islam, instead of Christianity, "discovered" unknown
land and people, not only might America not have been America, but
it would not have been the fourth part of the world because, from the
perspective of Islamic geography and cartography, the earth was not
divided in three parts. Economic expansion, technology, and power,
rather than truth, characterized European cartography early on, and
national cartography of the Americas at a later date.

From the point of view of the Amerindians of the past as well as of
the present, their cosmographic and cosmologic traditions were and
are what really count as territorial organization. Urton has shown the
continuity of Inca cosmology in contemporary Peru, and Gossen has
shown a similar pattern among the Chamulas of southern Mexico (fig.
6.26).[55] They provide good examples of communities for whom, even
today, the Americas does not have the same meaning it had for our
hypothetical European observer,[56] or for the intellectuals and nation
builders at the beginning of the nineteenth century who reversed the
European perspective by putting the Americas on the map not as
America in the New World but in the Western Hemisphere.[57]
Chamula, the city and the place, is at the center of the earth. For the
people who live in this cosmology, America is still not on the map.
They inhabit the same space, although they live in a different world
and in an alternative territory. Amerindians in South and Central
America as well as Native Americans in the United States have kept
their traditions alive and territorial organization is for them, as for
anybody else, a fundamental aspect of their cultural identity. They are
constantly teaching us not only that maps are not the territory, but also
that the process of inventing and putting the Americas on the map was
not an everlasting episode of the past, but an open process toward the
future.

Concluding Remarks

In this and the previous chapter I made an effort to understand colonization of space historically as well as theoretically. Historically, I
looked at the colonial expansion as the darker side of the European
Renaissance. Theoretically, I attempted, first, to displace questions
related to the representations of the colonized with questions related

to the performances at both end of the spectrum (colonizer and colonized) as well as in between (colonizer in exile, colonized in adaptation). Second, I made an effort to suggest—following O'Gorman's seminal works—to carve a locus of enunciation from which to look at the European Renaissance from the perspective of colonial and postcolonial worlds. Reversing a historical perspective is at the same time a theoretical and an ideological move. Theoretically, it requires a pluritopic hermeneutics; ideologically, it implies the creation of loci of enunciation parallel and opposite to the loci of enunciation created in the field of anthropology: instead of looking at marginal societies from the perspective of academic centers, it proposes to look at cultural and political centers from the academic margins. Loci of enunciation are only partially related to the physical domiciles and academic affiliation of speaking and writing subjects. They are constructed by both joining and detaching oneself from previous performances.[58] There is no reason to limit the question whether the

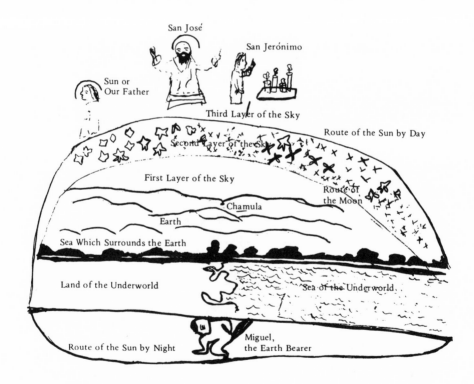

Fig. 6.26. Chamula's ordering of the world, in the second half of the twentieth century

subaltern can speak to the nonacademic world. One can witness every day in academic life a certain subalternity disguised under the label of "minorities," or in the way that publications are filtered out and fellowships are administered and awarded.

My efforts have been addressed to understanding some specific European (and not just Spanish) moves in putting the Americas on the map and administrating the Indies, as well as some Amerindian moves (from Mesoamerica and the Andes) in accommodating their perception and construction of territoriality to new social and cultural realities. I have also tried to avoid the idea that Spaniards' or European's misunderstanding or ignorance of Amerindian territorialities was a wrong representation of them, while Amerindians themselves were not allowed to tell their right part of the story. Instead, I have attempted to suggest that European moves in mapping and inventing a New World and Spanish moves toward administrating newly discovered lands and people were moves related to the need to justify their expansions, by spreading their knowledge and controlling territories. A similar view could be applied, certainly, to understanding Amerindian semiotic performances before, during, and after the conquest, except that, on the one hand, Amerindians (in Mesoamerica and the Andes) had no choice but to yield (counting also suppressed rebellions) to European and Spanish territorial control and that, on the other, their cosmopolitical uses of territoriality to organize and govern were overpowered by a territorial conception attached to complex bureaucracies and disguised sources of power that emptied spaces by ignoring previous existing territorialities. European maps and Spanish territorial administration historically became the "true representation" of a New World and the Indias Occidentales. Looking at them as social and semiotic interactions and territorial control instead of as representations of an ontological space (as López de Velasco described the Straits of Panama) opens up new ways of understanding in which cognitive patterns become embedded in social actions and representations become performances of colonization.

Afterword

On Modernity, Colonization, and the Rise of Occidentalism

What follows has emerged from notes taken in the process of writing the previous portion of this book. These notes have resulted in a list of issues I feel the need to address but have left out of the argument because they are too complex to be addressed in a footnote or would require significant diversions from the argument I have articulated. The underlying concern throughout the book has been undoing the Renaissance foundation Eurocentrism.

First of all, then, the need to understand the past in order to speak the present continued to haunt me as I tried to clarify for myself the differences between understanding the past and the practice of colonial cultural studies as a discipline. My research was a conscientious effort to understand the past, although I did not plan or feel, at any moment, that I was writing a history of New World colonization. I have written the book with the strong persuasion that the late European Renaissance (the early modern period), a landmark in the idea of modernity, was the beginning of an effort to constitute homogeneous linguistic, national, and religious communities, which have begun to disintegrate at the end of the twentieth century. The successful efforts made in the sixteenth and seventeenth centuries by Nebrija and Aldrete to think about territories on linguistic grounds, the complicity of historiography (of Spain and of the New World) and mapmaking in the configuration of cultural identities under the economic and legal rules of the empire (prolonged in the eighteenth and nineteenth centuries by England and France), are no longer useful to understand the connections between languages and territories at the end of the twentieth century. This is true, first, because Amerindian (in South and Central America) and Native American (in North America) cultural

315

and linguistic legacies are becoming part and parcel of the construction of multicultural and heterogeneous traditions and the emergence of new identities, all of which have been suppressed both by colonial regimes and postcolonial nation builders. Second, human migrations imply migrations of the languages and memories upon which human communities are built, communities that may flourish within a territorial structure alien to the language and culture of the migratory peoples. Such has been the case of Latinos or Hispanics in the United States, who are in the process of destabilizing not only the structure of traditional Anglo-American culture but also traditional Spanish American culture. It would certainly be a mistake to look at the Latino experience in Anglo America as an accomplishment of the expansion of the Spanish culture and not also as the end of Nebrija's and Aldrete's dream in the unity of language and territory. Since my explorations have centered on the colonial period, I have not paid much attention to the double bind of the ideologues of nation building in Spanish America during the nineteenth century, who played an important role in the conflictive process of negotiating the Spanish legacy and celebrating the Amerindians' pre-Spanish past while at the same time suppressing its burning present and flirting with new forms of economic (English and German) and cultural (French Enlightenment) imperialism.

In the context of the darker side of the Renaissance (or the early modern period), what I have tried to articulate throughout (while insisting on comparative analysis and pluritopic hermeneutics to chart the coexistence of differential loci of enunciation in colonial situations) could be recast in the influential description of modernity and the modern experience articulated by Berman:

> There is a mode of vital experience—experience of space and time, of the self and others, of life's possibilities and perils—that is shared by men and women all over the world today. I will call this body of experience "modernity." To be modern is to find ourselves in an environment that promises us adventure, power, joy, growth, transformation of ourselves and the world—and, at the same time, that threatens to destroy everything we have, everything we know, everything we are. Modern environments and experiences cut across all boundaries of geography and ethnicity, of class and nationality, of religion and ideology: in this sense, modernity can be said to unite all mankind. But it is a paradoxical unity, a unity of disunity: it pours us all into a maelstrom of perpetual disintegration and renewal, of struggle and contradiction, of ambiguity and anguish. To be modern is to be part of a universe in which, as Marx said, "all that is solid melts into air."[1]

Although I shared Perry Anderson's enthusiasm when I first read this paragraph,[2] I was also disappointed, as I was already well into the ideas that shaped this book. In Berman's description of "modernity" I missed its darker side, the differential experiences of space and time, of speech and writing, "shared by men and women all over the world" who lived in peripheral colonial and postcolonial situations. Even if one can accept that there are few remaining areas of the globe untouched by the expansion of the West, this does not mean that whoever is touched by Western expansion becomes automatically a Western person who experiences space and time, speech and writing in Kerala or in the Andes in the same way that a person experiences them in Paris, Bombay, or Buenos Aires. If one can assume, for instance, that territoriality is universally constructed according to similar human experiences of language, location, and memories, one can also argue that self-descriptions vary not only *across cultures* in colonial situations but *within* imperial and national environments as well. However, the Western expansion initiated in the sixteenth century brought to the foreground the need to negotiate differences across cultures and to rethink the links between differences and values. Although we human beings all inhabit the same world, not everyone lives in the same territory. Modernity is a period, in the history of the West, in which contact and domination between human cultures reached their peak. Thus, reflections on colonial experiences are not only corrective exercises in understanding the past but helpful tools in speaking the present. Critical perspectives on Western values and ways of thinking have much to gain from understanding colonial situations: the darker side of the European Renaissance and Western modernity, perhaps, but also the brighter side of a utopian future.[3]

The first half of the book deals with the basic issues of speech and writing and the second with space and time. Chapter 3 serves as a transition between the question of writing to writing history, invoking the concept of time. The last two chapters emphasize the notion of space as it centers on the mapping of the world. The four concepts—speech, writing, time, and space—together serve as a loose framework to analyze the spread of Western literacy and one of its major consequences, the Occidentalization of the globe. Such a larger set of concepts would require a much lengthier examination to trace the scholarly genealogy of each of them. I will limit myself, instead, to a few observations to contextualize the main arguments of the book.

Several times I have been asked to comment on Jacques Derrida's *De la grammatologie* (1967) in connection to my own approach to literacy and colonization. Derrida's pervasive analysis of a long-lasting philosophical construction of the relationship between speech and writing in the Western tradition (which is at the same time how the Western tradition came to be conceived as it is today) was an intervention into the language- and writing-oriented discussion that had been taking place in Paris since the late 1950s. If, on the one hand, Lévi-Strauss contributed to it with his "Leçon d'écriture"[4] the very notion of *écriture* (writing) began to dominate and move across disciplines and activities, from anthropology to metaphysics, from linguistics to literature, from literary criticism to the philosophy of language. Thus, Derrida's concern with writing merged a dominant linguistic and semiotic tradition defining the sign as a compound of signifier and signified as well as a philosophy of language that conceived of writing as a surrogate of speech. To demolish (or deconstruct) a long-lasting conception of writing that impinges on epistemology as well as on metaphysics, Derrida created a set of concepts (well known by now, although not necessarily well understood) and chose a few key examples. Among his examples, there is a big chronological leap: from Plato and Aristotle, at one end of the spectrum, to Rousseau, in the eighteenth century, before reaching Saussure and Lévi-Strauss in the twentieth century. Being a French philosopher himself (born in Algeria), it is natural that Derrida preferred to begin with the history of metaphysics in Greek philosophy and to skip over the Italian and Spanish Renaissance in order to arrive at Rousseau and the French Enlightenment and Hegel and German philosophy.[5] Nor is it a surprise that from Rousseau he made another jump to Ferdinand de Saussure and Claude Lévi-Strauss, since these two authors provided him with telling examples of the survival of the Western logos and the secondary role attributed to writing over speech. The Italian and Spanish Renaissance of the fifteenth and sixteenth centuries, however, offered an interesting approach to the philosophy and practice of writing that prevailed in the colonization of languages during the sixteenth and seventeenth centuries.

Part I of *On Grammatology,* entitled "Writing before the Letter," suggests, on the one hand, that Derrida is working within an evolutionary concept of writing (i.e., that once the letter was invented, alternative forms of writing lost importance) and, on the other, suggests from the beginning who his enemy is: alphabetic writing and its aftermath. One soon realizes, however, that it is not alphabetic writing that is Derrida's main concern, but the emerging idea of the sign divided into a signifier and a signified, and the complicity between alphabetic writing and Western foundations of knowledge. Nothing is said about non-Western alphabetic writing and alternative organizations of knowledge, such as the Arabic language and culture. References are made to Hebrew, although he employs examples from the

Western Jewish tradition and not from Hebrew writing before the configuration of the modern idea of the West, a configuration that could be traced back to the eleventh century, when the Christian West had to affirm itself in order to confront the increasing expansion of the Islamic world.

My main debt to Derrida, then, is his emphasis on the ideology of alphabetic writing and its dislocation of the very notion of writing in Western modernity. My first departure from his explorations is in the attempt to go beyond the evolutionary model still dominant in the various histories of writing and from which Derrida did not completely escape. The title of the first part of *On Grammatology* ("Writing before the Letter") suggests that with the invention of the alphabet the history of writing took a new path and alternative forms of writing were superseded. I prefer to emphasize a coevolutionary model and the idea of writing *without* letters,[6] which acknowledges both nonalphabetic forms of writing and alternatives to Greco-Roman alphabets. My second departure is by selecting Nebrija, instead of Rousseau, as a cue of the Western philosophy and ideology of alphabetic writing. For Nebrija the question of the letter was not related to the representation of the voice—one of Derrida's primary concerns—but to the taming of the voice, crucial for both the constitution of territoriality in modern imperial states and nation-states as well as in the colonization of non-Western languages (chap. 1). Nebrija's concern with alphabetic writing was political (in the narrow sense of the word), rather than philosophical or cognitive. My third departure from Derrida stems from the fact that the example chosen in his deconstruction of logocentrism remains within the tradition he deconstructs. Looking at conflicting writing systems during the early colonial expansion and the confrontation between people practicing different kinds of writing (some of them loosely related to the representations of speech sounds) brings new light to the ideology of the letter in the Western tradition. My fourth departure is that the discontinuity of the classical tradition (in all its forms) is of the essence to understanding colonial situations; and that Western logocentrism shows its limits when confronted with forms of knowledge and understanding built upon alternative philosophies of language, and alternative speaking practices and writing systems. My fifth departure is located in disciplinary configurations and the history of problems proper to each discipline. Derrida's main concern is the history of Western philosophy and in the ways that metaphysics functioned in the foundation of Western knowledge and the concept of science. For a philologist and a comparatist interested in colonial and postcolonial situations, attention is located in understanding and comparing alternative forms of knowledge and the structure of power that allowed the practice of alphabetic writing and its ideology to create a hierarchy across cultures that was fairly successful in spreading the image of its superiority.

This having been said, I do not intend here to construct my five departures as a criticism of or radical alternative to Derrida's proposal; nor am I so foolish as to embark on a self-promotional campaign by comparing myself with Derrida. I am interested in clarifying my agenda and in satisfying the almost obvious natural questions when someone decides to explore issues such as speech and writing. The agenda underlying my research is the understanding of the role played by the practice and the philosophy of writing in spreading Western literacy and colonizing non-Western languages and memories. The paradigmatic Western examples are, on the one hand, Nebrija and the European Renaissance instead of Rousseau and the European Enlightenment and, on the other, colonial situations in the margins of the Western world instead of a long-lasting European trajectory moving from Greece to Geneva and Paris, serving as a guiding principle to understand trajectories going from Seville to Mexico or from London to Bombay.

One more important observation should be made in relation to Derrida's concept of writing. One of his main efforts was to dissolve the distinction between speech and writing and to conceive of writing as the production of *differances* (differences and deferrals). Writing in Derrida's conception is not necessarily related to visible signs but to the production of *différance,* which is also achieved by means of sounds. For reasons that should be clear in the book, I needed to move in a different direction. Since I placed a heavy accent on the materiality of cultures and on human beings' (as individuals and communities) own self-description of their life and work, I needed to maintain the distinction between semiotic interactions involving the mouth and the ears from those involving the hands and the eyes. That these two activities do not have to be practiced successively, but that they can take place at the same time is certainly obvious. Now recognizing the material difference between these two kinds of activities does not force you to call writing the latter and not the former, as a Derridean logic will suggest. But there is no need to use *writing* to refer to the production of *différance* in either form, outside of a specific agenda whose goal is to destabilize a Western concept of writing strictly dependent on speech. One only need remember that writing was related, in Latin, to plowing and in other Western languages to scratching (chap. 2) to be liberated of a regional and restricted notion of writing as dependent on the sounds of speech.

A few years before the publication of Derrida's influential *On*
Grammatology, a no less influential article on the consequences of
literacy, "The Consequences of Literacy," was published by Jack
Goody and Ian Watt. This article and its aftermath are more relevant
to the question of the philosophy, politics, and materiality of writing I
raised in the first two chapters. The article caught my attention during
a seminar in anthropology, taught by José Cruz in 1964 at the University of Córdoba, in Argentina. We read it in connection with Lévi-Strauss's "Leçon d'écriture." Since I had also recently had a seminar in semiology with Luis Prieto, I was transfixed by this article as I began to see the scope of writing beyond speech and became intrigued by what alphabetic writing could have done for the history of humanity. When several years later I began to read colonial texts, I suddenly ran into the Spanish concern about Amerindian writing systems and its implications. A sign of postcolonial peripheries is the strong attraction from the centers, and as students in the College of Philosophy and Letters in Córdoba in the late 1960s, we also read Derrida's *De la grammatologie* outside of the classroom and discussed it not without passion, although perhaps with limited understanding. However, it had a less decisive influence on my thinking, even when I ended up in disagreement with most of the basic thesis advanced by Goody and Watt. These authors oriented my thinking toward the social and political dimension of writing rather than to its metaphysical underpinnings; and they also opened up for me new vistas in nonalphabetic writing systems. Perhaps it was easier for me to relate the consequences of literacy formulated by Goody and Watt with the problem of colonization raised by Frantz Fanon's *Los condenados de la tierra* [The wretched of the earth], whose first edition in Spanish was published in 1963 (the second in 1965); and with the social dimension of literature and intellectual life raised by Antonio Gramsci's *Letteratura e vita nazionale* (Literature and national life) (1952) and *Gli intelletuali e l'organizzazione della cultura* (The intellectuals and the organization of culture) (1955), translated into Spanish in 1961 and 1960, respectively, and eagerly read by my fellow students.

It was not until the early 1980s that Goody and Watt's article, which remained dormant for almost fifteen years in my unconscious, began to reemerge. I began to realize, at the same time, the ideological difficulties involved in the conception of literacy advanced therein. Literacy became a popular and truly interdisciplinary issue following the publication of that seminal article. In 1981 Harvey Graff was able to compile a volume of almost four hundred pages of titles published during that time span.[7] He needed fifteen sections in order to organize the different approaches, areas, methodologies, and so on, of research dealing with the topic. Despite its enormous complexity, Scribner was successful in presenting literacy in (and reducing it to) three metaphors: literacy as adaptation, as power, and as a state of grace.[8] By literacy as adaptation, Scribner refers to the pragmatic aspects of literacy and conceives it, broadly, "as the level of proficiency necessary for effective performance in a range of settings and customary activities." Contrary to "literacy as adaptation," which stresses the significance of literacy at the individual level, "literacy as power" put the accent on the group or community advancement. Scribner mentions Paulo Freire's view of literacy as a means to create a "critical consciousness through which a community can analyze its conditions of social existence and engage in effective action for a just society." Finally by "literacy as a state of grace," Scribner stresses some of the particular values (sacred and secular) that connect literacy with power, respect, high culture, civilization, intelligence, and so on. Scribner observes that older religious written traditions—such as Hebraic and Islamic—have "invested the written word with great power and respect." The question of writing is further complicated, in such cases, with the question of scriptures; with the distinction between the written signs of human beings and the written signs of gods. Western tradition has emphasized the values of "literateness" and construed it as synonymous with being cultured and civilized.

"In the 'literacy-as-state-of-grace' concept," Scribner states,

> the power and functionality of literacy is not bounded by political or economic parameters but in a sense transcends them; the literate individual's life derives its meaning and significance from intellectual, aesthetic, and spiritual participation in the accumulated creations and knowledge of humankind, made available through the written word.[9]

I would hurry to add that Scribner's description corresponds to one ideology of literacy, the ideology of those who constructed literacy as a state of grace, detached from political and economic parameters. Literacy as a state of grace, in other words, erases its links with economic structures and with literacy as power, because the exercise of power dwells, precisely, in its apparent disconnection with it. Literacy as a state of grace is perhaps one of the most lasting legacies of the European Renaissance and one of the most powerful ideologies in the process of colonization, extending itself to the European Enlightenment.

Perhaps it is the third of Scribner's metaphors that best summarizes the mythic Western story of literacy as the quantum leap in the history of human civilization and the great divide between Western reason and non-Western ways of thinking. One of the most blatant formulations comes from Marshall McLuhan:

> A single generation of alphabetic literacy suffices in Africa today, as in Gaul two thousand years ago, to release the individual initially, at least, from the tribal web. This fact has nothing to do with the content of the alphabetized word; it is the result of the sudden breach between the auditory and the visual experience of man. Only the phonetic alphabet makes such a sharp division in experience, giving to its user an eye for an ear, and freeing him from the tribal trance of reasoning word magic and the web of kinship. . . . The phonetic alphabet, alone, is the technology that has been the means of creating "civilized" man—the separate individuals equal before a written code of law. Separateness of the individual, continuity of space and time, and uniformity of codes are the primer marks of literate and civilized societies. . . . Typography ended parochialism and tribalism [and] had psychic and social consequences that suddenly shifted previous boundaries and patterns of cultures.[10]

Ruth Finnegan builds on that quotation and emphasizes the Western-centered perspective of the model: a developmental myth based on the predominance of communication in words and, in particular, of alphabetic writing and print.[11] The myth, Finnegan observes, played an important role in the organization and control of society as well as in the distribution of power, first during the imperial expansion, later in the era of nation building, and currently at the time of homogenizing the globe by spreading a literacy that suppresses diversity. How to go beyond it? Finnegan suggests creating a new myth with a wider view of communication and human interactions, and the demystification of the ideology of the written word, the power of literacy-as-state-of-grace. It is needed to get away from the evolutionary model at the basis of the consequences of literacy thesis and to learn from comparative studies and from cultural coevolution. This, in general, is my starting point regarding literacy and imperial expansion during the sixteenth century.

Regarding studies of the darker side of the late European Renaissance (or early modern period), the question of occidentalization and occidentalism have seldom been discussed by Renaissance scholars.[12] The reconfiguration of space and time becomes relevant here. If, in current discussions in the United States, Occidentalism was a natural response to Edward Said's *Orientalism* (1978), in Latin America it was already being discussed in the late 1950s, when Edmundo O'Gorman published his *La invención de America: La universalisación de la cultura occidental* (1958) (*The Invention of America: An Inquiry into the Historical Nature of the New World and the Meaning of Its History,* 1961). Leopoldo Zea devoted a chapter to the same topic in his *America en historia* and focused on liberal institutions and the industrial system of commodities and comfort as two features of the Western model. O'Gorman, instead, emphasized the Occidentalization of Western cultures in connection to the colonization of the Americas. More recently Serge Gruzinski, a French ethnohistorian working on the colonization of Mexico, published his *La colonisation de l'imaginaire: Sociétés indigènes et occidentalisation dans le Mexique espagnol, XVIe–XVIIIe siècles* (The colonization of the imaginary: Indigenous societies and occidentalizations in New Spain) (1988). And the Brazilian historian Janice Theodoro devoted two studies to the connections between Renaissance, "discoveries," and Occidentalization (*Descobrimentos e colonizacao* [Discovery and colonization], [1989] and *Descobrimentos e renascimento* [Discovery and the Renaissance], [1991]). Seen from the perspective of Latin American scholarship (or French scholars working in close connection with Latin American ones, such as Gruzinski), the European Renaissance and its relation to colonial expansion look different from the classic perspective of the European Renaissance scholars whose field of inquiry was mainly Italy (as in Paul Oskar Kristeller's *Renaissance Thought and the Arts,* 1980), as well as from the Spanish perspective of José Antonio Maravall,[13] justifying the Spanish contribution to the European Renaissance. Occidentalization was not an issue in these studies. And the attention that Maravall paid to the "discovery of America" in the context of the European Renaissance did not bring to the foreground the expansion of the West in terms of the universalization of occident, as did Zea, O'Gorman, Gruzinski, or Theodoro. Naturally, it is not just the perspective (a way of seeing) that is at stake but the locus of enunciation (a way of saying). What I am proposing here and throughout the entire book is that we must look for the place (physical as well as theoretical) from which a given statement (essays or book) is being pronounced. What are the desires, the interests, the alliances, and, briefly, the politics of intellectual inquiry implied in a scholarly work as well as in a political discourse? If Maravall cannot completely embrace Kristeller's perspective, neither can Zea embrace Maravall's. Maravall was mainly interested in charting the distinctive Spanish contribution to the European (mainly Italian) Renaissance, which had been downplayed (and continues to be) in the scholarly tradition of Renaissance studies. The fact that Spain produced neither a Hobbes nor a

Locke, nor a social contract or industrial revolution, was taken as proof that Spain remained untouched by the Renaissance and the Reformation.[14] In a nutshell, occidentalization is an issue for those who place themselves at its margins, not for those who place themselves at its center. However, such a dichotomy is not clear-cut, for, as Maravall's work bears witness, Spain in the sixteenth century—and at the peak of its glory—began to lose its position in the configuration of modern Europe and began to be placed—borrowing Leopoldo Zea's expression—"at the margin of the West." But Zea's interest is located in America, not in Europe and Spain.

It is not by chance, then, that occidentalization and Occidentalism as a distinctive feature of sixteenth-century European expansion (and its aftermath) were brought to the foreground by philosophers of cultures thinking from "marginalization and barbarism" and from European ethnohistorians studying colonial Mexico.[15] Recently, it has been a common topic of discussion among anthropologists in this country.[16] Before Orientalism developed as a massive discursive formation during the eighteenth and nineteenth centuries, a similar imaginary construction flourished with the inclusion of Indias Occidentales in the map and the subsequent invention of America. Spain and the rest of Europe began to look West to build an extension of their own destiny by enacting the ambiguity between Indias Orientales and Indias Occidentales. From the point of view of the Spanish Crown, overseas possessions were always conceived, from beginning to end, as Indias Occidentales and not as America, as could be seen in all relevant legal documents. One of the most significant collections of official documents was called *Recopilación de las Leyes de Indias* (Compilation of the laws of the Indies), in force from their first compilation, in 1542, until the end of the Spanish empire. The Indias Occidentales, we should remember, were not limited to the so-called New World but included part of the "Old World" as well. The Philippines were part of the Spanish empire and were located among the Indias del Poniente (or East Indies). The sixteenth century was a crucial moment in the consolidation of the idea of Europe as Christian and Western.

If the idea of the West was not properly born during the sixteenth century, it was certainly shaped in a lasting fashion. During the nineteenth century, the expansion of the French Empire under Napoleon I generated among the intellectuals the name of Amerique Latine,[17] which integrated the Spanish-speaking independent nations, as well as Brazil and the recently conquered Martinique, Guadalupe, and part of the Guyanas. Parallel to it, starting at the beginning of the eighteenth century, the idea of the Western Hemisphere began to take shape among American intellectuals (both north and south), geared toward distinguishing themselves from Europe and the idea of the West as it was associated only with Europe.[18] The tensions and conflicts during the nineteenth century between the idea of Latin America and that of the Western Hemisphere are too complex to be analyzed here (although they do come up in the last chapter). When, toward the end of the nineteenth century, the Cuban writer and political activist José Martí launched the expression "Our America" to distinguish North from South, one cannot forget that Europe as the "enemy" of both Americas was too recent to have been completely forgotten. The example provided by the "Indias Occidentales" through the politic of languages, the writing of history, and mapping and its transformation into "Latin America," "Western Hemisphere," and "Nuestra America" is a picture that should be kept in mind, while the construction of the idea of Europe and Europe as the West is at the other end of the spectrum. The coincidence of the final expulsion of the Moors in March of 1492 by the Spanish monarchs and the "discovery" of the Indias Occidentales in October of the same year are emblematic moments tracing the end of an era (the threat of the Islamic East to the Christian West). The unification of Castile was a landmark in the consolidation of Christian (or Western) Europe.

Perhaps one of the best ways to summarize the complex process leading to the transformation of the mythical idea of Europe into the land of Japheth (Christendom in the Middle Ages) and later on into an identification of the *republica christiana* (in the Renaissance) with Europe is to begin by mentioning the gigantic figure of Enea Sylvio de Piccolomini. When he became pope (Pius II) in 1458, he became an instrumental figure in placing the idea of a Christian community (*republica christiana*) in consonance with a geographical area, Europe. In 1459 Pius II convened a congress in Florence to discuss the Turkish menace. Castile was still a few decades away from the beginning of the era of the Catholic monarchs, and Portugal was consistently resisting the Moors. The Christian world had in Pius II its most perceptive ideologue, while Portugal and Spain boasted the most valuable armies on the frontier with the Muslim world. If *republica christiana* became located geographically in Europe, Europe would not only become more and more located in the West as opposed to the East occupied by the Islamic world but would create a distinction between Western and Eastern Christians.[19] Thus Indias Occidentales became both a geographical location and a location where the Western *republica christiana* would continue to grow.

Let's then bring the difficult issue of cultural relativism to the foreground. Leon Olive has distinguished between situations in which the notion of cultural relativism applies and similar situations in which it does not. It is appropriate to talk about cultural relativism, Olive argues, when there is some degree of *incommensurability* between two or more conceptual frameworks. Otherwise, cultural diversity or pluralism would be a more appropriate term to refer to heterogeneous communities with dissimilar beliefs and value systems, but with similar conceptual frameworks. One could ask, according to such a distinction, whether from the beginning of the colonization the history of the Americas is the history of the transformation of cultural relativism into cultural diversity. To turn the question into a hypothesis, one has to assume that both Amerindian and Native American legacies and the American version (North, South, and the Caribbean) of Western civilization have been transformed to the degree in which the initial incommensurability between conceptual frameworks has been converted into cultural diversity by means of dialogues between rational individuals, violence between communities generated by the possessive needs of Western economic expansion, and confrontations between conceptual frameworks.

One can accept, then, that in the Americas, during the sixteenth and seventeenth centuries, the problem of cultural relativism as confrontations of *incommensurable* conceptual frameworks was indeed the case. It is in such a context that the denial of coevalness is justified. However, a new problem arises at this point. In order to make the cultural relativism understandable one has to suppose a third party or observer who does not belong to any of the two or more conceptual frameworks in question and who can determine their incommensurability. One can ask how could that be possible, since the observer cannot be detached from one (or more) conceptual framework(s). The historical problem turns here into a logical one. Before elaborating on it, let's go back to the historical situation of the colonizing process. From which locus of enunciation was the denial of coevalness possible? Who was converting differences between conceptual frameworks into successive stages in the history of humanity? The answer is certainly obvious: those who described themselves as carrying civilization and Christianity over the world and who were able to accept the connection between Christianity and civilization. What is less obvious is why time became a factor in recognizing the value of diverse conceptual frameworks. If we can imagine a thought experiment in which the Maya had arrived in Europe and encountered an unknown continent and unknown people, it is not sure that the Maya would have interpreted the differences in conceptual frameworks in terms of different stages in time, in such a way that less civilized was equivalent to "back in time." Western expansion and colonization, in the sixteenth century, coincided with a radical transformation of the concept of time that impinged on the concept of history and created the necessary condition to place different conceptual frameworks somewhere in a temporal scale that had its point of arrival in the present, sixteenth-century Christian European civilization. To Mesoamerican people discovering the land of Japheth, translating differences into values based on a time frame would have been impossible because the Maya placed more emphasis in a cyclical calculus of time and the computation of human life according to the rhythm of the universe, rather than in the progressive story of human life itself (e.g., self, autobiography), as was the case in the European Renaissance.[20] To move beyond cultural relativism implies dealing with both the question of the observer and the spatialization of time.

First, then, the question of the observer. Currently there is a significant amount of knowledge about pre-Columbian civilization in the modern-day Americas, although the way in which Amerindians and Native Americans from the early sixteenth century on imagined Europeans in their conceptual framework is far less documented than is the reverse. One of the most important reasons for this is the incommensurability between the European humanist and the Amerindian and Native American concepts and uses of knowledge and wisdom. The literate legacies of Spaniards as well as northern Europeans are certainly massive. What is more important, however, is not the quantity but the ways in which negotiations between participants and observers have been handled. The dialectic between Europeans as participants *in* the process of colonization and Europeans as observers *of* the process was constant and persistent. As *participants,* Spaniards and Europeans in general lived and acted according to goals, desires, and needs prompted by a given conceptual framework (or, if you wish, a set of conceptual frameworks). As *observers,* Spanish and European literati became the judges able to compare and evaluate incommensurable conceptual frameworks. One of the crucial points in the construction of otherness was, precisely, this disguised movement between describing oneself as belonging to a given framework and describing oneself as belonging to the *right* one. Scholars of today, inheritors of the humanist legacy, have not only the ethical obligation of describing incommensurable conceptual frameworks, but also the hermeneutically difficult task of reestablishing the lost equilibrium between what, at one level, were alternative conceptual frameworks and, at the other, became organized in a hierarchy of values established by those who were at the same time participants and observers. By playing both roles at the same time, European intellectuals were able to implement (from Europe or from the New World) their observer's descriptions and to tie them up with the exercise of imperial power. Thus, practicing a pluritopic hermeneutics may be a way of detaching our descriptions as observers from our descriptions as participants by underlining and maintaining the discontinuity between "our" (as scholars educated in the Western traditions and practitioners of academic disciplines) conceptual framework and that of "our" ancestors. Thus, constructing loci of enunciation and building, on the one hand, on the discontinuity of the Western tradition as enacted in colonial situations and, on the other, on the discontinuity of Amerindian legacies were transformed and became part of the lived experiences (or, better, of the domains of interactions constructed as lived experiences) in the Americas during the colonial period. Constructing such loci of enunciation implies that the rules of the disciplinary practices (literary studies, philosophy, history, anthropology, etc.) are grounded in the personal (auto)biography of the scholar or social scientist. This brought to scholarship the heavy load of participation in everyday life that was chased out on the glorious day when scholarly and scientific pursuits were conceived as detached from the personal story of the scholar and the scientist. A pluritopic hermeneutics assumes a constant movement between the scholar as observer and participant as well as between the moments of discontinuity of past and present conceptual frameworks.

And what of the second part of the equation, the question of spatializing time? The overall conception of this book, more clearly developed in the final two chapters, is to read temporal arrangements (e.g., denial of coevalness) into geographical distributions. Let me say, before expanding on this idea, that the difficulties of attaching conceptual frameworks to geographical spaces in what Berman calls "a mode of vital experience" and in our postmodern age of constant migrations and relocations of communities were not necessarily present during the early modern period. Conceptual frameworks were indeed more attached to geographical locations than they are now; such was the effort made by imperial intellectuals and by nation builders. Thus, one of my main efforts was to postulate a denial of the denial of coevalness by spatializing time and by suggesting coevolutionary histories as alternatives to evolutionary ones told from a locus of enunciation constructed as the master locus. The construction of a Western perspective was then the construction of a master locus of enunciation in which the very conception and writing of universal history became entrenched with colonial expansion and warranted imperial and the nation-state apparatus.

At this point the question of spatializing time becomes related to the question of the observer, pluritopic hermeneutics, and the politics of intellectual inquiry. The processes of colonial expansion that began in the sixteenth century run parallel to the growing consolidation of the knowing and understanding subject placed in a given geography, constructed over the ruins of two Western languages attached to knowledge and wisdom (Greek and Latin), and situated in a growing idea of a progressive or evolutionary time frame. Such a development ruled out the possibility of imagining that alternative loci of enunciation and coevolutionary histories were also possible. From the early modern period to the eighteenth century the consolidation of a way of knowing as a mirror of nature, critically reviewed by Richard Rorty, was put in place.[21] My assumption in this book is that such a consolidation of ways of knowing implies the complicity between the regional locus of enunciation of a participant in Western European culture and the universal locus of enunciation of science and philosophy of a subject placed outside time and space. This is more precisely what I have earlier (and elsewhere) called the universalization of the regional concepts of science, philosophy, and knowledge. What one witnessed in the sixteenth century during the early encounters between European literati and intellectuals of non-European cultures grew, coalesced, and reached its peak after the eighteenth century, with the expansion of the British and French empires.[22] Certainly, universal ways of knowing have been called into question from within the Western tradition (Nietzsche, Heidegger, Derrida) and not only from the colonial periphery. At this point "from" is not just a geographical location, but mainly a geography of experiences "from people living there," "who cannot live there," or "who would like to live there." Scholarship and social sciences, at this point, approach the position developed by literary writers engaged with "the language and the place."

One example is provided by George Lamming. In an article written in the late 1950s, he asked why West Indian writers from Barbados, Trinidad, and Jamaica preferred living in London to the British Caribbean, and from there negotiating the place of the writer and her or his literature in relation to his or her language and region. I am more interested in the second paragraph, but the first is necessary to understand the second more fully:

> In the Caribbean we have a glorious opportunity of making some valid and permanent contribution to man's life in this century. But we must stand up; and we must move. The novelists have helped; yet when the new Caribbean emerges it may not be for them. It will be, like the future, an item on the list of possessions which the next generation of writers and builders will claim. I am still young by ordinary standards (thirty-two, to be exact), but already I feel that I have had it (as a writer) where the British Caribbean is concerned. I have lost my place, or my place has deserted me.

This may be the dilemma of the West Indian writer abroad: that he hungers for nourishment from a soil which he (as an ordinary citizen) could not at present endure. The pleasure and paradox of my own exile is that I belong wherever I am. My role, it seems, has rather to do with time and change than with the geography of circumstances; *and yet there is always an acre of ground in the New World which keeps growing echoes in my head.* I can only hope that these echoes do not die before my work comes to an end.[23]

A second example is provided by persons placed in between different languages and traditions, contrary to the case of Lamming in which the language of the colony is the "same" as the language of the metropolitan center. When the scholar-scientist (and writer) as observer is placed in a space in between, the space in which the universality of Western reason encounters different rationalities, cultural relativism becomes transformed: from relative conceptual frameworks that could be compared and analyzed, to hybrid conceptual frameworks from which new ways of knowing emerge. At this point the question is no longer how to use the enlightening guidance of Western notions of rationality in order to understand colonial, postcolonial, and Third World experiences but, rather, how to think from hybrid conceptual frameworks and spaces in between. This has been the lesson for me of colonial situations, complemented and expanded today by writers and artists (African-Americans, Latinos, women of color, etc.) and by former intellectuals from the margins, like Frantz Fanon or Césaire in the Caribbean or Rodolfo Kusch in Argentina.

I proposed a comparative and philological methodology and a pluritopic hermeneutics as justification, in order to deal with problems related to cultural relativism, construction of the other, and understanding subject. My main assumption is that in order to deal with cultural differences cultural relativism is necessary but not sufficient. While a philological approach allows me to understand the best I can culture-relative constructs, comparatism allows me to go beyond and to understand *differences* in the context of commonality of *similarities of human agency*. And it allows me to identify specific issues in which Amerindian cultures were misunderstood and misinterpreted by European literati precisely because of their recognition of universal similarities in human beings. (Although the reverse certainly took place as well, it was not symmetric and we do not have the same quantity of records.)

Representation is a notion I have tried to avoid as much as possible in my argument. If I say that I was interested in how European peoples and communities constructed the idea of the self-same instead of in how they "represented the other," it is because my interests are located more in *enactment* than in *representation;* or, if you wish, in *representation as enactment.*[24] But this formula may defeat the purpose of changing the perspective of analysis by changing the premises under which the analysis is carried out. *Representation* in the humanities rests on a denotative philosophy of language according to which names represent things and maps represent the territories. There is a second meaning of representation, more common in the social sciences, used to refer to persons speaking or being in place of others. In this case there is not a relation of "conceptual or visual likeness" that bounds the representation to the represented but a relation of what both notions have in common, namely "being in place of something else." The first focuses on the similarities between the representation and what is represented, while the second rests on the delegation of responsibility from a larger group of people to one person or to a smaller number of "representatives." Going back to the notion of representation in the humanities, the concern with the representation of the colonized (its accuracy or inaccuracy, its rights and wrongs) emerged from within the same *episteme* for which the notion of representation is such a crucial one. Thus, the concern with the representation of the colonized focuses on the discourse of the colonizer, and one forgets to ask how the colonized represent themselves, how they depict and conceive themselves as well as how they speak for themselves without the need of self-appointed chronists, philosophers, missionaries, or men of letters to represent (depict as well as speak for) them. To ask how the Mexica represented the Spanish is a difficult question, first because of the lack of documentation and second because it is not clear that such a notion was established among the Mexica. It is unfair to ask members of a culture different from ours how they do something we do. It is not fair because it assumes that whatever we do has a universal value and, as such, every culture on earth has to do it, one way or another, if they pretend to be human.

And this brings us back to the question of cultural relativism. If we assume that every culture in the world has to have activities similar to ours, although differently conceptualized, we have a false start, since one culture (the one to which the humanities and the social sciences belong) is attributed a universal value, and the possibility of looking at things otherwise is automatically ruled out. Thus, while comparisons continue to be made from the European perspective, questions in a different direction are seldom asked. How, for instance, did Europeans conceive what among the Mexica was referred to as *amoxtli* or *huehuetlatolli?* So cultural relativism is not enough, if all there is to it is that different cultures are different. To go beyond relativism is neces-

sary, first, to question the locus of enunciation from which the notion of cultural relativism has been produced; second, to question the
model or culture used as a reference point to illustrate cultural relativ-
ism and to constantly change the topos of comparison; and finally, to
explore cultural relativism in colonial situations where cultures are not
only different but struggle for imposition, resistance, adaptation, and
transformation.

Thus,the notion of enactment instead of representation focuses on
the locus of enunciation where representations are produced instead
of the configuration of what is being represented. By enactment I
mean, first, an alternative conception of cognition. While cognition as
representation presupposes a world outside the organism that is either
mentally or graphically represented, cognition as enactment implies
that the organism constitutes and places itself in the world by constructing an environment through a dynamic domain of interaction—
neither the world first and then the organism's mind representing it,
nor the organism first representing what is outside of it. The old alternative between realism and idealism vanishes as soon as one recog-
nizes that *the organism is not outside of the world but part of it* and that,
therefore, the question whether the organism represents the world or
the world leaves its imprints in the organism has to be transcended. An
organism is such not only because of its structural organization but
also because of its coupling with other elements of the world out of
which the organism creates its *environment.*

If we take this general assumption to the realm of living organisms
known as human beings and to the domain of interactions known as
culture, the preference for enactment over representation can be better understood. If human beings are conceived not as the mirror of
nature (e.g., being in and knowing of a world outside themselves) but
as developing activities in order to avoid death, to reproduce, to have
pleasure, and to expand their domain of interactions (in any of the
diverse possible forms such an expansion may take), then the realm of
enactments rather than the realm of representations takes precedence
in understanding human cultures.

In what sense could enactment be more useful than representation
in understanding colonial situations? One of the particularities in colonization processes is that people from quite different cultures come
face to face and fight to preserve or appropriate territories, both as
possessions and conceptualizations of space. Thus, understanding
colonial situations implies understanding different kinds of *activities*
performed by persons belonging to different communities and, consequently, with different programmed needs and domains of interaction. If one looks at representations instead of at enactments, one can

*OnModernity,
Colonization,
and the Rise of
Occidentalism*

say—as colonizers from the sixteenth to the twentieth centuries, from Spain to Britain said—that certain representations or lifestyles are inferior or barbarous. If one looks at enactments instead of representations, and cognition as enactment, one can not only escape the hierarchical description of culture but, more important, look at *activities* across cultures in a different light. For instance, a twentieth-century observer can surmise, when comparing an illuminated medieval codex or a wonderful Renaissance book to a painted Mexica codex, that while the latter is a piece to be admired, it cannot be put at the same level as the medieval codex or the Renaissance book. Books, in the West, became entrenched with writing and with truth, be it the truth of God by divine revelation in the Holy Book, or be it the truth of human beings by written narratives in historical books. The Mexica codices, instead, remained as curious objects related to devilish designs or mythical imagination. If one looks at cultural objects as results of activities responding to human needs rather than artifacts by means of which the mirror of nature is extended and the nature of the world is captured in visible signs, then enactment becomes more relevant than representation. What one can achieve by this means is to look, first, at colonial situations from the perspective of cognitive enactments and human activities in different societies and, second, to look at the transformations of activities and cognitive enactments into instruments of power, control, and domination. Thus, the book is about such transformations in the domain of speech and writing, in the domain of interpreting the past and anticipating the future, and in the domain of charting space and building territories, during the early modern period, as well as about the transformations of ways of seeing, saying, and understanding, today and in the future.

Notes

INTRODUCTION

Unless otherwise indicated, all translations are my own.

1. The changes in literacy scholarship inviting a rethinking the field of literary studies have been examined in the context of North American and European scholarship by Leah Marcus, "Renaissance/Early Modern Studies," in *Redrawing the Boundaries of Literary Study in English* New York: Modern Language Association, (1992), 41–63. A forceful argument in favor of revisiting the notion of Renaissance, to account for Western colonial expansion as one of its distinctive features, has been advanced by David Wallace, "Carving Up Time and the World: Medieval-Renaissance Turf Wars; Historiography and Personal History," (working paper 11, Center for Twentieth-Century Studies, University of Wisconsin, Milwaukee, 1991). I have examined recent scholarly works on and in the New World that have contributed to rethinking the Renaissance in literary scholarship in "The Darker Side of the Renaissance: Colonization and the Discontinuity of the Classical Tradition," *Renaissance Quarterly* 45, no. 4 (1993): 808–28.

2. Robert L. Collison, *Encyclopaedias: Their History throughout the Ages* (New York: Hafner Publishing Company, 1964).

3. I am thinking of Cornel West's persuasive articulation of the politics of intellectual inquiry in "The New Cultural Politics of Difference," in *Marginalization and Contemporary Cultures,* ed. R. Fergusson et al., 19–38 (New York: Museum of Contemporary Art; Cambridge: MIT Press, 1990).

4. Michel Foucault, *L'archéologie du savoir* (Paris: Gallimard, 1969).

5. Patricia Seed, "Colonial and Postcolonial Discourse" (review essay), *Latin American Research Review* 26, no. 3 (1991): 181–200; Walter D. Mignolo, "Colonial and Postcolonial Discourse: Cultural Critique or Academic Colonialism?" (comments on Seed's essay), *Latin American Research Review* 28, no. 3 (1993): 120–34, and "Darker Side."

6. Peter Hulme, *Colonial Encounters: Europe and the Native Caribbean,*

1492–1797 (New York: Methune 1986); and "Subversive Archipelagos: Colonial Discourse and the Break-up of Continental Theory," *Dispositio,* special issue on Colonial Discourse, ed. R. Adorno and Walter D. Mignolo, 36–38 (1989): 1–24.

7. *Pop Wuj: Libro del tiempo,* trans. Adrián I. Chávez (Buenos Aires: Ediciones Sol, 1987). An anthology of Mayan literature with commentaries is *Literatura Maya,* ed. Mercedes de la Garza (Caracas: Biblioteca Ayacucho, 1980). For an English translation see *Popol Vuh,* trans. Dennis Tedlock (New York: Simon and Schuster, 1985).

8. Or "discourse of colonialism," in Homi K. Bhabha's expression, "The Other Question: Difference, Discrimination, and the Discourse of Colonialism," in *Literature, Politics, and Theory: Papers from the Essex Conference 1976–1984,* F. Baker et al., 148–72 ed. (New York: Methuen, 1986).

9. For a thorough description of the quipus, see Marcia Ascher and Robert Ascher, *Code of the Quipu: A Study in Media, Mathematics, and Culture* (Ann Arbor: University of Michigan Press, 1981).

10. *Colonial semiosis* is not suggested to replace the notion of colonial discourse but to create a wider context of description, of which colonial discourse is an important component. Colonial semiosis is suggested, finally, with the intention of redrawing the boundaries of a field of study mainly inhabited by texts alphabetically written by the colonizers or in their languages, in order to open it up to a wider spectrum of semiotic interactions in Amerindian languages and in nonalphabetic scripts.

11. The forgotten connections between text and textile have been exploited by Dennis Tedlock and Barbara Tedlock, "Text and Textile: Language and Technology in the Arts of the Quiché Maya," *Journal of Anthropological Research* 41, no. 2 (1985): 121–46.

12. The Latin alphabet introduced by the Spaniards, the picto-ideographic writing systems of Mesoamerican cultures, and the quipus in the Andes delineate particular systems of interactions that took place during the colonial period. If we were to limit the use of the term *discourse* to oral interactions and reserve *text* for written interactions, we would need to expand the latter term beyond the range of alphabetically written documents to embrace all material sign inscriptions. By doing so we would honor the etymological meaning of text ("weaving," "textile") and justify the insertion of the quipus into a system in which writing had always been understood as scratching or painting on solid surfaces, but not as weaving. Two metaphors come to mind: the Latin analogy between writing and plowing, on the one hand, and the modern similarities between text and textile. As an activity, writing has been conceived and compared with plowing; as a product, the text has been conceived and compared with the intricacies of textiles.

13. I am using throughout this book the dichotomy center/periphery. I am not using it on the assumption that there is one ontological center (Europe) and various ontological peripheries (the colonies). I hope to show that the center is movable (see chap. 5), as is the personal pronoun "I," and as are the notions *same* and *the other.* It so happened, however, that during the sixteenth century Europe began to be construed as the center and colonial

expansion as movement toward the peripheries—that, of course, from the perspective of a European observer (see Chapter 6). From the perspective of the European peripheries, the center remained where it was, although in danger of radical transformations. I take the center/periphery dichotomy from Immanuel Wallerstein, *The Modern World-System: Capitalist Agriculture and the Origins of the European World-Economy in the Sixteenth Century* (New York: Academic Press, 1974), vol. 1, although I am aware of the criticism to which Wallerstein has been subjected, mainly for denying to peripheral formations their own histories. See, for instance, Ernesto Laclau, "Feudalism and Capitalism in Latin America," *New Left Review* 67 (1971): 19–38 and Robert Brenner, "The Origins of Capitalist Development: A Critique of Neo-Smithian Marxism," *New Left Review* 104 (1977): 25–93. One of the main goals of this study is, precisely, to bring to the foreground the "histories" and the "centers" that European missionaries and men of letters denied to people from colonial peripheries. Only within an evolutionary model of history could center and periphery be fixed and ontologized. Within a coevolutionary model and a pluritopic hermeneutics, centers and peripheries coexist in a constant struggle of power, domination, and resistance.

14. José Ortega y Gasset, "The Difficulties of Reading (trans. Clarence E. Parmenter)," *Diogenes* No. 28 (1959); 1–17, and *Man and People* (New York: W. W. Norton, 1963); M. M. Bakhtin's concerns with philology and with language in action, relevant to the present discussion, are expressed in "The Problem of Speech Genres" and "The Problem of the Text in Linguistics, Philology, and the Human Sciences: An Experiment in Philosophical Analysis," in *Speech Genres and Other Late Essays,* trans. V. W. McGee, 60–131 (Austin: University of Texas Press, 1986).

15. I am indebted to Alton Becker for calling to my attention Ortega y Gasset's "new philology" and for showing to me its significance for understanding semiotic practices across cultural boundaries. See Alton Becker, "Text-Building, Epistemology, and Aesthetics in Javanese Shadow Theatre," *Dispositio* 13–14 (1980): 137–68.

16. Michel Foucault, *Les mots et les choses: Une archéologie des sciences humaines* (Paris: Gallimard, 1966), 355–98.

17. Paul Ricoeur, *Hermeneutics and the Human Sciences: Essays on Language, Action, and Interpretation,* ed. and trans. John B. Thompson (Cambridge and Paris: Cambridge University Press; Paris: Editions de la Maison des Sciences de l'Homme, 1981).

18. A social science approach to colonial situations was proposed by George Balandier, "La situation coloniale: Approache théorique" (1951), trans. D. Garman as "The Colonial Situation: A Theoretical Approach," in *The Sociology of Black Africa: Social Dynamics in Central Africa* (New York: Praeger, 1970), 34–61. Recent developments have been collected and edited by George W. Stocking, Jr., *Colonial Situations: Essays on the Contextualization of Ethnographic Knowledge* (Madison: University of Wisconsin Press, 1991), esp. 3–6 and 314–24. For a more developed argument on the contribution of the human sciences (or humanities) to understanding colonial situations, see Walter D. Mignolo, "On the Colonization of Amerindian Lan-

guages and Memories: Renaissance Theories of Writing and the Discontinuity of the Classical Tradition," _Comparative Studies in Society and History_ 34, no. 2 (1992): 301–30.

19. See Donald Robertson, _Mexican Manuscript Painting of the Early Colonial Period: The Metropolitan Schools_ (New Haven: Yale University Press, 1959), 179–90.

20. Hans-George Gadamer, _Philosophical Hermeneutics,_ trans. and ed. David E. Linge (Berkeley: University of California Press, 1976).

21. Kurt Mueller-Vollmer, "Language, Mind, and Artifact: An Outline of Hermeneutic Theory since the Enlightenment," in _The Hermeneutics Reader: Texts of the German Tradition from the Enlightenment to the Present,_ ed. Kurt Mueller-Vollmer, 1–52 (New York: Continuum, 1985).

22. Raimundo Panikkar, "What Is Comparative Philosophy Comparing?" in _Interpreting across Boundaries: New Essays in Comparative Philosophy,_ ed. G. J. Larson and E. Deutsch, 116–36 (Princeton: Princeton University Press, 1988).

23. Enrique D. Dussel, _Philosophy of Liberation,_ trans. Aquilina Martinez and Christine Morkovsky (Maryknoll, N.Y.: Orbis, 1985).

24. Horacio Cerutti Guldberg, _Filosofía de la liberación latinoamericana_ (Mexico City: Fondo de Cultura Económica, 1983).

25. I would like to note, for the reader not familiar with Dussel's work, that there is no contradiction between his hermeneutic and Marxist reflections. Dussel's detailed reading of Marx's _Grundrisse_ (_La producción teórica de Marx: Un comentario a los "Grundrisse"_ [Mexico City: Siglo XXI, 1985]), is contextualized in Dussel's own concept of "a Latinamerican Marxism" grounding "a Latinamerican liberation philosophy." What may sound like a contradiction from the point of view of continental European philosophy (how could one mix hermeneutics and Marxism?) seems to be a common philosophical practice in the postcolonial Americas. Cornel West has convincingly analyzed this phenomenon in North American philosophy in _The American Evasion of Philosophy: A Genealogy of Pragmatism_ (Madison: University of Wisconsin Press, 1989).

26. Dussel, _La producción teórica,_ 108–31. See also "Teología de la liberación y marxismo," _Cuadernos Americanos,_ n.s. 12, no. 1 (1989): 138–59, and keep in mind that Dussel develops two parallel arguments: Marxism and philosophy of liberation and Marxism and theology of liberation.

I am indebted to Mario Saenz, who perceived the similarities between my idea of a pluritopic hermeneutics and Dussel's analectics. Our personal conversations have been complemented by my reading of some of his unpublished papers, in particular, "Memory, Enchantment, and Salvation: Latin American Philosophies of Liberation and the Religions of the Oppressed" (October 1991, mimeographed).

27. The specification "disciplinary postcolonial loci of enunciation" underlines the fact that it is in the disciplines (e.g., the human sciences) where the construction of authoritative voices beyond the universalization of Western epistemology was, and still is, difficult. The practice of literature has been, in general, the possibility for postcolonial intellectuals to make their voices heard. And, in general, literary writers have been more successful than scholars

in the human sciences in escaping universalization, dominated as scholars have been by modern European paradigms for the acquisition, organization, and distribution of knowledge.

28. For a detailed critique of Dussel's liberation philosophy vis-à-vis Marxism, see Ofelia Schutte, "Origins and Tendencies of the Philosophy of Liberation in Latin American Thought: A Critique of Dussel's Ethic," *Philosophical Forum* 22, no. 3 (1991): 270–95.

29. Ngugi wa Thiong'o lectured on "Resistance in the Literature of the African Diaspora: Post-Emancipation and Post-Colonial Discourses," and Edward K. Brathwaite read his poetry in the 1991–92 workshop series The Inventions of Africa: Africa in the Literatures of the Continent and the Diaspora, Center for Afro-American Studies, University of Michigan, April 17, 1992. See also Ngugi Wa Thiong'O, *Decolonizing the Mind: The Politics of Language in African Literature* (London: J. Currey, 1986); and Edward K. Brathwaite, *History of the Voice: The Development of Nation Language in Anglophone Caribbean Poetry* (London: New Beacon, 1984). For a critical analysis of Ngugi Wa Thiong'Os position, see Kwame Anthony Appiah, "Topologies of Nativism," in *In My Father's House: Africa in the Philosophy of Culture* (London: Methuen 1992), 47–72.

30. Michelle Cliff, *The Land of Look Behind* (Ithaca, N.Y.: Firebrand Books, 1985), 13.

31. Gloria Anzaldúa, *Borderlands/La frontera: The New Mestiza* (San Francisco: Spinsters/Aunt Lute, 1987).

32. I am referring here mainly to Rodolfo Kusch, *América profunda* (Buenos Aires: Hachette, 1962), and *El pensamiento indígena y popular en America* (Buenos Aires: Hachette, 1973).

33. Roger Chartier has underscored the fact that we can no longer postulate in our understanding a general subject such as "the French man," and we have to work on the particularities of multiple subjects. However, Chartier has limited his observations to the "subject of study or to be understood" and has not emphasized the need to take a similar position vis-à-vis the knowing or understanding subject. See "Intellectual History or Sociocultural History? The French Trajectories," in *Modern European Intellectual History: Reappraisals and New Perspectives,* ed. D. La Capra and S. L. Kaplan, 13–46 (Ithaca: Cornell University Press, 1982). A source of Chartier's position could be found in Pierre Bourdieu, *La distinction: Critique sociale du jugement* (Paris: Minuit, 1979), 13–46.

34. The distinction was introduced by Habermas (1970) in his reply to Gadamer: "Hermeneutics refers to a 'capability' which we acquire to the extent that we come to 'master' a natural language. . . . The art of interpretation is the counterpart of the art of convincing and persuading in situations where practical questions are brought to decision. . . . Philosophical hermeneutics is a different matter: it is not an art but a critique—that is, it brings to consciousness in a reflective attitude experiences that we have of language in the exercise of our communicative competence and thus in the course of social interaction with others through language." Jürgen Habermas, "On Hermeneutics's Claim to Universality," in Mueller-Vollmer, *The Hermeneutics Reader,* 2.

My position vis-à-vis Habermas will be similar to the position I am taking vis-à-vis Gadamer. Habermas's concepts of "communicative competence" and "universal pragmatics" have been articulated without taking into account cross-cultural communication and alternative locus of enunciation. See, for instance, "What Is Universal Pragmatics?" in *Communication and the Evolution of Society,* trans. Thomas McCarthy, 1–68 (Boston: Beacon Press, 1979).

35. Panikkar, "What Is," 131; italics mine.

36. Hans-George Gadamer, "On the Scope and Function of Hermeneutical Reflection" (1976), in *Philosophical Hermeneutics,* 28; italics mine.

37. Edmundo O'Gorman, *La invención de América: El universalismo de la cultura occidental* (Mexico City: Universidad Nacional Autónoma de México, 1958), translated as *The Invention of America: An Inquiry into the Historical Nature of the New World and the Meaning of Its History* (Bloomington: Indiana University Press, 1961). Recent perspectives on the universalization of Western culture have been developed in Mexico by Leopoldo Zea, *Discurso desde la marginacón y la barbarie* (Barcelona: Anthropos, 1988); and in Egypt by Samir Amin, *Eurocentrism,* trans. Russell More (New York: Monthly Review Press, 1989). I mention these two books here because Leopoldo Zea belongs to the same intellectual milieu as O'Gorman and because Samir Amin's book was translated into Spanish and published in Mexico by the same group of intellectuals (*El eurocentrismo: Crítica de una ideología,* traducción de Rosa Cusminsky de Cendrero [Mexico: Siglo XXI, 1989]). More recently, Vasilis Lambropoulos, *The Rose of Eurocentrism: Anatomy of Interpretation* (Princeton, N.J., Princeton University Press, 1992).

38. Edmundo O'Gorman, *Crisis y porvenir de la ciencia histórica* (Mexico City: Imprenta Universitaria, 1947). The Spanish translation of Heidegger's *Sein und Zeit* (1927) was published in 1951, in Mexico. It was translated by José Gaos, a Spanish philosopher in exile under Franco, who was very influential in Mexico. O'Gorman's critique of the positivistic conception of history owes much to section 1, chapter 5 and section 2, chapter 5. His deconstruction of European history on the "discovery of América" emerged from the theoretical position he developed from Heidegger (*La idea del descubrimiento de América: Historia de esa interpretación y crítica de sus fundamentos* [Mexico City: Universidad Nacional Autónoma de México, 1951]). *The Invention of America* stemmed from the same foundation.

39. Hans-George Gadamer, "On the Discrediting of Prejudice by the Enlightenment," in Mueller-Vollmer, *The Hermeneutics Reader,* 259.

40. Hans-George Gadamer, "The Hermeneutics of Suspicion," in *Hermeneutics: Questions and Prospects,* ed. Gary Shapiro and Alan Sica (Amherst: University of Massachusetts Press, 1984), 57.

41. Sylvia Winter, "Ethno or Socio Poetics," in *Ethnopoetics: A First International Symposium,* ed. M. Benamou and R. Rothemberg, 78–94 (Boston: Boston University Press, 1976); Michele Duchet, *Anthropologie et historie au siècle des lumières* (Paris: Maspero, 1971); Anthony Pagden, *The Fall of Natural Man: The American Indian and the Origins of Comparative Ethnology* (Cambridge: Cambridge University Press, 1982).

42. Francois Hartog, *The Mirror of Herodotus: An Essay on the Representation of the Other* (Berkeley and Los Angeles: University of California Press, 1988), 212–59.

43. Eric Lenneberg, *Biological Foundations of Language* (New York: Wiley, 1967); Eleanor Rosch, "Principle of Categorization," in *Cognition and Categorization,* ed. Eleanor Rosch and B. B. Lloyd, 28–49 (Hillsdale, N.J.: Lawrence Erlbaum, 1978), "Wittgenstein and Categorization Research in Cognitive Psychology," in *Meaning and the Growth of Understanding: Wittgenstein's Significance for Developmental Psychology,* ed. M. Chapman and R. Dixon (Hillsdale, N.J.: Lawrence Erlbaum, 1987).

44. Mary Elizabeth Smith, *Picture Writing from Ancient Southern Mexico* (Norman: University of Oklahoma Press, 1973).

45. David Wallace, "Carving Up Time," 1.

46. Ernst von Glasersfeld, "An Introduction to Radical Constructivism," and Heiz von Foerster, "On Constructing a Reality," in *The Invented Reality: How Do We Know What We Believe We Know? Contributions to Constructivism,* ed. P. Watzlawick, 17–40 and 41–61 (New York: W. W. Norton, 1984).

47. I am borrowing "enactive" from Francisco Varela, *Conocer: Las ciencias cognitivas* (Barcelona: Gedisa, 1990), 87–116, although the concept of cognition thus baptized has already been proposed in Umberto Maturana and Francisco Varela, *The Tree of Knowledge: The Biological Roots of Human Understanding* (Boston: New Science Library, 1987). More recently, these ideas have been recast in Francisco Varela, Evan Thompson, and Eleanor Rosch et al., *The Embodied Mind: Cognitive Science and Human Experience* (Cambridge: MIT Press, 1991), 147–84.

48. See, for instance, Clifford Geertz, *Local Knowledge: Further Essays in Interpretive Anthropology* (New York: Basic Books, 1983); David Harvey, *The Condition of Postmodernity: An Inquiry into the Origins of Cultural Change* (Cambridge, Mass.: Basil Blackwell, 1989); Pauline Marie Rosenau, *Post-Modernism and the Social Sciences. Insights, Inroads, and Intrusions* (Princeton, N.J.: Princeton University Press, 1992).

49. Juri Lotman et al., "Theses on the Semiotic Study of Cultures (as Applied to Slavic Texts," in *Structure of Texts and Semiotics of Culture,* ed. Jan van der Eng and Mormi Grigar, 1–28 (The Hague: Mouton, 1973); Juri Lotman and Boris Ouspenski, eds., *Travaux sur les systemes de signes* (Brussels: Editions Complexes, 1976); Yuri M. Lotman, *Universe of the Mind: A Semiotic Theory of Culture,* trans. Ann Shukman (Bloomington: Indiana University Press, 1990).

50. M. M. Bakhtin, *The Dialogic Imagination: Four Essays,* ed. Michael Holquist, trans. Caryl Emerson and Michael Holquist (Austin: University of Texas Press, 1981), and *Speech Genres.*

51. Jacques Derrida, *De la grammatologie* (Paris: Minuit, 1967), "Semiologie et grammatologie," in *Essays in Semiotics,* ed. Julia Kristeva, J. Rey-Debove, and D. J. Umiker, 11–27 (The Hague: Mouton, 1971), *Marges de la philosophie* (Paris: Minuit, 1972); Claude Lévi-Strauss, *Anthropologie structurale,* 2 vols. (Paris: Plon, 1958; 1969).

52. Michel Foucault, *L'archéologie du savoir* (Paris: Gallimard, 1969) and *L'ordre du discours* (Paris: Gallimard, 1971).

53. Humberto Maturana, "Biology of Language: The Epistemology of Reality," in *Psychology and Biology of Language and Thought: Essays in Honor of*

Eric Lenneberg, ed. G. A. Miller and Eric Lenneberg, 27–64 (New York: Academic Press, 1978).

54. Maturana, "Biology of Language," 29. For a more detailed discussion of this topic see Walter D. Mignolo, "(Re)modeling the Letter: Literacy and Literature at the Intersection of Semiotics and Literary Studies," in *On Semiotic Modeling,* ed. M. Anderson and F. Merrell, 357–94 (Berlin: de Gruyter, 1991).

55. Abundant have been the publications on the topic in the past decade. I have benefited from the reading of George W. Stocking, Jr., ed., *Observers Observed: Essays on Ethnographic Field Work* (Madison: University of Wisconsin Press, 1983); James Clifford and George E. Marcus, eds., *Writing Culture: The Poetics and Politics of Ethnography* (Berkeley and Los Angeles: University of California Press, 1986); George E. Marcus and Michael M. J. Fischer, *Anthropology as Cultural Critique: An Experimental Moment in the Human Sciences* (Chicago: University of Chicago Press, 1986); James Clifford, *The Predicament of Culture: Twentieth-Century Ethnography, Literature, and Art* (Cambridge: Harvard University Press, 1988); Jean-Loup Amselles, *Logiques métisses. Anthropologie de l'identité en Afrique et ailleurs* (Paris: Payot, 1990).

CHAPTER I

1. Bernardo José de Aldrete, *Del origen y principio de la lengua castellana o romance que oi se usa en España,* ed. Lidio Nieto Jiménez (Madrid: Consejo Superior de Investigaciones Científicas, 1972–75). Subsequent references are given in the text.

2. See, for instance, the anthology compiled by German Bleiberg, *Antología de elogios de la lengua española* (Madrid: Ediciones de Cultura Hispánica, 1951). In the eighteenth century, the well-known grammarian and historian Gregorio Mayans y Siscar published his own narrative of origins, preceded by a compilation of previous writing about the same topic (*Orígenes de la lengua española* [Madrid: Ediciones Atlas, 1981]).

3. Historians have divided the period of the invasion of northern communities into the Iberian Peninsula in three stages: 409 to 506, a century of chaos, the disintegration of the Roman Empire, and the invasion and settlement of northern communities; 507 to 624, power increasingly moving to the hands of the Visigoths, who settled in Toledo; 625 to 711, a century in which Visigoths took control of power and ended Roman imperial domination. The year 711 also marks the beginning of the Islamic invasion from the south. *Historia de España y América: Social y económica,* coordinated by J. Vicens Vives (Madrid: Editorial Vicens-Vives, 1971), 1:178–80.

4. I translate as "West Indies" the Spanish expression of the time, Indias Occidentales (sometimes Indias), used quite consistently during the sixteenth and early seventeenth centuries by Spanish writers. The "West Indies" were the entire Spanish possessions, from Florida and Mexico in the north to Patagonia in the south; from Santo Domingo in the east to the Philippines in the West. In chapter 6 I will discuss the contexts in which "West Indies" and "America" were used.

5. Bernardo José Aldrete, *Varias antiguedades de España, Africa y otras provincias* (Amberes: A Costa de Iuan Hasrey, 1614), 73.

6. *Runa:* human being, person; *Simi:* mouth, words (sounds emerging

from the mouth). Domingo de Santo Tomás, *Lexicon o vocabulario de la lengua general del Perú* (Lima: Edición del Instituto de Historia, 1951).

7. Purist "literacy" scholars are troubled by the confusion between language and literacy. I am less concerned here with maintaining the purity of the distinction than with the fact that, on the one hand, learning to read and write in Castilian went together with learning to speak Castilian and, on the other, that Castilian learned orally implied illiteracy. So, in both cases, language and literacy are two sides of the same coin.

8. Huayna Capac, Inca king, was the father of Huáscar and Atahualpa. The conquest of Peru began in 1532 when Francisco Pizarro arrested the latter and killed him in Cajamarca.

9. Manuscript at the John Carter Brown Library, Brown University.

10. Antonio de Herrera y Tordesillas, *Historia general de los hechos de los castellanos en las Islas de Tierra Firme del mar océano,* 8 vols. (Madrid: Imprenta Real, 1601–15).

11. I am paraphrasing and commenting on the following quotation: "Por que conuiene aduertir, que los Romanos hallaron mui de otra manera a España, que los Españoles hallaron las Indias, en las quales ninguna nacion estrangera auia entrado primero, que ellos, i assi aquellas gentes carecian de toda suerte de letras, i consiguientemente de las ciencias, i estudios dellas, i de la policia, que las acompaña, i biuian a guisa de fieras desnudos" (book 1, chap. 12).

12. It has been reported that Queen Isabella's last wish was to "convert them to our Holy Catholic faith" and to send prelates and clergy "to indoctrinate them and to teach them good customs." Quoted by Carlos Pereyra, *Breve historia de América* (Santiago: Editorial Universitaria, 1938), 1:208–9.

13. Vives's *De ratione studii puerilis* (1523); Erasmus's *De civilitate morum puerilium* (1530), in which signs of changes in social behavior could be seen next to the preservation of medieval manners.

14. Norbert Elías, *The Civilizing Process,* trans. E. Jephcott (New York: Urizen Books, 1978), 1:78–79.

15. Elías observes that "The concept of *civilité* received the specific stamp and function . . . in the second quarter of the sixteenth century." He attributes to Erasmus's treatise *De civilitate morum puerilium* a fundamental importance in redefining the term. The treatise focuses on the way people look: "Bodily carriage, gestures, dress, facial expressions—this 'outward' behavior with which the treatise concerns itself is the expression of the inner, the whole man." *The Civilizing Process,* 1:56.

16. By the second half of the sixteenth century two influential grammars of Nahuatl and Quechua had already been published. In Mexico Alonso de Molina published his *Arte de la lengua mexicana y castellana* (1571); and in Peru Domingo de Santo Tomás published his *Gramática o arte de la lengua general de los Indios de los Reynos del Perú* (1560). In both cases the discrepancy between the sounds of Amerindian languages and the codification of the Latin alphabet became apparent, as did the tensions between the logic of grammar and the ideology of conversation. See Walter D. Mignolo, "Nebrija in the New World: The Question of the Letter, the Colonization of Amerindian Languages, and the Discontinuity of the Classical Tradition," *L'Homme* 122–24 (1992): 187–209.

17. It is accepted today among historians of writing that the Latin alphabet was derived from Etruscan. See Mauro Cristofani, "L'alphabeto etrusco," in *Popoli e civilta dell'Italia antica,* vol. 6, *Lingue e dialetti* (Rome: Biblioteca di Storia Patria, 1978), 403–6, and "Recent Advances in Etruscan Epigraphy and Language," *Italy before the Romans* (London: Academic Press, 1979), 378–80; Rex Wallace, in "The Origins and Development of the Latin Alphabet," in *The Origins of Writing,* ed. Wayne Senner, 121–36 (Lincoln: University of Nebraska Press, 1989).

18. The supremacy or the tyranny of the letter is perceived today as an obstacle to understanding histories of literacy and of semiotic transactions and owes much of its force to the European Renaissance legacy. See Geoffrey Sampson, *Systems of Writing* (London: Longman, 1987); Roy Harris, *The Origin of Writing* (La Salle, Ill.: Open Court, 1986); Walter D. Mignolo, "Teorías renacentistas de la escritura y la colonización de las lenguas nativas," in *I Simposio de filología Iberoamericana* (Zaragoza: Libros Pórticos, 1990), 171–201.

19. Humanism underlined the relevance of "literary studies" in the sense of interpretation of the written word (*littera*) in education. Humanists drew from the Roman grammarians and developed the idea that grammar is *intellectu poetarum* and *recti scribendi loquendive ratione.* Francisco Rico, *Nebrija contra los bárbaros: El canon de gramáticos nefastos en las polémicas del humanismo* (Salamanca: Universidad de Salamanca, 1978). On Nebrija's project see also Luis Gil Fernández, *Panorama social del humanismo español (1500–1800)* (Madrid: Alhambra, 1981), 98–117.

20. *Gramática de la lengua castellana* (Salamanca, 1492; London: Oxford University Press, 1926).

21. See, for instance, Eugenio Ascensio, "La lengua compañera del imperio: Historia de una idea de Nebrija en España y Portugal," *Revista de Filología Española* 43 (1960): 399–413; Jaime García de la Concha, ed., *Nebrija y la introducción del renacimiento en España* (Salamanca: Actas de la Academia Literaria Renacentista, 1981).

22. Nebrija, *Gramática castellana,* preface.

23. A good example of the network of processes by which the missionaries appropriated and tamed Amerindian language is the Jesuits' "reduction" of Guarani and the transformation of it to a lingua franca in the Jesuit mission quite different from the Guarani spoken by the Amerindian population. See Bartomeu Meliá, *El Guaraní conquistado y reducido: Ensayos de ethnohistoria,* vol. 6, Biblioteca Paraguaya de Antropología (Asunción: Universidad Católica, 1985).

24. *The City of God,* trans. Eva Mathews Sanford (Cambridge: Harvard University Press, 1970), book 16, chap. 11.

25. Juan Luis Vives, *De tradendis disciplines* (1531) (Totowa, N.J.: Rowman and Littlefield, 1971).

26. See, for instance, Antonio Vázquez de Espinosa's narrative (1620) in which he "naturally" harmonized the history of Amerindian languages with the confusion of tongues after Babel and the migration of the ten tribes of

Israel to the New World (*Compendio y descripción de las Indias Occidentales* [Madrid: Ediciones Atlas, 1969], 3:14).

27. Ascensio, "La lengua."

28. Lorenzo Valla, "In sex libros elegantiarum preafatio" in *Prosatori Latini al Quattrocento,* ed. E. Garin (Milan: Mondadori, 1952).

29. With the exception of the union of Philip the Handsome and Juana la Loca, who gave birth to Charles, future Charles I of Aragon and Castile and emperor of the Holy Roman Empire, the rest were unsuccessful.

30. Nebrija, *Gramática castellana,* book I, chap. 10, *Reglas de la ortografía en la lengua castellana* (1517), second principle.

31. Nebrija, *Gramática castellana,* book I, chap. 2.

32. Nebrija, *Reglas de ortografía,* book I, chap. 2; italics mine.

33. Condillac, *Traité des sensations* (1754); Jean-Jacques Rousseau, *Essais sur l'origine des langues* (1756); Maupertius, *Reflexions philosophiques sur l'origine des langues et de la signification des mots* (1748). See also Hans Aarsleff, "The Tradition of Condillac: The Problem of the Origin of Language in the Eighteenth Century and the Debate in the Berlin Academy before Herder" and "An Outline of Language-Origins Theory since the Renaissance," in *From Locke to Saussure: Essays on the Study of Language and Intellectual History* (Minneapolis: University of Minnesota Press, 1982), 146–209, 278–92.

34. "Barbarae sive Barbaricae linguae praeter Graecam et Latinam dicuntur mores. Nos etiam Hebraican excipimus, quod ea cum anqiquissima ac instar parentis aliarum tum sacra et divina sit lingua," Konrad von Gesner, *Mithridates,* cited by Claude Gilbert-Dubois, *Mythe et language au seizième siècle* (Paris: Editions Ducros, 1970), 64.

35. Nebrija, *Gramática castellana,* book I, chap. 2.

36. Juan Bautista Pomar, *Relación de Tezcoco,* ed. Joaquín García Icazbalceta (Mexico City: Biblioteca Enciclopédica del Estado de México, 1975), chap. 16. See chapter 6 for the general context in which the *relaciones de Indias* were written.

37. Translated by Maureen Dyokas.

38. Joaquín García Icazbalceta, *Nueva colección de documentos para la historia de México. Vol. 2. Códice Franciscano* (Mexico City: Editorial Salvador Chavez, 1941).

39. Thus, the question of *to read.* In Nahuatl, for instance, *amoxitoa* can be translated as "to read." The word comes from *amoxtli* (a kind of tree that flourished in the lakes, in the Valley of Mexico) and *toa* (a verb that could be translated as "to narrate" or "to tell"). The members of a culture without letters tell or narrate what they see written on a solid surface, although they do not necessarily read in the sense we attribute to this word today. Eugenio Coseriu pointed out to me that the case is similar in Latin: *legere* means basically "to discern." The synonymity between *to discern* and *to read* came about when the use of the verb was restricted and applied to "discern" the written words (see chap. 2).

40. Horacio Carochi, *Arte de la lengua mexicana* (Mexico City: Juan Ruyz, 1540), chap. 1, secs. 1–2.

41. Santo Tomás, *Gramática*, 10.

42. Ascensión León-Portilla, *Tepuztlahcuilolli: Impresos en Náhuatl* (Mexico City: Universidad Nacional Autónoma de México, 1988), 1:6.

43. Ignacio Osorio Romero, *Colegios y profesores Jesuitas que enseñaron Latin in Nueva España 1572–1767* (Mexico City: Universidad Nacional Autónoma de México, 1979), *Las biblioteca novohispanas* (Mexico City: Secretaría de Educación Pública, 1986).

44. Miguel Mathes, *Santa Cruz de Tlatelolco: La primera biblioteca académica de las Américas* (Mexico City: Archivo Histórico Mexicano, 1982); Ignacio Osorio Romero, *Las biblioteca novohispanas,* and *Historia de las bibliotecas en Puebla* (Mexico City: Secretaría de Educación Pública, 1986).

45. Francisco Rico, "Lección y herencia de Elio Antonio de Nebrija," in Concha, *Nebrija*, 9.

46. Ottavio Di Camillo, *El humanismo castellano del siglo XV* (Valencia: Fernando Torres, 1976); Gil Fernández, *Panorama*, 98–186.

47. Valla, "In sex libros elegantiarum preafatio" (Six books on the elegance of the Latin language); Ascencio, "La lengua"; Ottavio Besomi and Marigneli Regoliosi, *Lorenzo Valla e l'humanesimo italiano* (Padova: Editrice Antenore, 1986).

48. José Antonio Maravall, "La concepción del saber en una sociedad tradicional," in *Estudios de historia del pensamiento español* (Madrid: Ediciones Cultura Hispánica, 1967), 1:201–60.

49. Martín de la Cruz, *Libellus de medicinalibus indorum herbis* (1552), trans. Juan Badiano (Mexico City: Instituto Mexicano del Seguro Social, 1964).

50. We should remember, in this context and in relation to our previous analysis of Nebrija's program and Aldrete's concern about teaching Castilian to Amerindians, the ideological celebration of Castilian language as well as the critical perspective that it is necessary to take today regarding the continuity of the language of the empire in postcolonial independent nations. Regarding the first aspect, the classical studies are by A. Morel Fatio, "L'espagnol langue universelle," *Bulletin hispanique* 15 (1913): 207–23; Ramón Menéndez Pidal, *La lengua de Cristóbal Colón* (Madrid: Austral, 1942), 101–19, and *Castilla, la tradición y el Idioma* (Madrid: Austral, 1945), 169–216; and Manuel García Blanco, "La lengua española en la época de Carlos V," *Discurso de clausura del curso de extranjeros de la Universidad Menéndez Pelayo* [1958] (Madrid: Escelicer, 1967), 11–43. For the second aspect, see Eugenio Coseriu, "El español de America y la unidad del idioma," *I Simposio de Filología Iberoamericana* (Zaragoza: Libros Portico, 1990), 43–76.

51. Both the Crown's politics of language and its educational practices have been studied. For the politics of language in Mexico, see Rómulo Velasco Ceballos and Miguel Maldonado Huerta, eds., *La alfabetización en la Nueva España: Leyes, cédulas reales, ordenanzas, bandos, pastoral y otros documentos* (Mexico City: Secretaría de Educación, 1945); Shirley Brice Heath, *La política del lenguaje en México: De la colonia a la nación* (Mexico City: Secretaría de Educación, 1972). For the politics of language in Peru, see Bruce Mannheim, *The Language of the Inca since the European Invasion* (Austin: University of Texas Press, 1990). For the educational Franciscan practice in America, Lino

Gómez Canedo, *Evangelización y conquista: Experiencia franciscana en*
América (Mexico City: Porrúa, 1977); Pilar Gonzalbo Aizpuru, *Historia de la*
educación en México en la época colonial: El mundo indígena (Mexico City: El
Colegio de México, 1990), hereafter *El mundo indígena;* Ignacio Osorio
Romero, *La enseñanza del latin a los Indios* (Mexico City: Universidad Nacio-
nal Autónoma de México, 1990).

52. It is useful to keep in mind the linguistic distribution according to the
religious orders. What follows should not be taken as a clear-cut distribution
with rigid frontiers but, rather, a general tendency. Thus, the Dominicans
concentrated on languages of southern Mexico and Guatemala, like Mixtec,
Chabañal, Mixe, Tzotzil, Zapotec. Franciscans devoted themselves to the
major Amerindian languages, like Maya, Nahuatl, and Otomi in Mesoamerica
and Quiche in Peru. The Jesuits, who arrived in Mexico in 1572, devoted
themselves to minor languages like Tarahumara and Totonac. See Irma Contreras García, *Bibliografía sobre la castellanización de los grupos indígenas de la*
República Mexicana, vol. 2 (Mexico City: Universidad Nacional Autónoma
de México, 1985).

53. Robert Ricard, *La conquista espiritual de México: Ensayos sobre el apos-*
tolado y los métodos misioneros de las órdenes mendicantes en la Nueva España
de 1523–24 a 1572, trans. A. María Garibay (Mexico City: Fondo Cultura
Económica, 1986); José María Kobayashi, *La educación como conquista: Em-*
presa franciscana en México (Mexico City: El Colegio de México, 1974).

54. Alberto María Carreño, *La real y Pontificia Universidad de México,* 2
vols. (Mexico City: Universidad Nacional Autónoma de México, 1963).

55. Javier Gómez Robledo, *Humanismo en México en el siglo xvi: El sis-*
tema del colegio de San Pedro y San Pablo (Mexico City: Jus, 1954); I. Osorio
Romero, *Colegios y profesores Jesuitas.*

56. *Recopilación de Leyes de los reinos de las Indias, mandadas imprimir y*
publicar por la Magestad catolica del rey Don Carlos II (Madrid: Boix, 1841),
libro I, 211–12; libro I, tit. xxiii, ley ii.

57. Ceballos and Huerta, *La alfabetización;* Heath, *La política del*
lenguaje, 68–96; Gonzalo Aguirre Beltrán, *Lenguas vernáculas: Su uso y desuso*
en la enseñanza (Mexico City: Ediciones de la Casa Chata, 1968), 45–66.

58. Teaching Latin was mainly devoted to the children of Spanish descent,
all over the New World. In Colombia (or New Grenada), it was studied in
detail by José Manuel Rivas Sacconi, and a chapter of his work is devoted to
the influence of Nebrija's Latin grammar and vocabulary in the New World.
See *El Latín en Colombia: Bosquejo histórico del humanismo colombiano*
(Bogotá: Instituto Caro y Cuervo, 1949), 141–54. Teaching Latin to the
Amerindian was limited in place (mainly to the Colegio Santa Cruz de
Tlatelolco) and in time (after 1560, under Philip II). For more detail about
this topic, however, see Ignacio Osorio Romero, *La enseñanza del Latín a los*
Indios (Mexico City: Universidad Nacional Autónoma de México, 1990).

59. The ethnic and social distinctions are quite interesting in this quotation: "siguiendo en toda la autoridad del Concilio Tridentino manda . . . a los
españoles y a los negros esclavos, aún a los que son solo por parte de uno de sus
padres (mulatos) y a los chichimecas, enséñese la doctrina en lengua

castellana; más a los Indios en su propia lengua materna" (Mariano Galván Rivera, *Concilio III Provincial Mexicano* (1585) (Mexico City: Maillefert, 1859), 187. Chichimeca, as a category distinct from Indians, seems to keep alive the distinction, made by the Mexica of Mexico City–Tenochtitlán, between them and the "barbarian" Chichimecas.

60. Ceballos and Huerta, *La alfabetización;* Richard Konetzke, *Colección de documentos para la historia de la formación social de Hispano-América, 1493–1810* (Madrid: Consego Superior de Investigaciones Científicas y Ténicas, 1953) 1:30–41, 272–75, 571; 602–3, etc.

61. Pilar Gonzalbo Aizpurú, *El mundo indígena,* and *Historia de la educación en México en la época colonial: La educación de los criollos y la vida urbana* (Mexico City: El Colegio de México, 1990), hereafter *La educación.*

62. Heath, *La política del lenguaje,* 52–53.

63. Mathes, *Santa Cruz de Tlatelolco.*

64. Another revealing example is the phrase by Don Pablo Nazareo, "indios latinista," in his Latin letters addressed to Charles V, cited by Osorio Romero, *La enseñanza del Latín,* 1–34.

65. Osorio Romero, *Colegios y profesores Jesuitas,* 152.

66. Aldo Scaglioni, *The Liberal Arts and the Jesuit College System* (Amsterdam: John Benjamins Publishing Company, 1986).

67. The Jesuits were also concerned with teaching Spanish to the Amerindians (Romero, *La enseñanza del Latin,* 59). However, their efforts to achieve this goal did not reach the same splendor as their achievements in higher education. Furthermore, a clear social distinction was made between "popular" and "high" education (Gonzalbo Aizpurú, *El mundo indígena* and *La educación;* Canedo, *Evangelización y conquista*).

68. A second aspect of the value attributed to the letters could be seen in their use beyond the realm of the voice. Geoffroy Tory worked on the relations between the letter and the human body (*Champ fleury: Auquel est contenu l'art et science de la deue et vraye proportion des lettres attiques, qu'on dit autrement lettres antiques et vulgairement lettres romaines proportionées selon le corps et visage humain* [Paris, 1529]). Albrecht Dürer looked into the geometrical proportion of the letters (*Institutionum geometricarum libris* [Paris, 1535]). And, in the age of the printing press, handwriting acquired a new dimension in the pedagogical and civilizing process. See Jonathan Goldberg, *Writing Matter: From the Hands of the English Renaissance* (Stanford: Stanford University Press, 1990). See also Berhard Teuber, "Europäisches und Amerikanisches im frühneuzeiltlichen Diskurs über Stimme und Schrift," in *Romanistik in Geschichte und Gegenwart* (Hamburg: Helmut Buske Verlag, 1989) 24:47–59.

69. Francisco Antonio Lorenzana y Buitrón, *Cartas pastorales y edictos* (Mexico City: Imprenta Superior de Gobierno, 1770). Translations from Lorenzana are by Maureen Dyokas.

70. Louis-Jean Calvet, *Linguistique et colonialisme: Petit traité de glottophagie* (Paris: Payot, 1974), and *La guerre des langues et les politiques linguistiques* (Paris: Payot, 1987); Maurice Bloch, "Literacy and Enlightenment," in *Literacy and Society,* ed. Karen Schousboe and Mogens Trolle

Larsen, 15–37 (Copenhagen: Akademiske Forlag, 1989); J. R. Clammer, *Literacy and Social Change: A Case Study of Fiji* (Leiden: E. Brill, 1976); and V. Y. Mudimbe, *The Invention of Africa: Gnosis, Philosophy, and the Order of Knowledge* (Bloomington: Indiana University Press, 1988).

71. *Bibliotheca Mexicana sive eruditorum historia virorum qui in America Boreali nati, vel alibi geniti, in ipsam Domicilio aut Studijs asciti, quavis lingua scripto aliquid tradiderun* (Mexico City: Ex nova Typographia in Aedibus Authoris editioni Ejusdem Bibliothecae destinata, 1770). The *bibliotheca* is introduced with a series of prologues (*anteloquia*). And the entire work was introduced by Vincentio Lopez (*Aprilis dialogus,* Autore Patre Vincentio Lopez, Corduvensi, theologo, e Societate Jesu, apud Tribunal fidei censore), a Jesuit from Andalusia, who moved to Mexico in 1730 to teach reading and writing in the Colegio de San Gregorio, devoted to the children of the Amerindian population.

72. Such tension is not among persons born here or there, but between ideologies embraced by persons born here or there. Lopez's *Aprilis dialogus* is a case in point. Lopez was a peninsular who supported Eguiara y Eguren against the position defended by Manuel Martí.

73. Ramón Pané, *Relación de las antiguedades de los indios* (1493), ed. Juan José Arrom (Mexico City: Fondo de Cultura Económica, 1974); Juan de Torquemada, *Monarquía indiana* (1615), 6 vols. (Mexico City: Universidad Nacional Autónoma de México, Instituto de Investigaciones Filológicas, 1977), 1:3. We should remember, in this context, the thesis advanced by Erasmus in his *De recta Graeci et Latini sermonis pronunciatione* (1528). The dialogue between Urus and Leo develops in such a way that the reader is convinced that the "humanity" of human beings depends on the letters. Ursus, for instance, departs from the fact that the Latin word to designate speech is *sermo*. He proves that, etymologically, *sermo* comes from *serendo,* which means "to sow." Consequently, the analogy between "to sow" and "to speak" allows for the interpretation of speech as the sowing of the letters. We are facing a near-total inversion, in which the letter takes precedence over the voice and justifies, indirectly, the belief that "humanness" depends on the letter and alphabetic writing rather than the voice and speech. This Renaissance meaning is in striking contrast with the medieval analogy between *writing* and *plowing* (Ernst Robert Curtius, *European Literature and the Latin Middle Ages,* trans. Willard E. Trask [New York: Pantheon Books, 1953]), which underlines the physical aspect of scratching solid surfaces in the act of writing, rather than the relationship between the voice and the letter (Walter Mignolo, "Signs and Their Transmission: The Question of the Book in the New World," in *Writing without Words: Alternative Literacies in Mesoamerica and the Andes,* ed. Walter D. Mignolo and Elizabeth H. Boone [Durham, N.C.: Duke University Press, 1994], 220–70).

74. Take, for instance, Bartolomé de las Casas's four kinds of barbarians: "La segunda manera o especie de bárbaros es algo más estrecha, y en está son aquellos que *carecen* de literal locución que responda a su lenguaje como responde a la nuestra la lengua latina; finalmente, que *carazcan de ejercicios y estudio de las letras,* y estos tales se dicen ser bárbaros *secundum quid,* conviene a saber, según alguna parte o calidad que les falta para no ser bárbaros."

Apologética historia sumaria, ed. Edmundo O'Gorman (Mexico City: Instituto de Investigaciones Históricas, 1967), 2:638; italics mine.

75. The bibliography in this respect is quite large. A sample from the Yucatán peninsula (both in Guatemala and Mexico) are the works of Judith Friedlander, *Being Indian in Hueyapan: A Study of Forced Identity in Contemporary Mexico* (New York: St. Martin's Press, 1975); and Kay B. Warren, *The Symbolism of Subordination: Indian Identity in a Guatemalan Town* (Austin: University of Texas Press, 1978). Several articles in the volume edited by Carol A. Smith are relevant to this issue: *Guatemalan Indians and the State: 1540 to 1988* (Austin: University of Texas Press, 1990). An overview of the question in Latin America is in Greg Urban and Joel Sherzer, eds., *Nation-States and Indians in Latin America* (Austin: University of Texas Press, 1991).

76. Gary Gossen, *Chamulas in the World of the Sun: Time and Space in a Maya Oral Tradition* (Cambridge: Harvard University Press, 1974); Beltrán, *Lenguas vernáculas;* Joanne Rappaport, "Mythic Images, Historical Thought, and Printed Texts: The Paez and the Written Word," *Journal of Anthropological Research* 43, no. 1 (1987): 43–61.

77. From the perspective of the tensions between an idiomatically defined Hispanic America and a culturally conceived Latin America, it is helpful to remember the three main stages of Castilian languages from the colonial period to the present. The first stage, the colonial period, is explored in this chapter; the second stage could be framed as the period of nation building and the coalition between the Spanish language and national identities; the third stage, whose beginning we are currently witnessing, brings to the fore the multilingual and pluricultural nature of Latin America and can be illustrated with examples of an emerging linguistic-cultural paradigm: Chicano literature as exemplified, among others, by Gloria Anzaldúa, *Borderlands/La Frontera;* the cultural unity of the Caribbean beyond its linguistic diversity, as illustrated by Brathwaite, *History of the Voice;* the pluricultural nature of countries such as Peru, brought into focus in Vargas Llosa's novel *El hablador* (1987).

CHAPTER 2

1. Alejo Venegas, *Primera parte de las diferencias de libros que hay en el universo* (Toledo, 1546; reprint Barcelona, Puvill Libros, 1983).

2. This idea is far from original in Venegas. It has a long and rich history, related both to Jewish and Arabic holy traditions. Widengren has summarized the trajectory of the idea of the archetype or heavenly book from Babylonian Tablets of Destiny to Jewish literature, to the Koran. He has also traced the trajectory of the manifestation of the Heavenly Book in outward form (the metagraph book), in Venegas's conception: "There are accordingly two different conceptions of the outward form in which the Heavenly Writing is written: it is *either* written as a sheet, or a scroll, or as a *kitab,* a real book, or even in a way—at least partly—identical with a special Jewish-Christian Book, the single zabur, or this Heavenly Scripture is not a book, but tablets, or rather one tablet, *lauh.* George Widengren," "Holy Book and Holy Tradition in Iran, in *Holy Book and Holy Tradition,* ed. F. F. Bruce and E. G. Rupp (Grand

Rapids, Mich.: William B. Erdmans Publishing Company, 1968), 215–16.

3. Jean Glenisson, *Le livre au Moyen Age* (Paris: Presse Universitaire de CNRS, 1988); Lucien Febvre and Henri-Jean Martin, *L'apparition du livre, 1450–1800* (Paris: Albin Michel, 1958).

4. Frederic G. Kenyon, *Books and Readers in Ancient Greece and Rome* (Oxford: Clarendon Press, 1932), 86–119; L. D. Reynolds and N. G. Wilson, *Scribes and Scholars: A Guide to the Transmission of Greek and Latin Literature* (Oxford: Clarendon Press, 1991), 122–63.

5. Thomas Skeat, "Early Christian Book Production: Papyrus and Manuscripts," in *The Cambridge History of the Bible,* ed. G. N. Lampe, 54–79 (New York: Cambridge University Press, 1969).

6. Screen-folded, scroll, and wall-hanging narratives from China and Japan are reproduced and described in the National Gallery's catalog edited by J. A. Levenson, *Circa 1492: Art in the Age of Exploration* (Washington, D.C.: National Gallery of Art; New Haven: Yale University Press, 1991), 305–62. But, alas, they are presented as art and painting not as books. This image was already in place in fifteenth-century Europe. Roger Bacon observed that "The people in Cathay to the east write with the same instrument with which painters paint, forming in one character groups of letters [!], each group representing a sentence." *The Opus Majus of Roger Bacon,* trans. R. B. Burke (New York: Russell and Russell, 1962), 389.

7. Among the many examples available to illustrate this assertion, the best comes from the Canadian-Australian movie *Black Robe,* about the Jesuit mission among the Hurons, around 1630. Black Robe, the French missionary, writes down on a piece of paper a sentence pronounced by an Amerindian and then takes the piece of paper to another French member of the expedition to read. He reads it out loud, surprising the Amerindians, who do not understand how the words spoken could have been carried that distance and pronounced by someone who did not hear them.

8. Diego de Landa, *Yucatan before and after the Conquest,* trans. and ed. William Gates (New York: Dover Publications, 1978), 82.

9. Landa, *Yucatan,* 13.

10. Michael D. Cole, in his helpful *The Maya Scribe and His World* (New York: Grolier Club, 1973), provides several examples of different surfaces on which writing was inscribed. He includes also a description of the *Grolier Codex,* one of the four supposedly pre-Columbian codices from the Yucatán peninsula (the other three are *Dresden, Madrid,* and *Paris,* which is a folding screen painted on bark paper coated with stucco [150]).

11. Toribio de Motolinía, *Memoriales* (Mexico City: Luis García Pimentel, 1903), translated by Francis Borgia Steck as *Motolinía's History of the Indians of New Spain* (Washington, D.C.: Academy of American Franciscan History, 1951).

12. Landa, *Yucatan,* 13.

13. Manuel García Pelayo, "Las culturas del libro," *Revista de Occidente* 24–25 (1965): 45–70; S. G. F. Brandon, "The Holy Book, the Holy Tradition, and the Holy Ikon," in Bruce and Rupp, *Holy Book,* 1–20; Widengren, "Holy Book," 210–36; Johannes Pederson, *The Arabic Book,* ed. Robert Hill-

enbrand, trans. Geoffrey French (Princeton: Princeton University Press, 1984), 12–20.

14. Cole has observed: "Maya hieroglyphs are obviously highly pictorial. . . . Because of these factors, *the Maya calligrapher was basically a painter, and probably both professions were joined in the same man.* This is reminiscent of China, of course. As in China, brush pens of various sizes were used. It is likely that for the relief carving of a text the master calligrapher would first brush on the characters, the rest of the job being finished by the sculptor; in the case of carved pottery, the calligrapher himself may have incised the still-damp clay" (Cole, *Maya Scribe,* 8; italics mine). David N. Keightley has observed that "Literacy in China involved not only a profound knowledge of the written classics but also the ability to wield a brush effectively, either to paint a landscape, usually with a poem inscribed at its side, or to write Chinese characters in their meaning but also their aesthetic vitality and the taste of their composer." "The Origins of Writing in China: Scripts and Cultural Contexts," in *The Origins of Writing,* ed. W. Senner (Lincoln: University of Nebraska Press, 1989), 171–72. If indeed the Maya were fully literate, to be literate in such a society meant something different than being literate in the European Middle Ages. The materiality of signs, communicative interactions, and the discourse about them had a different configuration.

15. Antonio de Ciudad Real, *Relación breve y verdadera de algunas cosas de las muchas que sucedieron al Padre Fray Alonso de Ponce* (Madrid: Imprenta de la Viuda de Calero, 1873), 2:392.

16. David Diringer, *Writing* (New York: F. A. Praeger, 1962), 84.

17. David Diringer, *The Book before Printing* (1953) (New York: Dover Publications, 1982).

18. Diringer, *Writing,* 86.

19. A. L. Oppenheim, *Ancient Mesopotamia* (Chicago: University of Chicago Press, 1964), 230ff.; Piotr Michalowski, "Early Mesopotamian Communicative Systems: Art, Literature, and Writing," in *Investigating Artistic Environments in the Ancient Near East,* ed. Ann C. Gunter, 53–69 (Washington, D.C.: Smithsonian Institution, 1990). A clear presentation of Egyptian writing is Henry George Fischer, *L'écriture et l'art de l'Egypte ancienne: Quatre leçons sur la paléographie et l'épigraphie pharaoniques* (Paris: Presses Universitaires de France, 1986).

20. A roll was conceptualized in terms of the frame where either it stopped or was cut and was called *tómos* (a cutting); hence our idea of "tomes," Spanish *tomos.* The Romans translated it as *volumen,* a thing that is rolled or wound up. Since long inscriptions, such as those dealing with the law or theological narratives, needed more than one volume, they were called "voluminous." The Greeks also coined the word *bibliothéke* to name the place (boxes or rooms) in which *biblos* or *papyrus* rolls were kept. The ancient Mexicans also named the object after the material it was made from, *amoxtli,* and they derived from it the name for the place where it was stored, *amoxpialoya, amotlacentecoyan.* The logic of naming is the same: the name of the object

derives from the material of which it is made, plus the name designating a place in which the object is stored.

21. One can surmise, after this collection of words, that there was a moment in the configuration of the system of representation of different cultures in which the name of a tree was used to designate the medium in which graphic signs were inscribed and transmitted. The Spanish *Diccionario de autoridades,* published in the eighteenth century, describes *book* (*libro*) as volume of paper sawed and covered with parchment or something else. It is quite interesting to note that eighteenth-century Spanish has already eliminated the connection between Latin *liber* (the inner bark of a tree on which surface the ancients wrote) and has retained only the equivalence between *book* and *work* (*obra*) or *treatise.* Here I have in mind the comment made by Diringer after drawing the etymological map of the word *book:* "The exact connection," says Diringer, "between 'book' and 'beech tree' is not known" (*The Book before Printing,* 24–25). The comment draws attention to the semantic and not to the phonetic aspect of the word. I suspect a connection could be suggested by departing from the system of representation associated with the words, instead of taking into account only the change of their meanings.

22. Curtius, *European Literature,* quotes a Greek epigram engraved on a stone of a *bibliothéke* that reads: "Say that this grove is dedicated to us, the Muses, and point to the books (*ta biblios*) over there *by the plane tree-grove.* We guard them here; but let him who truly loves us come to us: We will crown him with ivy" (306; italics mine).

23. Remi Siméon, *Dictionnaire de la langue Nahuatl ou Mexicaine* (Paris: Imprimerie Nationale, 1885), gives as a first meaning of *amoxtli,* "Plante abondante dans le lac de Mexico" and, as second meaning, "livre, ouvrage."

24. I cannot resist the temptation to recall that according to Curtius (*European Literature,* 313), *exarare* (to plough up) could also mean "to write," which, on the one hand, explains the comparison between book and field and, on the other, the fact that *legere* is used in noncultivated Latin in the sense of "gathering and collecting."

25. Curtius, *European Literature,* 315.

26. "Lingua mea calamus scribae velociter scribentis" (My tongue is the pen of a ready writer). Curtius, *European Literature,* 311.

27. Jacques Le Goff, *Les intellectuels au Moyen Age* (Paris: Editions du Seuil, 1957); 90–97; Glenisson, *Le livre,* 115–63.

28. Jack Goody, *The Interface between the Written and the Oral* (New York: Cambridge University Press, 1987), 5.

29. José de Acosta, *Historia natural y moral de las Indias* (1590), ed. Edmundo O'Gorman (Mexico City: Fondo de Cultura Económica, 1940), book 6, 285–90.

30. Translated by Maureen Dyokas.

31. Acosta, *Historia,* book 6, chap. 8; italics mine.

32. Translated by Maureen Dyokas.

33. Ascher and Ascher, *Code of the Quipu,* 61–62.

34. Paul Zumthor, *La lettre et la voix: De la "literature" médiévale* (Paris:

Editions du Seuil, 1987), 107–54; also Jean-Claude Schmitt, *La raison des gestes dans l'Occident médiéval* (Paris: Gallimard, 1990), 239–51.

35. *Instruccion del Ynga D. Diego de Castro Tito Cussi Yupangui,* ed. Maria del Carmen Martin Rubio (Madrid: Ediciones Atlas, 1988), 128.

36. *Amauta,* which Garcilaso de la Vega (*Comentarios reales de los Incas,* ed. Angel Rosenblatt [Buenos Aires: Emecé, 1943], book 2, chap. 27) translates as "philosopher," is not clear. The word is not registered before Garcilaso. Some Andeanists surmise that it might have been Garcilaso's invention. Either that or, because of the image of the *letrado* (men of letters) in Spanish society, early missionaries failed to see the similarities between those, in the Andes, who had the wisdom of the word (which Garcilaso called *amautas*) and those, in Castile, who possessed the written word.

37. Bernardino de Sahagún, *Florentine Codex* (1578), trans. and ed. Charles E. Dibble, Arthur Anderson, and J. O. Anderson, 13 vols., bilingual edition (Salt Lake City: University of Utah Press; Santa Fe: School of American Research, 1956–69), book 6. In this edition, each volume corresponds to one of the twelve books.

38. Sahagún, *Florentine Codex,* book 9. For more details, see chapter 4.

39. An area located southeast of Mexico-Tenochtitlán, between Mexico and Puebla. In colonial times Chalco was under the administration of Mexico, both in economic and religious matters.

40. Don Francisco de San Antón Muñón Chimalpaín Cuahtehuanitzin, *Relaciones originales de Chalco Amaquemecan,* ed. and trans. Silva Rendón (Mexico City: Fondo de Cultura Económica, 1982), 20–21.

41. Translated by Maureen Dyokas.

42. Chimalpaín, *Relaciones originales,* 20–21.

43. Fernando de Alva Ixtlilxóchit, *Obras históricas,* ed. Edmundo O'Gorman (Mexico City: Universidad Nacional Autónoma de México, 1975), 1:527.

44. Translated by Maureen Dyokas.

45. José Pau y Martí, ed., "El libro perdido de las pláticas o Coloquios de los doce primeros misioneros de México," in *Estratto della Miscellanea Fr. Ehrle III* (Rome: Tipografia del Senato, del Dottore G. Bardi, 1924).

46. "The Aztec-Spanish Dialogues 1524," trans. J. Jorge Klor de Alva, *Alcheringa/Ethnopoetics* 4, no. 2 (1980): 52–193; *Los diálogos de 1524 según el texto de Fray Bernardino de Sahagún y sus colaboradores indígenas,* ed. Miguel León-Portilla (Mexico City: Universidad Nacional Autónoma de México, 1986). In Klor de Alva's translation, the first verse quoted here has the number 770 instead of 761.

47. *Breath* designates oral discourse, speech. In the codices it is generally indicated by the depiction of air escaping from the mouth.

48. Sahagún, *Coloquios y Doctrina Christiana* (1565), trans. and intro. Miguel León-Portilla (Mexico City: Universidad Nacional Autónoma de México), 1981, chap. 6, B; italics mine.

49. Translated by Maureen Dyokas.

50. Alonso de Molina, *Vocabulario en lengua castellana y mexicana y mexicana castellana* (1571) (Mexico City: Editorial Porrúa, 1971); Simeon, *Dictionnaire.*

51. Miguel León-Portilla, "El testimonio de la historia prehispánica en

náhuatl," in *Toltecayótl: Aspectos de la cultura náhuatl* (Mexico City: Fondo de Cultura Económica, 1980), 53–71.

52. There are no unified criteria specifying the name of the person in charge of the military apparatus and the sovereign head of a well-organized religious and military community. Some suggest *tlatoani;* others *tlatoqui* (plural *tlatoque*). What is important, however, is that both are skillful in speaking and their names have the same root, *tlatoa,* which means "to speak," and also to sing (Siméon, *Dictionnaire*). The relationship between being skillful in speaking and being in a power position is well known in case studies of the ethnography of speaking.

53. Johannes Fabian, *Time and the Other: How Anthropology Makes Its Object* (New York: Columbia University Press, 1983).

54. Martín de Murúa, *Historia general del Perú* (1590), ed. Manuel Ballesteros (Madrid: Historia 16, 1986), book 2, chap. 11.

55. Translated by Maureen Dyokas.

56. It has been observed that in the European Middle Ages "reading" was an activity quite different from that understood today. See Pierre Riché, *Ecole et enseignement dans le haut Moyen Age* (Paris: Denöel, 1979); François Richaudeau, *La lisibilité* (Paris: Denöel, 1969); Zumthor, *La lettre.*

57. Sahagún, *Coloquios,* 90A; italics mine.

58. Although according to the Christian idea the verb does not become book (as is believed by Jews and Muslims, Pedersen, *The Arabic Book*) but flesh, and it reveals itself in the words and deed of Christ, the idea of writing and the book is incorporated into Christian ideology with the New Testament (Pelayo, "Las culturas del libro").

59. Curtius, *European Literature,* 301–48.

60. Alfredo López Austin, *Educación mexica: Antologia de documentos sahaguntinos* (Mexico City: Universidad Nacional Autónoma de México, 1985).

61. "Otherness," like personal pronouns, is an empty and movable category. It is not just Europe, the "self-same," and the rest, the "others"! See Walter D. Mignolo, "Anáhuac y sus otros: La cuestión de la letra en el Nuevo Mundo," *Revista Latinoamericana de Crítica Literaria* 28 (1988): 28–53; also Fritz Krammer, "The Otherness of the European," *Culture and History* 16 (1989): 107–23.

62. Sabine MacCormack, "Atahualpa and the Book," *Dispositio* 14 (1989): 36–38. Henry L. Gates has perceived a similar phenomenon in nineteenth-century slave narratives and used the metaphor of the talking book to describe communicative situations across writing boundaries. Gates's essay indirectly shows that similar episodes related to the interpretation of written signs repeat themselves in colonial situations. The talking book is an ur-trope of the Anglo-American tradition that reveals the tensions between the Black vernacular and the literate white text, between the oral and the printed form of literary discourse: "Literacy, the very literacy of the printed book, stood as the ultimate parameter by which to measure the humanities of authors struggling to define the African self in Western letters." *The Signifying Monkey* (New York: Oxford University Press, 1989), 131.

63. Clammer, *Literacy and Social Change;* Mudimbe, *The Invention*

of Africa; Bloch, "Literacy and Enlightenment"; Calvet, Linguistique et colonialisme; Martine Astier Loutfi, Littérature et colonialisme: L'expansion coloniale vue dans la littérature romanesque francaise, 1871–1914 (Paris: Mouton, 1971).

64. Sahagún, "Rhetoric and Moral Philosophy," Florentine Codex, book 6.

65. The Spanish version of this expression reads: "Todas las naciones, por barbaras, y de baxo metal que ayan sido." Sahagún, Florentine Codex, 1:65.

66. Sahagún, "Rhetoric and Moral Philosophy," part 7.

67. Torquemada, Monarquía indiana, book 13, chap. 6.

68. Translated by Noel Fallows.

69. Juan Bautista Huehuetlatolli: Testimonios de la antigua palabra (1600), trans. Libando Silva Galeano (Mexico City: Secretaría de Educación Pública, 1991).

70. Nahuatl specialists have studied these authors in relation to the huehuetlatolli in a precolonial context: Josefina García Quintana, "Exhortación de un padre a su hijo: Texto recogido por Andrés de Olmos," Estudios de Cultura Náhuatl 11 (1974): 137–82; Angel María Garibay, Historia de la literatura náhuatl, 2 vols. (Mexico City: Porrúa, 1954); Thelma Sullivan, "The Rhetorical Orations, or Huehuetlatolli," in Sixteenth-Century Mexico: The Work of Sahagún, ed. Munro S. Edmonson, 79–110 (Albuquerque: University of New Mexico Press, 1974); Don Paul Abbott, "The Ancient Word: Rhetoric in Aztec Culture," Rhetorica 3 (1987): 251–64.

71. See also Angel Garibay, La literatura náhuatl, vol. 1.

72. See note 69. See also Walter D. Mignolo and Colleen Ebacher, "Alfabetización y literatura: Los huehuetlatolli como ejemplo de semiosis colonial," Actas del XXII Congreso de Literatura Iberoamericana 1992, ed. José Ortega, (forthcoming).

73. Maurice Bloch, ed., Political Language and Oratory in Traditional Society (London: Academic Press, 1975).

74. Garibay, La literatura náhuatl, 1:426.

75. Translated by Noel Fallows.

76. Maravall, "La concepción del saber," 201–60; Roy P. Mottahedeh, The Mantle of the Prophet: Religion and Politics in Iran (New York: Simon and Schuster, 1985); Pedersen, The Arabic Book.

77. Maravall, "La concepción del saber, 227–31, 239–50.

78. Pelayo, "Las culturas del libro," Revista de Occidente; Roger Chartier "Distinction et divulgation: La civilité et ses livres," Lectures et lecteurs dans la France de l'Ancien Régime (Paris: Editions du Seuil, 1987) 45–86; Ulrich Gumbrecht, "The Body versus the Printing Press: Media in the Early Modern Period, Mentalities in the Reign of Castile, and Another History of Literary Forms," Poetics 14, nos. 3–4 (1985): 209–27; Mignolo, "Signs and Their Transmission."

79. Sahagún, Florentine Codex, book 6, chap. 22.

80. Sahagún, Florentine Codex, book 6, chap. 22.

81. An argument could be made that we human beings do not have speech but that we are speech. This principle cannot be easily reconciled with the "instrumentalist" view of speech because both have always been presented as

either/or positions. I perceive a complementary rather than a contradictory relation between them. At one level, it is possible to say that "we human beings are speech," taking speech as one of the features that distinguish different species of living nervous systems. At another level, it seems quite obvious that human beings have turned speech into an instrument of human semiotic interactions, including the organization and transmission of knowledge and education, the organization of society, the expression of agreements and disagreements, the control of people and exercise of social power, and so on.

82. Derrida, *De la grammatologie.*

83. Jonathan Goldberg, *Writing Matters: From the Hands of the English Renaissance* (Stanford: Stanford University Press, 1990); Mignolo "Colonization of Amerindian Languages."

84. This is nothing new. The fact that Aztec books were different from Spanish books is quite obvious. Robertson, for instance, places the word within quotation marks, but then proceeds to compare pre-Columbian painting with the European Renaissance(!). The problem does not lie in the "perception" of the different but in thinking within its framework. Robertson does perceive the difference, although his description of the Aztecs' "books" makes one doubtful. See *Mexican Manuscript Painting*, 29ff.

85. For a perspective on the practice, transmission, and conceptualization of writing in the Arabic world, see the wonderful book by Pederson, *The Arabic Book*. Pederson is writing for a Western audience and naturally uses the word *book* in the title. According to the previous discussion, the title should have been *The Arabic Kitab and al-Kitab,* where the emphasis is put on human and holy writing rather than on the object that results from the inscription of graphic signs.

86. Ananda Wood has transcribed several autobiographical accounts from Kerala, in which learning the alphabet was coupled with the ritual of having the letters inscribed on the tongue. *Knowledge before Printing and After: The Indian Tradition in Changing Kerala* (Bombay: Oxford University Press, 1985).

87. John C. Ecles, *Evolution of the Brain: Creation of the Self* (London: Routledge, 1989), 71–97; Derek Bickerton, *Language and Species* (Chicago: University of Chicago Press, 1990), 164–97. I am following the approach developed by Maturana and Varela, *The Tree of Knowledge,* in particular, "Linguistic Domains and Human Consciousness," 205–39.

88. By "restructuring of thought" I am not referring to the supposed qualitative jump achieved by alphabetic writing. One of the difficulties of this thesis is that the paradigmatic example is always the classical tradition in the West (see, for instance, Erick Havelock, "The Aftermath of the Alphabet," in *The Literate Revolution in Greece* [Princeton: Princeton University Press, 1982], 314–50). I am rather referring to the extension of brain function once visual means for recording and classifying information began to be developed in human cultures. See Robert Claiborne, *The Birth of Writing* (New York: Time-Life, 1974). And for a more sophisticated approach, although heavily rooted in the ideology of the consequences of (Western) literacy and in Greek

"beginnings," see D. De Kerchove and Charles J. Lumdsen, eds., *The Alphabet and the Brain: The Lateralization of Writing* (London: Verlag, 1988), in particular, 235–321.

CHAPTER 3

1. An overview of this debate is presented in the collection edited by Patrick Gardiner, *Theories of History* (Glencoe, Ill.: Free Press, 1964), 344–540.

2. Hayden White, *The Tropics of Discourse* (Baltimore: Johns Hopkins University Press, 1978). More recently, and from the perspective of literary studies, Lionel Gossman, *Between History and Literature* (Cambridge: Harvard University Press, 1990). A more extensive exposition of my own views on the interrelations between history, literature, fiction, and truth could be found in Walter D. Mignolo, "Dominios borrosos y dominios teóricos," *Filología* 20 (1985): 21–40, and "Lógica de las semejanzas y políticas de las diferencias: Sobre la literatura que parece historia y antropología, y viceversa." *Literatura e História na América Latina,* ed. L. Chiappini and Flavio Wolf de Aguiar (São Paulo: EDUSP, 1993), 115–34.

3. Walter D. Mignolo, "Literacy and the Colonization of Memory: Writing Histories of People without History," in *Literacy: Interdisciplinary Conversations,* ed. Deborah Keller-Cohen (Norwood, N.J.: Ablex, 1994), 91–114.

4. Ranajit Guha, "On Some Aspects of the Historiography of Colonial India," in *Selected Subaltern Studies,* ed. Ranajit Guha and Gayatri C. Spivak (New York: Oxford University Press, 1988), 7–46.

5. For a reflection on the historiography of colonial India, see Gayatri C. Spivak, "Subaltern Studies: Deconstructing Historiography," in Guha and Spivak, *Selected Subaltern Studies,* 3–44.

6. Edouard Glissant, *Caribbean Discourse: Selected Essays* (1981; reprint Charlottesville: University Press of Virginia, 1989), 64, 75, 76.

7. Pané, *Relacion;* Torquemada, *Monarquía indiana.*

8. Torquemada, *Monarquía indiana,* book I, chap. II; italics mine.

9. Nebrija, *Reglas de ortografía,* prologue.

10. Las Casas, *Apologética historia,* 2:638; trans. Noel Fallows.

11. The opinion that history is made up of words and things ran through those who merged a rhetorical philosophy of history grounded on Cicero with a denotative philosophy of language predicated by Plato. For a summary of such perspective in the Italian Renaissance, see Giorgio Spini, "I trattatisti dell'arte storica nella Controriforma italiana," in *Contributi alla storia del Concilio di Trento della Controriforma* (Florence: Vallecchi, 1948), 109–36; Girolamo Cotroneo, "*I trattatisti dell'* Ars historica" (Naples: Francesco Giannini Editore, 1971). On New World historiography, see Walter D. Mignolo, "El metatexto historiográfico y la historiografia indiana," *Modern Language Notes* 96 (1981): 358–402.

12. I am indebted here to Elizabeth Hill Boone's lecture on "Aztec Pictorial Histories: Record Keeping without Words" (delivered at Dumbarton Oaks on March 22, 1991, published in *Writing without Words: Alternative Literacies in Mesoamerica and the Andes,* ed. E. H. Boone and W. D. Mignolo [Durham,

N.C., Duke University Press, 1994], 45–66). See also her "Migration Histories as Ritual Performance," in *To Change Place: Aztec Ceremonial Landscapes*, ed. D. Carrasco, 121–51 (Niwot: University Press of Colorado, 1991).

13. It is understandable that the practices of decoding signs would be conceived according to the materiality of coding signs and that in an alphabetically oriented society, decoding will mean decoding letters (see, for instance, Richaudeau, *La lisibilité*). The point I am trying to make throughout this book is that the universalization of regional semiotic practices is relative to a locus of enunciation constructed in the process of analysis and not of a transcendent or objective perspective.

14. Tovar's letter to Acosta has been reproduced in Joaquín García Icazbalceta, *Don Fray Juan de Zumárraga, Primer Obispo y Arzobispo de México* (Mexico City: Antigua Librería de Andrade y Morales, 1881), 2:263–67.

15. Such a perspective could be found in every standard history of writing. As we saw in chapter 1, note 67, Geoffroy de Tory correlates "les lettres *attiques*" with "les lettres *antiques*." A cultural perspective has been developed more recently by Erick Havelock in *The Muse Learns to Write: Reflections on Orality and Literacy from Antiquity to the Present* (New Haven: Yale University Press, 1986) and *The Literate Revolution in Greece and Its Cultural Consequences* (Princeton: Princeton University Press, 1982).

16. Joseph Naveh, *Early History of the Alphabet: An Introduction to West Semitic Epigraphy and Paleography* (Jerusalem: Magnes Press, 1982); Harris, *The Origin of Writing*; Senner, *The Origins of Writing*.

17. Ibn Khaldun, *The Muqaddimah: An Introduction to History,* trans. Franz Rosenthal, 3 vols. (New York: Pantheon Books, 1958).

18. Titus Livius, *Ab urbe condita,* trans. B. O. Foster (Cambridge: Harvard University Press, Loeb Classical Library, 1919), 1:4–11; Flavio Biondo, *Historiarum ab inclinatione romanorum decades* (Venice, 1484), translated by Achille Crespi as *Le decadi* (Forlì: Zauli, 1963). On Biondo's concept of history, see Eric W. Cochrane, *Historians and Historiography in the Italian Renaissance* (Chicago: University of Chicago Press, 1981), 34–41. On las Casas's concept of history see his introduction to *Historia de las Indias* (written toward 1560).

19. Eric W. Cochrane, *Historians and Historiography,* and *Florence in the Forgotten Centuries, 1527–1800: A History of Florence and the Florentines in the Age of the Grand Dukes* (Chicago: University of Chicago Press, 1973); Donald J. Wilcox, *The Development of Florentine Humanist Historiography in the Fifteenth Century* (Cambridge: Harvard University Press, 1969); Nancy Struever, *The Language of History in the Renaissance: Rhetoric and Historical Consciousness in Florentine Humanism* (Princeton: Princeton University Press, 1970).

20. An overview of this process from the perspective of the Arabic world is Amin, *Eurocentrism*, 89–117. The impact of the "discovery" of America in the construction of Eurocentrism has been discussed extensively in O'Gorman, *The Invention of America.*

21. Isidore of Seville, *Etymologies,* ed. Jacques André (Paris: Les Belles Lettres, 1981). Spanish translation by J. González Cuenca (Salamanca: Universidad de Salamanca, 1983).

22. Marcus Terentius Varro, *On the Latin Language,* trans. Roland G. Kent, 2 vols. (Cambridge: Harvard University Press, 1951).

23. Isidore, *Etymologies,* book 1, chap. 3.

24. A splendid overview of literacy and education during these centuries could be found in Pierre Riché, *Education et culture dans l'Occident barbare, 6e–8e siecles* (Paris: Editions du Seuil, 1962), translation by John Contreni as *Education and Culture in the Barbarian West, Sixth through Eighth Centuries* (Columbia: University of South Carolina Press, 1976). Chapter 6 is devoted to education of laymen in Gaul and Spain. This chapter, as well as the book, offers a contemporary perspective on many of the issues addressed by Aldrete in his study on the origin of Castilian language.

25. Isidore, *Etymologies,* book 1, chap. 4.

26. When Isidore has to identify the origin of history, he does not rank Herodotus in first place. Since he has established that Greek and Latin letters both originated in Hebrew (book 1, chap. 3), it was natural to consider Moses the first historian who wrote about the beginning of the world: Herodotus was *just* the first Greek historian.

27. There are early formulations of this problem in Alan Dundes, "Meta-folklore and Oral Literary Criticism" *Monist* 50, no. 4 (1966): 505–16; Dan Ben-Amos, "Analytical Categories and Ethnic Genres," *Folklore Genres* 28 (1976): 215–42; and Geneviève Calame-Griaule, *Ethnologie et langage: La parole chez le Dogon* (Paris: Gallimard, 1965). An approach to genre criticism from this perspective is found in Walter D. Mignolo, "Qué clase de textos son géneros? Fundamentos de tipología textual," *Acta Poética* 4–5 (1982–83): 25–51, and "Semiosis, Coherence, and Universes of Meaning," in *Text and Discourse Connectedness,* ed. Maria-Elizabeth Conte, J. S. Petofi, and E. Sozer, 483–505 (Amsterdam: John Benjamin, 1989).

28. Miguel León-Portilla, *Toltecáyotl: Estudios de cultura náhuatl* (Mexico: Fondo de Cultura Económica, 1982). Of particular interest for our purposes are the following chapters: "Toltecáyotl, conciencia de una herencia de cultura," 15–35; "El México antiguo, capítulo de la historia universal?" 36–52; "El testimonio de la historia pre-hispánica en Náhuatl," 53–71; "Una categorización de la historiografía Náhuatl y de la que a ésta siguió en el siglo XVI," 72–100.

29. Tula was the center of Toltec civilization around the ninth century, preceding the Mexica development, in the Valley of Mexico, between the thirteenth and the beginning of the sixteenth centuries.

30. León-Portilla, *Toltecáyotl,* 23; italics mine.

31. León-Portilla, *Toltecáyotl,* 18.

32. *A Latin Dictionary,* rev. Charlton T. Lewis and Charles Short (Oxford: Clarendon Press, 1980).

33. "La sociedad náhuatl prehispánica se sentía verdaderamente en posesión de una herencia (*topializ*), de plena significación cultural (*yuhcatiliztli*), fruto de la acción de los antepasados que debía proseguirse para fortalecer lo más valiosos del propio ser." [The prehispanic Nahuatl society felt in possession of a legacy (*topializ*), of full cultural signification (*yuhcatiliztli*). They also felt that their mission was to preserve and to continue such a legacy in order to strengthen their own mode of being.] León-Portilla, *Toltecáyotl,* 17.

34. León-Portilla, *Toltecáyotl*, 58ff.

35. Siméon translates *tlatollótl* as: "Historie, procès, vie, biographie" and makes the distinction between different ways of referring to the "biography" of different linguistic roles involved in the process of communication: "notlatollo, mon procès, ma biographie; motlatollo, ton procès; itlatollo, son procès." And he translates *tetlatollo* as "procès, vie, histoire de quelqu'un" (*Dictionnaire*). What all this amounts to is the problematic concept of the self in Western and Mexican culture. Klor de Alva ("Contar vidas: La auto-biografía confesional y la reconstrucción del ser nahua," *Arbor* 515–16 [1988]: 49–78) suggests that the Western concept of self was transmitted to Amerindians through the Christian confession.

36. León-Portilla, *Toltecáyotl*, 60; italics mine.

37. Translated by Maureen Dyokas.

38. The distinction I am using here between discursive types and discursive configurations (or "formation") has been developed elsewhere (Mignolo, "Qué clase," and "Semiosis"), together with the notion of discursive structures. The reason behind this distinction is to have a vocabulary that would allow us to compare discursive landscapes in different cultures, without getting into the difficulties of using culturally loaded Western categories (history or literature, as discursive configurations; biography or novel, as discursive types) as theoretical constructs.

39. Marcelino Menéndez Pelayo, *Historia de las ideas estéticas en España*, 2 vols. (Madrid: Consejo Superior de Investigaciones Científicas, 1974); Antonio García-Berrio, *Formación de la teoría literaria moderna*, 2 vols. (Madrid: Planeta, 1977–80).

40. Several discursive types in several Amerindian languages are described and presented in Munro S. Edmonson, ed., *Literatures: Supplement to the Handbook of Middle American Indians* (Austin: University of Texas Press, 1985). The term *literature* here is certainly a misnomer, according to the perspective I am developing in this chapter. The discursive practice that in the West after the eighteenth century has been baptized literature is, like history, a regional discursive practice whose universality went together with the spread of Western literacy. In sixteenth-century Europe *poetry* was the term to identify a discursive practice that became "literature" (belles lettres). For more details, see Walter D. Mignolo, "Discursos pronunciados con el corazón caliente: Teorías del habla, del discurso y de la escritura," in *America Latina: Palabra, cultura, literatura,* ed. Ana Pizarro (São Paulo: Memorial de America Latina, 1994).

41. This section departs from research I pursued in the late 1970s and two papers published during the early 1980s. See "El metatexto" and "La historia de la escritura y la escritura de la historia," in *De la crónica a la nueva narrative mexicana,* ed. M. H. Forster and J. Ortega, 13–28 (Mexico City: Oasis, 1986).

42. Bernardo Boturini Benaducci, *Idea de una nueva historia general de la America Septentrional* (1746) (Paris: Centre de Documentation "Andre Thevet," 1933).

43. All quotations are from *Tutte le opere di Giambattista Vico* (Milan: Arnoldo Mondadori Editore, 1957). *PSN* refers to the 1744 edition *Principi di*

Scienza Nuova, and *SNP* to the 1730 edition, *La scienza nuova prima.* English translation by Thomas Goddard Bergin and Max Harold Fisch as *The New Science of Giambattista Vico,* from the 3d ed., 1744 (Ithaca: Cornell University Press, 1948).

44. "Alla qual lingua corrispondono i geroglifici degli egizi, overo i loro caratteri sagri (de' quali s' intendevano i soli sacerdoti) . . . talche appo gli egizi, greci e latini, si fatti parlari divini dovettero essere ritruovati da' poeti teologi, che furono quelli della prima etá poetica, che fondarono queste tre nazioni" (*SNP,* book 3, chap. 25, 927–28).

45. Vico, *New Science,* book 4, chap. 5, 306.

46. Vico, *New Science,* 307.

47. The language of the age of gods is expressed in hieroglyphs; the language of the age of heroes in symbols or heroic enterprises (*PSN,* book 2, chap. 4, 186). Vico is not clear on this point in the *SNP.* It is helpful to read *PSN* ("La seconda fu per impresse eroiche, con le quali parlano l'armi; la cual favella, come abbiam sopra detto, reto alla militar disciplina"). The language of the age of men (or human beings), which Vico perceives in every nation at his own time, is the articulated language, "la lingua volgare" (prose), and the "letteri volgari" (alphabet).

48. C. A. Burland, *The Four Directions of Time: An Account of Page One of Codex Fejervary Mayer* (Santa Fe: Museum of Navajo Ceremonial Art, 1950), Burr Cartwright Brundage, *The Fifth Sun: Aztec Gods, Aztec World* (Austin: University of Texas Press, 1979), 3–30. In chapter 5 I will return to this topic in relation to organization of space.

49. There are unquestionably striking similarities between Vico's and Derrida's concepts of writing, and it would be interesting to know how much the anxiety of influence made Derrida bring Rousseau to the foreground and relegate Vico to a couple of footnotes on the margin of the page. See Jurgen Trabant, "*Parlare scrivendo:* Deconstructive Remarks on Derrida's Reading of Vico," in *New Vico Studies* (New York: Institute for Vico Studies, 1989), 7:43–58.

50. The diagram indirectly shows how alphabetically oriented are most of the current discussions on orality and literacy.

51. *PSN,* book 2, chap. 4, 190; italics mine.

52. Vico, *New Science,* book 2, chap. 4, par. 435.

53. Boturini, *Idea,* 2.

54. Boturini, *Idea,* 5.

55. On encyclopedias and their complicity with alphabetic writing, see the following chapter on genres and organization of knowledge. For an introduction to the nature and functions of Egyptian writing system, Henry George Fischer, *L'écriture et l'art de l'Egypte ancienne: Quatre leçons sur la paléographie et l'épigraphie pharaoniques* (Paris: Presses Universitaires de France, 1986) and "The Origins of Egyptian hieroglyphs," in Senner, *The Origins of Writing,* 59–76.

56. Boturini, *Idea,* 7.

57. "Mutos si difinisce 'narrazion vera,' e pure resto a significare 'favola,'

che e stata da tutti finor creduta 'narrazione falsa.' Logos (λόγος) si deffinisce 'vero parlare,' e volgarmente significa 'origine' overo 'istoria di voci'; e l'etimologie, quali ci sono pervenute finor, di assai poco soddisfano l'intendimento per le vere istorie dintorno all'origini delle cose da esse voci significate" (*SNP,* book 3, chap. 1, 895–96). Thus, if the Greek meaning of *favola* could be translated into the Latin *mutus,* and the *favole* were the first expressions of the primal human being, Vico concludes that this was a "parlar immutabile."

58. Boturini here is obviously referring to *SNP* (book 3, chap. 5, 899–90), in which Vico explains the discovery of the principle of abstraction ("caratteri poetici"), which was the vocabulary of the "naciones gentiles" [heathen nations]. Vico gives the example of the letter *a,* which indicates a diversity of similar sounds produced on different occasions and in different ways; or the triangle, a geometric abstraction that indicates the diversity of similar forms produced on different occasions and in different ways.

59. *SNP,* book 2, chap. 1.

60. Boturini, *Idea,* 32; italics mine.

61. For more detail about this topic see chapter 2.

62. It is time to remind the reader that Vico, writing during the first half of the eighteenth century, was rethinking some of the basic premises of humanist and Renaissance men of letters. See the classic study by Andrea Sorrentino, *La retorica e la poetica di Vico: Ossia la prima concezione estetica del linguagio* (Turin: Fratelli Bocca, Editori, 1927), 1–73. In this regard, he could be linked to Valla's and Nebrija's philosophy of language.

63. Juan José de Eguiara y Eguren, *Bibliotheca mexicana* . . . (Mexico City: Ex Nova Typographia in Aedibus Authoris Editioni Ejustem Bibliothecae Destinata, 1770; reprint Mexico City: Universidad Nacional Autónoma de México, 1986), 1:56.

64. Translated by Maureen Dyokas.

65. When discussing the conditions of truthfulness, sixteenth- and seventeenth-century theoreticians of historiography accentuated the need to match the truth of the narrative with the truth of the things (or events) themselves. From the belief that the truth is both in the narrative and in the events, it followed that history was made of both words and events. Good examples in the Spanish world are provided by Cabrera de Córdoba, *De historia para entenderla y escribirla* (1611), ed. Santiago Montero Díaz (Madrid: Instituto de Estudios Políticos, 1948); and Jerónimo de San José, *Genio de la historia* (1651), ed. Higinio de Santa Teresa (Vitoria: El Carmen, 1957). For a general discussion of the topic, see Mignolo, "El metatexto."

66. Francesco Patritio, *Della historia diece dialogui: Ne' qvali si ragiona di tute le cose appartenenti all'historia, e allo scriverla, e all'osservarla* (Venetia: Andrea Arrivabene, 1560).

67. Jean Bodin, *Methodus ad facilem historiarum cognitionem* (Paris: M. Iuuenem, 1566). For the place of Jean Bodin in the sixteenth century and his influence in eighteenth-century concept of history, see Julian H. Franklin, *Jean Bodin and the Sixteenth-Century Revolution in the Methodology of Law and History* (New York: Columbia University Press, 1963); see also,

Cotroneo, *I trattatisti,* 343–84; and, more recently, Simone Goyard-Fabre, *Jean Bodin et le droit de la République* (Paris: Presses Universitaires de France, 1989).

68. On Patrizi see Spini, "I trattatisti"; and Cotroneo, *I trattatisti,* 205–64.

69. A masterful summary is Elena Artaza, *El ars narrandi en el siglo XVI español: Teoría y práctica* (Bilbao: Universidad de Deusto, 1989).

CHAPTER 4

1. Pedro Martir de Anglería, *Epistolario: Documentos inéditos para la historia de España,* ed. and trans. José López de Toro (Madrid: Imprenta Góngora, 1953), letter 129, January 5, 1493, 9:235–36.

2. Gil Fernández, *Panorama,* 231–90.

3. Javier Malagón-Barceló, "The Role of *Letrado* in the Colonization of America," *Americas* 18 (1961): 1–17.

4. Vega, *Comentarios,* part 1, ix, 29.

5. *Ars rhetorica,* in *Rhetores latini minores,* ed. Charles Halm, 371–448 (Frankfurt: Minerva, 1964).

6. James V. Murphy, "*Ars dictaminis:* The Art of Letter-Writing," in *Rhetoric in the Middle Ages* (Berkeley and Los Angeles: University of California Press, 1974), 194–268; John Siegel, "From *Dictatores* to the Humanists," in *Rhetoric and Philosophy in Renaissance Humanism* (Princeton: Princeton University Press, 1968); Carmen Castillo, "La epistola como género literario: De la antigüedad a la edad media latina," *Estudios Clásicos* 18 (1974): 427–42; J. N. H. Lawrence, "Nuevos lectores y nuevos géneros: Apuntes y observaciones sobre la epistolografía en el primer Renacimiento español," *Academia Literaria Renacentista* 5 (1988): 81–99.

7. See, for instance, Judith Rice Henderson, "Defining the Genre of the Letter: Juan Luis Vives' *De Conscribendis Epistolis,*" *Renaissance and Reformation* 19, no. 2 (1983): 89–105.

8. Paul Oskar Kristeller, *Renaissance Thought and the Arts* (Princeton: Princeton University Press, 1980), 9.

9. Peter Martyr, *De orbe novo decades* (Alcalá de Henares, 1530). Trans. Joaquín Torres Asensio as *Décadas del Nuevo Mundo* (1892; reprint, Buenos Aires: Bajel, 1944), 105.

10. Translations from Martyr are by Maureen Dyokas.

11. Martir de Anglería, *Epistolario,* letter 130, May 14, 1493, 9:236–37.

12. Chimalpaín, *Relaciones originales,* 114.

13. Translated by Maureen Dyokas.

14. Francesco Guicciardini, *The History of Italy* (1561), trans. and ed. Sidney Alexander (Princeton: Princeton University Press, 1969), book 1.

15. Martir de Anglería, *Epistolario,* letter 92, March 11, 1492, 9:171–72.

16. Martir de Anglería, *Epistolario,* letter 114, September 1, 1492, 9:210–11.

17. Martir de Anglería, *Epistolario,* letter 121, October 11, 1492, 9:220. Curiously enough, this letter, predicting the Italian ruin and wondering about the French attitude, was written the day before Columbus's landing.

18. On Alfonso el Sabio, see Robert Burns, ed., *Emperor of Culture: Al-*

delphia: University of Pennsylvania Press, 1990). On El Gerundense, see Benito Sánchez Alonso, *Historia de la historiografía española: Ensayo de un exámen de conjunto* (Madrid: Cultura Hispánica, 1944), vol. 1; Robert Brian Tate, *Ensayos sobre la historiografía peninsular del siglo XV,* trans. Jesús Díaz (Madrid: Editorial Gredos, 1970).

19. On the historians and historiography under Charles I of Spain and Charles V of the Holy Roman Empire, see A. Morel-Fatio, *Historiographie de Charles Quint* (Paris: H. Champion, 1913).

20. Edmundo O'Gorman, *Cuatro historiadores de Indias, siglo XVI: Pedro Mártir de Anglería, Gonzálo Fernández de Oviedo y Valdés, Bartolomé de las Casas, Joseph de Acosta* (Mexico City: Secretaría de Educación Pública, 1972), 13.

21. O'Gorman, *Cuatro historiadores de Indias,* 15.

22. Wilcox, *Florentine Humanist Historiography.*

23. Cochrane, *Historians and Historiography,* 15–30. See also Hans Baron, *From Petrarch to Leonardo Bruni: Studies in Humanistic and Political Literature* (Chicago: Newberry Library and University of Chicago Press, 1968).

24. Martír de Anglería, *Décadas del Nuevo Mundo,* decade 7, book 1, chap. 1.

25. Martír de Anglería, *Décadas del Nuevo Mundo,* decade 7, book 1, chap. 1.

26. Juan Bautista Avalle-Arce, "Las memorias de Gonzálo Fernández de Oviedo," in *Dintorno de una época dorada* (Madrid: Porrúa Turanzas, 1978), 101–19.

27. Cochrane, *Historians and Historiography,* 15–16.

28. Lisa Jardine, *Francis Bacon: Discovery and the Art of Discourse* (Cambridge: Cambridge University Press, 1974).

29. Collison, *Encyclopaedias.*

30. Sahagún, *Florentine Codex,* 1:105–6; italics mine. The fact that Sahagún's manuscript ended up in Florence should come not as a surprise after the previous discussion.

31. Alfredo López Austin, "The Research Method of Fray Bernardino de Sahagún: The Questionnaires," in Edmonson, *Sixteenth-Century Mexico,* 111–49.

32. Sahagún, *Florentine Codex,* 1:105–6.

33. Luis Nicolau d'Olwer, *Fray Bernardino de Sahagún (1499–1590),* trans. Mauricio J. Mixco (Salt Lake City: University of Utah Press, 1987).

34. Sahagún, *Florentine Codex,* 1:106–7; italics mine.

35. John B. Glass, *Sahagún: Reorganization of the Manuscrito de Tlatelolco, 1566–1569,* Contributions to the Ethnohistory of Mexico, no. 7 (Lincoln Center, Mass.: Conemex Associates, 1978).

36. Sahagún, *Florentine Codex,* 1:31–32; italics mine.

37. See chapter 6 for more details about Juan de Ovando's contribution to gathering and organizing information about the Spanish Indies.

38. Donald Robertson, "The Sixteenth-Century Mexican Encyclopedia of Fray Bernardino de Sahagún," *Cahiers d'Historie Mondiale* 9, no. 3 (1966): 617–26.

39. F. G. Ritsch, *De M. Terentii Varronis Disciplinarum libris commentarious* (Bonnae, 1845), *opusc.* 3, 352–402.

40. Gonzálo Fernández de Oviedo y Valdés, *General y natural historia de las Indias, islas y tierra-firme del mar océano,* 4 vols. (Madrid: Imprenta de la Real Academia de la Historia, 1855). Two of the classical articles on Oviedo y Valdés are O'Gorman, *Cuatro historiadores de Indias,* 47–86; and Juan Bautista Avalle-Arce, *Dintorno de una epoca dorada* (Madrid: Porrúa Turanzas, 1978), 101–36. For the place of Oviedo y Valdés in the context of New World historiography, see Walter D. Mignolo, "Cartas, crónicas y relaciones del descubrimiento y la conquista," in *Historia de la literatura hispanoamericana: Época colonial,* ed. Iñigo Madrigal, 57–116 (Madrid: Cátedra, 1982). On the organization of and other discursive aspects of the *Historia general,* see Stephanie Merrim, "'Un *Mare Magno* e Oculto': Anatomy of Fernández de Oviedo's *Historia general y natural de las Indias,*" *Revista de estudios hispánicos* 11 (1984): 101–19; and on its encyclopedic character, the chapter that José Rabasa devotes to Oviedo y Valdés in his *Inventing America* (Norman: University of Oklahoma Press, 1993).

41. Francisco Hernández, *Historia natural de Cayo Plinio Segundo,* trans. Francisco Hernández (Mexico City: Universidad Nacional Autónoma de México, 1966). A master summary of scientific practice in colonial Mexico and the role played by Hernández can be found in Elias Trabulse, "Tres momentos de la heterodoxia científica en el México colonial," *Revista Latinoamericana de Historia de las Ciencias y la Tecnología* 5, no. 1 (1988): 7–18.

42. Ritsch, *Disciplinarum libris commentarius;* Francesco Della Corte, *Varrone, il terzo gran lume romano* (Genoa: Francesco M. Bozzi, 1954); Jacques Fontaine, *Isidore de Seville et la culture classique dans l'Espagne wisigothique* (Paris: Etudes Agustiniennes, 1983).

43. Francis Bacon, *Novum Organum* (1620), vol. 4 of *The Works of Francis Bacon,* ed. J. Spedding, R. L. Ellis, and D. D. Heath (London, 1857–74), 292–93; italics mine. This very idea was already expanded on in *The Advancement of Learning* (1605), book 2, chap. 1, and further developed in *De Augmentis Scientiarum* (1623), book 1, chap. 1. I have benefited mainly from two studies on Bacon and the organization of knowledge: Jardine, *Francis Bacon;* and Antonio Pérez-Ramos, *Francis Bacon's Idea of Science and the Maker's Knowledge Tradition* (Oxford: Clarendon Press, 1988).

44. For a useful overview of *Ilm al-Tarijh,* an expression embracing both annals and biographical narratives, from the third to the thirteen century, see Hamilton A. R. Gibb, *Studies on the Civilization of Islam* (Princeton: Princeton University Press, 1982), 109–37.

45. For the meaning of *kitab* and its social and ideological dimensions in the Arab tradition, see Pederson, *The Arabic Book,* 12–19.

46. Gonzalbo Aizpurú, *El mundo indígena;* Romero, *La enseñanza del Latín.*

47. See the masterful summary by Enrique Florescano, "La reconstrucción histórica elaborada por la nobleza indígena y sus descendientes mestizos," in *La memoria y el olvido* (Mexico City: Secretaría de Educación Pública, 1985), 11–20.

48. There is another dimension of literacy and resistance illustrated by the documentation related to testaments, land litigations, and other forms of legal disputes whose integration in my argument would force a long detour. See, however, F. Karttunen, "Náhuatl Literacy," in *The Inca and Aztec States: 1400–1800,* ed. G. A. Collier, R. Rosaldo, and J. D. Wirth (New York: Academic Press, 1982), 395–417; and A. Anderson et al., *Beyond the Codices: The Nahuatl View of Colonial Mexico* (Berkeley and Los Angeles: University of California Press, 1976). I am limiting my examples to the philosophy of writing (and therefore to the sphere of "high culture") and the frame it provided for writing grammars of Amerindian languages and histories of Amerindian cultures, rather than to the consequences manifested in particular cases in which Spanish grammarians and historians could have been transformed by intercultural experiences. At the same time, I am limiting my examples of resistance to the sphere of interactions framed by members and representatives of Spanish literate culture. While I hope that my argument does not convince the reader that I am celebrating "high culture," at the same time I hope the reader will understand that a critical examination of its phenomena is no less relevant than exploring more "popular" ones.

49. Some of the basic studies on the issue are Bernard Weinberg, *History of Literary Criticism in the Italian Renaissance* (Chicago: University of Chicago Press, 1961); Antonio García Berrio, *Formación de la teoría literaria moderna: Renacimiento Europeo* (Madrid: Planeta, 1977); and Barbara Kiefer Lewalski, ed., *Renaissance Genres: Essays on Theory, History, and Interpretation* (Cambridge: Harvard University Press, 1986).

50. European intellectuals and political leaders are becoming aware of the challenge of a multiethnic world to the classical tradition. Former British prime minister Margaret Thatcher, in her Burger speech, invoked the common experience rooted in the European classical tradition and celebrated (without apologies) the story of how Europeans explored, colonized, and civilized much of the world, as a venture of talent, skill, and courage (see Yasmin Alibhai "Community Whitewash," *Guardian,* January 23, 1989). A telling example of the perpetuation of fractured symbolic worlds in colonial situations is provided by Lucy R. Lippard, *Mixed Blessings: New Art in a Multicultural America* (New York: Pantheon Books, 1990).

51. Mercedes de la Garza, *Literatura maya* (Caracas: Biblioteca Ayacucho, 1980), prologue; Victoria Bricker, "Yucatecan Maya Literature," In *Literatures,* supplement to *Handbook of Middle American Indians* (Austin: University of Texas Press, 1985), 3:44–63.

52. Recent editions of these two well-known *Books of Chilam Balam,* Munro S. Edmonson, ed. and trans., *The Ancient Future of the Itza: The Book of Chilam Balam of Tizimin* (Austin: University of Texas Press, 1982), and *Heaven Born Merida and Its Destiny: The Book of Chilam Balam of Chumayel* (Austin: University of Texas Press, 1986).

53. Ralph L. Roys, *The Book of Chilam Balam of Chumayel* (Washington, D.C.: Carnegie Institution of Washington, 1933).

54. Royce, *Book of Chilam Balam,* 3.

55. Ramón Arzápalo Marín, "The Indian Book in Colonial Yucatán" (pa-

per presented at the conference The Book in the Americas, John Carter Brown Library, Providence, R.I., June 18–21, 1987, mimeo).

56. José María López Piñero, *Ciencia y técnica en la sociedad española de los siglos XVI y XVII* (Barcelona: Labor Universitaria, 1979), 192–96.

57. Marín, "Indian Book."

58. Gerónimo de Mendieta, *Historia eclesiástica indiana* (1597) (Mexico City: Porrúa, 1954), book 2, chap. 20.

59. Maravall, "La concepción del saber," 1:220ff.

60. While this kind of perspective is understandable in the sixteenth century, its persistence in the twentieth century is more troublesome (Abbott, "The Ancient Word"). It suggests that in the realm of linguistic behavior, as well as in other aspects of the colonization, sixteenth-century images of the Amerindian are still alive and well.

61. León-Portilla, *Toltecayótl*, and "Nahuatl Literature," in Edmonson, *Literatures*, 3:7–43.

62. Folklorists have provided useful insights into the general issue of discourse classification while avoiding Western genre history and theory. See, for instance, Dundes, "Metafolklore"; and Ben-Amos, "Analytical Categories." I find Bakhtin's perspective as expressed in *Speech Genres*, 60–102, akin to Dundes and Ben-Amos. I have dealt with some of the theoretical problems of discourse classification, taking Dundes, Ben-Amos, and Bakhtin as a starting point, in "Qué clase de textos son géneros? Fundamentos de tipología textual," *Acta Poética* 4–5 (1982–83): 25–51, and in "Semiosis."

63. Mignolo, "(Re)modeling the Letter," 357–94.

64. Dennis Tedlock, *The Spoken Word and the Art of Interpretation* (Philadelphia: University of Pennsylvania Press, 1982).

65. If, on the one hand, there is a general agreement on the nonexistence of "metalanguages" (and prejudice against them), the use of language (or discourse) to describe the uses of language (or discourse) is different from the uses of language to give order or to describe nonlinguistic (semiotic) interactions. On the other hand, the logic of the diagram does not work according to the standard "semiotic square": conceptualizations of oral and written interactions, being themselves either oral or written, cannot be interpreted as contradictory with the level of oral and written interactions.

66. This thesis has been advanced in the influential article by Jack Goody and Ian Watt, "The Consequences of Literacy," *Comparative Studies in Society and History* 5 (1963): 304–45. Some of the ideas have been revised and expanded in Goody, *Interface*. In the humanities, the question was considered by Walter J. Ong, *Orality and Literacy: The Technologizing of the Word* (London: Methuen, 1982). For critiques of the position defended by Goody and Ong, see Brian V. Street, *Literacy in Theory and Practice* (New York: Cambridge University Press, 1984), 19–128; and Ruth Finnegan, *Literacy and Orality: Studies in the Technology of Communication* (Oxford: Blackwell, 1988).

67. Maurice Bloch has traced contemporary thinking about the consequences of literacy back to eighteenth-century French philosophes and encyclopedists in "Literacy and Enlightenment." It is not difficult to perceive

the similarities between the current ideology on the magical power of literacy with those of French encyclopedists and Spanish missionaries and men of letters.

68. Roland Scollon and Suzanne Scollon, *Linguistic Convergence: An Ethnography of Speaking at Fort Chipewyan* (New York: Academic Press, 1979); Calame-Griaule, *Ethnologie et langage;* Richard Bauman and Joel Sherzer, eds., *Explorations in the Ethnography of Speaking* (Cambridge: Cambridge University Press, 1974); Gary Gossen, "To Speak with a Heated Heart: Chamula Canons of Style and Good Performance," in Bauman and Sherzer, *Explorations,* 389–413.

69. Victoria Bricker, "The Ethnographic Context of Some Traditional Mayan Speech Genres," in Bauman and Sherzer, *Explorations,* 369–87. More recently, the question of genres in the Yucatán peninsula has been undertaken by William Hanks. See, for instance, his "Discourse Genres in Theory and Practice," *American Ethnologist* 14, no. 4 (1987): 668–92, and "Elements of Maya Style," in *Word and Image in Maya Culture: Explorations in Language, Writing, and Representation,* ed. William F. Hanks and Don S. Rice, 92–111 (Salt Lake City: University of Utah Press, 1989). For Bakhtin, see *Speech Genres,* 60–102; and Mignolo, "Semiosis."

70. Gary Gossen, "Chamula Genres of Verbal Behavior," in *Toward New Perspectives in Folklore,* ed. A. Paredes and R. Bauman, 145–67 (Austin: University of Texas Press, 1972).

71. Gossen, *Chamulas,* 89.

72. Gossen, "To Speak," 412.

CHAPTER 5

1. Pasquale d'Elia, ed., *Il mappamondo cinese del p. Matteo Ricci* (Pechino, 1602) (Vatican City: Biblioteca Apostolica Vaticana, 1938), 25; *Fonti Ricciane* (Rome: Edizione nazionale delle opere edite e inedite di Matteo Ricci, 1942), vol. 1.

2. d'Elia, *Il mappamondo cinese,* 27.

3. Ricci's world map as reprinted in d'Elia, *Il mappamondo cinese,* 25.

4. Joseph Needham and Wang Ling, *Science and Civilization in China* (Cambridge: Cambridge University Press, 1959), 3:501ff.

5. For a more detailed, sophisticated analysis of the "nested square map," in the context of ancient Chinese cosmology, see John S. Major, "The Five Phases, Magic Squares, and Schematic Cosmography," in *Explorations in Early Chinese Cosmology, Journal of the American Academy of Religion Studies* 2(1984): 133–66.

6. Giovanni Francesco Gemelli Carreri (1651–1725), *Giro del Mondo* (Napoli, 1699); my reference is to the French translation, *Voyage du tour du monde* (Paris: E. Ganeau, 1719), vol. 4.

7. I have to resist the temptation to compare the conversations between the Franciscan friars and the Mexica *principales* with the conversation in China between the Jesuits and the Chinese mandarins, almost a century later. See Bernard Hung-Kay Luk, "A Serious Matter of Life and Death: Learned

Conversations at Foochow in 1627," in *East Meets West: The Jesuits in China, 1582–1773*, ed. Ch. E. Ronan and Bonnie B. C. Oh, 173–207 (Chicago: Loyola University Press, 1988).

8. The invention of the globe to depict the shape of the earth emphasizes the mobility of the geometric center. This example does not contradict my argument but rather reinforces it. This is so, first, because the mobility of the geometric center attained in the terraqueous globe cannot hide the fact that the globe was a Western invention at a particular point of its history (toward the end of the fifteenth century and at the beginning of the age of explorations). Second, when the globe is depicted on a flat surface some place has to occupy the center. Ricci's move suggests that the center is not only determined by ethnic and cognitive reasons, but by political strategies as well.

9. David Woodward has described a drastic change in the European ordering of space toward the beginning of the fifteenth century with the translation into Latin of Ptolemy's *Geography*, the increasing uses of geometric projections, as well as the flourishing period of transoceanic explorations. See his "Maps and the Rationalization of Geographic Space," in Levenson, *Circa 1492*, 83–87. This fact does not place European cartographers in any privileged position, however. Needham and Ling, *Science and Civilization*, 533–61, move away from a uniform and evolutionary history of human civilization and compare diverse rhythms of cultural developments in China and Europe. Quantitative and geometric ordering of space was not alien to the Chinese, although they did not use it in the same way that Europeans did. The Chinese did not have the interrupted tradition of geometric cartographic projection described by Woodward, but a continuous one from the first century A.D. to the arrival of the Jesuits. Ptolemy, on the other hand, was known in the Arab world much sooner than in Christian Europe. See below, the section on Ibn Khaldun.

10. See Helen Wallis, "The Influence of Father Ricci on Far Eastern Cartography," *Imago Mundi* 19 (1965): 38–45; Kenneth Ch'en, "Matteo Ricci's Contribution to, and Influence on, Geographical Knowledge in China," *Journal of the American Oriental Society* 59 (1939): 325–509; Edward Heawood, "The Relationships of the Ricci Maps," *Geographical Journal* 50 (1917): 271–76. For a general account of the Jesuits in China see George H. Dunne, *Generations of Giants: The Story of the Jesuits in China in the Last Decades of the Ming Dynasty* (West Lafayette, Ind.: University of Notre Dame Press, 1962).

11. Wallis, "Influence of Father Ricci," 42–43.

12. Ch'en, "Ricci's Contribution"

13. Chang Wei-hua, quoted by Ch'en, "Ricci's Contribution," 348.

14. Fabian, *Time and the Other*.

15. This image is preserved, perhaps unwittingly, when scholars pay attention only to the European side of the coin, studying, for example, the European impact in China (Theodore N. Foss, "A Western Interpretation of China: Jesuit Cartography," and Harriet Vanderstappen, "Chinese Art and the Jesuits in Peking," both articles collected in Ronan and Oh, *East Meets West*, 209–51 and 103–27, respectively) without looking at the resistance to it or the Chinese's own uses, adaptations, and transgressions of European borrowing as well as the Chinese impact on European culture.

16. John Brian Harley, "Maps, Knowledge, and Power," in *The Iconography of Landscapes: Essays on the Symbolic Representation, Design, and Use of Past Environments,* ed. D. Cosgrove and S. Daniels, 277–312 (London: Cambridge University Press, 1988), and "Deconstructing the Map," *Cartographica* 26, no. 2 (1989): 1–20. See also Walter D. Mignolo, "Comments on Harley's 'Deconstructing the Map,'" *Cartographica* 26, no. 3 (1989): 109–13.

17. For the changing conception of time during the thirteenth century and the emergence of the idea of progress, see Robert Nisbet, *History of the Idea of Progress* (New York: Basic Books, 1980), 77–100. For the changing conception of space toward the end of the fifteenth century, see W. G. L. Randles, *De la terre plate au globe terrestre: Une mutation épistémologique rapide 1480–1520* (Paris: Armand Colin, 1980).

18. Alexander Marshack, *The Roots of Civilization: The Cognitive Beginning of Man's First Art, Symbol, and Notation* (New York: McGraw-Hill, 1972).

19. Rudolf Arnheim, *The Power of the Center: A Study of Composition in the Visual Arts,* 2d ed. (Berkeley and Los Angeles: University of California Press, 1988), 1–12, 36–50.

20. The dialectic between place as a reference point and space as a network of places and emptiness has been discussed by Yi-Fu Tuan, *Space and Place: The Perspective of Experience* (Minneapolis: University of Minnesota Press, 1977), 34–50.

21. Charles Lumsden and Edward Wilson, *Promethean Fire: Reflections on the Origin of Mind* (Cambridge: Harvard University Press, 1983). For a more suggestive formulation of the problem I am trying to sketch here, see Varela, Thompson, and Rosch, *The Embodied Mind,* 147–84. I will come back to this issue in the Afterword.

22. Leo Bagrow and R. A. Skelton, *History of Cartography* (Cambridge: Cambridge University Press, 1964), 33, reported that a manuscript by a Milesian scholar from the sixth century B.C. was recently discovered and that this manuscript describes the supposed composition of the earth in seven parts: head and face in the Peloponnesus, backbone in the isthmus, diaphragm in Ionia, legs in the Hellespont, feet in the Thracian and Cimmerian Bosphorus, epigastrium in the Egyptian sea, hypogastrium and rectum in the Caspian.

23. Armin Wolf, "News on the Ebstorf World Map: Date, Origin, Authorship," in *Géographie du monde au Moyen Age et à la Renaissance,* ed. Monique Pelletier, 51–68 (Paris: CTHS, 1989), and "Die Ebstorfer Welkkarte als Denkmal eines Mittelalterlichen Welt- und Geschichtsbildes," *Geschichte in Wissenschaft und Unterricht* 8 (1957): 316–34; Aaron Gurevich, *Categories of Medieval Culture* (London: Routledge and Kegan Paul, 1985), 41–92.

24. A. C. Graham, "The Date and Composition of Liehtzyy." *Asia Major,* n.s., 8 (1961): 139–98.

25. A. C. Graham, *The Book of Lieh-tzu* (London: Murray, 1960), 67–68.

26. On the center in religious thought, see Mircea Eliade, *Patterns in Comparative Religion* (New York: Harper Torchbooks, 1958), 367–87; and

James Dougherty, *The Fivesquare City: The City in the Religious Imagination* (West Lafayette, Ind.: University of Notre Dame Press, 1980). For the Andes see Joseph W. Bastien, *Mountain of the Condor: Metaphor and Ritual in an Andean Ayllu* (Minneapolis: West Publishing, 1978); and Lawrence Sullivan, "Above, Below, or Far Away: Andean Cosmogony and Ethical Order," in *Cosmogony and Ethical Order: New Studies in Comparative Ethics,* ed. R. W. Lovin and F. Reynolds, 98–131 (Chicago: University of Chicago Press, 1985). For the relationships established by humans between the structure of the cosmos and record keeping, see Mircea Eliade, *Cosmos and History* (New York: Harper and Row, 1959).

27. Alfredo López Austin, *Cuerpo humano e ideología: Las concepciones de los antiguos náhuas* (Mexico City: Universidad Nacional Autónoma de México, 1980), 1:397–99.

28. Cosmas Indicopleustes, *Topographie chrétienne* (A.D. 547–49), ed. Wanda Wolska-Conus (Paris: Les Editions du Cerf, 1968), 1: book 2, pars. 24–28.

29. See Denys Hay, *Europe: The Emergence of an Idea* (Edinburgh: University of Edinburgh Press, 1957).

30. Isidore of Seville, *Etimologiarum sive originum: Libri X,* ed. W. M. Lindsay (1911; rpt. London: Oxford University Press, 1957).

31. Also Indicopleustes, *Topographie chrétienne,* 1:book 2, par. 24, for the naming of the three continents. T/O maps were one of the four types of maps or "*descriptio.*" See David Woodward, "Medieval *Mappamundi,*" in *The History of Cartography,* ed. B. Harley and David Woodward, 1:286–369 (Chicago: University of Chicago Press, 1987). I emphasize them because they are largely responsible for the sixteenth-century idea that a fourth part of the world had been discovered. Neither the Chinese nor the Arabs conceived the world divided in three parts.

32. Diego Durán, *Book of the Gods and Rites and the Ancient Calendar* (1581) trans. and ed. Fernando Horcasitas and Doris Heyden (Norman: University of Oklahoma Press, 1971).

33. A classical description of the first page of the *Codex Féjérvary-Mayer,* which depicts the four (or five) directions of time, is in Burland, *Four Directions of Time.* A reconstruction of it, placing the Templo Mayor, is in Eduardo Matos Moctezuma, *The Aztecs* (New York: Rizzoli, 1989), 93–110. For a general discussion of the "shape of time" as applied to Mesoamerican cultures, see Clemency Coggins, "The Shape of Time: Some Political Implications of the Four-Part Figure," *American Antiquity* 45 (1980): 727–39. A detailed description also appears in Miguel León-Portilla, "Códice mesoamericano *Féjérvary-Mayer,*" in *Tonalamatl de los Pochtecas* (Mexico City: Celanese Mexicana, 1985), 29–31.

34. The reader may be wondering what is the justification for bringing an Arabic thinker into the discussion. There are several. First, Columbus brought a translator who knew Arabic on his first voyage; second, the discussion on Aldrete in the first chapter underlined the presence of the Arabic world in Christian Spain. And, finally, one of my goals in writing this book is to work across cultures, in a nonevolutionary way, looking at coexisting writing sys-

tems, record keeping, and territorial ordering. In this regard it is important to

keep in mind, for instance, what we could call the "two Ptolemaic traditions."
In the Arabic world, Ptolemy was rehearsed by Al-Idrisi (born around the
beginning of the twelfth century), while he entered the "West" toward the
second half of the fifteenth century. See S. Maqbul Ahmad, "Cartography of
al-Sharīf-al-Idrīsī," in *The History of Cartography: Cartography in the Traditional Islamic and South Asian Societies,* ed. J. B. Harley and D. Woodward
(Chicago: University of Chicago Press, 1992), 2:156–74.

35. See A. I. Wensinck, *The Ideas of the Western Semites Concerning the
Navel of the Earth,* Verhandelingen der Koninklijke Akademie van Weternschappen te Amsterdam, n.s., vol. 17, no. 1 (Amsterdam: Afdeeling Letterkunde, 1916).

36. Bernard Lewis, *The Muslim Discovery of Europe* (New York: W. W.
Norton, 1982), 59–60.

37. On the significance of Ibn Khaldun's history writing, see the previous
chapter, and Yves Lacoste, *Ibn Khaldun: The Birth of History and the Past of the
Third World* (London: Verso, 1984).

38. The plan of Tenochtitlán appeared in the first edition of Cortes's letters published in Nuremberg in 1524. The information was supposedly provided by Cortés himself.

39. Hernán Cortés, *Cartas de Relación de la Conquista de la Nueva España al Emperador Carlos V, 1529–27,* trans. A. Pagden as *Hernan Cortes:
Letters from Mexico* (New York: Grossman, 1971), hereafter cited as *Letters
from Mexico.*

40. On the possible connections between the Spanish administrators
(Council of the Indies) and the Roman tradition of mapping and land sur-
veyors, see the next chapter. Regarding the Roman innovations in land survey-
ing, see O. A. W. Dilke, *The Roman Land Surveyors: An Introduction to the
Agrimensores* (Newton Abbot: David and Charles, 1971), and "Maps in the
Service of the State: Roman Cartography to the End of the Augustan Era," in
Harley and Woodward, *The History of Cartography,* 201–11.

41. "I immediately set about building four brigantines, which I finished
very quickly, and they were made so that they could carry three hundred men
to the shore, and bring the horses whenever the need arose." Cortés, *Letters
from Mexico.*

42. Nigel Cameron and Brian Blake, *Peking: A Tale of Three Cities* (New
York: Harper and Row, 1965), 119. For useful comparisons between
ceremonial centers in China and the New World (among others), see Paul
Wheatley, *The Pivot of the Four Quarters: A Preliminary Enquiry into the
Origins and Character of the Ancient Chinese City* (Chicago: Aldine, 1971),
225–43.

43. What Wheatley calls "cosmo-marginal thought" I here refer to as
"ethnic rationalization of space." I am interested in underlining alternative
modes of rationalizing space instead of looking at it in chronological, evolutionary, and hierarchical order. For a useful comparison of ancient Chinese
and ancient Mesoamerican cosmologies, see John Carlson, "A Geometric
Model for the Interpretation of Mesoamerican Sites: An Essay in Cross-

Cultural Comparison," in *Mesoamerican Sites and World-Views,* ed. Elizabeth P. Benson, (Washington, D.C.: Dumbarton Oaks Research Library and Collections, 1981) 143–216.

44. David Carrasco, "City as Symbol in Aztec Thought: The Clues from the Codex Mendoza," *History of Religions* 20 (1981): 199–223.

45. The Western four cardinal points are an easy way to place the colors and symbols of Aztec cosmovision, but they are also misleading because they belong to a different worldview. From a Western perspective, one runs the risk of believing in the ontology of the four cardinal points and saying that, in Durán's calendar, "Unlike the European system, east appears to the north" (Durán, *Book of the Gods,* 329).

46. Wheatley, *Pivot,* 428.

47. Edward Calneck, "The Internal Structure of Tenochtitlan," in *The Valley of Mexico,* ed. Eric Wolf (Albuquerque: University of New Mexico Press, 1976), 287–302; Miguel León-Portilla, *Aztec Thought and Culture* (Norman: University of Oklahoma Press, 1963), 44–50; Brundage, *The Fifth Sun,* and *Two Heavens, Two Earths: An Essay Contrasting the Aztecs and the Incas* (Albuquerque: University of New Mexico Press, 1975), 20–34.

48. Dilke, "Maps," 201–12; and Claude Nicolet, *Space, Geography, and Politics in the Early Roman Empire* (Ann Arbor: University of Michigan Press, 1991), 189–208.

49. A manuscript copy of the *Descripción* can be found at the John Carter Brown Library, Brown University.

50. Rómulo Carbia, *La crónica oficial de las Indias Occidentales: Estudio histórico y crítico acerca de la historiografía mayor de Hispano América en los siglos XVI a XVIII* (Buenos Aires: Ediciones Buenos Aires, 1940), 109–49.

51. The *Relaciones geográficas de Indias* have been recently studied by Howard Cline in "The *Relaciones geográficas* of the Spanish Indies, 1577–1586," *Hispanic American Historical Review* 3 (1964): 341–74, and "The *Relaciones geográficas* of Spain, New Spain, and the Spanish Indies: An Annotated Bibliography," in *Handbook of Middle American Indians,* gen. ed. Robert Wauchope (Austin: University of Texas Press, 1964–76, vols. 12–15, *Guide to Ethnohistorical Sources,* ed. Howard F. Cline, 12:370–95. For the significance of the *Relaciones geográficas* in the context of colonial letters and textual production, see Mignolo, "Cartas," 61–66, "El mandato y la ofrenda: La *Descripción de la provincia y ciudad de Tlaxcala,* de Diego Muñoz Camargo y las *Relaciones de Indias*," *Nueva Revista de Filología Hispánica* 35, no. 2 (1987): 451–84, and "La grafía, la voz y el silencio," *Insula* 552 (1990): 11–12.

52. López de Velasco. *Geografía y descripción universal de las Indias, recopilada por el cosmógrafo cronista, Juan López de Velasco, desde el año 1571 a 1574.* Published for the first time in *Boletín de la Sociedad Geográfica de Madrid* (Madrid: Justo Zaragoza, 1871).

53. Herrera y Tordesillas was appointed official chronist in 1596. He used and expanded López de Velasco's *Description* in one volume of the *Historia general.*

54. Jimenez de la Espada published several *relaciones geográficas* of Peru. Since then the *relaciones geográficas* have received more attention from

scholars. Acuña between 1984 and 1989 published over 150 *relaciones* of Mexico, all of them from the sixteenth century. Solano edited a considerable number of *relaciones geográficas* from the seventeenth and eighteenth centuries.

55. Studies such as those of Gary Urton, *At the Crossroads of the Earth and
the Sky* (Austin: University of Texas Press, 1981), and *The History of a Myth:
Pacaritambo and the Origin of the Inkas* (Austin: University of Texas Press,
1990), are telling examples of such survivals. See also Alfonso Villa Rojas, "Los
conceptos de espacio y tiempo entre los grupos mayances contemporáneos,"
in *Tiempo y realidad en el pensamiento Maya,* ed. Miguel León-Portilla, 119–
68 (Mexico City: Universidad Nacional Autónoma de México, 1986); and
Gossen, *Chamulas.*

56. See, for instance, R. V. H. Dover, Katharine Seibold, and J. H.
McDowell, eds., *Andean Cosmologies through Time: Persistence and Emergence* (Bloomington: Indiana University Press, 1992).

57. Fabian, *Time and the Other,* 27.

58. Anthony Aveni, *Empires of Time: Calendars, Clocks, and Cultures*
(New York: Basic Books, 1989).

59. Clemency Chase Coggins, "The Zenith, the Mountain, the Center,
and the Sea," and Johanna Broda, "Astronomy, *Cosmovision,* and Ideology in
Pre-Hispanic Mesoamerica, both in *Ethnoastronomy and Archaeoastronomy
in the American Tropics,* ed. Anthony Aveni and Gary Urton, 111–24 and 81–
110 (New York: New York Academy of Science, 1982). An analysis of the Maya
space directions, based on the movement of the sun (independent of the four
Western cardinal directions, East, West, South, and North), is Coggins, "The
Shape of Time."

60. Nancy M. Farriss, "Remembering the Future, Anticipating the Past:
History, Time, and Cosmology among the Maya of Yucatan," *Comparative
Studies in Society and History* 29 (1989): 566–93; see also Clemency Chase
Coggins, "The Birth of the Baktun at Tikal and Seibal," in *Vision and Revision
in Maya Studies,* ed. Flora S. Clancy and Peter D. Harrison, 77–98 (Albuquer-
que: University of New Mexico Press, 1990).

61. León-Portilla, *Tiempo y realidad,* 131. Of particular interest in the same
volume is the chapter by Rojas, "Los conceptos de espacio."

62. Wayne Elzey, "Some Remarks on the Space and Time of the 'Center'
in Aztec Religion," *Estudios de Cultura Náhuatl* 12 (1976): 318–26. A similar
cosmological conception could be found in ancient India, where the center
was located in Mount Meru (on Sumeru), commonly identified with Mount
Kailasa (Kailas) in Tibet, considered as the *axis mundi.* See Joseph E.
Schwartzberg, "Cosmological Mapping," in *Cartography in the Traditional
Islamic and South Asian Societies,* ed. J. B. Harley and D. Woodward
(Chicago: University of Chicago Press, 1992), 2:332–87.

63. Elzey, "Remarks," 319.

64. Vega, *Comentarios,* book 1, chap. 11.

65. Urton, *Crossroads;* R. T. Zuidema, *The Ceque System of Cuzco: The
Social Organization of the Capital of the Inca,* trans. Eva M. Hoykaas (Leiden:
E. J. Brill, 1964).

66. Urton, *Crossroads,* 4.

67. Natham Wachtel, "Structuralisme et histoire: A propos de l'organiza-tion sociale du Cuzco, _Annales_ 21(1966): 71–94, and "Pensée sauvage et ac-culturation: L'espace et le temps chez Felipe Guaman Poma de Ayala et l'Inca Garcilaso de la Vega," _Annales_ 26(1971): 793–837.

68. Tom Zuidema (personal conversations, April and May of 1992) doubts whether the quatripartite division in the _mappamundi_ comes from Andean cosmology or from European (in his words) tradition. As in the case of Ixtlilxochitl (see next chapter), I tend to believe that such cosmographic and cosmologic grids are common to different cultural traditions, not that a world, kingdom, or empire conceived in four parts was an Amerindian adapta-tion of ancient models imported by Franciscans, Dominicans, or Jesuits.

69. See, for instance, Martellus's world map, fig. 6.1.

70. For an in-depth analysis of the correlations between the structuring of the _mappamundi_ and the rest of Guaman Poma's text, see Rolena Adorno's insightful studies, "Paradigm Lost: A Peruvian Indian Surveys Spanish Col-onial Society," _Studies in the Anthropology of Visual Communication_ 5, no. 2 (1979): 11–27, "On Pictorial Language and the Typology of Culture in a New World Chronicle," _Semiotica_ 36, nos. 1–2 (1981): 51–106, and _Guaman Poma: Writing and Resistance in Colonial Peru_ (Austin: University of Texas Press, 1986), 92ff.

71. John de Mandeville recognized, before Ricci, the conflict between the ideological and geometric dimensions of ethnic centers. Based on a pure geo-metric calculus, he questioned the idea that Jerusalem occupied the center of the earth:

> Car si nous considerons la largeur estimée de la terre entre les deux poles, il es certain que la Judee n'est pas au milieu, car alor elle serait sout le cercle equatorial, et le jour y serait l'egal de la nuit, et l'un et l'autre poles seraient a l'horizont, ce que n'est nullement le cas, parce que pour ceux qui habi-tent la Judee, le pole articque est tres au dessus de l'horizon. En sens contraire, si nous considerons la largeur estimee de la terre depues le Pa-radis terrestre, c'est-a-dire depues le lieu le plus digne et le plus eleve, jusqua son nadir, c'est-a-dire jusqu'au lieu qui lui es oppose sur la sphere de la terre come si la Judee etait aux antipodes du Paradis, il apparait qu'il n'en est pas ainsi parce que, alors, pour un voyageur allant de Judee au Paradis, la longeur de la route serait la meme, qui'il se dirige vers l'orient ou vers l'occident. Mais cela n'est ni vraisemblable ni vrai, ainsi que l'a prouve l'experience de beaucoup de gens. Quan a moi, il me semble que dans la susdite inscription prophetique, l'expression "au milieu de la terre", c'est a dire "pres du milieu de notre oecumene" peut etre interprete de la facons suivante, a savoir que la judee est exactemente situe entre le Paradis et les antipodes du Paradis, e qu'e lle est eloignee de 90 aussi bien du Paradis en direction de l'orient que des antipodes du Paradis en direction de l'occi-dent.
>
> Ou bien cette expression peut etre intepretee aisin, a savoir que Daivd, qui etait roid de Judee, a dit "au milieu de la terre" c'est a dire "dan la

principale cite de son royaume", Jerusalem, qui etait la cite royale et sacer-
dotale de la Judee. A moing que, peut etre, l'Esperit Saint, qui parlait para
la bouche du prophete, n'ait voulu donner a cette expression aucun sens
material ou spatial, mai exclusivemente un sens spirituel. De cette facon de
penser, je n'ecrirai rien pur le moment.

72. Pagden, *Fall of Natural Man;* Fabian, *Time and the Other.*

73. Juan Antonio Maravall, *Los factores de la idea de progreso en el Renacimiento español* (Madrid: Real Academia de Historia, 1963). Maravall opposes
the idea developed by Bury, according to which the idea of progress, an
eighteenth-century invention, cannot be found in the Renaissance (J. B.
Bury, *The Idea of Progress: An Inquiry into Its Origin and Growth* [London:
Macmillan, 1932]). Maravall also advances and opposes the more radical
claim that the Renaissance lacked a sense of progress developed by Nisbet in
Idea of Progress. In the context of my argument, the idea of progress emerges
in the domain of alphabetic writing, the idea of history and mapping in
conjunction with the denial of coevalness. Bury's and Nisbet's idea of progress seems to correspond very much to its nineteenth-century formulation.
One classical example is Lewis H. Morgan, "Ethical Periods," in the first
chapter of his *Ancient Society, or Researches in the Lines of Human Progress
from Savagery through Barbarism to Civilization* (Chicago: Charles H. Kerr,
1910). For a more recent discussion of the idea of progress, see David H.
Hopper, *Technology, Theology, and the Idea of Progress* (Louisville: John Knox
Press, 1991).

CHAPTER 6

1. Robert David Sack, *Human Territoriality: Its Theory and History* (New
York: Cambridge University Press, 1986), 28–51.

2. See, for instance, Jonathan T. Lanman, "The Religious Symbolism of
the T in T-O Maps," *Cartographica* 4 (1981): 18–22; David Woodward, "Reality, Symbolism, Time, and Space in Medieval World Maps," *Annals of the
Association of American Geographers* 75, no. 4 (1985): 510–21, and "Medieval
Mappaemundi."

3. A more detailed account of mapping, Columbus, and the age of
discovery is Kenneth Nebenzahl, *Atlas of Columbus and the Great Discoveries*
(Chicago: Rand McNally, 1990).

4. Edward Said, *Orientalism* (New York: Vintage, 1978).

5. Roger Barlow, *A Brief Summe of Geographie* (1540), ed. E. G. R.
Taylor (London: Hakluyt Society, 1932), a translation of Martín Fernández de
Enciso, *Suma de geografia* (Seville, 1519) (Madrid: Joyas Bibliográficas, 1948).

6. Francisco Hernández, *Historia natural de Nueva Espana,* ed. German
Somolinos (Mexico City: Universidad Nacional Autónoma de México, 1959),
3:296.

7. Michèle Duchet et al., *L'Amérique de Théodore de Bry: Une collection
de voyages protestante du XVIe. siècle* (Paris: Editions du Centre National de la
Recherche Scientifique, 1987).

8. The first edition comprised thirteen units of books (*pars*). A selection of the entire work has been published in French by Duchet et al., *L'Amérique;* and in English, by Michael Alexander, *Discovering the New World* (New York: Harper and Row, 1976).

9. See the Introduction for a detailed explanation of these notions.

10. Ambroise Paré, *Des monstres et prodige,* ed. Jean Ceard (Geneva: Librarie Droz, 1971), English translation by Janis L. Pallister, *On Monsters and Marvels* (Chicago: University of Chicago Press, 1982).

11. On Bry's uses of monsters interpreted as a way of placing Asia and America at the same level, see the interesting article by Daniel Defert, "Collections et nations au xvie. siecle," in Duchet et al., *L'Amerique,* 47–67. On the sixteenth-century theorization of monsters and prodigies, see Arnold I. Davidson, "The Horror of Monsters," in *The Boundaries of Humanity: Humans, Animals, Machines,* ed. James J. Sheehan and Morton Sosna (Berkeley and Los Angeles: University of California Press, 1991), 36–68. For a general background, see, of course, Jean Delumeau, *La peur en Occident: Une citte assigie* (Paris: Fayard, 1978), and *Le péché et la peur: La culpabilisation en Occident* (Paris: Fayard, 1983).

12. Between 1615 and 1621, Rubens devoted a great deal of time to painting hunting scenes in which horses, of course, played a great role. See David Rosand, "Rubens's Munich *Lion Hunt:* Its Sources and Significance," *Art Bulletin* 51 (1969): 29–41. I am thankful to Laurie Winter for calling this article to my attention.

13. Maps with paneled borders on three or four sides were popular toward the first half of the seventeenth century. They were issued separately or bound in large atlas volumes.

14. The distinction between space and place has been theorized, recently, by Tuan in *Space and Place.* Bill Hillier and Julienne Hanson have offered important insights on the logical organization of space from a perspective of urban planning in *The Social Logic of Space* (New York: Cambridge University Press, 1984). See also the issue of *Cultural Anthropology* (7 [1992]) devoted to *Space, Identity, and the Politics of Difference.*

15. Juan López de Velasco, *Geografía y descripción universal de las Indias* (Madrid, 1894).

16. Carbia, *La crónica oficial.*

17. Herrera y Tordesillas, *Historia general.*

18. Juan López de Velasco, *Descripción y demarcación de las Indias Occidentales* (1574), published for the first time in *Colección de documentos inéditos, relativos al descubrimiento, conquista y organización de las antiguas posesiones españolas de América y Oceanía, sacados de los Archivos del Reino, y muy especialmente del de Indias* (Madrid: José María Pérez, 1871), 405; italics mine.

19. Andreas Homen's *Universe ac navigabilis totius Terrarum orbis Descriptio* (1559) covers the same earth surface as López de Velasco's *Descripción* (1574). However, Homen is charting Atlantic and Pacific navigations rather than the possessions of the Spanish kingdom. A reproduction and description of Homen's planisphere can be found in Monique de la Roncière

and Michel Mollat Jourdin's *Les portulans: Cartes marines du xiiième au xviième siècle* (Fribourg, Switzerland: Nathan, 1984), plate 55, 235–36.

20. Velasco, *Descripción*, 407.

21. Although I am not exploring this aspect here, it should be remembered that one important function of maps is finding one's way. The so-called portolands are precisely of this kind. See Roncière and Jourdin, *Les portulans*.

22. Alonso de Santa Cruz, *Obra cosmográfica* (1560), ed. Mariano de la Cuesta (Madrid: Consejo Superior de Investigaciones Científicas, 1983), 288.

23. German Latorre, *La enseñanza de la geografía en la Casa de Contratación* (Madrid: Establecimiento Tipográfico de Jaime Rates Martin, 1915); E. L. Stevenson, "The Geographic Activities of the Casa de Contratación," *Annals of the Association of American Geographers* 7, no. 2 (1927): 39–60; Ernesto Schafer, *El consejo real y supremo de las Indias: Su historia, organización y labor administrativa hasta la terminación de la Casa de Austria*, 2 vols. (Seville: Publicaciones del Centro de Estudios de Historia de América, 1935).

24. O'Gorman, *La invención de América*, 28.

25. M. B. Parkes, "The Literacy of the Laity," in *The Medieval World*, ed. David Daiches and A. Thorlby, 555–77 (London: Aldous, 1973). For more detail, see his *Scribes, Scripts, and Readers: Studies in the Communication, Presentation, and Dissemination of Medieval Texts* (London: Hambledon Press, 1991); José Antonio Maravall, "La formación de la conciencia estamental de los letrados," *Revista de estudios políticos* 70 (1953), reprinted as "Los 'hombres de saber' o letrados y la formación de la conciencia estamental," in *Estudios de historia del pensamiento español* (Madrid: Ediciones de Cultura Hispánica, 1967), 345–80; Michael T. Clanchy, "Looking Back from the Invention of Printing," in *Literacy in Historical Perspective*, ed. Daniel P. Resnick (Washington, D.C.: Library of Congress, 1983), 7–22, and *From Memory to Written Record: England 1066–1307* (London: Edward Arnold, 1979).

26. Gil Fernández, *Panorama*, 231–98; Maravall, "Los 'hombres de saber.'"

27. Maravall, "Los 'hombres de saber,'" 334.

28. Malagón-Barceló, "The Role of 'Letrado.'"

29. Cline, "*Relaciones Geográficas*, 1577–1586," "*Relaciones* of Spain," and "The *Relaciones Geográficas* of the Spanish Indies, 1577–1648," in Cline, *Guide to Ethnohistorical Sources*, 12:183–242.

30. Mignolo, "Cartas," and "El mandato"; and Serge Gruzinski, *La colonization de l'imaginarie* (Paris: Gallimard, 1988), 101–38.

31. Mignolo, "El mandato," 456–62.

32. Quoted by Cline, "Relaciones geográficas, 1577–1648," 12:233.

33. Teuber, "Europäisches und Amerikanisches"; Mignolo; "Colonization of Amerindian Languages."

34. For a modern edition of this text, see Paul Kirchhoff, Lina Odena Guemes, and Luis Reyes, eds. and trans., *Historia tolteca-chichemeca* (Mexico City: CISINAH, 1976). For a study of the maps of Cuauhtinchán, see Bente Bittman Simons, *Los mapas de Cuauhtinchán y la historia tolteca-chichimeca*

(Mexico City: Instituto Nacional de Antropología e Historia, 1968); and Keiko Yoneda, *Los mapas de Cuauhtinchan y la historia cartográfica prehispánica* (Mexico City: Archivo General de la Nación, 1981).

35. John B. Glass, "A Survey of Native Middle American Pictorial Manuscripts," in Cline, *Handbook,* 14:3–80; and John B. Glass and Donald Robertson, "A Census of Native Middle American Pictorial Manuscripts," in Cline, *Handbook,* 14:81–252; Eulalia Guzmán, "The Art of Map-Making among the Ancient Mexicans," *Imago Mundi* 3 (1939): 1–6.

36. More examples of these kinds of "maps" can be found in Robertson, *Mexican Manuscript Painting,* 134–41, 179–82, and "The 'pinturas' (maps) of the *Relaciones geográficas,* with a catalog," in Cline, *Guide to Ethnohistorical Sources,* 12:243–78.

37. See, for instance, Ducio Sacchi, "Imagen y percepción del territorio según los mapas mixtecos (1595–1617)," *Historia* 15 (1986): 19–30; Serge Gruzinski, "Colonial Indian Maps in Sixteenth-Century Mexico," *Res* 13 (1987): 46–61; Joyce Baddel Bailey, "Map of Texupa (Oaxaca, 1579): A Study of Form and Meaning," *Art Bulletin* 54 (1972): 452–72; Arthur G. Miller, "Transformations of Time and Space: Oaxaca, México, circa 1500–1700," in *Images of Memory: On Remembering and Representation,* ed. S. Kuchler and W. Melion, 141–75 (Washington, D.C.: Smithsonian Institution Press, 1991).

38. Angel García Conde, "Aztlán y Tenochtitlán, o sea breve ensayo paleográfico de las peregrinaciones Nahoas," *Memorias de la Sociedad Científica Antonio Alzate* 45 (1926): 309–52.

39. Bernardo García Martínez, *Los pueblos de la sierra: El poder y el espacio entre los indios del norte de Puebla hasta 1700* (Mexico City: El Colegio de México, 1987).

40. Paul Radin, *The Sources and Authenticity of the History of the Ancient Mexicans* (Berkeley: University Publications of American Archeology and Ethnology, 1920), 17:1.

41. Christian Duverger, *L'origine des Azteques* (Paris: Editions du Seuil, 1983).

42. Simons, *Los mapas de Cuauhtinchán;* Yoneda, *Los mapas de Cuauhtinchán.*

43. Cuauhtinchán is a town adjacent to Puebla and the place of origin of both the *mapas* and the *Historia. Historia* is not, of course, the original name of this text. The Nahuatl name employed was *xiutlapoualli* or "counting of the years." The so-called *mapa* no. 1 traced the Chichimec conquests. *Mapa* no. 2, like the *Mapa Sigüenza* and the *Tira,* tracked the peregrination from Chicomoztoc (another name for Aztlán) to Cuauhtinchán. *Mapa* no. 3 traces community migrations, and *mapa* no. 4 draws the boundaries of the *señorio* of Cuauhtinchán.

44. According to the typology established by Woodward in "Reality, Symbolism."

45. Carmen Blacker and Michael Loewe, eds., *Ancient Cosmologies* (London: Allen and Unwin, 1975).

46. Ixtlilxochitl, *Obras históricas,* 2:295–96.

47. Louis Jacobs, "Jewish Cosmology," in Blacker and Loewe, *Ancient Cosmologies,* 66–84.

48. Charles Gibson, *The Aztecs under the Spanish Rules: A History of the Indians of the Valley of Mexico, 1519–1810* (Stanford: Stanford University Press, 1964); Nancy M. Farriss, *Maya Society under Colonial Rules: The Collective Enterprise of Survival* (Princeton: Princeton University Press, 1984); Karen Spaulding, *Huarochiri: An Andean Society under Inca and Spanish Rules* (Stanford: Stanford University Press, 1984); Birgit Scharlau and Mark Munzel, *Quelqay: Mundliche Kultur und Schrifttradition bei Indianeren Lateinamerikas* (Frankfurt am Main: Campus Verlag, 1987); Gruzinksi, *La colonization.*

49. Gossen, *Chamulas,* and Gary Gossen, ed., *Symbol and Meaning beyond the Closed Community: Essays in Mesoamerican Ideas* (Austin: University of Texas Press, 1986).

50. Cline, "*Relaciones geográficas, 1577–1586,*" 366; italics mine.

51. Marshack, *The Roots of Civilization;* Lanman, "Religious Symbolism."

52. René Acuña, ed., *Relaciones geográficas del siglo xvi: México* (Mexico City: Universidad Nacional Autónoma de México, 1985), 6:159.

53. Gisela von Wobeser, *La formación de la hacienda en la época colonial* (Mexico City: Universidad Nacional Autónoma de México, 1983); Bailey, "Map of Texupa."

54. *Tahuantinsuyu,* let's remember, means "the four corners of the world unified among themselves." More specifically, *tasa* means "four," *suyo* means "place," and *ntin* means the "unification of what is different." The Spaniards translated it as "empire." Compare the notion of *altepetl,* the organization of land, space, and memory, in the Nahuatl-speaking world.

55. Urton, *Crossroads,* and Gossen, *Chamulas.*

56. Thomas Abercrombie, "To Be Indian, to Be Bolivian: 'Ethnic' and 'National' Discourses of Identity," in Urban and Sherzer, *Nation-States and Indians.*

57. Arthur Preston Whitaker, *The Western Hemisphere Idea: Its Rise and Decline* (Ithaca: Cornell University Press, 1954); Lesler D. Langley, *America and the Americas: The United States in the Western Hemisphere* (Athens: University of Georgia Press, 1989).

58. For a particular example of this case, see José Piedra, "The Game of Critical Arrival," *Diacritics* 19 (1989): 34–61; Fernando Coronil, "Discovering America Again: The Politics of Selfhood in the Age of Post-Colonial Empires," *Dispositio* 36–38 (1989): 315–31.

Afterword

The final version of the conclusion was written toward the end of the fall semester 1992, while I was teaching an interdisciplinary graduate seminar, Beyond Occidentalism: Rethinking How the West Was Born, at the University of Michigan with Fernando Coronil. Since parts of this book were discussed in the seminar, I benefited enormously from the discussion. I am indebted to Coronil as well as to the twenty-four students enrolled, whose enthusiasm, commitments, and critical skills taught me to see my own project in a new light.

1. Marshall Berman, *All That Is Solid Melts into Air: The Experience of Modernity* (New York: Simon and Schuster, 1982), 15.

2. Perry Anderson, "Modernidad y revolución," in *El debate modernidad/post-modernidad,* ed. Nicolás Casullo, 92–116 (Buenos Aires: Punto Sur, 1989).

3. I am thinking of Cornel West's persuasive articulation of the politics of intellectual inquiry, in his "New Cultural Politics."

4. Claude Lévi-Strauss, *Tristes tropiques* (Paris: Flammarion, 1958).

5. Goldberg's *Writing Matters* makes a case for seeing the philosophy of (hand)writing in the English Renaissance within the framework advanced by Derrida. I take a different road, according to which the concept of writing, as articulated by Nebrija, is no longer a surrogate of speech but a way of taming the voice.

6. For more details about this position, see Elizabeth H. Boone and Walter D. Mignolo, eds., *Writing without Words: Literacies in Mesoamerica and the Andes* (Durham, N.C.: Duke University Press, 1994).

7. Harvey Graff, *Literacy in History: An Interdisciplinary Research Bibliography* (New York: Garland, 1981).

8. Sylvia Scribner, "Literacy in Three Metaphors," *Journal of American Education* 93 (1986): 6–21.

9. Scribner, "Literacy in Three Metaphors," 16.

10. Marshall McLuhan, *Understanding Media: The Extension of Man* (London: Sphere Books, 1967), 93–94.

11. Ruth Finnegan, "The Myth of Literacy" (paper presented at the conference Literacy, Culture, and Mind, University of Michigan, October 1991).

12. See Mignolo, "Darker Side."

13. José Antonio Maravall, *Los factores de la Idea de Progreso en el Renacimiento español* (Madrid: Real Academia de la Historia, 1963).

14. Bernice Hamilton, *Political Thought in Sixteenth-Century Spain* (Oxford: Oxford University Press, 1963); Otis H. Green, *Spain and the Western Tradition* (Madison: University of Wisconsin Press, 1968), vol. 3.

15. Leopoldo Zea, *América en la historia* (Mexico City: Fondo de Cultura Económica, 1958), and *Discurso.*

16. Fernando Coronil, "Beyond Occidentalism" (paper presented at the conference Power: Thinking across Disciplines, University of Michigan, January 1992), *Critical Inquiry,* forthcoming.

17. Arturo Ardao, *El nombre y la idea de América Latina* (Caracas: Instituto Andres Bello, 1978).

18. Arthur Preston Whitaker, *The Western Hemisphere Idea: Its Rise and Decline* (Ithaca, N.Y.: Cornell University Press, 1954).

19. Francis M. Rogers, *The Quest for Eastern Christians: Travels and Rumors in the Age of Discovery* (Minneapolis: University of Minnesota Press, 1962).

20. Farriss, *Maya Society.*

21. Richard Rorty, *Philosophy and the Mirror of Nature* (Princeton, N.J.: Princeton University Press, 1981).

22. A recent overview is provided by the articles collected in Nicholas B. Dirks, ed., *Colonialism and Culture* (Ann Arbor: University of Michigan Press, 1992).

23. George Lamming, "The Occasion for Speaking," in *The Pleasures of Exile* (1960; rpt. Ann Arbor: University of Michigan Press, 1992), 2–50; italics mine.

24. While in the Introduction of this book I exploited some of the ideas advanced by Humberto Maturana and Francisco Varela, in this conclusion I mainly benefited from Rosch et al., *The Body's Mind*.

Bibliography

Aarsleff, Hans. "An Outline of Language-Origins Theory since the Renaissance." In *From Locke to Saussure: Essays on the Study of Language and Intellectual History*. Minneapolis: University of Minnesota Press, 1982.

———. "The Tradition of Condillac: The Problem of the Origin of Language in the Eighteenth Century and the Debate in the Berlin Academy before Herder." In *From Locke to Saussure: Essays on the Study of Language and Intellectual History*. Minneapolis: University of Minnesota Press, 1982.

Abbot, Don Paul. "The Ancient Word: Rhetoric in Aztec Culture." *Rhetorica* (1987): 251–64.

Abercrombie, Thomas. "To Be Indian, to Be Bolivian: 'Ethnic' and 'National' Discourses of Identity." In *Nation-States and Indians in Latin America*, ed. Greg Urban and Joel Sherzer. Austin: University of Texas Press, 1991.

Acosta, José de. *Historia Natural y Moral de las Indias*. 1590. New edition introduction by E. O'Gorman. Mexico: F.C.E., 1940.

Acuña, René, ed. *Relaciones geográficas del siglo xvi: México*. Mexico City: Universidad Nacional Autónoma de México, 1985.

Adorno, Rolena. *Guaman Poma: Writing and Resistance in Colonial Peru*. Austin: University of Texas Press, 1986.

———. "On Pictorial Language and the Typology of Culture in a New World Chronicle." *Semiotica* 36, nos. 1–2 (1981): 51–106.

———. "Paradigm Lost: A Peruvian Indian Surveys Spanish Colonial Society." *Studies in the Anthropology of Visual Communications* 5, no. 2 (1979): 11–27.

Aguirre Beltrán, Gonzalo. *Lenguas vernáculas: Su uso y desuso en la enseñanza*. Mexico City: Ediciones de la Casa Chata, 1968.

Aldrete, Bernardo José. *Del origen y principio de la lengua castellana o romance que oi se usa en España*. Ed. Lidio Nieto Jiménez. Madrid: Consejo Superior de Investigaciones Científicas, 1972–75.

———. *Varias antiguidades de España, Africa y otras provincias*. Amberes: A Costa de Iuan Hasrey, 1614.

Alexander, Micha. *Discovering the New World*. New York: Harper and Row, 1976.

Alibhai, Yasmin. "Community Whitewash." *Guardian*, January 23, 1989.

Alva Ixtlilxóchitl, Fernando de. *Obras históricas*. Ed. Edmundo O'Gorman. Mexico City: Universidad Nacional Autónoma de México, 1975.

Amin, Samir. *Eurocentrism*. Trans. Russell Moore. New York: Monthly Review Press, 1989.

———. *El eurocentrismo: Crítica de una ideología*. Trans. Rosa Cusminsky de Cendrero. Mexico City: Siglo XXI, 1989.

Amselle, Jean-Loup. *Logiques métisses. Anthropologie de l'identité en Afrique et ailleurs* (Paris: Payot, 1990).

Anderson, A., et al. *Beyond the Codices: The Nahuatl View of Colonial Mexico*. Berkeley and Los Angeles: University of California Press, 1976.

Anderson, Perry. "Modernidad y revolución." In *El debate modernidad/postmodernidad*. Comp. Nicolás Casullo, 92–116. Buenos Aires: Punto Sur, 1989.

Andrews, E. A. *A Latin Dictionary*. Revised by Charlton T. Lewis and Charles Short. Oxford: Clarendon Press, 1980.

Anzaldúa, Gloria. *Borderlands/La frontera: The New Mestiza*. San Francisco: Spinsters/Aunt Lute, 1987.

Appiah, Kwame Anthony. "Topologies of Nativism." In *In My Father's House: Africa in the Philosophy of Culture*. London: Oxford University Press, 1992.

Ardao, Arturo. *El nombre y la idea de América Latina*. Caracas: Instituto Andres Bello, 1978.

Arnheim, Rudolf. *The Power of the Center: A Study of Composition in the Visual Arts*. 2d ed. Berkeley and Los Angeles: University of California Press, 1988.

Artaza, Elena. *El ars narrandi en el siglo XVI español: Teoría y práctica*. Bilbao: Universidad de Deusto, 1989.

Arzápalo Marín, Ramón. "The Indian Book in Colonial Yucatán." Paper presented at the conference The Book in the Americas. John Carter Brown Library, Brown University, June 18–21, 1987.

Ascensio, Eugenio. "La lengua compañera del imperio: Historia de una idea de Nebrija en España y Portugal." *Revista de Filología Española* 43 (1960): 399–413.

Ascher, Marcia, and Robert Ascher. *Code of the Quipu: A Study in Media, Mathematics, and Culture*. Ann Arbor: University of Michigan Press, 1981.

Avalle-Arce, Juan Bautista. "Las memorias de Gonzálo Fernández de Oviedo." In *Dintorno de un época dorada*. Madrid: Porrúa Turanzas, 1978.

Aveni, Anthony. *Empires of Time: Calendars, Clocks, and Cultures*. New York: Basic Books, 1989.

Bacon, Francis. *The Advancement of Learning*. 1605. Vol. 2 of *Complete Works of Francis Bacon*. Ed. J. Spedding, R. L. Ellis, and D. D. Heath. London, 1857–74.

———. *De Augmentis Scientiarum*. 1623. Vol. 1 of *Complete Works*. London, 1857–74.

———. *Novum Organum*. 1620. Vol. 4 of *Complete Works*.

Bacon, Roger. *The Opus Majus of Roger Bacon*. Trans. R. B. Burke. New York: Russell and Russell, 1962.

Bagrow, Leo, and R. A. Skelton. *History of Cartography*. Cambridge: Cambridge University Press, 1964.

Bailey, Joyce Baddel. "Map of Texupa (Oaxaca, 1579): A Study of Form and Meaning." *Art Bulletin* 54 (1972): 452–72.

Bakhtin, M. M. *The Dialogic Imagination: Four Essays*. Ed. Michael Holquist. Trans. Caryl Emerson and Michael Holquist. Austin: University of Texas Press, 1981.

———. *Speech Genres and Other Late Essays*. Trans. V. W. McGee. Austin: University of Texas Press, 1986.

Balandier, George. "The Colonial Situation: A Theoretical Approach." In *The Sociology of Black Africa: Social Dynamics in Central Africa*. Trans. D. Garman. New York: Praeger Publishers, 1970.

Barlow, Roger. *A Brief Summe of Geographie*. 1540. Ed. E. G. R. Taylor. London: Hakluyt Society, 1932. A translation of Martín Fernández de Enciso's *Suma de geografía*. Seville, 1519. Madrid: Joyas Bibliográficas, 1948.

Baron, Hans. *From Petrarch to Leonardo Bruni: Studies in Humanistic and Political Literature*. Chicago: Newbury Library and University of Chicago Press, 1968.

Bastien, Joseph W. *Mountain of the Condor: Metaphor and Ritual in an Andean Ayllu*. Minneapolis: West Publishing, 1978.

Bauman, Richard, and Joel Sherzer, eds. *Exploration in the Ethnography of Speaking*. Cambridge: Cambridge University Press, 1974.

Becker, Alton. "Text-Building, Epistemology, and Aesthetics in Javanese Shadow Theatre." *Dispositio* 13–14 (1980): 137–68.

Ben-Amos, Dan. "Analytical Categories and Ethnic Genres." In *Folklore Genres*. Austin: University of Texas Press, 1976.

Berman, Marshall. *All That Is Solid Melts into Air: The Experience of Modernity*. New York: Simon and Schuster, 1982.

Besomi, Ottavio, and Marigneli Regolisi. *Lorenzo Valla e l'humanesimo italiano*. Padova: Editrice Antenore, 1986.

Bhabha, Homi K. "The Other Question: Difference, Discrimination, and the Discourse of Colonialism." In *Literature, Politics, and Theory: Papers from the Essex Conference, 1976–1984*, ed. F. Baker et al., 148–72. New York: Methuen, 1986.

Bibliografía sobre la castellanización de la grupos indígenas de la República Mexicana. Vol. 2. Mexico City: Universidad Nacional Autónoma de México, 1985.

Bickerton, Derek. *Language and Species*. Chicago: University of Chicago Press, 1990.

Biondo, Flavio. *Historiarum ab inclinatione romanorum decades*. Venice, 1484.

Black Robe. 100 min. Distributed by Samuel Goldwyn, Los Angeles, 1991.

Blacker, Carmen, and Michael Loewe, eds. *Ancient Cosmologies*. London: Allen and Unwin, 1975.

Bleiberg, German, comp. *Antología de elogios de la lengua española*. Madrid: Ediciones de Cultura Hispánica, 1951.

Bloch, Maurice. "Literacy and Enlightenment." In *Literacy and Society,* ed. Karen Schousboe and Mogens Trolle Larsen, 15–37. Copenhagen: Akademiske Forlag, 1989.

———, ed. *Political Language and Oratory in Traditional Society.* London: Academic Press, 1975.

Bodin, Jean. *Methodus ad facilem historiarum cognitionem.* Paris: M. Iuuenem, 1566.

Boone, Elizabeth H. "Aztec Pictorial Histories: Record Keeping without Words." In *Writing without Words: Literacies in Mesoamerica and the Andes,* ed. Elizabeth H. Boone and Walter D. Mignolo, 45–66. Durham: Duke University Press, 1994.

———. "Migration Histories as Ritual Performances." In *To Change Place: Aztec Ceremonial Landscapes,* ed. David Carrasco, 121–51. Niwot: Colorado University Press, 1991.

Boone, Elizabeth H., and Walter D. Mignolo, eds. *Writing without Words: Alternative Literacies in Mesoamerica and the Andes.* Durham, N.C.: Duke University Press: 1994.

Boturini Benaducci, Bernardo. *Idea de una nueva historia general de la America septentrional.* 1746. Paris: Centre de Documentation "Andre Thevet," 1933.

Bourdieu, Pierre. *La distinction: Critique sociale du jugement.* Paris: Minuit, 1979.

Brandon, S. G. F. "The Holy Book, the Holy Tradition, and the Holy Ikon." In *Holy Book and Holy Tradition,* ed. F. F. Bruce and E. G. Rupp, 1–20. Grand Rapids: William B. Eerdmans, 1968.

Brathwaite, Edward K. *History of the Voice: The Development of National Language in Anglophone Caribbean Poetry.* London: New Beacon, 1984.

Brenner, Robert. "The Origins of Capitalist Development: A Critique of Neo-Smithian Marxism." *New Left Review* 104 (1977): 25–93.

Bricker, Victoria. "The Ethnographic Context of Some Traditional Mayan Speech Genres." In *Exploration in the Ethnography of Speaking,* ed. Richard Bauman and Joel Sherzer, 369–87. Cambridge: Cambridge University Press, 1974.

———. "Yucatecan Maya Literature." In *Literatures.* Supplement to the *Handbook of Middle American Indians.* Austin: University of Texas Press, 1985.

Broda, Johanna. "Astronomy, *Cosmovision,* and Ideology in Pre-Hispanic Mesoamerica." In *Ethnoastronomy and Archaeoastronomy in the American Tropics,* ed. Anthony Aveni and Gary Urton, 81–110. New York: New York Academy of Science, 1982.

Brundage, Burr Cartwright. *The Fifth Sun: Aztec Gods, Aztec World.* Austin: University of Texas Press, 1979.

———. *The Two Heavens, Two Earths: An Essay Contrasting the Aztecs and the Incas.* Albuquerque: University of New Mexico Press, 1975.

Burland, C. A. *The Four Directions of Time: An Account of Page One of Codex Féjérvary-Mayer.* Santa Fe: Museum of Navajo Ceremonial Art, 1950.

Burns, Robert, ed. *Emperor of Culture: Alfonso X the Learned of Castile and His Thirteenth-Century Renaissance,* Philadelphia: University of Pennsylvania Press, 1990.

Bury, J. B. *The Idea of Progress: An Inquiry into Its Origin and Growth.* New York: Macmillan, 1932.

Cabrera de Córdoba, Luis. *De historia para entenderla y escribirla.* 1611. Ed. Santiago Montero Díaz. Madrid: Instituto de Estudios Políticos, 1948.

Calame-Griaule, Geneviève. *Ethnologie et langage: La parole chez le Dogon.* Paris: Gallimard, 1965.

Calneck, Edward. "The Internal Structure of Tenochtitlan." In *The Valley of Mexico,* ed. Eric Wolf, 287–302. Albuquerque: University of New Mexico Press, 1976.

Calvet, Louis-Jean. *La guerre des langues et les politiques linguistiques.* Paris: Payot, 1987.

———. *Linguistique et colonialisme: Petit traité de glottophagie.* Paris: Payot, 1974.

Cameron, Nigel, and Brian Blake. *Peking: A Tale of Three Cities.* New York: Harper and Row, 1965.

Camillo, Ottavio di. *El humanismo castellano del siglo XV.* Valencia: Fernando Torres, 1976.

Carbia, Rómulo. *La crónica oficial de las Indias Occidentales: Estudio histórico y crítico acerca de la historiografía mayor de Hispano América en los siglos XVI a XVIII, con una introducción sobre la crónica oficial de Castilla.* Buenos Aires: Ediciones Buenos Aires, 1940.

Carlson, John. "A Geometric Model for the Interpretation of Mesoamerican Sites: An Essay in Cross-Cultural Comparison." In *Mesoamerican Sites and World-Views,* ed. Elizabeth P. Benson, 143–216. Washington, D.C.: Dumbarton Oaks Research Library and Collections, 1981.

Carochi, Horacio. *Arte de la lengua Mexicana.* Mexico City: Juan Ruyz, 1540.

Carrasco, David. "City as Symbol in Aztec Thought: The Clues from the Codex Mendoza." *History of Religions* 20 (1981): 199–223.

Carreño, Alberto María. *La real y Pontificia Universidad de México.* 2 vols. Mexico City: Universidad Nacional Autónoma de México, 1963.

Casas, Bartolomé de las. *Apologética historia sumaria,* ed. Edmundo O'Gorman. Mexico City: Instituto de Investigaciones Históricas, 1967.

———. *Historia de las Indias.* Mexico City: Fondo de Cultura Económica, 1965.

Castillo, Carmen. "La epistola como género literario: De la antigüedad a la edad media latina." *Estudios Clásicos* 18 (1974): 427–42.

Cerutti Guldberg, Horacio. *Filosofía de la liberación latinoamericana.* Mexico City: Fondo de Cultura Económica, 1983.

Cevallos-Candau, Francisco Javier, et al., eds. *Coded Encounters: Writing, Gender and Ethnicity in Colonial Latin America.* Amherst: University of Massachusetts Press, 1994.

Ch'en, Kenneth. "Matteo Ricci's Contribution to, and Influence on, Geographical Knowledge in China." *Journal of the American Oriental Society* 59 (1939): 325–509.

Chartier, Roger. "Distinction et divulgation: La civilité et ses livres." In *Lectures et lecteurs dans la France de d'Ancien Régime*. Paris: Seuil, 1987.

———. "Intellectual History or Sociocultural History? The French Trajectories." In *Modern European Intellectual History: Reappraisal and New Perspectives,* ed. D. La Capra and S. L. Kaplan. Ithaca: Cornell University Press, 1982.

Chavez, Adrián I., trans. *Pop Wuj: Libro del tiempo*. Buenos Aires: Ediciones Sol, 1987.

Chimalpaín Cuahtehuanitzin, Francisco de San Antón Muñón. *Relaciones originales de Chalco Amaquemecan*. Ed. and trans. Silva Rendón. Mexico City: Fondo de Cultura Económica, 1982.

Ciudad Real, Antonio de. *Relación breve y verdadera de algunas cosas de las muchas que sucedieron al padre Fray Alonso de Ponce*. Madrid: Imprenta de la Viuda de Calero, 1873.

Clairborne, Robert. *The Birth of Writing*. New York: Time-Life, 1974.

Clammer, J. R. *Literacy and Social Change: A Case Study of Fiji*. Leiden: E. Brill, 1976.

Clanchy, Michael T. *From Memory to Written Record: England 1066–1307*. London: Edward Arnold, 1979.

———. "Looking Back from the Invention of Printing." In *Literacy in Historical Perspective,* ed. Daniel P. Resnick, 7–22. Washington, D.C.: Library of Congress, 1983.

Cliff, Michelle. *The Land of Look Behind*. New York: Firebrand Books, 1985.

Clifford, James. *The Predicament of Culture: Twentieth-Century Ethnography, Literature, and Art*. Cambridge: Harvard University Press, 1988.

Clifford, James, and George E. Marcus, eds. *Writing Culture: The Poetics and Politics of Ethnography*. Berkeley and Los Angeles: University of California Press, 1986.

Cline, Howard. "The *Relaciones Geográficas* of Spain, New Spain, and the Spanish Indies: An Annotated Bibliography." In *Guide to Ethnohistorical Sources,* ed. Howard Cline, vols. 12–15 of *Handbook of Middle American Indians,* 12:370–95. Austin: University of Texas Press, 1972.

———. "The *Relaciones Geográficas* of Spanish Indies, 1577–1586." *Hispanic American Historical Review* 3 (1964): 341–74.

Cochrane, Erich W. *Florence in the Forgotten Centuries, 1527–1800: A History of Florence and the Florentines in the Age of the Grand Dukes*. Chicago: University of Chicago Press, 1973.

———. *Historians and Historiography in the Italian Renaissance*. Chicago: University of Chicago Press, 1981.

Coe, Michael D. *The Maya Scribe and His World*. New York: Grolier Club, 1973.

Coggins, Clemency Chase. "The Birth of the Baktun at Tikal and Seibal." In *Vision and Revision in Maya Studies,* ed. Flora S. Clancy and Peter D. Harrison, 77–97. Albuquerque: University of New Mexico Press, 1990.

————. "The Shape of Time: Some Political Implications of the Four-Part Figure." *American Antiquity* 45, no. 4 (1980): 727–39.

————. "The Zenith, the Mountain, the Center, and the Sea." In *Ethnoastronomy and Archaeoastronomy in the American Tropics,* ed. Anthony Aveni and Gary Urton, 111–24. New York: New York Academy of Sciences, 1982.

Cole, Michael D. *The Maya Scribe and His World.* New York: Grolier Club, 1973.

Colegios y profesores Jesuitas que enseñaron Latín en Nueva España (1572–1767). Mexico City: Universidad Nacional Autónoma de México, 1979.

Collison, Robert L. *Encyclopaedias: Their History throughout the Ages.* New York: Hafner, 1964.

Condillac, Etienne Bonnot de. *Traité des sensations.* 1754. Paris: Fayard, 1984.

Contreras García, Irma. *Bibiografía sobre la castellanización de los grupos indígenas de la República Mexicana.* Vol. 2. Mexico City: Universidad Nacional Autónoma de México, 1985.

Coronil, Fernando. "Beyond Occidentalism." Paper presented at the conference Power: Thinking across Disciplines, University of Michigan, January 1992 *Critical Inquiry,* forthcoming.

————. "Discovering America Again: The Politics of Selfhood in the Age of Post-Colonial Empires," *Dispositio* 14 (1989): 315–31.

————. "Transculturation and the Politics of Theory: Countering the Center, Cuban Counterpoint." Introduction to the English translation of Fernando Ortiz's *Cuban Counterpoint: Tobacco and Sugar.* Durham: Duke University Press, forthcoming.

Cortés, Hernán. *Hernan Cortes: Letters from Mexico.* Trans. Anthony Pagden. New York: Grossman, 1971.

Coseriu, Eugenio. "El español de América y la unidad del idioma." In *I Simposio de Filología Iberoamericana.* Zaragoza: Libros Portico, 1990.

Cotroneo, Girolamo. *I trattatisti dell'Ars Historica.* Napoli: Francesco Giannini Editore, 1971.

Cristofani, M. "L'alphabeto etrusco." In *Lingue e dialetti,* vol. 6 of *Popoli e civilta dell'Italia antica.* Rome: Biblioteca di Storia Patria, 1978.

————. "Recent Advances in Etruscan Epigraphy and Language." In *Italy before the Romans,* 378–80. London: Academic Press, 1979.

Cruz, Martín de la. *Libellus de medicinalibus indorum herbis.* 1552. Trans. Juan Badiano. Mexico City: Instituto Mexicano del Seguro Social, 1964.

Curtius, Ernst Robert. *European Literature and the Latin Middle Ages.* Trans. Willard R. Trask. 1948. Reprint, New York: Pantheon Books, 1953.

Davidson, Arnold I. "The Horror of Monsters." In *The Boundaries of Humanity: Humans, Animals, Machines,* ed. James J. Sheehan and Morton Sosna, 36–68. Berkeley and Los Angeles: University of California Press, 1991.

De Kerchove, Derrick, and Charles J. Lumdsen, eds. *The Alphabet and the Brain: The Lateralization of Writing.* London: Verlag, 1988.

d'Elia, Pasquale, ed. *Il mappamondo cinese del p. Matteo Ricci.* Pechino, 1602. Vatican City: Biblioteca Apostolica Vaticana, 1938.

Defert, Daniel. "Collections et nations au xvie. siècle." In *L'Amerique de Theodore de Bry: Une collection de voyages protestants du xvie siècle,* ed. Michèle Duchet, 47–67. Paris: Editions du Centre Nationale de la Recherche Scientifique, 1987.

Della Corte, Francesco. *Varrone, il terzo gran lume romano.* Genoa: Francesco M. Bozzi, 1954.

Delumeau, Jean. *Le péché et la peur: La culpabilisation en Occident.* Paris: Fayard, 1983.

———. *La peur en Occident: Une citté assigie.* Paris: Fayard, 1978.

Derrida, Jacques. *De la grammatologie.* Paris: Minuit, 1967.

———. *Marges de la philosophie.* Paris: Minuit, 1972.

———. "Semiologie et grammatologie." In *Essays in Semiotics,* ed. Julia Kristeva, J. Rey-Debove, and D. J. Umiker, 11–27. The Hague: Mouton, 1971.

Dilke, O. A. W. "Maps in the Service of the State: Roman Cartography to the End of the Augustan Era." In *The History of Cartography,* ed. John B. Harley and David Woodward, 201–11. Chicago: University of Chicago Press, 1987.

———. *The Roman Land Surveyors: An Introduction to the Agrimensores.* Newton Abbot: David and Charles, 1971.

Diringer, David. *The Book before Printing: Ancient, Medieval, and Oriental.* 1953. Reprint, New York: Dover Publications, 1982.

———. *Writing.* New York: F. A. Praeger, 1962.

Dirks, Nicholas B., ed. *Colonialism and Culture.* Ann Arbor: University of Michigan Press, 1992.

Dougherty, James. *The Fivesquare City: The City in the Religious Imagination.* West Lafayette, Ind.: University of Notre Dame Press, 1980.

Dover, R. V. H., Katherine Seibold, and J. H. McDowell, eds. *Andean Cosmologies through Time: Persistence and Emergence.* Bloomington: Indiana University Press, 1992.

Duchet, Michèle. *Anthropologie e historie au siècle des lumières.* Paris: Maspero, 1971.

Duchet, Michèle, et al. *L'Amérique de Théodore de Bry: Une collection de voyages protestante du xvie siècle.* Paris: Editions du Centre National de la Recherche Scientifique, 1987.

Dundes, Alan. "Metafolklore and Oral Literacy Criticism." *Monist* 50, no. 4 (1966): 505–16.

Dunne, George H. *Generations of Giants: The Story of the Jesuits in China in the Last Decades of the Ming Dynasty.* West Lafayette, Ind.: University of Notre Dame Press, 1962.

Durán, Diego. *Book of the Gods and Rites and the Ancient Calendar.* 1581. Trans. and ed. Fernando Horcasitas and Doris Heyden. Norman: University of Oklahoma Press, 1971.

Dürer, Albrecht. *Institutionem geometricarum libris.* Paris, 1535.

Dussel, Enrique. "Eurocentrism and Modernity." *boundary 2,* 20/3 (1993): 65–76.

———. *Philosophy of Liberation.* Trans. Aquilina Martinez and Christine Morkovsky. New York: Orbis Book, 1985.

————. *La producción teórica de Marx: Un comentario a los Grundrisse.* Mexico City: Siglo XXI, 1985.

————. "Teología de la liberación y marxismo." *Cuadernos Americanos,* n.s., 12, no. 1 (1989): 138–59.

Duverger, Christian. *L'origine des Azteques.* Paris: Seuil, 1983.

Ecles, John C. *Evolution of the Brain: Creation of the Self.* London: Routledge, 1989.

Edmonson, Munro S., ed. and trans. *The Ancient Future of the Itza: The Book of Chilam Balam of Tizimin.* Austin: University of Texas Press, 1982.

————, ed. *Heaven Born Merida and Its Destiny: The Book of Chilam Balam Chumayel.* Austin: University of Texas Press, 1986.

————, ed. *Literatures: Supplement to the Handbook of Middle American Indians.* Austin: University of Texas Press, 1985.

Eguiara y Eguren, Juan José de. *Bibliotheca mexicana sive eruditorum historia virorum qui in America Boreali nati, vel alibi geniti, in ipsam Domicilio aut Studiis asciti, quavis lingua scripto aliquid tradiderun.* Mexico City: Ex Nova Typographia in Aedibus Authoris Editioni Ejustem Bibliothecae Destinata, 1770. Rpt. Mexico City: Universidad Nacional Autónomo de México, 1986.

Eliade, Mircea. *Cosmos and History.* New York: Harper and Row, 1959.

————. *Patterns in Comparative Religion.* New York: Harper Torchbooks, 1958.

Elías, Norbert. *The Civilizing Process.* Trans. E. Jephcott. New York: Urizen Books, 1978.

Elzey, Wayne. "Some Remarks on the Space and Time of the 'Center' in Aztec Religion." *Estudios de Cultura Náhuatl* 12 (1976): 318–26.

Erasmus. *De civilitate morum puerilium.* 1530. London: W. de Worde, 1532.

————. *De recta Graeci et Latini sermonis pronunciatione.* 1528.

Fabian, Johannes. *Time and the Other: How Anthropology Makes Its Object.* New York: Columbia University Press, 1983.

Farriss, Nancy M. *Maya Society under Colonial Rules: The Collective Enterprise of Survival.* Princeton: Princeton University Press, 1984.

————. "Remembering the Future, Anticipating the Past: History, Time, and Cosmology among the Maya of Yucatan." *Comparative Studies in Society and History* 29 (1989): 566–93.

Febvre, Lucien, and Henri-Jean Martin. *L'apparition du livre, 1450–1800.* Paris: Albin Michel, 1958.

Finnegan, Ruth. *Literacy and Orality: Studies in the Technology of Communication.* Oxford: Blackwell, 1988.

————. "The Myth of Literacy." Paper presented at the conference Literacy, Culture, and Mind, University of Michigan, October 1991.

Fischer, Henry George. *L'écriture et l'art de l'Egypte ancienne: Quatre leçons sur la paléographie et l'épigraphie pharaoniques.* Paris: Presses Universitaires de France, 1986.

————. "The Origins of Egyptian Hieroglyphs." In *The Origins of Writing,* ed. Wayne Senner, 59–76. Lincoln: University of Nebraska Press, 1989.

Florescano, Enrique. "La reconstrucción histórica elaborada por la nobleza indígena y sus descendientes mestizos." In *La memoria y el olvido*. Mexico City: Secretaría de Educación Pública, 1985.

Foerster, Heiz von. "On Constructing a Reality." In *The Invented Reality: How Do We Know What We Believe We Know?* ed. P. Watzlawick, 41–61. New York: W. W. Norton, 1984.

Fontaine, Jacques. *Isidore de Seville et la culture classique dans l'Espagne isigothique*. Paris: Etudes Agustiniennes, 1983.

Fonti Ricciane. Rome: Edizione Nazionale delle opere edite e inedite di Matteo Ricci, 1942.

Foss, Theodore N. "A Western Interpretation of China: Jesuit Cartography." In *East Meets West: The Jesuits in China, 1582–1773*, ed. C. E. Ronan and Bonnie B. C. Oh, 209–51. Chicago: Loyola University Press, 1982.

Foucault, Michel. *L'archaeologie du savoir*. Paris: Gallimard, 1969.

———. *Les mots et les choses: Une archeologie des sciences humaines*. Paris: Gallimard, 1966.

———. *L'ordre du discours*. Paris: Gallimard, 1971.

Franklin, Julian H. *Jean Bodin and the Sixteenth-Century Revolution in the Methodology of Law and History*. New York: Columbia University Press, 1963.

Friedlander, Judith. *Being Indian in Hueyapan: A Study of Forced Identity in Contemporary Mexico*. New York: St. Martin's Press, 1975.

Gadamer, Hans-George. "The Hermeneutics of Suspicion." In *Hermeneutics: Questions and Prospects,* ed. Gary Shapiro and Alan Sica, 54–65. Amherst: University of Massachusetts Press, 1984.

———. "On the Discrediting of Prejudice by the Enlightenment." In *The Hermeneutics Reader: Texts of the German Tradition from the Enlightenment to the Present,* ed. Kurt Mueller-Vollmer, 257–60. New York: Continuum, 1985.

———. "On the Scope and Function of Hermeneutical Reflection." In *Philosophical Hermeneutics*.

———. *Philosophical Hermeneutics*. Trans. and ed. David E. Linge. Berkeley and Los Angeles: University of California Press, 1976.

Galsersfeld, Ernst von. "An Introduction to Radical Constructivism." In *The Invented Reality: How Do We Know What We Believe We Know?* ed. P. Watzlawick, 17–40. New York: W. W. Norton, 1984.

Galván Rivera, Mariano. *Concilio III Provincial Mexicano*. 1585. Mexico City: Maillefert, 1859.

García-Berrio, Antonio. *Formación de la teoría literaria moderna*. 2 vols. Madrid: Planeta, 1977–80.

García-Blanco, Manuel. "La lengua española en la época de Carlos V." In *Discurso de clausura del curso de extranjeros de la Universidad Menéndez Pelayo* [1958]. Madrid: Escelicer, 1967.

García de la Concha, Jaime, ed. *Nebrija y la introducción del Renacimiento en España*. Salamanca: Actas de la III Academia Literaria Renacentista, 1981.

García Icazbalceta, Joaquín. *Don Fray Juan de Zumárraga, Primer Obispo y*

Arzobispo de México. Vol. 2. *Códice Franciscano.* Mexico City: Antigua Librería de Andrade y Morales, 1881.

————. *Nueva colección de documentos para la historia de México: Códice Franciscano.* Mexico City: Editorial Salvador Chavez, 1941.

García Martínez, Bernardo. *Los pueblos de la sierra: El poder y el espacio entre los indios del norte de Puebla hasta 1700.* Mexico City: El Colegio de México, 1987.

García Pelayo, Manuel. "Las culturas del libro." *Revista de Occidente* 24–25 (1965): 45–70.

García Quintana, Josefina. "Exhortación de un padre a su hijo: Texto recogido por Andrés de Olmos." *Estudios de Cultura Náhuatl* 11 (1974): 137–82.

Garcilaso de la Vega, Inca. *Comentarios reales de los Incas.* 1607. Ed. Angel Rosenblat. Buenos Aires: Emece, 1943.

Gardiner, Patrick. *Theories of History.* Glencoe, Ill.: Free Press, 1964.

Garibay, Angel María. *Historia de la literatura Náhuatl.* Mexico City: Porrúa, 1954.

Garza, Mercedes de la, comp. *Literatura Maya.* Caracas: Biblioteca Ayacucho, 1980.

Gates, Henry L. *The Signifying Monkey.* New York: Oxford University Press, 1989.

Gemelli Careri, Giovanni Francesco. *Voyage du tour du monde,* Vol. 4. Paris: E. Ganeau, 1719. Originally published as *Giro del Mondo* (Napoli, 1699).

Gibb, Hamilton A. R. *Studies on the Civilization of Islam.* Princeton: Princeton University Press, 1982.

Gibson, Charles. *The Aztecs under the Spanish Rules: A History of the Indians of the Valley of México, 1519–1810.* Stanford: Stanford University Press, 1964.

Gil Fernández, Luis. *Panorama social del humanismo español, 1500–1800.* Madrid: Alhambra, 1981.

Gilbert-Dubois, Claude. *Mythe et language au seizième siècle.* Paris: Editions Ducros, 1970.

Glass, John B. *Sahagún: Reorganization of the Manuscrito de Tlatelolco, 1566–1569.* Part 1. Mass.: Lincoln Center; Mexico City: Contributions to the Ethnology of Mexico, 1978.

————. "A Survey of Native Middle American Pictorial Manuscripts." In *Handbook of Middle American Indians,* gen. ed. Robert Wauchope, 14: 3–80. Austin: University of Texas Press, 1964–76.

Glass, John B., and Donald Robertson. " A Census of Native Middle American Pictorial Manuscripts." In *Handbook of Middle American Indians,* gen. ed. Robert Wauchope, 14: 81–252. Austin: University of Texas Press, 1964–76.

Glenisson, Jean. *Le livre au Moyen Age.* Paris: Press Universitaire de Centre National de la Recherche Scientifique, 1988.

Glissant, Edouard. *Caribbean Discourse: Selected Essays.* 1981; reprint Charlottesville: University Press of Virginia, 1989.

Goldberg, Jonathan. *Writing Matters: From the Hands of the English Renaissance*. Stanford: Stanford University Press, 1990.

Gómez Canedo, Lino. *Evangelización conquista: Experiencia Franciscana en América*. Mexico City: Porrúa, 1977.

Gómez Robledo, Javier. *Humanismo en México en el siglo xvi: El sistema del colegio de San Pedro y San Pablo*. Mexico City: Jus, 1954.

Gonzalbo Aizpurú, Pilar. *Historia de la educación en la época colonial: El mundo indígena*. Mexico City: El Colegio de México, 1990.

———. *Historia de la educación en México en la época colonial: La educación de los criollos y la vida urbana*. Mexico City: El Colegio de México, 1990.

Goody, Jack. *The Interface between the Written and the Oral*. New York: Cambridge University Press, 1987.

Goody, Jack, and Ian Watt. "The Consequences of Literacy." *Comparative Studies in Society and History* 5 (1963): 304–45.

Gossen, Gary. "Chamula Genres of Verbal Behavior." In *Toward New Perspectives in Folklore*, ed. A. Paredes and Richard Bauman, 145–67. Austin: University of Texas Press, 1972.

———. *Chamulas in the World of the Sun: Time and Space in a Maya Oral Tradition*. Cambridge: Harvard University Press, 1974.

———. "To Speak with a Heated Heart: Chamula Canons of Style and Good Performance." In *Exploration in the Ethnography of Speaking*, ed. Richard Bauman and Joel Sherzer, 389–413. Cambridge: Cambridge University Press, 1974.

———, ed. *Symbol and Meaning beyond the Closed Community: Essays in Mesoamerican Ideas*. Austin: University of Texas Press, 1986.

Gossman, Lionel. *Between History and Literature*. Cambridge: Harvard University Press, 1990.

Goyard-Fabre, Simone. *Jean Bodin et le droit de la République*. Paris: Presses Universitaires de France, 1989.

Graff, Harvey. *Literacy in History: An Interdisciplinary Research Bibliography*. New York: Garland, 1981.

Graham, A. C. *The Book of Lieh-tzu*. London: Murray, 1960.

———. "The Date and Composition of Liehtsy." *Asia Major*, n.s., 8 (1961): 139–98.

Green, Otis H. *Spain and the Western Tradition*. Vol. 3. Madison: University of Wisconsin Press, 1968.

Gruzinski, Serge. "Colonial Indian Maps in Sixteenth-Century Mexico." *Res* 13 (1987): 46–61.

———. *La colonisation de l'imaginarie. Sociétés indigènes et occidentalisation dans le Mexique espagnol, xviie–xviii siècles*. Paris: Gallimard, 1988.

Guha, Ranajit. "On Some Aspects of the Historiography of Colonial India." In *Selected Subaltern Studies*, ed. Ranajit Guha and Gayatri C. Spivak, 37–46. New York: Oxford University Press, 1988.

Guicciardini, Francesco. *Storia d'Italia*. 1561. Trans. and ed. Sidney Alexander under the title *The History of Italy* (Princeton: Princeton University Press, 1969).

Gumbrecht, Ulrich. "The Body Versus the Printing Press: Media in the Early Modern Period, Mentalities in the Reign of Castile, and Another History of Literary Forms." *Poetics* 14, nos. 3–4 (1985): 209–27.

Gurevich, Aaron. *Categories of Medieval Culture*. London: Routledge and Kegan Paul, 1985.

Guzmán, Eulalia. "The Art of Map-Making among the Ancient Mexicans." *Imago Mundi* 3 (1939): 1–6.

Habermas, Jürgen. "On Hermeneutics's Claim to Universality." In *The Hermeneutics Reader: Texts of the German Tradition from the Enlightenment to the Present*, ed. Kurt Mueller-Vollmer, 294–319. New York: Continuum, 1985.

———. "What Is Universal Pragmatics?" In *Communication and the Evolution of Society*, trans. Thomas McCarthy. Boston: Beacon Press, 1976.

Halm, Karl Felix von. *Ars rhetorica*. In *Rhetores latini minores*, ed. Charles Halm, 371–448. Frankfurt am Main: Minerva, 1964.

Hamilton, Bernice. *Political Thought in Sixteenth-Century Spain*. Oxford: Oxford University Press, 1963.

Hanks, William. "Discourse Genres in Theory and Practice." *American Ethnologist* 14, no. 4 (1987): 668–92.

———. "Element of Maya Style." In *Word and Image in Maya Culture: Explorations in Language, Writing, and Representation*, ed. William F. Hanks and Don S. Rice, 92–III. Salt Lake City: University of Utah Press, 1989.

Harley, John Brian. "Deconstructing the Map." *Cartographica* 26, no. 2 (1989): 1–20.

———. "Maps, Knowledge, and Power." In *The Iconography of Landscapes: Essay on the Symbolic Representation, Design, and Use of Past Environments*, ed. D. Cosgrove and S. Daniels, 277–312. London: Cambridge University Press, 1988.

Harris, Roy. *The Origin of Writing*. LaSalle, Ill.: Open Court, 1986.

Hartog, Francois. *The Mirror of Herodotus: An Essay on the Representation of the Other*. Berkeley and Los Angeles: University of California Press, 1988.

Havelock, Erick. "The Aftermath of the Alphabet." In *The Literate Revolution in Greece and Its Cultural Consequences*, 314–50.

———. *The Literate Revolution in Greece and Its Cultural Consequences*. Princeton: Princeton University Press, 1982.

———. *The Muse Learns to Write: Reflections on Orality and Literacy from Antiquity to the Present*. New Haven: Yale University Press, 1986.

Hay, Denys. *Europe: The Emergence of an Idea*. Edinburgh: Edinburgh University Press, 1957.

Heath, Shirley Brice. *La política del lenguaje en México: De la colonia a la nación*. Mexico City: Secretaría de Educación, 1972.

Heawood, Edward. "The Relationships of the Ricci Maps." *Geographical Journal* 50 (1917): 271–76.

Heidegger, Martin. *El ser y el tiempo*. 1927. Trans. José Gaos. Mexico City: Fondo de Cultura Económica, 1951.

Henderson, Judith Rice. "Defining the Genre of the Letter: Juan Luis Vives' *De Conscribendis Epistolis.*" *Renaissance and Reformation* 19, no. 2 (1983): 89–105.

Hernández, Francisco. *Historia natural de Nueva España.* Ed. German Somolinos. Mexico City: Universidad Nacional Autónoma de México, 1959.

———, trans. *Historia natural de Cayo Plinio Segundo.* Mexico City: Universidad Nacional Autónoma de México, 1966.

Herrera y Tordesillas, Antonio. *Historia general de los hechos de los castellanos en las Islas de Tierra Firme del mar océano, por Antonio de Herrera coronista mayor de Su Majestad, de las Indias y su coronista de Castilla, en cuatro décadas desde el año de 1492 hasta el de 1531.* 8 vols. Madrid: Imprenta Real, 1601–15.

Hillier, Bill, and Julienne Hanson. *The Social Logic of Space.* New York: Cambridge University Press, 1984.

Homen, Andreas. *Universe ac navigabilis totius Terrarum orbis Descriptio.* 1559.

Hopper, David H. *Technology, Theology, and the Idea of Progress.* Louisville, Ky.: John Knox Press, 1991.

Hulme, Peter. *Colonial Encounters: Europe and the Native Caribbean, 1492–1797.* New York: Methuen, 1986.

———. "Subversive Archipelagos: Colonial Discourse and the Break-up of Continental Theory." *Dispositio* 14 (1989): 1–24.

Indicopleustes, Cosmas. *Topographie Chretienne.* A.D. 547–49. Ed. Wanda Wolska-Conus. Vol. 1. Paris: Les Editions du Cerf, 1968.

Isidore of Seville. *Etimologiarum sive originum: Libri X.* Ed. W. M. Lindsay. 1911. Reprint, London: Oxford University Press, 1957.

———. *Etymologies.* Drafted, translated, and annotated by Jacques André. Paris: Les Belles Lettres, 1981.

Jacobs, Louis. "Jewish Cosmology." In *Ancient Cosmologies,* ed. C. Blacker and Michael Loewe, 66–84. London: Allen and Unwin, 1975.

Jardine, Lisa. *Francis Bacon: Discovery and the Art of Discourse.* Cambridge: Cambridge University Press, 1974.

Juan Bautista, comp. *Huehuetlatolli: Testimonios de la antigua palabra,* trans. Librado Silva Galeano. Mexico City: Secretaría de Educación Pública, 1991.

Karttunen, F. "Náhuatl Literacy." In *The Inca and Aztec States: 1400–1800,* ed. G. A. Collier, R. Rosaldo, and J. D. Wirth. New York: Academic Press, 1982.

Keightley, David N. "The Origins of Writing in China: Scripts and Cultural Contexts." In *The Origins of Writing,* ed. W. Senner, 171–202. Lincoln: University of Nebraska Press, 1989.

Keller-Cohen, Deborah, ed. *Literacy: Interdisciplinary Conversations.* New Jersey: Hampton Press, 1994.

Kenyon, Frederic G. *Books and Readers in Ancient Greece and Rome.* Oxford: Clarendon Press, 1932.

Khatibi, Abdelkhebir. *Love in Two Languages*. Minneapolis: University of Minnesota Press, 1990.

Khaldun, Ibn. *The Muqaddimah: An Introduction to History*. Trans. Franz Rosenthal. 3 vols. New York: Pantheon Books, 1958.

Kirchhoff, Paul, Lina Odena Guemes, and Luis Reyes, eds. and trans. *Historia tolteca-chichemeca*. Mexico City: CISINAH, 1976.

Klor de Alva, J. Jorge, "Contair vidas: La autobiografía confesional y la recon-strucción del ser nahua." *Arbor* 515–16 (1988): 49–78.

———, trans. "The Aztec-Spanish Dialoques of 1524." *Alcheringa/Ethno-poetics* 4, no. 2 (1980): 52–193.

Kobayashi, José María. *La educación como conquista: Empresa franciscana en Méxicano*. 1933. Mexico City: El Colegio de México, 1974.

Konetzke, Richard. *Colección de documentos para la historia de la formación social de Hispano-América, 1493–1810*. Vol. 1. Madrid: Consejo Superior de Investigaciones Cientíﬁcas y Técnicas, 1953.

Krammer, Fritz. "The Otherness of the European." *Culture and History* 16 (1989): 107–23.

Kristeller, Paul Oskar. *Renaissance Thought and the Arts*. Princeton, N.J.: Princeton University Press, 1980.

Kusch, Rodolfo. *América profunda*. Buenos Aires: Hachette, 1962.

———. *El pensamiento indígena y popular en América*. Buenos Aires: Hachette, 1973.

la Roncière, Monique de, and Michel Mollat du Jourdin. *Les portulans: Cartes marines du xiiième au xviième siècle*. Fribourg, Switzerland: Nathan, 1984.

Laclau, Ernesto. "Feudalism and Capitalism in Latin America." *New Left Review* 67 (1971): 19–38.

Lacoste, Yves. *Ibn Khaldun: The Birth of History and the Past of the Third World*. London: Verso, 1984.

Lamming, George. "The Occasion for Speaking." In *The Pleasures of Exile*. 1960. Rpt. Ann Arbor: University of Michigan Press, 1992.

Landa, Diego de. *Yucatan before and after the Conquest*. Trans. and ed. William Gates. New York: Dover Publications, 1978.

Langley, Lesler D. *America and the Americas: The United States in the Western Hemisphere*. Athens: University of Georgia Press, 1989.

Lanman, Jonathan T. "The Religious Symbolism of the T in T-O Maps." *Cartographica* 18 (1981): 18–22.

Latorre, German. *La enseñanza de la geografía en la Casa de Contratación*. Madrid: Establecimiento Tipográﬁco de Jaime Rates Martin, 1915.

Lawrance, J. N. H. "Nuevos lectores y nuevos géneros: Apuntes y observa-ciones sobre la epistolografía en el primer Renacimiento español." *Academia Literaria Renacentista* 5 (1988): 81–99.

Le Goff, Jacques. *Les intellectuels au Moyen Age*. Paris: Seuil, 1957.

———. *Le livre au Moyen Age*. Paris: Presses du Centre National de la Recherche Scientifique, 1988.

Lenneberg, Eric. *Biological Foundations of Language*. New York: Wiley, 1967.

León-Portilla, Ascensión. *Tepuztiahcuilolli: Impresos en Náhuatl.* Vol. i. Mexico City: Universidad Nacional Autónoma de México, 1988.

León-Portilla, Miguel. *Aztec Thought and Culture.* Norman: University of Oklahoma Press, 1963.

———. "Códice mesoamericano *Féjérvary-Mayer.*" In *Tonalamatl de los Pochtecas.* Mexico City: Celanese Mexicana, 1985.

———. "Nahuatl Literature." In *Literatures.* Supplement to the *Handbook of Middle American Indians,* ed. Howard Cline. Austin: University of Texas Press, 1985.

———. "El testimonio de la historia prehispánica en náhuatl." In *Toltecayótl: Aspectos de la cultura náhuatl.* Mexico City: Fondo de Cultura Económica, 1980.

———. *Tiempo y realidad en el pensamiento maya.* Mexico City: Universidad Nacional Autónoma de México, 1986.

———. *Tolecáyotl: Estudios de cultura Náhuatl.* Mexico City: Fondo de Cultura Económica, 1982.

Levenson, Jay A. *Circa 1492: Art in the Age of Exploration.* New Haven: Yale University Press; Washington, D.C.: National Gallery of Art, 1991.

Lévi-Strauss, Claude. *Anthropologie structurale.* Paris: Plon, 1958.

———. *Tristes Tropiques.* Paris: Flammarion, 1958.

Lewalski, Barbara Kiefer, ed. *Renaissance Genres: Essays on Theory, History, and Interpretation.* Cambridge: Harvard University Press, 1986.

Lewis, Bernard. *The Muslim Discovery of Europe.* New York: W. W. Norton, 1982.

Lippard, Lucy R. *Mixed Blessings: New Art in a Multicultural America.* New York: Pantheon Books, 1990.

Livius, Titus (ca. 59 B.C.–A.D. 17) *Ab Urbe Condita.* Trans. B. O. Foster, Vol. i. Cambridge: Harvard University Press, Loeb Classical Library, 1919.

López, Vincentio. *Aprilis Dialogus.* Introduction and translation into Spanish by Silvia Vargas Alquicira. Mexico City: Universidad Nacional Autónoma de México, 1987.

López Austin, Alfredo. *Cuerpo humano e ideología: Las concepciones de los antiguos náhuas.* Vol. i. Mexico City: Universidad Nacional Autónoma de México, 1980.

———. *Educación Mexica: Antologia de documentos sahaguntinos.* Mexico City: Universidad Nacional Autónoma de México, 1985.

———. "The Research Method of Fray Bernardino de Sahagún: The Questionnaires." In *Sixteenth-Century Mexico: The Work of Sahagún,* ed. Munro S. Edmonson, iii–149. Albuquerque: University of New Mexico Press, 1974.

López Piñero, José María. *Ciencia y técnica en la sociedad española de los siglos XVI y XVII.* Barcelona: Labor Universitaria, 1979.

López de Velasco, Juan. *Descripción de las Indias Occidentales.* 1574. Manuscript. John Carter Brown Library, Brown University.

———. *Descripción y demarcación de las Indias Occidentales.* 1574. Published in *Colección de documentos inéditos, relavitos al descubrimiento, conquista y organización de las antiguas posesiones españoles de América y Oceanía, sacados de los Archivos del Reino, y muy especialmente del de Indias.* Madrid: José María Pérez, 1871.

————. *Geografía y descripción universal de las Indias.* Madrid: 1894. Rpt. Madrid: Ediciones Atlas, 1971.

Lorenzana y Buitrón, Francisco Antonio. *Cartas pastorales y edictos.* Mexico City: Imprenta Superior de Gobierno, 1770.

Lotman, Juri M. *Universe of the Mind: A Semiotic Theory of Culture.* Trans. Ann C. Shukman. Bloomington: Indiana University Press, 1990.

Lotman, Juri M., and Boris Ouspenski, eds. *Travaux su les systèmes de signes.* Brussels: Editions Complexes, 1976.

Lotman, Juri, et al. "Theses on the Semiotic Study of Cultures as Applied to Slavic Texts." In *Structure of Texts and Semiotics of Culture,* ed. Jan van der Eng and Mormit Grigar, 1–28. The Hague: Mouton, 1973.

Loutfi, Martine Astier. *Litterature et colonialisme: L'expansion coloniale vue dans la littérature romanesque française, 1871–1914.* Paris: Mouton, 1971.

Luk, Bernard Hung-Kay. "A Serious Matter of Life and Death: Learned Conversations at Foochow in 1627." In *East Meets West: The Jesuits in China, 1582–1773,* ed. Ch. E. Ronan and Bonnie B. C. Oh, 173–207. Chicago: Loyola University Press, 1982.

Lumsden, Charles, and Edward Wilson. *Promethean Fire: Reflections on the Origin of Mind.* Cambridge: Harvard University Press, 1983.

MacCormack, Sabine. "Atahualpa and the Book." *Dispositio* 14 (1989): 36–38.

Major, John S. "The Five Phases, Magic Squares, and Schematic Cosmology." *Journal of the American Academy of Religious Studies* 2 (1984): 133–66.

Malagón-Barceló, Javier. "The Role of *Letrado* in the Colonization of America." *Americas* 18 (1961): 1–17.

Mannheim, Bruce. *The Language of the Incas since the European Invasion.* Austin: University of Texas Press, 1990.

Magbul Ahmad, S. "Cartography of al-Sharīf-al-Idrīsī." In *The History of Cartography in the Traditional Islamic and South Asian Societies,* ed. J. B. Harley and D. Woodward, vol. 2. 156–74. Chicago: University of Chicago Press, 1992.

Maravall, José Antonio. "La concepción del saber en una sociedad tradicional." *Cuadernos Hispanoamericanos* 197–98 (1966). Reprinted in *Estudios de historia del pensamiento español,* 201–60. Madrid: Ediciones de Cultura Hispánica, 1967.

————. *Los factores de la idea de progreso en el Renacimiento español.* Madrid: Real Academia de Historia, 1963.

————. "La formación de la conciencia estamental de los letrados." *Revista de estudios políticos* 70 (1953). Reprinted as "Los 'hombres de saber' o letrados y la formación de la concienca estamental." In *Estudios de historia del pensamiento español,* 345–80. Madrid: Ediciones de Cultura Hispánica, 1967.

Marcus, George E., and Michael M. J. Fischer. *Anthropology as Cultural Critique: An Experimental Moment in the Human Sciences.* Chicago: University of Chicago Press, 1986.

Marcus, Leah. "Renaissance/Early Modern Studies." In *Redrawing the Boundaries of Literary Study in English,* ed. Stephen Greenblatt and Giles Gunn, 41–63. New York: Modern Language Association, 1992.

Marshack, Alexander. *The Roots of Civilization: The Cognitive Beginnings of Man's First Art, Symbol, and Notation.* New York: McGraw-Hill, 1972.

Martin Rubio, María del Cármen, ed. *Instrucción del Ynga D. Diego de Castro Tito Cussi Yupangui.* Madrid: Ediciones Atlas, 1988.

Martyr, Peter [Martir de Anglería, Pedro]. *De orbe novo decades.* Alcalá de Henares, 1530. Trans. D. Joaquín Torres Asensio as *Décadas del Nuevo Mundo,* 1892. Rpt. Buenos Aires: Editorial Bajel, 1944.

———. *Epistolario: Documentos inéditos para la historia de España.* Ed. and trans. José López de Toro. Madrid: Imprenta Góngora, 1953.

Mathes, Miguel. *Santa Cruz de Tlateloloco: La primera biblioteca académica de las Américas.* Mexico City: Archivo Histórico Mexicano, 1982.

Matos Moctezuma, Eduardo. *The Aztecs.* New York: Rizzoli, 1989.

Maturana, Humberto. "Biology of Language: The Epistemology of Reality." In *Psychology and Biology of Language and Thought: Essays in Honor of Eric Lenneberg,* ed. G. A. Miller and Eric Lenneberg, 27–64. New York: Academic Press, 1978.

Maturana, Humberto, and Francisco Varela. *The Tree of Knowledge: The Biological Roots of Human Understanding.* Boston: New Science Library, 1987.

Maupertuis. *Reflexions philosophiques sur l'origine des langues et de la significa-tion des mots.* 1748. In *Maupertuis, Turgot et Maine de Biran sur l'origine du langage,* ed. Ronald Grimsley. Geneva: Droz, 1971.

Mayans y Siscar, Gregorió. *Orígenes de la lengua española.* 1737. Madrid: Ediciones Atlas, 1981.

McLuhan, Marshall. *Understanding Media: The Extension of Man.* London: Sphere Books, 1967.

Melía, Bartomeu. *El guaraní conquistado y reducido: Ensayos de ethnohistoria.* Vol. 6. Asunción: Biblioteca Paraguaya de Antropología Asunción, Universidad Católica, 1985.

Mendieta, Gerónimo de. *Historia eclesiástica indiana.* 1597. Mexico City: Porrúa, 1954.

Menéndez Pelayo, Marcelino. *Historia de las ideas estéticas en España.* 2 vols. Madrid: Consejo Superior de Investigaciones Científicas, 1974.

Menéndez Pidal, Ramón. *Castilla, la tradición y el idioma.* Madrid: Austral, 1945.

———. *La lengua de Cristóbal Colón.* Madrid: Austral, 1942.

Merrim, Stephanie. "'Un *Mare Magno* e oculto': Anatomy of Fernández de Oviedo's *Historia general y natural de la Indias." Revista de Estudios His-pánicos* II (1984): 101–19.

Michalowski, Piotr. "Early Mesopotamia Communicative Systems: Art, Liter-ature, and Writing." In *Investigating Artistic Environments in the Ancient Near East,* ed. Ann C. Gunter, 53–69. Washington, D.C.: Smithsonian Institution, 1990.

Mignolo, Walter D. "Anáhuac y sus otros: La cuestión de la letra en el Nuevo Mundo." *Revista Latinoamericana de Crítica Literaria* 28 (1988): 28–53.

———. "Cartas, crónicas y relaciones del descubrimiento y la conquista." In *Historia de la literatura hispanoamericana: Época colonial,* ed. Iñigo Madrigal, 57–116. Madrid: Cátedra, 1982.

———. "Colonial and Postcolonial Discourse: Cultural Critique or Academic Colonialism?" *Latin American Research Review* 28, no. 3 (1993): 120–34.

———. "Comments on Harley's 'Deconstructing the Map.'" *Cartographica* 26, no. 3 (1989): 109–13.

———. "The Darker Side of the Renaissance: Colonization and the Discontinuity of the Classical Tradition." *Renaissance Quarterly* 45, no. 4 (winter 1992): 808–28.

———. "Discursos pronunciados con el corazón caliente: Teorías del habla, del discurso y de la escritura." In *América Latina: Palabra, cultura, literatura,* coordinated by Ana Pizarro, 527–62. São Paulo: Memorial de América Latina, 1994.

———. "Dominios borrosos y dominios teóricos." *Filología* 20 (1985): 21–40.

———. "La grafía, la voz y el silencio." *Insula* 552 (1990): 11–12.

———. "La historia de la escritura y la escritura de la historia." In *De la crónica a la nueva narrativa mexicana,* ed. M. H. Forster and J. Ortega, 13–28. Mexico City: Oasis, 1986.

———. "Literacy and the Colonization of Memory: Writing Histories of People without History." In *Literacy: Interdisciplinary Conversations,* ed. Deborah Keller-Cohen, 91–114. Norwood, N.J.: Ablex, 1994.

———. "Lógica de las semejanzas y políticas de las diferencias: Sobre la literatura que parece historia y antropología, y viceversa." *Literatura e História na América Latina,* 115–62. São Paulo: EDUSP, 1993.

———. "El mandato y la ofrenda: La *Descripción de la provincia y ciudad de Tlaxcala,* de Diego Muñoz Camargo y las *Relaciones de Indias.*" *Nueva Revista de Filología Hispánica* 35, no. 2 (1987): 451–84.

———. "El metatexto historiográfico y la historiografía indiana." *Modern Language Notes* 96 (1981): 358–402.

———. "Nebrija in the New World: The Question of the Letter, the Colonization of Amerindian Languages, and the Discontinuity of the Classical Tradition." *L'Homme* 122–24 (1992): 187–209.

———. "On the Colonization of Amerindian Languages and Memories: Renaissance Theories of Writing and the Discontinuity of the Classical Tradition." *Comparative Studies in Society and History* 34, no. 2 (1992): 301–30.

———. "The Postcolonial Reason: Colonial Legacies and Postcolonial Theories." Mimeo in *Globalization and Culture,* Conference Reader (Nov. 9–12, 1994) Duke Center for Critical Theory. Forthcoming in Kalpana Seshadri-Crooks and Fawzia Afzal-Khan, eds. *Dimensions of Postcolonial Studies.*

————. "Qué clase de textos son géneros? Fundamentos de tipología textual." *Acta Poética* 4–5 (1982–83): 25–51.

————. "Re(modeling) the Letter: Literacy and Literature at the Intersection Semiotics and Literacy Studies." In *On Semiotic Modeling,* ed. M. Anderson and F. Merrell. Berlin: de Gruyter, 1991.

————. "Semiosis, Coherence, and Universes of Meaning." In *Text and Discourse Connectedness,* ed. Maria-Elizabeth Conte, J. S. Petofi, and E. Sozer, 483–505. Amsterdam: John Benjamin, 1989.

————. "Signs and Their Transmission: The Question of the Book in the New World." *Writing without Words: Alternative Literacies in Mesoamerica and the Andes,* ed. E. Boone and W. Mignolo, 220–70. Durham, N.C.: Duke University Press, 1994.

————. "Teorías renacentistas de la escritura y la colonización de las lenguas nativas." In *I Simposio de filología Iberoamericana,* 171–201. Zaragoza: Libros Pórticos, 1990.

Mignolo, Walter D., and Colleen Ebacher, "Alfabetización y literatura: Los *huehueltatolli* como ejemplo de semiosis colonial." *Actas de XXII Congreso de Literatura Iberoamericana,* ed. José Ortega, forthcoming.

Miller, Arthur G. "Transformations of Time and Space: Oaxaca, México, circa 1500–1700." In *Images of Memory: On Remembering and Representation,* ed. S. Kuchler and W. Melion, 141–75. Washington, D.C.: Smithsonian Institution Press, 1991.

Molina, Alonso de. *Arte de la lengua mexicana y castellana.* 1571. Madrid: Ediciones Cultura Hispanica, 1945.

————. *Vocabulario en lengua castellana y mexicana y mexicana castellana.* 1571. Mexico City: Editorial Porrúa, 1971.

Morel-Fatio, Alfred. "L'espagnol langue universelle." *Bulletin hispanique* 15 (1913): 207–23.

————. *Historiographie de Charles Quint.* Paris: H. Champion, 1913.

Morgan, Lewis H. *Ancient Society, or Researches in the Lines of Human Progress from Savagery through Barbarism to Civilization.* Chicago: Charles H. Kerr, 1910.

Motolinía, Toribio de. *Memoriales.* Mexico City: Luis García Pimentel, 1903. *Motolinía's History of the Indians of New Spain,* trans. Francis Borgia Steck. Washington, D.C.: Academy of American Franciscan History, 1951.

Mottahedeh, Roy P. *The Mantle of the Prophet: Religion and Politics in Iran.* New York: Simon and Schuster, 1985.

Mudimbe, V. Y. "For Said. Why Even the Critic of Imperialism Labors under Western Skies." *Transition* 63 (2995): 34–50.

————. *The Invention of Africa: Gnosis, Philosophy, and the Order of Knowledge.* Bloomington: Indiana University Press, 1988.

Mueller-Vollmer, Kurt. "Language, Mind, and Artifact: An Outline of Hermeneutic Theory since the Enlightenment." In *The Hermeneutics Reader: Texts of the German Tradition from the Enlightenment to the Present,* ed. Kurt Mueller-Vollmer, 1–52. New York: Continuum, 1985.

Murphy, James J. "*Ars dictaminis:* The Art of Letter-Writing." In *Rhetoric in the Middle Ages: A History of Rhetorical Theory from Saint Augustine to the Renaissance.* Berkeley and Los Angeles: University of California Press, 1974, 194–268.

Murúa, Martín de. *Historia general del Perú.* 1590. Ed. Manuel Ballesteros. Madrid: Historia 16, 1986.

Naveh, Joseph. *Early History of the Alphabet: An Introduction to West Semitic Epigraphy and Paleography.* Jerusalem: Magnes Press, 1982.

Nebenzahl, Kenneth. *Atlas of Columbus and the Great Discoveries.* Chicago: Rand McNally, 1990.

Nebrija, Elio Antonio de. *Gramática de la lengua castellana.* Salamanca, 1492. London: Oxford University Press, 1926.

———. *Reglas de la ortografía castellana.* Salamanca, 1517.

Needham, Joseph, and Wang Ling. *Science and Civilization in China.* Cambridge: Cambridge University Press, 1959.

Nicolau d'Olwer, Luis. *Fray Bernardino de Sahagún (1499–1590).* Trans. Mauricio J. Mixco. Salt Lake City: University of Utah Press, 1987.

Nicolet, Claude. *Space, Geography, and Politics in the Early Roman Empire.* Ann Arbor: University of Michigan Press, 1991.

Nisbet, Robert. *History of the Idea of Progress.* New York: Basic Books, 1980.

O'Gorman, Edmundo. *Crisis y porvenir de la ciencia histórica.* Mexico City: Imprenta Universitaria, 1947.

———. *Cuatro historiadores de India, siglo XVI: Pedro Mártir de Anglería, Gonzalo Fernández de Oviedo y Valdés, Bartolomé de la Casas, Joseph de Acosta.* Mexico City: Secretaría de Educación Pública, 1972.

———. *La idea del descubrimiento de América: Historia de esa interpretación y crítica de sus fundamentos.* Mexico City: Universidad Nacional Autónoma de México, 1951.

———. *La invención de América: La universalisación de la cultura occidental.* Mexico City: Universidad Nacional Autónoma de México, 1958.

———. *The Invention of America: An Inquiry into the Historical Nature of the New World and the Meaning of Its History.* Bloomington: Indiana University Press, 1961.

Ong, Walter J. *Orality and Literacy: The Technologizing of the Word.* London: Methuen, 1982.

Oppenheim, A. L. *Ancient Mesopotamia: A Portrait of a Dead Civilization.* Chicago: University of Chicago Press, 1964.

Ortega y Gasset, José. "The Difficulties of Reading." Trans. Clarence E. Parmenter. *Diogenes* no. 28 (1954): 1–17.

———. *Man and People.* New York: W. W. Norton, 1963.

Osorio Romero, Ignacio. *Las bibliotecas novohispanas.* Mexico City: Secretaría de Educación Pública, 1986.

———. *Colegios y profesores Jesuitas que enseñaron Latin en Nueva España (1572–1767).* Mexico City: Universidad Nacional Autónoma de México, 1979.

————. *La enseñanza del latín a los Indios*. Mexico City: Universidad Nacional Autónoma de México, 1990.

————. *Historia de las bibliotecas en Puebla*. Mexico City: Secretaría de Educación Pública, 1988.

Oviedo y Valdés, Gonzálo Fernández de. *Historia general y natural de las Indias, islas y tierra-firme del mar océano*. 4 vols. Madrid: Imprenta de la Real Academia de la Historia, 1855.

Pagden, Anthony. *The Fall of Natural Man: The American Indian and the Origins of Comparative Ethnology*. Cambridge: Cambridge University Press, 1982.

Pané, Ramón. *Relación de las antiguedades de los indios*. 1493. Ed. Juan José Arrom. Mexico City: Fondo de Cultura Económica, 1974.

Panikkar, Raimundo. "What Is Comparative Philosophy Comparing?" In *Interpreting across Boundaries: New Essays in Comparative Philosophy*, ed. G. J. Larson and E. Deutsch, 116–36. Princeton: Princeton University Press, 1988.

Paré, Ambroise. *Des monstres et prodiges*. Ed. Jean Céard. Geneva: Librarie Droz, 1971. English trans. Janis L. Pallister, *On Monsters and Marvels*. Chicago: University of Chicago Press, 1982.

Parkes, M. B. "The Literacy of the Laity." In *The Medieval World*, ed. David Daiches and A. Thorlby, 555–77. London: Aldous Book, 1973.

————. *Scribes, Scripts and Readers: Studies in the Communication, Presentation, and Dissemination of Medieval Texts*. London: Hambledon Press, 1991.

Patrizi [Patritio], Francesco. *Della historia diece dialoghi: Ne' qvali si ragiona de tute le cose appretenenti all'historia, e allo scriverla, e all'osservarla*. Venice: Andrea Arrivabene, 1560.

Pau y Marti, José María. "El libro perdido de las pláticas o Coloquios de los doce primeros misioneros de México." In *Estratto della Miscellanea Fr. Ehrle III*. Rome: Tipografia del Senato, del Dottore G. Bardi, 1524.

Pederson, Johannes. *The Arabic Book*. Ed. Robert Hillenbrand. Trans. Geoffrey French. Princeton: Princeton University Press, 1984.

Pereyra, Carlos. *Breve historia de América*. Vol. 1. Santiago: Editorial Universitaria, 1938.

Pérez-Ramos, Antonio. *Francis Bacon's Idea of Science and the Maker's Knowledge Traditions*. Oxford: Clarendon Press, 1988.

Piedra, José. "The Game of Critical Arrival." *Diacritics* 19 (1989): 34–61.

Pomar, Juan Bautista. *Relación de Tezcoco* (Siglo XVI). Ed. Joaquín García Icazbalceta. Mexico City: Biblioteca Enciclopédica del Estado de México, 1975.

Rabasa, José. *Inventing America*. Norman: Oklahoma University Press, 1993.

Radin, Paul. *The Sources and Authenticity of the History of the Ancient Mexicans*. Berkeley: University Publications of American Archeology and Ethnology, 1920.

Randles, W. G. L. *De la terre plate au globe terrestre: Une mutation épistémologique rapide 1480–1520*. Paris: Armand Colin, 1980.

Rappaport, Joanne. "Mythic Images, Historical Thought, and Printed Texts: The Paez and the Written Word." *Journal of Anthropological Research* 43, no. 1 (1987): 43–61.

Real Academica Española. *Diccionario de Autoridades.* Edición Facsimilar. Madrid: Editorial Gredos, 1964.

Recopilación de Leyes de los reinos de las Indias, mandadas imprimir y publicar por la Magestad católica del rey Don Carlos II. Madrid: Boix, 1841.

Reynolds, L. D., and N. G. Wilson. *Scribes and Scholars: A Guide to the Transmission of Greek and Latin Literature.* Oxford: Clarendon Press, 1991.

Ricard, Robert. *La conquista espiritual de México: Ensayos sobre el apostolado y los métodos misioneros de las órdenes mendicantes en la Nueva España de 1523–24 a 1572.* Trans. Angel María Garibay. Mexico City: Fondo de Cultura Económica, 1986.

Richaudeau, Francois. *La lisibilité.* Paris: Denöel, 1969.

Riché, Pierre. *Ecole et enseignement dans le haut Moyen Age.* Paris: Denöel, 1979.

———. *Education et culture dans l'Occident barbare, 6e–8e siècles.* Paris: Editions du Seuil, 1962. Trans. John Contreni. *Education and Culture in the Barbarian West, Sixth through Eighth Centuries.* Columbia: University of South Carolina Press, 1976.

Rico, Francisco. "Lección y herencia de Elio Antonio de Nebrija." In *Nebrija y la introducción del renacimiento en España,* ed. Victor García de la Concha. Salamanca: Actas de la Academia Literaria Renacentista, 1991.

———. *Nebrija contra los bárbaros: El canon de gramáticos nefastos en las polémicas del humanismo.* Salamanca: Universidad de Salamanca, 1978.

Ricoeur, Paul. *Hermeneutics and the Human Sciences: Essays on Language, Action, and Interpretation,* ed. and trans. John B. Thompson. Cambridge: Cambridge University Press; Paris: Editions de la Maison des Sciences de l'Homme, 1981.

Ritsch, F. G. *De M. Terentii Varronis Disciplinarum Libris Commentarious. Oposc III,* 352–402. Bonnae, 1845.

Rivas Sacconi, José Manuel. *El latín en Colombia Bosquejo histórico del humanisno colombiano.* Bogotá: Instituto Caro y Cuervo, 1949.

Robertson, Donald. *Mexican Manuscript Painting of the Early Colonial Period.* New Haven: Yale University Press, 1959.

———. "The 'Pinturas' (Maps) of the *Relaciones geográficas,* with a Catalog." In *Handbook of Middle American Indians,* ed. Howard Cline, 12:243–78. Austin: University of Texas Press, 1972.

———. "The Sixteenth-Century Mexican Encyclopedia of Fray Bernardino de Sahagún." *Cahiers d'Historie Mondiale* 9, no. 3 (1966): 617–26.

Rogers, Francis M. *The Quest for Eastern Christians: Travels and Rumors in the Age of Discovery.* Minneapolis: University of Minnesota Press, 1962.

Rorty, Richard. *Philosophy and the Mirror of Nature.* Princeton: Princeton University Press, 1981.

Rosand, David. "Rubens's Munich *Lion Hunt:* Its Sources and Significance." *Art Bulletin* 51 (1969): 29–41.

Rosch, Eleanor. "Principle of Categorization." In *Cognition and Categorization*, ed. Eleanor Rosch and B. B. Lloyd, 28–49. Hillsdale, N.J.: Lawrence Erlbaum, 1978.

———. "Wittgenstein and Categorization Research in Cognitive Psychology." In *Meaning and the Growth of Understanding: Wittgenstein's Significance for Developmental Psychology*, ed. M. Chapman and R. Dixon. Hillsdale, N.J.: Lawrence Erlbaum, 1987.

Rousseau, J. J. *Essais sur l'origine des langues*. 1756. Trans. John H. Moran and Alexander Gode. Chicago: Chicago United Press, 1966.

Roys, Ralph L. *The Book of Chilam Balam of Chumayel*. Washington, D.C.: Carnegie Institution of Washington, 1933. Norman: University of Oklahoma Press, 1967.

Sacchi, Ducio. "Imagen y percepción del territorio según los mapas mixtecos, (1595–1617)." *Historia* 15 (1986): 19–30.

Sack, Robert David. *Human Territoriality: Its Theory and History*. New York: Cambridge University Press, 1986.

Saenz, Mario. "Memory, Enchantment, and Salvation: Latin American Philosophies of Liberation and the Religions of the Opressed." Mimeo. October, 1991.

Sahagún, Bernardino de. *Coloquios y doctrina Christiana*. 1565. Trans. and Intro. Miguel León-Portilla. Mexico City: Universidad Nacional Autónoma de México, 1981.

———. *Florentine Codex*. 1578. Trans. and ed. Charles E. Dibble, Arthur Anderson, and J. O. Anderson. 13 vols. Bilingual edition Salt Lake City: University of Utah Press. Santa Fe: School of American Research, 1956–69.

———. *Los diálogos de 1524 según el texto de Fray Bernardino de Sahagún y sus colaboradores indígenas*. Ed. and trans. Miguel León-Portilla. Mexico City: Universidad Nacional Autónoma de México, 1986.

Said, Edward. *Culture and Imperialism*. New York: Alfred A. Knopf, 1993.

———. *Orientalism*. New York: Vintage Books, 1978.

Sampson, Geoffrey. *Systems of Writing*. London: Longman, 1987.

San José, Jerónimo. *Genio de la historia*. 1651. Ed. Higinio de Santa Teresa. Vitoria, Spain: El Carmen, 1957.

Sánchez Alonso, Benito. *Historia de la historiografía española: Ensayo de un examen de conjunto*. Vol. 1. Madrid: Cultura Hispánica, 1944.

Santa Cruz, Alonso de. *Obra cosmográfica* 1560. Ed. Mariano de la Cuesta. Madrid: Consejo Superior de Investigaciones Científicas, 1983.

Santo Tomás, Domingo de. *Gramática o arte de la lengua general de los Indios de los Reynos del Perú*. 1560. Ed. R. Porras Barrenchea. Lima: Edición del Instituto de Historia, 1951.

———. *Lexicon o vocabulario de la lengua general del Perú*. Ed. R. Porras Barrenchea. Lima: Edición del Instituto de Historia, 1951.

Scaglioni, Aldo. *The Liberal Arts and the Jesuit College System*. Amsterdam: John Benjamins, 1986.

Schafer, Ernesto. *El consejo real y supremo de las Indias: Su historia, organización y labor administrativa hasta la terminación de la Casa de Austria*. 2

vols. Seville: Publicaciones del Centro de Estudios de Historia América, 1935.

Scharlau, Birgit, and Mark Munzel. *Quelqay: Mundliche Kultur und Schrift-tradition bei Indianeren Lateinamerikas.* Frankfurt am Main: Campus Verlag, 1987.

Schmitt, Jean-Claude. *La raison des gestes dans l'Occident médiévale.* Paris: Gallimard, 1990.

Schutte, Ofelia. "Origins and Tendencies of the Philosophy of Liberation in Latin American Thought: A Critique of Dussel's Ethic." *Philosophical Forum* 22, no. 3 (1991): 270–95.

Schwartzbert, Joseph E. "Cosmological mapping." In *The History of Cartography in the Traditional Islamic and South Asian Societies,* ed. J. B. Harley and D. Woodward, vol. 2, 332–87. Chicago: University of Chicago Press, 1992.

Scollon, Roland, and Suzanne Scollon. *Linguistic Convergence: An Ethnography of Speaking at Fort Chipewyan.* New York: Academic Press, 1979.

Scribner, Sylvia. "Literacy in Three Metaphors." *Journal of American Education* 93 (1986): 6–21.

Seed, Patricia. "Colonial and Postcolonial Discourse." *Latin American Research Review* 26, no. 3 (1991): 181–200.

Senner, Wayne, ed. *The Origin of Writing.* Lincoln: University of Nebraska Press, 1989.

Siegel, John. "From *Dictatores* to the Humanists." In *Rhetoric and Philosophy in Renaissance Humanism.* Princeton: Princeton University Press, 1968.

Simeon, Remi. *Dictionnaire de la langue Náhuatl ou Mexican.* Paris: Imprimerie Nationale, 1885. Graz: Akademische Druck-U Verlagsanstalt, 1963.

Simons, Bente Bittman. *Los mapas de Cuauhtinchán y la historia tolteca-chichimeca.* Mexico City: Instituto Nacional de Antropología e Historia, 1968.

Skeat, Thomas. "Early Christian Book Production: Paper and Manuscripts." In *The Cambridge History of the Bible,* ed. G. N. Lampe, 2:54–79. New York: Cambridge University Press, 1969.

Smith, Carol A., ed. *Guatemalan Indians and the State: 1540 to 1988.* Austin: University of Texas Press, 1990.

Smith, Mary Elizabeth. *Picture Writing from Ancient Southern Mexico.* Norman: University of Oklahoma Press, 1973.

Sorrentino, Andrea. *La retorica e la poetica di Vico: Ossia la prima concezione estetica del linguagio.* Turin: Fratelli Bocca, editori, 1927.

Spaulding, Karen. *Huarochiri: An Andean Society under Inca and Spanish Rules.* Stanford: Stanford University Press, 1984.

Spini, Giorgio. "I trattatisti dell'arte storica nella Controriforma italiana." In *Contributi alla storia del Concilio di Trento della Controriforma.* Florence: Vallechi, 1948.

Spivak, Gayatri C. "Subaltern Studies: Deconstructing Historiography." In

Selected Subaltern Studies, ed. Ranajit Guha and Gayatri C. Spivak, 3–33. New York: Oxford University Press, 1988.

Stevenson, E. L. "The Geographic Activities of the Casa de Contratación." *Annals of the Association of American Geographers* 7, no. 2 (1927): 39–60.

Stocking, George W., Jr. *Colonial Situations: Essays on the Ethnographic Knowledge.* Madison: University of Wisconsin Press, 1991.

———, ed. *Observers Observed: Essays on Ethnographic Field Work.* Madison: University of Wisconsin Press, 1983.

Street, Brian V. *Literacy in Theory and Practice.* New York: Cambridge University Press, 1984.

Struever, Nancy. *The Language of History in the Renaissance: Rhetoric and Historical Consciousness in Florentine Humanism.* Princeton: Princeton University Press, 1970.

Sullivan, Lawrence. "Above, Below, or Far Away: Andean Cosmology and Ethical Order." In *Cosmology and Ethical Order: New Studies in Comparative Ethics,* ed. R. W. Lovin and F. Reynolds, 98–132. Chicago: University of Chicago Press, 1985.

Sullivan, Thelma. "The Rhetorical Orations, or *Huehuetlatolli.*" In *Sixteenth-Century Mexico: The Work of Sahagún,* ed. Munro S. Edmonson, 79–110. Albuquerque: University of New Mexico Press, 1974.

Tate, Robert Brian. *Ensayos sobre la historiografía peninsular del siglo XV.* Trans. Jesús Díaz. Madrid: Editorial Gredos, 1970.

Tedlock, Dennis. *The Spoken Word and the Art of Interpretation.* Philadelphia: University of Pennsylvania Press, 1982.

———, trans. *Popul Vuh: The Definitive Edition of the Mayan Book of the Dawn of Life and the Glories of Gods and Kings.* New York: Simon and Schuster, 1985.

Tedlock, Dennis, and Barbara Tedlock. "Text and Textile: Language and Technology in the Arts of the Quiché Maya." *Journal of Anthropological Research* 41, no. 2 (1985): 121–46.

Teuber, Bernard. "Europäisches und Amerikanisches im frühneuzeitlichen Diskurs uber Stimme und Schrift." *Romanistik in Geschichte und Gegenwart.* Band 24, 47–59. Hamburg: Helmut Buske Verlag, 1989.

Thiong'O Ngugi Wa. *Decolonizing the Mind: The Politics of Language in African Literature.* London: J. Currey, 1986.

———. "Resistance in the Literature of the African Diaspora: Post-Emancipation and Post-Colonial Discourses." Paper given at the workshop series The Inventions of Africa: Africa in the Literatures of the Continent and the Diaspora, April 17, 1992, University of Michigan.

Torquemada, Juan de. *Monarquía Indiana.* 1615. 6 vols. Ed. Miguel León-Portilla. Mexico City: Universidad Nacional Autónoma de México, Instituto de Investigaciones Filológicas, 1977.

Tory, Geoffroy. *Champ fleury: Auquel est contenu l'art et science de la deue et vraye proportion des lettres attiques, qu'on dit autrement lettres antiques et vulgairement lettres romaines proportionees selon le corps et visage humain.* Paris, 1529.

Trabant, Jurgen. "*Parlare Scrivendo:* Deconstructive Remarks on Derrida's Reading of Vico." Trans. Martha B. Helfer. In *New Vico Studies,* 43–58. New York: Institute for Vico Studies, 1989.

Trabulse, Elias. "Tres momentos de la heterodoxia científica en el México colonial." *Revista Latinoamericana de Historia de las Ciencias y la Tecnología* 5, no. 1 (1988): 7–18.

Tuan, Yi-Fu. *Space and Place: The Perspective of Experience.* Minneapolis: University of Minnesota Press, 1977.

Urbar, Greg, and Joel Sherzer, eds. *Nation-States and Indians in Latin America.* Austin: University of Texas Press, 1991.

Urton, Gary. *At the Crossroads of the Earth and the Sky: An Andean Cosmology.* Austin: University of Texas Press, 1981.

———. *The History of a Myth: Pacaritambo and the Origin of the Inkas.* Austin: University of Texas Press, 1990.

Valla, Lorenzo. "In sex libros elegantiarum praefatio." 1442? In *Prosatori Latini del Quattrocento.* Ed. E. Garin. Milano: Mondadori, 1952.

Vanderstappen, Harrie. "Chinese Art and the Jesuits in Peking." In *East Meets West: The Jesuits in China, 1582–1773,* ed. C. E. Ronan and Bonnie B. C. Oh, 103–27. Chicago: Loyola University Press, 1982.

Varela, Francisco. *Conocer: Las ciencias cognitivas.* Barcelona: Gedisa, 1990.

Varela, Francisco J., Evan Thompson, and Eleanor Rosch. *The Embodied Mind: Cognitive Science and Human Experience.* Cambridge: MIT Press, 1991.

Vargas Llosa, Mario. *El hablador.* Barcelona: Seix Barral, 1987.

Varonnis, Terentii. *Disciplinarum libris commentarius.*

Varro, Marcus Terentius. *On the Latin Language.* Trans. Roland G. Kent. 2 vols. Cambridge: Harvard University Press, 1951.

Vázquez de Espinosa, Antonio. *Compendio y descripción de las Indias Occidentales III.* 1620. Madrid: Ediciones Atlas, 1969.

Velasco Ceballos, Rómulo, and Miguel Maldonado Huerta, eds. *La alfabetización en la Nueva España: Leyes, cédulas reales, ordenanzas, bandos, pastoral y otros documentos.* Mexico City: Secretaría de Educación, 1945.

Venegas, Alejo. *Primera parte de las diferencias de libros que hay en el universo.* Toledo, 1546. Rpt. Barcelona: Puvill Libros, 1983.

Vicens Vives, Jaime, comp. *Historia de España y América:* Social y Económica. Madrid: Editorial Vicens-Vives, 1971.

Vico, Giambattista. *Tutte le opere di Giambattista Vico.* Milan: Arnoldo Mondadori Editore, 1957. Trans. Thomas Goddard Bergin and Max Harold Fisch as *The New Science of Giambattista Vico.* Ithaca: Cornell University Press, 1948.

Villa Rojas, Alfonso. "Los conceptos de espacio y tiempo entre los grupos mayances contemporáneos." In *Tiempo y realidad en el pensamiento maya,* ed. Miguel León-Portilla, 119–68. Mexico City: Universidad Nacional Autónoma de México, 1986.

Vives, Juan Luis. *De ratione studii puerilis.* 1523.

————. *De tradendis disciplines.* 1531. Totowa, N.J.: Rowman and Littlefield, 1971.

Von Foerster, Heinz. "On Constructing a Reality." In *The Invented Reality,* ed. P. Watzlowick, 41–61. New York: W. W. Norton, 1984.

Von Glasersfeld, Ernst. "*An Introduction to Radical Constructivism.*" In *The Invented Reality,* ed. P. Watzlowick, 17–40. New York: W. W. Norton, 1984.

Wachtel, Natham. "Pensée sauvage et acculturation: L'espace et le temps chez Felipe Guaman Poma de Ayala et l'Inca Garcilaso de la Vega." *Annales* 26 (1971): 793–837.

————. "Structuralisme et histoire: A Propos de l'organization sociale du Cuzco." *Annales* 21 (1966): 71–94.

Wallace, David. "Carving Up Time and the World: Medieval-Renaissance Turf Wars; Historiography and Personal History." Working paper no. 11, Center for Twentieth-Century Studies, University of Wisconsin, Milwaukee, 1991.

Wallace, Rex. "The Origins and Development of the Latin Alphabet." In *The Origins of Writing,* ed. Wayne Senner, 121–36. Lincoln: University of Nebraska Press, 1989.

Wallerstein, Immanuel. *The Modern World-System: Capitalist Agriculture and the Origins of the European World-Economy in the Sixteenth Century.* New York: Academic Press, 1974.

Wallis, Helen. "The Influence of Father Ricci on Far Eastern Cartography." *Imago Mundi* 19 (1965): 38–45.

Warren, Kay B. *The Symbolism of Subordination: Indian Identity in a Guatemalan Town.* Austin: University of Texas Press, 1978.

Weinberg, Bernard. *History of Literary Criticism in the Italian Renaissance.* Chicago: University of Chicago Press, 1961.

Wensinck, A. I. *The Ideas of the Western Semites Concerning the Navel of the Earth.* Verhandelingen der Koninklijke Akademie van Weternschappen te Amsterdam, vol. 17, no. 1 Amsterdam: Afdeeling Letterkunde, 1916.

West, Cornel. *The American Evasion of Philosophy: A Genealogy of Pragmatism.* Madison: University of Wisconsin Press, 1989.

————. "The New Cultural Politics of Difference." In *Marginalization and Contemporary Cultures,* ed. R. Fergusson et al., 19–38. New York: Museum of Contemporary Art; Cambridge: MIT Press, 1990.

Wheatley, Paul. *The Pivot of the Four Quarters: A Preliminary Enquiry into the Origins and Character of the Ancient Chinese City.* Chicago: Aldine, 1971.

Whitaker, Arthur Preston. *The Western Hemisphere Idea: Its Rise and Decline.* Ithaca: Cornell University Press, 1954.

White, Hayden. *The Tropics of Discourse.* Baltimore: Johns Hopkins University Press, 1978.

Widengren, Geo. "Holy Book and Holy Tradition in Iran." In *Holy Book and Holy Tradition: International Colloquium held in the Faculty of Theology University of Manchester,* ed. F. F. Bruce and E. G. Rupp, 210–36. Grand Rapids: William B. Eerdmans, 1968.

Wilcox, Donald J. *The Development of Florentine Humanist Historiography in the Fifteenth Century.* Cambridge: Harvard University Press, 1969.

Winter, Sylvia. "Ethno or Socio Poetics." In *Ethnopoetics: A First International Symposium,* ed. M. Benamou and R. Rothemberg, 78–94. Boston: Boston University Press, 1976.

Wobeser, Gisela von. *La formación de la hacienda en la época colonial.* Mexico City: Universidad Nacional Autónoma de México, 1983.

Wolf, Armin. "Die Ebstorfer Welkkarte als Denkmal eines Mittelalterlichen Welt- und Geschichtsbildes." *Geschichte in Wissenschaft und Unterricht* 8 (1957): 316–34.

———. "News on the Ebstorf World Map: Date, Origin, Authorship." In *Géographie du Monde au Moyen Age et à la Renaissance,* ed. Monique Pelletier, 51–68. Paris: Editions du CTHS, 1989.

Wood, Ananda. *Knowledge before Printing and after: The Indian Tradition in Changing Kerala.* Bombay: Oxford University Press, 1985.

Woodward, David. "Maps and the Rationalization of Geographic Space." In *Circa 1492: Art in the Age of Exploration,* ed. J. A. Levenson, 83–87. Washington, D.C.: National Gallery of Art; New Haven: Yale University Press, 1991.

———. "Medieval *Mappamundi.*" In *The History of Cartography.* Vol. 1, *Cartography in Prehistoric, Ancient, and Medieval Europe and the Mediterranean,* ed. B. Harley and David Woodward, 286–369. Chicago: University of Chicago Press, 1987.

———. "Reality, Symbolism, Time, and Space in Medieval World Maps." *Annals of the Association of American Geographers* 75, no. 4 (1985): 510–21.

Yoneda, Keiko. *Los mapas de Cuahtinchán y la historia cartográfica prehispánica.* Mexico City: Archivo General de la Nación, 1981.

Zea, Leopoldo. *América en la historia.* Mexico City: Fondo de Cultura Económica, 1958.

———. *Discurso desde la marginación y la barbarie.* Barcelona: Anthropos, 1988.

Zuidema, R. T. *The Ceque System of Cuzco: The Social Organization of the Capital of the Inca.* Trans. Eva M. Hoykaas. Leiden: E. J. Brill, 1964.

Zumthor, Paul. *La lettre et la voix: De la "literature" médiévale.* Paris: Editions du Seuil, 1987.

Index

415

Illustration Credits

Fig. 1.1. Reprinted from S. Gregorius Magnus, *Moralia in Job,* Cîteaux, twelfth century. Courtesy Bibliothèque Municipale, Dijon. Fig. 1.2a. Reprinted, by permission, from Albrecht Dürer, *Of the Just Shaping of Letters.* New York: Dover, 1965. Fig. 1.2b. Reprinted, by permission, from Jesus Yhmoff Cabrera, *Los impresos mexicanos del siglo XVI en la Biblioteca Nacional de México.* Mexico City: Universidad Nacional Autónoma de México, 1990. Fig. 1.3. Reprinted by permission from Geoffroy Tory, *Champ Fleury.* Paris, 1529, British Library. Fig. 1.4. Reprinted from *Codex Vaticanus,* plate 3738, by permission of Biblioteca Apostolica Vaticana, Rome. Fig. 1.5. Reprinted from Michael Coe, Dean Snow, and Elizabeth Benson, *Atlas of Ancient America.* Oxford: Andromeda, 1986. Photo courtesy of Michael Holford. Fig. 1.6. Reprinted from Martin de la Cruz, *Libellus de medicinalibus indorum herbis.* Mexico City: Instituto Mexicano del Seguro Social, 1964. Fig. 1.7. Reprinted, by permission, from Mary Elizabeth Smith, *Picture Writing from Ancient Southern Mexico: Mixtec Place Signs and Maps.* Copyright © 1973 by the University of Oklahoma Press. Fig. 1.8. Reprinted, by permission, from Diego de Landa, *Relación de las cosas de Yucatán.* Madrid: Real Academía de la Historia, 1985. Fig. 1.9. Reprinted from Juan Jose de Eguiara y Eguren, *Biblioteca mexicana sive eruditorum historia virorum qui in America Nati.* Mexico City: Universidad Nacional Autónoma de México, 1986.

Chapter 2

Fig. 2.1. Reprinted, with permission, from Jean Glenisson, *Le Livre au Moyen Age.* Paris: Press Universitaire de CNRS, 1988. Fig. 2.2a. Reprinted, by permission, from Henry G. Fischer, *L'Ecriture et l'art de l'Egypte ancienne.* Paris: Presses Universitaires de France, 1986. Fig. 2.2bc. Reprinted from Michael D. Coe, *The Maya Scribe and His World.* New York: Grolier Club, 1973. Fig. 2.4a. From the Museo National de Antropología, Peru. Reprinted from Marcia Ascher and Robert Ascher, *Code of the Quipu.* Ann Arbor: University of Michigan Press, 1981. Fig. 2.4b. Cushion Cover with Coat of Arms. Charles Potter Kling Fund. Courtesy, Museum of Fine Arts, Boston. Fig. 2.5. Reprinted, by permission, from Felipe Guaman Poma de Ayala, *Nueva coronica y buen gobierno,* ca. 1615. The Royal Library, Copenhagen. Fig. 2.6. Reprinted from Virgil, *Georgics,* plate 493. Courtesy Bibliothèque Municipale, Dijon. Fig. 2.7. Reprinted from Albrecht Dürer, *Erasmus of Rotterdam.* Photo © 1993, courtesy National Gallery of Art, Washington, D.C. Fig. 2.8. Reprinted, by permission, from Felipe Guaman Poma de Ayala, *Nueva coronica y buen gobierno.* The Royal Library, Copenhagen. Fig. 2.9. Reprinted, by permission, from Bernardino de Sahagún,

Codice Florentino, vol. 2, book 6, folio 50. Archivo General de la Nación y Biblioteca Laurentiana, Rome, 1979. Fig. 2.10abc. Reprinted from *Codex Mendoza*, folio 70r. Bodleian Library, Oxford. Fig. 2.11. Reprinted from Bernardino de Sahagún, *Coloquios y Doctrina Cristiana*, 1524. Universidad Nacional Autónoma de México, Mexico City. Fig. 2.12a. Reprinted from Bernardino de Sahagún, *Codice Florentino*. Archivo General de la Nación y Biblioteca Laurentiana, Rome, 1979. Fig. 2.12b. Reprinted, by permission, from Bernardino de Sahagún, *Florentine Codex*. The School of American Research and the University of Utah. Illustration by Francisco del Paso y Troncoso.

Chapter 3

Fig. 3.1a. *Codex Selden*, Bodleian Library, Oxford. Figs. 3.1b and 3.2. Reprinted from Museo Nacional de Antropología, Peru. Fig. 3.3. Reprinted from Bernardo Boturini Benaducci, *Idea de una nueva historia general de la América septentrional*. Paris: Centre de Documentation "Andre Thevet," 1933. Fig. 3.4. Reprinted from Diego de Durán's *Historia de las indias de Nueva España*. Biblioteca Nacional, Madrid. Fig. 3.5ab. Reprinted, by permission, from Fray Diego Durán, *Book of the Gods and Rites and The Ancient Calendar*. Copyright © University of Oklahoma Press, 1971. Fig. 3.6. Reprinted from *Codex Féjérvary-Mayer*, courtesy The Board of Trustees of the National Museums and Galleries on Merseyside (Liverpool Museum). Fig. 3.7. Reprinted from the *Codex Borgia*. Biblioteca Apostolica Vaticana, Rome. Fig. 3.8. Reprinted from *Biblioteca Mexicana*. Fig. 3.9. Reprinted from the frontispiece of Francesco Patrizi, *Della historia dieci dialoghi*. Venice: Andrea Arrivabene, 1560. The Newberry Library, Chicago.

Chapter 4

Fig. 4.1ab. Reprinted, by permission, from Bernardino de Sahagún, *Historia Universal de las Cosas de la Nueva España*, Biblioteca del Palacio de Madrid. Fig. 4.2. Reprinted, by permission, from Bernard de Tuy, *Chroniques*, Bibliothèque Municipale, Besançon. Fig. 4.3. Reprinted, by permission, from Bernardino de Sahagún, *Florentine Codex*. The School of American Research and the University of Utah. Illustration by Francisco del Paso y Troncoso. Fig. 4.4. Reprinted, by permission, from *Book of the Chilam Balam of Chumayel*, Princeton University Libraries. Fig. 4.5. Reprinted, by permission, from Ralph Roys, *Book of the Chilam Balam of Chumayel*. Copyright © 1967 by the University of Oklahoma Press. Fig. 4.6. Reprinted, by permission, from Bernadino Sahagún, *Florentine Codex*. The School of American Research and the University of Utah. Illustration by Francisco del Paso y Troncoso. Fig. 4.7. Diagram by Walter Mignolo. Fig. 4.8. Reprinted, by permission, from Gary Gossen, "Chamula Genres of Verbal Behavior," in *Toward New Perspectives in Folklore*, ed. A. Paredes and R. Bauman, 1972. The American Folklore Society from the *Journal of American Folklore* 84 (January–March 1971), 331. Not for further reproduction.

Chapter 5

Fig. 5.1. Courtesy of the Edward E. Ayer Collection, The Newberry Library, Chicago. Fig. 5.2. Reprinted from J. Needham and L. Wang, *Science and Civilization in China, Vol. III,* 1959. Reprinted with the permission of the Cambridge University Press. Fig. 5.3. Biblioteca Vaticana, Rome. Fig. 5.5. Reprinted, by permission, from Matsutaro Namba, *Old Maps in Japan*. Map by Kobayashi Koho. Osaka: Sogensha, 1973. Figs. 5.6 and 5.7. Reprinted from Armin Wolf, "News on the Ebstorf World Map: Date, Origin, Authorship," in *Géographie du monde au moyen âge et à la renaissance,* ed. Monique Pelletier. Paris: Comité des Travaux Historiques et Scientifiques, 1989. Fig. 5.8. Reprinted, by permission, from Isidore of Seville, *Etimologiarum sive originum,* 1911. Photo courtesy Bibliothèque National, Paris. Fig. 5.9a. Biblioteca Laurentiana-

Vaticana, Rome. Fig. 5.9b. Reprinted, by permission, from Bartholomeus Anglicus, *De proprietaribum rerum*, 1492. Biblioteca Apostolica Vaticana, Rome. Fig. 5.10a. Reprinted from Eduardo Matos Moctezuma, *The Aztecs*. New York: Rizzoli, 1989. Fig. 5.10b. John Carter Brown Library at Brown University, Providence, R.I. Fig. 5.11. Reprinted from Eduardo Matos Moctezuma, *The Aztecs*. New York: Rizzoli, 1989. Fig. 5.12. Reprinted, by permission, from Ibn-Khaldun, *The Muqaddimah: An Introduction to History*. Princeton, N.J.: Princeton University Press, 1958. Fig. 5.13a. The Newberry Library, Chicago. Fig. 5.13b. Frontispiece to the sixth part of Theodor DeBry's *Grands Voyages*. Courtesy of the John Carter Brown Library at Brown University, Providence, R.I. Fig. 5.13c. Reprinted from Paul Wheatley, *The Pivot of the Four Quarters: A Preliminary Enquiry into the Origins and Character of the Ancient Chinese City*. Chicago: Aldine, 1971. Fig. 5.14. Frontispiece of the *Codex Mendoza*. Bodleian Library, Oxford. Figs. 5.15 and 5.16. Illustration by López de Velasco from Antonio Herrera y Tordesillas, *Historia general de los hechos de los castellanos en las Islas de Tierra Firme del mar océano*. 8 vols. Madrid: Imprenta Real, 1601–15. Fig. 5.17. Reprinted, by permission, from Gary Urton, *At the Crossroads of the Earth and the Sky: An Andean Cosmology*. Copyright © 1981. By permission of the author and the University of Texas Press. Figs. 5.18 and 5.19. Reprinted, by permission, from Guaman Poma de Ayala, *Nueva coronica y buen gobierno*, 1587–1615. The Royal Library, Copenhagen. Fig. 5.20. Reprinted from Johannes Fabian, *Time and the Other: How Anthropology Makes Its Object*. New York: Columbia University Press, 1983.

Chapter 6

Fig. 6.1. Henricus Martellus Germanus's world map, 1490. Courtesy of The British Library, London. Fig. 6.2a. The Newberry Library, Chicago. Fig. 6.2b. Biblioteca Nazionale Centrale. Fig. 6.3. Reprinted, by permission, from Ptolomaeus's *Geographia*. The Newberry Library, Chicago. Fig. 6.4. Studio Editions, Ltd., London. Fig. 6.5. Reprinted from C. Julius Solinius, *Ioannis Comentis Minori*. The Newberry Library, Chicago. Fig. 6.6. Courtesy of the James Ford Bell Library, University of Minnesota. Fig. 6.7. Courtesy of the John Carter Brown Library at Brown University, Providence, R.I. Fig. 6.8. Courtesy of the Newberry Library, Chicago. Fig. 6.9. Courtesy of the Royal Geographical Society, London. Fig. 6.10. Courtesy of the Huntington Library, San Marino, Calif. Fig. 6.11. Claes Janszoon Visscher, Bibliothèque Nationale, Paris. Figs. 6.13 and 6.14. Courtesy of the John Carter Brown Library at Brown University, Providence, R.I. Fig. 6.15. The Newberry Library, Chicago. Figs. 6.16 and 6.17. Courtesy of the John Carter Brown Library at Brown University, Providence, R.I. Fig. 6.18. Reprinted from M. Cuesta Domingo, *Alonso de Santa Cruz y Su Obra Cosmografica*. Madrid: Consego Superior de Investigaciones Cientificas, "Instituto Gonzalo Fernandez de Oviedo." Fig. 6.19. Sebastiano del Piombo, *Portait of a Humanist*. Samuel H. Kress Collection, © 1994 Board of Trustees, National Gallery of Art, Washington, D.C. Fig. 6.20. Sebastiano del Piombo, *Cardinal Bandinello Sauli, His Secretary, and Two Geographers*. Samuel H. Kress Collection, © 1994 Board of Trustees, National Gallery of Art, Washington, D.C. Fig. 6.21. Archivo General de la Nación. Fig. 6.22. Museo Nacional de Antropología, Peru. Fig. 6.23. Archivo General de Indias, Seville. Fig. 6.24. Reprinted by permission of the Benson Latin American Collection, The University of Texas at Austin. Fig. 6.25ab. Reprinted, by permission, from Guaman Poma de Ayala, *Nueva coronica y buen gobierno*, ca. 1615. The Royal Library, Copenhagen. Fig. 6.26. Reprinted from Gary Gossen, *Chamulas in the World of the Sun: Time and Space in a Maya Oral Tradition*. Cambridge, Mass., Harvard University Press, 1974.